WHO'S WHO OF EVERTON

WHO'S WHO OF

EVERTON

Tony Matthews

MAINSTREAM
PUBLISHING
EDINBURGH AND LONDON

First published in Great Britain in 2004 by
MAINSTREAM PUBLISHING COMPANY (EDINBURGH) LTD
7 Albany Street
Edinburgh EH1 3UG

ISBN 1 84018 819 7

A catalogue record for this book is available from the British Library

Typeset in Caslon and Gill Condensed
Printed and bound in Great Britain by
Antony Rowe Ltd, Chippenham, Wiltshire

CONTENTS

ACKNOWLEDGEMENTS

First and foremost I must say a special big 'thank you' to four people: Bill Campbell, Graeme Blaikie and Ailsa Bathgate of Mainstream Publishing (Edinburgh) and Everton statistician Gavin Buckland, who has checked and re-checked the players' write-ups.

Also thank you to David Barber (FA) and Zoe Ward (Premier League) and to Gordon Locke, Charlie Poultney, Dennis Clareborough and Mark Rowan (Everton Press Office) who have loaned certain pictures.

Thank you, also – and 'sorry' darling for the inconvenience caused – to my loving wife Margaret, who once again has endured the tedious tapping of a computer keyboard and seeing scores of reference books, programmes and magazines scattered all over the floor.

IMPORTANT NOTICE

The majority of pictures in this book have come via scrapbooks, albums and certain programmes/magazines owned by ex-players, Everton fans and collectors of soccer memorabilia. I have been unable to establish clear copyright on some of these pictures and therefore both myself and the publishers would be pleased to hear from anyone whose copyright has been unintentionally infringed.

INTRODUCTION

I am positively certain that all supporters of Everton Football Club, young and old, male and female, have, at some time or another, been involved in an argument concerning a player, whether from the past or present!

In pubs, clubs, cafés, bars and restaurants, schools, colleges and universities, at home, in the office, out walking or shopping, at a ground, in a car, on a train, bus or plane and on the beach, discussions have taken place about one or more players, even managers, who have been associated with Everton down the years.

Some of these discussions have turned into heated arguments with questions being asked but no definite answer given. As a result, wagers have been laid as to who is right and who is wrong!

The questions are varied. When did a certain player join the club? Where did he come from? How many goals did he score? Who did he join after leaving Goodison? Did he play international football? Was he a defender or midfielder? Did he play in a cup final?

This *Who's Who* will answer most, if not all of these questions, as well as offering the fan loads more information besides. It will also satisfy that laudable curiosity without a shadow of doubt.

You will find multitudinous authentic personal details of every player who has appeared for Everton in a competitive match from October 1887, when the club first entered the FA Cup, up to May 2004.

At the end of the book, there are also details of the players who guested for the club during two world wars (see 'Wartime Guests' section), and information on managers (see 'Everton Managers' section).

The date and place of birth and death of players are given, where these can be verified. Occasionally, it has only been possible to ascertain the year when a player was born and when he died, and no information is available for the place of birth or death. In some instances the word 'Deceased' has been used to indicate that the exact date and place of death is not known.

Also included in the 'biog' are details of the junior and non-League clubs that a player served, any transfer fees involved (if known), honours won at club and international level, plus the respective senior appearance and goalscoring records (for Everton up to May 2004), which appears at the head of each individual player's write-up. Figures given for appearances and goals records take into account only senior competitive games. First-team friendlies, tour games, wartime fixtures etc. are not included.

Virtually throughout this book, the name of the club is referred to as Everton or the Blues. Very few abbreviations have been used, but among the more common ones are the obvious: FC (Football Club), FAC (FA Cup), FLC (Football League Cup), FMC (Full Members' Cup), FRT (Freight Rover Trophy), AWS (Auto Windscreen Shield), 'sub' (substitute) and n/c (non-contract). A plus sign (i.e. 100+3 apps) under a player's name indicates the number of substitute appearances made.

Where a single year appears in the text (when referring to an individual player's career) this indicates, in most cases, the second half of a season: i.e. 1975 is 1974–75. However, when the figures (dates) such as 1975–80 appear, this means seasons 1975–76 to 1979–80 inclusive and not 1974–80.

If you spot any discrepancies, errors and/or omissions, I would appreciate it if you would contact me (via the publishers) so that any amendments can be made in future publications regarding Everton FC. If you have anything to add, this too would be appreciated, as people tend to reveal unknown facts from all sources when football is the topic of conversation.

WHO'S WHO OF EVERTON, 1878—2004

ABBOTT, WALTER
Inside-left: 291 apps, 37 goals
Born: Small Heath, Birmingham, 7 December 1877 – *Died*: Birmingham, 1
    February 1941
Career: Rosewood Victoria, Small Heath/Birmingham (April 1896),
    EVERTON (July 1899), Burnley (July 1908), Birmingham (July 1910;
    retired May 1911)
Abbott started as a strong-running, tenacious inside-left with a cracking shot
before switching to wing-half with Everton, where he still managed to net his
fair share of goals. A dominant figure at times at the heart of the Blues' defence,
he played in successive FA Cup finals, gaining a winner's medal in 1906 and a
runner's-up prize a year later. Capped by England against Wales (1902), he also
represented the Football League on four occasions and holds the scoring record
for Birmingham for most goals in a season, netting 42 in 1898–99 (34 in 34
League games). He retired with a knee injury and later worked in the motor
industry at Longbridge, Birmingham. Abbott's son, also named Walter, played
for Grimsby (1920–21).

ABLETT, GARY IAN
Defender: 156 apps, 6 goals
Born: Liverpool, 19 November 1965
Career: Liverpool (apprentice, 1981; professional, November 1983), Derby
    County (loan, January 1985), Hull City (loan, September 1986), EVERTON
    (£750,000, January 1992), Sheffield United (loan, March 1996), Birmingham
    City (£390,000, June 1996), Wycombe Wanderers (loan, December 1999),
    Scunthorpe United (on trial), Blackpool (free, January 2000; retired May
    2001)
Composed left-sided defender, cool and calm under pressure, Gary Ablett made
over 300 appearances for the two Merseyside clubs. He spent four years at
Goodison Park, having his best season in 1994–95, when he occupied four
different positions. He partnered Matt Jackson at full-back in the FA Cup final,
having started the campaign with victory in the Charity Shield. Injuries began
to interrupt his performances during the latter stages of his Birmingham days
and he struggled to hold down a first-team place at Blackpool. Twice a League

championship-winner with Liverpool (1988, 1990), he also gained an FA Cup-winner's medal (1989), becoming the first player to achieve this feat with both Merseyside clubs, also helping the Reds lift the Charity Shield in 1988. Ablett won England caps at both 'B' and Under-21 levels.

ADAMS, JAMES
Full-back: 43 apps, 1 goal
Born: Edinburgh, 1864 – *Died*: New Jersey, USA, 24 April 1943
Career: Heart of Midlothian, EVERTON (April 1894), Heart of Midlothian (June 1896–May 1897); became a first-class referee before emigrating to the USA where he worked as a stonemason and sculptor

Adams was probably responsible for the penalty-kick being introduced! In 1890–91, playing for Hearts, he punched out a goal-bound shot and the resultant protest led to the Scottish FA proposing that a penalty-kick should be introduced for any similar future offence. It was therefore only appropriate that Adams should give away the first penalty conceded by Hearts in a later game. Regarded as one of Hearts' finest full-backs, he was fast, thoughtful and a hard tackler, whose performances often won applause, even in Glasgow. He helped Hearts win the Scottish Cup in 1891, was capped three times between 1889 and 1893, played twice for the Scottish League and represented the East of Scotland FA. He initially contested the right-back position with Bob Kelso at Everton before partnering 'Smart' Arridge during 1895–96.

ADAMS, NEIL JAMES
Winger: 26+6 apps, 1 goal
Born: Stoke, 23 November 1965
Career: Stoke City (apprentice, April 1982; professional, July 1985), EVERTON (£150,000, July 1986), Oldham Athletic (loan, January –February 1989, signed for £100,000, June 1989), Norwich City (£250,000, February 1994), Oldham Athletic (July 1999; retired July 2001)

An England Under-21 international (one cap), Neil Adams was a 1987 League championship winner with Everton (12 appearances) and a Second Division championship winner with Oldham in 1991. He struggled with injuries during his last two years with Norwich, breaking his collarbone and severely damaging his foot, never regaining full fitness. On his day he was a fine player, supplying a stream of crosses from the right, many delivered with perfection. He missed the first penalty of his career, the unlucky 13th for Norwich against Swansea, in a League Cup-tie in his last season at Carrow Road. He made 206 appearances for Norwich and 167 for Oldham.

ADAMSON, HUGH M.
Wing-half: 25 apps
Born: Scotland, *circa* 1881 – Deceased
Career: Dunfermline Athletic, Lochgelly United, EVERTON (May 1907), Bolton Wanderers (December 1909), South Liverpool (October 1910); did not play after the First World War

A well-built half-back, Adamson made 40 League appearances: 25 for Everton, 15 for Bolton. Signed as cover for Harry Makepeace, for whom he deputised in a handful of games during the first half of 1907–08, he later replaced Walter Abbott at left-half, moving on after Val Harris and Harry Makepeace became the two recognised wing-halves. He skippered South Liverpool.

AINSCOW, ALAN

Midfield: 25+5 apps, 3 goals
Born: Bolton, 15 July 1953
Career: Blackpool (apprentice, June 1969; professional, July 1971), Birmingham City (July 1971), EVERTON (August 1981), Barnsley (loan, November 1982), Eastern FC/Hong Kong (1983), Wolverhampton Wanderers (August 1984), Blackburn Rovers (December 1985), Rochdale (June 1989), Horwich RMI (August 1990), Flint Town United (July 1991), Ellesmere Port Town (coach, 1992–93); later ran a newspaper shop and is now a delivery driver for a bakery firm

An England youth international, Ainscow was a key figure in Birmingham's 1980 promotion race before scoring on his debut for Everton, ironically against his former club. Playing in the main as a probing right-sided midfielder, he had a good technique and his low, hard crosses led to many important goals being scored. He made 209 appearances for Blackpool, and was close to the 500 mark in League appearances when he left Rochdale.

ALEXANDERSSON, NICLAS

Wide right midfield: 55+11 apps, 6 goals
Born: Halmstad, Sweden, 29 December 1971
Career: Halmstad/Sweden (August 1988), IFK Gothenburg/Sweden (May 1996), Sheffield Wednesday (December 1997), EVERTON (£2.5m, July 2000); Swedish football (2003), IFK Gothenburg/Sweden (free transfer, July 2004)

A Swedish international (68 caps gained, seven goals scored up to 2004), Alexandersson scored against England in the 2002 World Cup finals. Signed after netting 12 goals in 88 games for Wednesday, he's a skilful footballer, passes the ball well and is a good finisher. He was troubled by injury in 2002–03, including tendonitis and inflammation behind the knee. Prior to joining the Owls he scored 38 goals in almost 200 League appearances in Sweden.

ALFORD, FRANCIS JOHN

Outside-left: 2 apps
Born: Swindon, 14 May 1901 – *Died*: 16 October 1982
Career: Junior football, Swindon Town (1914–19), Darwen (July 1920), Barrow (November 1920), EVERTON (£450 plus proceeds of a match, January 1921), Barrow (June 1923), Lincoln City (May 1925), Scunthorpe and Lindsey United (June 1926)

Frank Alford was a neat little player but not a great goalscorer, did well in Everton's reserves but played only twice for the first XI at Oldham in

October 1921 and Burnley in April 1922. He made 64 League appearances for Barrow.

ALLAN, JOHN
Right-half: 19 apps
Born: Carlisle, 11 May 1890 – Deceased
Career: Bedlington United, Carlisle United, EVERTON (December 1909), Leeds City (June 1912), Rochdale (1914–15), Coventry City (July 1919), Walsall (1920–21)
Basically a reserve at Goodison, Allan, well built, made his debut for Everton against Liverpool in February 1910. After that he made only fleeting appearances.

ALLEN, GRAHAM
Full-back: 2+4 apps
Born: Bolton, 8 April 1977
Career: EVERTON (apprentice, June 1993; professional, December 1994), Tranmere Rovers (free, August 1998)
An England youth international, Allen developed into an uncompromising, rock-steady defender after failing to establish himself at Goodison Park. He became captain at Prenton Park and, leading by example, had made over 220 career appearances up to 2004.

AMOKACHI, DANIEL OWEFEN
Striker: 42+12 apps, 13 goals
Born: Groko, Nigeria, 30 December 1972
Career: FC Bruges/Belgium, EVERTON (£3.2m, August 1994), Besiktas/Turkey (June 1996)
Daniel Amokachi became Everton's first £3m-rated player in 1994. An aggressive, all-action, lightning-fast striker with pace and a strong right-foot shot, he came off the subs' bench to score twice for the Blues in their 1995 FA Cup semi-final win over Spurs. He duly collected a winner's medal and also helped Everton lift the Charity Shield that same year. He drew up a fine understanding with Paul Rideout and then Duncan Ferguson at Goodison before leaving in 1996. An Olympic gold medal-winner with Nigeria in Atlanta (after leaving Everton), he played in almost 40 internationals for his country.

ANGELL, BRETT ASHLEY MARK
Striker: 16+5 apps, 1 goal
Born: Marlborough, 20 August 1968
Career: Portsmouth (apprentice, April 1985; professional, August 1986), Cheltenham Town (August 1987), Derby County (£40,000, February 1988), Stockport County (£33,000, October 1988), Southend United (£100,000, August 1990), EVERTON (loan, September 1993; signed for £500,000, January 1994), Sunderland (£600,000, March 1995), Sheffield United (loan, January 1996), West Bromwich Albion (loan, March–April 1996), Stockport

County (£120,000, August 1996), Notts County (loan, December 1999), Preston North End (loan, February 2000), Walsall (free, July 2000), Rushden and Diamonds (free, February 2002), Port Vale (free, August 2002), Queens Park Rangers (free, November 2002), Linfield (free, July 2003), Doncaster Rovers (scout, 2003–04)

A quarter of much-travelled striker Brett Angell's appearances for Everton came as a substitute. He made his League debut for Southend against Norwich in September 1993 when the Canaries won 5–1. He scored his only goal for Everton in a 6–2 home win over Swindon in February 1994 when he partnered hat-trick hero Tony Cottee up front. In a nomadic career, Angell, looking awkward at times, scored over 200 goals in almost 500 first-class matches, helping Stockport win the Second Division title in 2000.

ANGUS, JAMES ALEXANDER

Centre-forward/outside-left/goalkeeper: 17 apps
Born: Blythswood, Glasgow, 1 December 1868 – *Died*: Liverpool, April 1891
Career: Glasgow Central, EVERTON (December 1888–January 1889), King's Park, Sunderland Albion (February 1889), EVERTON (August 1890 until his death)

During the first season of League football (1888–89), Jack Angus, a deft and aggressive player, appeared in four games on the left-wing and once at centre-forward for Everton. He was converted into a goalkeeper by Sunderland Albion before returning for a second spell on Merseyside, appearing in 12 competitive games in the championship-winning campaign of 1891 before ill health let in David Jardine. There was another J.A. Angus playing around the same time. He scored 11 goals in 23 games for St Mary's (Southampton) from 1893 and also assisted Ardwick and Third Lanark.

ARCHER, JOHN WILLIAM

Half-back/outside-left: 15 apps, 2 goals
Born: Wednesbury, 1909 – *Died*: *circa* 1975
Career: Swan Athletic, Walsall (professional, August 1929), EVERTON (September 1932), Coventry City (July 1936), Plymouth Argyle (November 1938–September 1939); RAF during the Second World War (no further League clubs)

A well-built, strong-tackling left-half, Jack Archer, in the main, deputised for Jock Thomson during his four years at Goodison. He did, however, play on the left-wing during his last season with the club, scoring against Chelsea (won 5–1) and Blackburn (1–1). He made 138 League appearances in all.

ARNOLD, JAMES ALEXANDER

Goalkeeper: 59 apps
Born: Stafford, 6 August 1950
Career: Rising Brook FC/Stafford, Stafford Rangers, Sandbach Ramblers (loan), Blackburn Rovers (professional, June 1970), EVERTON (August 1981), Preston North End (loan, October–November 1982), Port Vale

(August 1985), Staffordshire Police Force (Recreation Officer, July 1986), Port Vale (n/c, September 1986–May 1987), later Kidderminster Harriers, Rochester, Workington (briefly), Stoke City (reserves); now lives in Stafford

Following his manager, Howard Kendall, to Goodison, Jim Arnold was 31 when he made his League debut for Everton at Birmingham in August 1981. Highly efficient, he possessed fine positional sense, could kick long and true and won England honours as a semi-professional. After retiring from senior football in 1986, he joined the police in a civilian capacity but came out of retirement when Port Vale had a goalkeeping problem.

ARRIDGE, SMART

Full-back: 56 apps

Born: Southwick, Sunderland, 1872 – *Died*: Bangor, North Wales, 20 October 1947

Career: Friars school (Bangor), Bangor (amateur, August 1888; professional, August 1891), Bootle (August 1892), EVERTON (August 1893), New Brighton Tower (July 1897), Stockport County (June 1901), Bangor (August 1903–May 1906; later part-time trainer at club); also ran a second-hand furniture business, worked on the *Clio*, an industrial training ship off Bangor pier, before becoming a stevedore in Penrhyn Port

Arridge started as an outside-left with Bangor and was described in newspapers as 'the smartest player on the field' and 'a smart mover'. He spent some time at sea before deciding to become a professional and was switched to full-back by Percy Hughes, the Bangor captain, in 1890. He never regretted the move and made an immediate impact. After 21 League outings for Bootle he transferred to Everton, establishing himself in the Blues' side in 1895–96. He played in all the early cup-ties the following season but missed the semi-final with double-chasing Aston Villa. Described as a 'gentleman footballer', Arridge was scrupulously fair with a solid shoulder charge. He had speed, kicked well with either foot and loved to assist his forwards. He was replaced in the Everton side by David Storrier. Arridge's brothers, Will and Jack, also played for Bangor.

ASHWORTH, ALEC

Inside-forward: 12 apps, 3 goals

Born: Southport, 1 October 1939 – *Died*: June 1995

Career: EVERTON (amateur, April 1955; professional, May 1957), Luton Town (October 1960), Northampton Town (July 1962), Preston North End (June 1963), Stockport County (loan, March–April 1965), Altrincham (May 1965; retired through injury, April 1966)

A well-built inside-forward with a powerful shot, Alex Ashworth netted 62 goals in a total of 148 League games for his four major clubs. He made his Everton debut at inside-left (in place of Derek Temple) against Sheffield Wednesday in April 1958 and scored twice in the opening ten minutes on his home debut a week later against Manchester City. He joined Luton Town as a makeweight for Billy Bingham and after grabbing 20 goals in 63 League outings for the Hatters (as partner to Gordon Turner), he moved to

Northampton after the Cobblers had failed to sign Terry Bly. He was a Third Division championship-winner in 1963 and a year later played in the FA Cup final for Preston against West Ham United. He was only 55 when he died.

ASHWORTH, SAMUEL BOLTON
Half-back: 11 apps
Born: Fenton, Stoke-on-Trent, March 1877 – *Died*: Stoke-on-Trent, 30 December 1925
Career: Stoke Alliance (1893), Fenton Town (1894), Stafford Wednesday (1895), Stafford Rangers (1897), Stoke Nomads (1899), Stoke (August 1901), Oxford City (August 1902), Reading (August 1903), Manchester City (September 1903), Reading (August 1904), EVERTON (September 1904), Burlsem Port Vale (October 1905), North Staffs Nomads (August 1906), Sheffield FC (1907), Richmond Association (1908), Northern Nomads (1910–11); later Stoke director (from 1920)

An amateur defender, Sam Ashworth made his debut for Everton in October 1904. An FA Cup winner and League championship runner-up with Manchester City, he was one of 17 City players (including Welsh international Billy Meredith) involved in a soccer scandal which eventually resulted in Ashworth being accused of earning money over and above the normal expenses allowed for amateurs. He was found guilty, fined £25 and ordered never to play for City again (although by the time the inquiry had ended, he was elsewhere, playing for Port Vale). A surveyor and architect by profession, he later became chief architect to the Stoke-on-Trent Education Committee, a position he held until his death at the age of 48.

ASPINALL, WARREN
Forward: 0+10 apps
Born: Wigan, 13 September 1967
Career: Wigan Athletic (junior, 1983; professional, August 1985), EVERTON (£150,000, February 1986), Wigan Athletic (loan, February 1986), Aston Villa (£300,000, February 1987), Portsmouth (£315,000, August 1988), Bournemouth (loan, August 1993), Swansea City (loan, October 1993), Bournemouth (£20,000, December 1993), Carlisle United (free, March 1995), Brentford (£50,000, November 1997), Colchester United (free, February 1999), Brighton and Hove Albion (free, September 1999; retired injured, November 2000; appointed scout, January 2001)

Warren Aspinall was a smart forward who developed into an efficient midfielder. An England youth international, he did very well at competitive level, scoring plenty of goals. He helped Wigan win the FRT in 1985, collected a winner's medal when Carlisle lifted the AWS in 1997 and gained promotion from Division Three with Colchester in 1999. His first game for Everton came in May 1986 – as a second-half 'sub' against West Ham. Aspinall amassed over 575 club appearances and scored 110 goals.

ATKINS, IAN LESLIE
Utility: 6+3 apps, 1 goal
Born: Sheldon, Birmingham, 16 January 1957
Career: Sheldon Heath School, Leafield Athletic (Central Warwickshire Boys League), Shrewsbury Town (apprentice, June 1973; professional, January 1975), Sunderland (August 1982), EVERTON (£70,000, November 1984), Ipswich Town (£100,000, September 1985), Birmingham City (loan, March 1988; signing permanently for £50,000, April 1988), Colchester United (player–manager, 1990–91), Birmingham City (assistant manager, season 1991–92), Cambridge United (player–manager, December 1992–May 1993), Sunderland (assistant manager, July–November 1993), Doncaster Rovers (manager, January–July 1994), Solihull Borough (guest player, July–August 1994), Redditch United (as a player, September–December 1994), Northampton Town (manager, January 1995–May 1999), Chester City (manager, July 1999–May 2000), Carlisle United (manager, season 2000–01); during August–October 2001, was an occasional match summariser for Sky Sport (football); Oxford United (manager, November 2001–October 2003), Bristol Rovers (manager, April 2004)

A Third Division championship and Welsh Cup winner with Shrewsbury in 1979, Ian Atkins was a competitive player with a ferocious tackle who was brought in as a utility player by Everton, playing mostly in defence. He enjoyed 15 years in top-class football, during which time he served with five different clubs, amassing over 550 League appearances, playing in 314 games and scoring 64 goals for Shrewsbury alone. He turned out for Birmingham against Peterborough in 1991 before his registration had been completed, an offence for which the St Andrew's club received a £10,000 fine. He resigned as Chester boss after relegation to the Conference in 2000 and during the early part of the 2003–04 season he had an awful lot of problems when managing Oxford!

ATTEVELD, RAYMOND
Full-back/Midfield: 53+10 apps, 2 goals
Born: Amsterdam, Holland, 8 September 1966
Career: RJC Haarlem/Holland, EVERTON (August 1989), West Ham United (loan, February 1992), Bristol City (March 1992, released May 1993)

Ray Atteveld took over at right-back from the injury-prone Ian Snodin a third of the way through the 1989–90 campaign, making his debut for Everton in a 2–0 home win over Coventry in December. He played in 22 games in his first season at Goodison and 26 in his second before losing his place to Neil McDonald.

ATTWOOD, ARTHUR ALBERT
Centre-forward: 3 apps
Born: Walsall, 1 December 1901 – *Died*: Walsall, 1974
Career: Walsall LMS, Walsall (October 1927), EVERTON (March 1929), Bristol Rovers (August 1930), Brighton and Hove Albion (June 1932), Northfleet (1933), Hove (1934; retired, May 1935)

In a useful League career that started late, Arthur Attwood scored 95 goals in 155 games including 55 in 87 outings for Brighton. Learning his football with the Army of Occupation on the Rhine when serving with the Shropshire Light Infantry during the First World War, he signed for Everton as one of the covering players for Dixie Dean. Unfortunately, he didn't have the greatest of debuts, the Blues losing 4–0 at home to West Ham in April 1929. After retiring, he resided and worked in Walsall.

BAARDSEN, PER ESPEN
Goalkeeper: 1 app.
Born: San Rafael, USA, 7 December 1977
Career: San Francisco All Blacks (1995), Tottenham Hotspur (free, July 1996), Watford (£1.25m, with Allan Nielsen, August 2000), EVERTON (free, December 2002–February 2003); later travelled the USA

A former USA youth international who went on to play for Norway in four full and 31 Under-21 matches, 6 ft 5 in. goalkeeper Espen Baardsen made 29 appearances during his four years at White Hart Lane, although he was a League Cup winner in 1999. He did much better with Watford before moving to Goodison Park halfway through the season as cover for injuries to reserves Paul Gerrard and Steve Simonsen. He made his debut for the Blues in unusual circumstances, taking over from regular keeper Richard Wright, who injured himself during the warm-up before a Premiership game against his former club, Spurs, in January 2003, making him the club's tallest ever player. He left when Richard Wright resumed between the posts.

BAILEY, JOHN ANTHONY
Left-back: 220+2 apps, 3 goals
Born: Liverpool, 1 April 1957
Career: EVERTON (junior trialist, 1971–72), Blackburn Rovers (apprentice, June 1973; professional, April 1975), EVERTON (£300,000, July 1979), Newcastle United (£80,000, October 1985), Bristol City (free, September 1988; retired January 1992), EVERTON (assistant coach), Sheffield United (coach/assistant manager)

A clever, attacking full-back, possessing a strong tackle, John Bailey gave Everton excellent service. In 1980, he was capped by England 'B' and represented the Football League, and gained both FA Cup and League championship winning medals in 1984 and 1985 while also playing in the losing League Cup final of 1984. A forward in his younger days, he was successfully converted into a defender at Blackburn, having been rejected by Everton as a lad. He made his debut for the Blues against Norwich on the opening day of the 1979–80 season, taking over at left-back from David Jones. The joker in the pack, he was something of an extrovert, being a very useful amateur boxer who fought in the ABA championships.

BAIN, DAVID
Centre-forward/centre-half: 43 apps, 3 goals
Born: Rutherglen, Scotland, 5 August 1900 – Deceased
Career: Rutherglen Glencairn, Manchester United (initially a trialist, signed as a professional, May 1922), EVERTON (£1,200, June 1924), Bristol City (June 1928), Halifax Town (August 1930), Rochdale (September 1932; retired May 1934)

After impressing as a trialist, David Bain went on to score nine goals in 23 senior games for Manchester United. A good striker of the ball, mainly right-footed, he won Scottish junior international honours with Rutherglen and was converted into a half-back by Everton, having made his League debut at centre-forward in place of Jack Cock in a 3–0 home defeat by Sunderland in October 1924. He played his first game at centre-half at Blackburn six weeks later. He lost his way during 1927–28, appearing in only two matches.

BAKAYOKO, IBRAHIMA
Striker: 20+8 apps, 7 goals
Born: Sequela, Ivory Coast, 31 December 1976
Career: Montpellier/France, Arsenal (trialist), EVERTON (£4.5m, October 1998), Olympique Marseille/France (£4m, June 1999)

A compact and decisive striker who occasionally showed flashes of unpredictable star quality, Ibrahima Bakayoko made his League debut for Everton against Liverpool in October 1998. Unfortunately, he failed to settle down at Goodison, never really adapting himself to the speed of the Premiership. He had won 17 caps for the Ivory Coast before his departure to France.

BAKER, BENJAMIN HOWARD
Goalkeeper: 13 apps
Born: Liverpool, 12 February 1892 – *Died*: 8 September 1987
Career: Marlborough Old Boys, Northern Nomads, Blackburn Rovers (reserves), Corinthians, Liverpool (amateur, March 1920), EVERTON (amateur, November 1920), Preston North End (amateur), Northern Nomads (February 1921), Chelsea (amateur, October 1921), Corinthians, EVERTON (amateur, July 1926), Oldham Athletic (amateur, March 1929), Lancashire County, Corinthians (1930–31)

A 1919 England amateur trialist at centre-half, Howard Baker quickly became a goalkeeper and went on to win ten caps at that level between 1921 and 1929 and two for the senior side (against Belgium in 1921 and against Ireland in 1925) as well as representing the Football League. One of the great all-round athletes of his day, he also starred for Great Britain in the high jump at the 1912 and 1920 Olympic Games, finishing sixth in the latter year, being the British record holder at this event. Besides his footballing activities, Baker was a useful cricketer for Liverpool CC, scoring two centuries; he kept goal for a local water polo team and was a fine lawn tennis player. He made his debut for the Blues in a 1–0 win at Chelsea in February 1921, deputising for Tom Fern. He played in

176 first-class games for the Corinthians and was a Welsh Cup winner with the Northern Nomads in 1921. The length of Baker's goal-kicks, his upfield sorties and his penalty-taking were all part of his remarkable repertoire.

BALL, ALAN JAMES
Midfield: 251 apps, 79 goals
Born: Farnworth, near Bolton, 12 May 1945
Career: Wolverhampton Wanderers (trial), Bolton Wanderers (amateur), Blackpool (apprentice, September 1961; professional, May 1962), EVERTON (£110,000, July 1966), Arsenal (£220,000, December 1971), Southampton (£60,000, December 1976), Philadelphia Fury/USA (player–coach, May 1978), Vancouver Whitecaps (June 1979), Blackpool (player–manager, July 1980–February 1981), Southampton (March 1981), FC Bulowa/Hong Kong (October 1982), Bristol Rovers (January 1983), Portsmouth (manager, May 1984–January 1989), Colchester United (assistant manager, February–October 1989), Stoke City (assistant manager, October–November 1989; manager, November 1989–February 1991), Exeter City (manager, August 1991–94), Manchester City (manager, July 1995–November 1996), Portsmouth (manager, January 1998–December 1999)
A tireless midfield firebrand, Alan Ball was 'Mr Perpetual Motion' on the pitch, covering acres of ground every time he played. He was excellent on the right for England in their 1966 World Cup triumph and scored eight goals in 72 international appearances (1965–75), gaining 39 caps with Everton. He also played in eight Under-23 matches, represented the Football League and participated in over 900 games for his major clubs (743 in the Football League), scoring 190 goals. A First Division championship winner with Everton (1970) and FA Cup runner-up twice with the Blues (1968) and Arsenal (1972), he succeeded Brian Labone as captain at Goodison in 1971. As manager, he guided Portsmouth to promotion from Division Two in 1987 and for six months (to August 1992) was on England's coaching staff (under Graham Taylor). When Ball joined Arsenal in 1971, it was for a then record British transfer fee, having earlier become Everton's first six-figure signing. He scored the winning goal on his Blues' debut at Fulham in August 1966 and was the first Everton player to score a hat-trick in a European game, doing so against Keflavik (Iceland) in September 1970. Ball's last game in the top flight was for Southampton against Everton in October 1982.

BALL, MICHAEL JOHN
Defender: 116+23 apps, 8 goals
Born: Liverpool, 2 October 1979
Career: EVERTON (apprentice, April 1995; professional, October 1996), Glasgow Rangers (August 2001)
Michael Ball was five days short of his 18th birthday when he scored for Everton against Arsenal in a Premiership game at Goodison in September 1997. Initially a midfielder, an injury crisis forced manager Walter Smith to switch him to left-back, where he performed majestically, going on to win his

first full England cap against Spain in 2000–01. A positive and totally committed footballer, he has also represented his country at schoolboy, youth and Under-21 levels, gaining seven caps in the latter category. Injury forced him to miss the greater part of his first two seasons at Ibrox.

BALMER, ROBERT
Full-back: 188 apps
Born: West Derby, Liverpool, 1881 – Deceased
Career: West Derby Schools, Liverpool junior football, EVERTON (amateur, April 1900; professional, 1902–May 1912)
Robert Balmer partnered his elder brother Walter (q.v.) at full-back in the 1907 FA Cup final, when Everton lost 2–1 to Sheffield Wednesday. Having made his League debut at home to Middlesbrough in January 1903, he gained a regular place in the side three years later. Often choosing to use the 'big kick' downfield to clear any danger, he was a very effective and hard-working defender, who had a fine understanding with his goalkeeper.

BALMER, WALTER
Full-back: 331 apps, 1 goal
Born: Liverpool, 1877 – *Died*: 1937
Career: Aintree Church, South Shore FC, EVERTON (August 1897), Croydon Common (1908–13), later Huddersfield Town (coach, 1919–21)
Walter Balmer, a thickset defender, played in successive FA Cup finals for Everton, gaining a winner's medal in 1906 and a runner's-up prize in 1907, the latter with his brother Robert (q.v.). A very consistent performer, he made his League debut for the Blues at West Bromwich in November 1897 and played his last game against Sunderland in April 1908. Possessing a crunching tackle, he could occupy both full-back positions and in 1905 won his only England cap against Ireland at Middlesbrough. He also represented the Football League. His solitary goal for Everton was a penalty in a 4–2 defeat at Nottingham Forest in February 1900.

BANKS, HERBERT ERNEST
Outside-left: 2 apps
Born: Coventry, 1874 – *Died*: Smethwick, 1947
Career: Coventry Highfield FC, 72nd Seaforth Highlanders (1894–97), EVERTON (March 1897), St Mirren (loan, August 1897), Third Lanark (September 1897), Millwall Athletic (June 1898), Aston Villa (April 1901), Bristol City (November 1901), Watford (May 1903), Coventry City (1904), Stafford Rangers (1905), Verity's Athletic (1906); later worked for a Birmingham engineering firm
Herbie Banks played his early football with the 'Highlanders', helping his regiment twice win the Simla Cup in India. Recruited out of the Army by Everton as a 23 year old, he made his League debut on the left-wing in place of Alf Milward in a 4–1 defeat at Preston in April 1897. A shortish, heavily built player with a bustling technique and strong shot, he had a varied career

spanning almost a decade. In that time he also played as an inside- or centre-forward and left-half, netting 70 goals in over 200 appearances, including 51 in 90 outings for Millwall and 18 in 43 for Bristol City. He scored twice in an England trial and was Millwall's first full international, capped against Ireland at Southampton in March 1901. In December 1899 he was suspended by Millwall for being overweight – just after scoring four goals in an FA Cup-tie against Clapton.

BARBER, ARTHUR WILLIAM
Outside-right: 2 apps
Born: Liverpool, *circa* 1915
Career: Local junior football, EVERTON (August 1938–September 1939); did not figure after the Second World War
Arthur Barber's two League appearances for Everton were against Wolves in October 1938 (his debut) and at Leeds in February 1939. He replaced Torry Gillick in both games.

BARDSLEY, JOHN CHARLES
Left-back: 1 app.
Born: Southport, March 1877 – Deceased
Career: Northern Nomads, EVERTON (September 1909), Manchester City (August 1911–May 1912)
Reserve defender Jack Bardsley was 32 when he made his only League appearance for Everton against Nottingham Forest in April 1910, deputising for John Maconnachie in a 4–0 defeat.

BARKER, GEORGE
Full-back: 10 apps
Born: Blakenhall, Wolverhampton, 12 February 1875 – *Died*: *circa* 1940
Career: Wolverhampton Wanderers (amateur, 1895–96), EVERTON (July 1896), Bristol City (August 1898), Wolverhampton Wanderers (December 1900; retired, injured, September 1901)
A well-built defender with a strong tackle, George Barker made the first of his ten appearances for the Blues against his former club, Wolves, at Molineux in September 1896, deputising for Smart Arridge at left-back. A well-respected reserve at both Goodison and Molineux, he made 36 appearances for Bristol City, gaining a Southern League runner's-up medal in 1899.

BARLOW, GEORGE HERBERT
Outside-left: 42 apps, 6 goals
Born: Wigan, 1885 – *Died*: Lancashire, 1921
Career: Wigan Central, Preston North End (August 1906), EVERTON (September 1908), Preston North End (October 1912–May 1915); didn't figure after the First World War
A short, dark-haired left-winger with good pace and an eye for goal, George Barlow did well at Deepdale before joining Everton, being a reliable

replacement for Harold Hardman. He scored on his debut against Middlesbrough (won 3–2) and had an excellent first season at Goodison before injuries disrupted his progress in 1909–10. Eventually losing out to George Bear, he went on to play in 94 senior games for Preston.

BARLOW, JOHN
Inside-right/outside-left: 4 apps
Born: Prescot, Lancashire, May 1875 – Deceased
Career: Prescot FC, EVERTON (February 1898), Reading (January 1899), Tottenham Hotspur (July 1901), Reading (March 1903), Leicester Fosse (May 1903–June 1904)
Jack Barlow made his League debut for Everton at Bolton Wanderers in March 1898 and had his outing six months later at West Bromwich Albion. He sampled Southern League fare with both Reading and Spurs and scored six times in 24 games for Leicester.

BARLOW, STUART
Forward: 31+57 apps, 13 goals
Born: Liverpool, 16 July 1968
Career: Sherwood Park, EVERTON (professional, June 1990), Rotherham United (loan, January 1992), Oldham Athletic (£450,000, November 1995), Wigan Athletic (£45,000, March 1996), Tranmere Rovers (free, July 2000–May 2003), Stockport County (August 2003)
A player with extraordinary acceleration, Stuart Barlow found it difficult to hold down a regular first-team place during his time at Goodison, the majority of his appearances coming as a substitute. He came off the bench for his League debut against Wimbledon in April 1991 and scored his first goals for the Blues in December 1992 against QPR. After leaving Everton, Barlow netted 32 times in 107 outings for the Latics, scored 52 goals in 106 games for Wigan and struck 27 in 115 appearances for Tranmere. He was an AWS winner with Wigan in 1999.

BARMBY, NICHOLAS JONATHAN
Forward/Midfield: 119+14 apps, 23 goals
Born: Hull, 11 February 1974
Career: Tottenham Hotspur (apprentice, June 1990; professional, April 1991), Middlesbrough (£5.25m, August 1995), EVERTON (£5.75m, November 1996), Liverpool (£6m, July 2000), Leeds United (£2.75m, August 2002), Nottingham Forest (loan, February–May 2004), Hull City (July 2004)
Able to play anywhere in midfield or as a striker, Nicky Barmby had chalked up more than 150 senior appearances with Spurs and Middlesbrough before moving to Goodison. He quickly started to produce the goods for Everton, scoring in his second outing (a 7–1 win over Southampton in mid-November 1996) having made his debut a fortnight earlier against Coventry. He continued to do well, having his best season in 1999–2000, when he netted ten times in 43 outings. Manager Terry Venables' first signing for Leeds, Barmby has 23

England caps to his credit, has also played in two 'B' and four Under-21 internationals, having earlier starred at youth and schoolboy levels. He was a treble winner with Liverpool in 2001 (League Cup, UEFA Cup and Charity Shield) and his departure to Liverpool is still a sore point with quite a few Everton fans!

BARNETT, GEOFFREY COLIN
Goalkeeper: 10 apps
Born: Northwich, Cheshire, 16 October 1946
Career: Verdin Grammar school (Winsford), EVERTON (amateur, October 1962; professional, May 1964), Arsenal (£35,000, October 1969–February 1976); publican (briefly), then Minnesota Kicks/NASL (1977, manager/coach, 1978–1980); returned to the UK as a publican in Cheshire
Geoff Barnett gained England schoolboy and youth international honours as an Everton teenager. A member of the Blues' 1965 FA Cup-winning team, he was given only ten senior games by the club, making his League debut against Sunderland in December 1965, when he took over from Andy Rankin. He played in the next eight matches before making his last appearance against West Ham in May 1968, when Gordon West was rested ahead of the FA Cup final. Barnett made 49 appearances for the Gunners, gaining an FA Cup runner's-up medal in 1972. His contract at Highbury was cancelled by mutual consent.

BARRETT, EARL DELLISER
Defender: 82+1 app.
Born: Rochdale, 28 April 1967
Career: Manchester City (amateur, June 1983; professional, April 1985), Chester City (loan, March 1986), Oldham Athletic (November 1987), Aston Villa (£1.7m, February 1992), EVERTON (£1.7m, January 1995), Sheffield United (loan, January 1998), Sheffield Wednesday (February 1998; retired, injured, July 1999)
Stylish defender, able to play at right-back or as a centre-back, Earl Barrett appeared in 150 games for Aston Villa (two goals) before transferring to Everton. Capped on three occasions by England, he also represented his country in four 'B' and four Under-21 internationals as well as assisting the Football League side. A Second Division championship winner in 1991 with Oldham, a League Cup winner with Villa in 1994 and a Charity Shield victor with Everton a year later, he was cup-tied and so missed Blues' FA Cup-winning triumph of 1995. He made over 400 League appearances during his career.

BARTON, JOHN STANLEY
Full-back: 23+2 apps
Born: Birmingham, 24 October 1953
Career: Boldmere St Michael's, Paget Rangers (1971), Sutton Coldfield Town, Worcester City, EVERTON (£30,000, December 1978), Derby County (March 1982), Kidderminster Harriers (player/assistant manager, August 1984–May 1988), Nuneaton Borough (manager, May 1993–March 1994),

Burton Albion (manager, April 1994–98); now lives in Derby and works as a PT instructor at Burton College

John Barton cost a record fee for a non-League player when he joined Everton in 1978. Having played in front of relatively low crowds for seven or eight years, he made his debut in the First Division (as a substitute) against Norwich in March 1979 in front of almost 27,000 fans. He never quite fitted the bill on Merseyside but later appeared in 82 matches for Derby. He helped Kidderminster reach the 1986 Welsh Cup final and win the FA Trophy a year later.

BATTEN, HERBERT GEORGE
Forward: 15 apps, 1 goal
Born: Bristol, 14 May 1898 – *Died*: 1956
Career: St James Welfare, Bristol City (August 1919), Plymouth Argyle (August 1921), EVERTON (August 1925), Bradford City (November 1926), Reading (June 1927), Clapton Orient (February 1928–May 1929)

After 100 appearances for Plymouth and a successful tour of Australia with the FA in 1925, Bert Batten was recruited by Everton in 1925. A utility forward, able to occupy most positions, he made his debut against Burnley in February 1926, but, with Dixie Dean, Jack O'Donnell, Alec Troup and Bobby Irvine to contend with, his senior outings were restricted to 15 before leaving for Valley Parade. During his career, Batten, strong and willing, made over 200 appearances (177 in the Football League) and netted 45 goals.

BEAGRIE, PETER SYDNEY
Forward/wide-midfield: 111+33 apps, 15 goals
Born: Middlesbrough, 29 November 1965
Career: Middlesbrough (April 1983; professional, September 1983), Sheffield United (£35,000, August 1986), Stoke City (£210,000, June 1988), EVERTON (£750,000, November 1989), Sunderland (loan, September 1991), Manchester City (£1.1m, July 1997), Bradford City (£50,000, July 1997), EVERTON (loan, March–April 1998), Wigan Athletic (free, February 2001), Scunthorpe United (July 2001)

Renowned for his back-flip somersault after scoring a goal, soccer journeyman Peter Beagrie has had a wonderful career. Capped twice by England at both 'B' and Under-21 levels, he's now netted over 80 goals in more than 725 appearances. He made his League debut as a substitute for Middlesbrough against Oldham in October 1984 and hit his first goal on the last day of that season against Shrewsbury. He had already played in over 200 games before moving to Everton, for whom he made his first appearance (as a 'sub') in a 6–2 defeat at Villa Park in November 1989. It was not until halfway through 1991–92 that he finally established himself as a regular in the Blues' side and that season played in 31 games (five goals).

BEARDSLEY, PETER ANDREW
Forward: 95 apps, 32 goals
Born: Longbenton, Newcastle-upon-Tyne, 18 January 1961
Career: Wallsend Boys' Club, Newcastle United (trialist, season 1977–78),
 Carlisle United (August 1979), Vancouver Whitecaps/NASL (May 1981),
 Manchester United (£300,000, September 1982), Vancouver Whitecaps
 (May 1983), Newcastle United (£120,000, September 1983), Liverpool
 (£1.9m, July 1987), EVERTON (£1m, August 1991), Newcastle United
 (£1.45m, June 1993), Bolton Wanderers (£450,000, August 1997),
 Manchester City (loan, February 1998), Fulham (March 1998), Hartlepool
 United (December 1998; retired May 1999); Newcastle United (Academy
 coach from 2000)

Peter Beardsley was a fine footballer with a wonderful technique. He assembled
a magnificent record of almost 1,000 appearances (club and country) and scored
over 275 goals. He won 59 caps for England (nine goals) and appeared in two
'B' internationals. He formed a splendid strike-partnership with Kevin Keegan
at Newcastle, with Ian Rush at Liverpool, figured prominently alongside Tony
Cottee for Everton and linked up splendidly with Gary Lineker for England.
He was twice a League championship winner with Liverpool, whom he also
helped lift the FA Cup and two Charity Shields (1988–90). He made his debut
for Everton against Nottingham Forest in August 1991 and played in the club's
first Premiership game against Sheffield Wednesday a year later. In 1998–99 he
was a member of Fulham's Second Division championship-winning side under
his former colleague Keegan.

BEARE, GEORGE
Winger: 118 apps, 19 goals
Born: Southampton, 2 October 1885 – *Died*: 1970
Career: Shirley Warren FC/Southampton, Southampton (July 1906), Blackpool
 (May 1908), EVERTON (November 1910), Cardiff City (June 1914),
 Bristol City (November 1921), Cardiff City (September–October 1922),
 Oswestry Town (November 1922–May 1924)

A quick, touchline dribbler, George Beare earned a huge reputation with
Blackpool, for whom he scored 18 goals in 80 appearances, having failed to
make an impression with Southampton (one game). He started his Everton
career with a 3–1 defeat at Bradford City but quickly got into action a week later
with two goals in a 6–1 win over Blackburn. He netted eight times in 29 games
in his first season, followed up with four strikes in 35 outings in 1911–12 and
scored seven times in 42 games in 1912–13, before losing his place to John
Houston. He left Goodison soon after Sam Chedgzoy had made a concerted
effort to grab the outside-right position. In 1921, a northern journalist wrote of
Beare: ' If he did not enjoy playing football he would probably have been one of
our leading music hall comedians, as he is an expert card manipulator, a trick
cyclist of no little repute and an excellent billiards player.'

BELFITT, RODERICK MICHAEL
Striker: 16+2 apps, 3 goals
Born: Doncaster, 30 October 1945
Career: Retford Town, Leeds United (professional, July 1963), Ipswich Town
(November 1971), EVERTON (November 1972), Sunderland (October
1973), Fulham (loan, November–December 1974), Huddersfield Town
(February 1975–May 1976); now a draughtsman, his original profession
before joining Leeds

Scorer of 45 goals in 210 League games, centre-forward Rod Belfitt, big and
strong, never really established himself with any one club, having perhaps his
best spell at Leeds, being a member of Don Revie's great squad of the late 1960s.
In 1967–68, he appeared in the Fairs Cup final and came on as a substitute
against Arsenal in United's League Cup final victory. He admitted that he did
not score as many goals as he would have liked but was nevertheless always a
handful for defenders. He played his first game for the Blues at Crystal Palace
in November 1972 and scored on his home debut a week later against
Manchester City.

BELL, JOHN
Outside-right: 199 apps, 70 goals
Born: Dumbarton, 6 October 1869 – Deceased
Career: Dumbarton Union, Dumbarton (1888), EVERTON (August 1892),
Tottenham Hotspur (briefly), Celtic (£250, August 1898), New Brighton
Tower (September 1900), EVERTON (July 1901), Preston North End
(August 1903; later PNE's first coach, appointed 1909); also chairman of the
first attempt at forming a Players' Union

John Bell – brother of Lawrie (q.v.) – was a brilliant dribbler, a sporting
craftsman, who loved to hug the right-hand touchline. A Scottish international,
gaining ten caps – his first and last against Ireland in 1890 and 1899 – he was a
sharpshooter, quick to pounce on a loose ball, yet he brought thought to his
game as well, creating openings galore for his colleagues at both club and
international level. He won successive League titles north of the border (1891,
1892) and was a Scottish Cup finalist in 1891. He played in the 1897 FA Cup
final for Everton against Aston Villa and was twice a Cup winner with Celtic in
1899 and 1900, later helping Preston take the Second Division title (1904). Bell
appeared in 308 League games in England and almost 100 in Scotland (35 with
Celtic), scoring more than 100 goals. In one First Division game Bell saved the
life of a fellow player when he repositioned the latter's dislocated neck with one
firm wrench using his massive hands.

BELL, ROBERT CHARLES
Centre-forward: 14 apps, 9 goals
Born: Birkenhead, 10 April 1911 – *Died*: 1988
Career: Carlton Athletic (June 1927), Tranmere Rovers (professional, April 1930),
EVERTON (£2,500, April 1936; retired May 1946); continued to work in a
shipping office and in his grocer's shop in Birkenhead, bought in 1936

After scoring 102 goals in 114 League games for Tranmere, including a record 35 in the Third Division (N) in 1933–34 and nine in the home game with Oldham on Boxing Day 1935, all-action striker Bob 'Bunny' Bell was snapped up by Everton, and signed as a possible replacement for Dixie Dean. He started off well by scoring on his debut against Leeds as Dean's deputy but struggled with his form and fitness at times and never got to grips with football in the top flight, although the Second World War certainly interrupted proceedings. He continued to play during the hostilities, netting seven goals in 14 outings before retiring at the age of 35.

BELL, STANLEY LAWRENCE THOMAS

Utility-forward: 48 apps, 20 goals
Born: Langbank, Renfrewshire, 5 May 1875 – *Died*: Scotland, 1955
Career: Langbank Schools, Langbank, Dumbarton (1892), Third Lanark (1893), Sheffield Wednesday (August 1895), EVERTON (August 1897), Bolton Wanderers (July 1899), Brentford (July 1903), West Bromwich Albion (June 1904), Hibernian (May 1905; retired May 1912)
Lawrie Bell was a much-travelled, constructive utility player who did well north of the border before gaining an FA Cup-winner's medal with Sheffield Wednesday (1896). He netted 13 goals in 54 games for the Owls and later notched 45 in 103 outings for Bolton. He had a few injury problems during his spell with WBA, but, after returning to Scotland, went on to reach the 300 mark in senior appearances. Rewarded with Scottish League representative honours as a Third Lanark player in 1895, he was twice named as reserve to the full international side. Bell scored twice on his League debut for Everton against Bolton in September 1897.

BENNETT, HENRY SYLVESTER

Wing-half: 3+1 apps
Born: Liverpool, 16 May 1949
Career: EVERTON (apprentice, June 1964; professional, March 1967), Aldershot (January 1971), Crewe Alexandra (July 1973–May 1974)
A reserve at Goodison for almost seven years, Harry Bennett made his First Division debut as a substitute in a 2–0 win at Leicester in September 1967, playing his last game for the club against Manchester City in a League Cup-tie in October 1969. He later appeared in 89 League games for Aldershot and 30 for Crewe.

BENT, MARCUS NATHAN

Forward: *apps, *goals
Born: Hammersmith, London, 19 May 1978
Career: Brentford (apprentice, June 1993; professional, July 1995), Crystal Palace (£150,000, January 1998), Port Vale (£375,000, January 1999), Sheffield United (£300,000, October 1999), Blackburn Rovers (£1.3m, November 2000), Ipswich Town (£3m, November 2001), EVERTON (£450,000, June 2004)
An England Under-21 international (two caps gained), Marcus Bent was signed

to replace the departed Tomasz Radzinski – having already scored over 80 goals in first-class football. His style of play is reminiscent of the traditional centre-forward, holding the ball up well and then spreading out to his wide man. Fast and direct, he will certainly add strength and power to the Blues' attack. Marcus and his younger brother, Darren Bent, were at Ipswich together from 2001 to 2004.

* New signing for 2004–05.

BENTHAM, STANLEY JOSEPH
Inside-right: 125 apps, 17 goals
Born: Leigh, 17 March 1915 – *Died*: May 2002
Career: Lowton St Mary's (Church team), Chesterfield (trial), Bolton Wanderers (trial), Wigan Athletic (professional, April 1932), EVERTON (with Terry Kavanagh, February 1934; retired as a player, May 1949, remained on backroom staff until 1962); Luton Town (coach); guest for Stockport County during the Second World War

Stan Bentham made a dream start with Everton, scoring twice on his senior debut at Grimsby in November 1935. An honest, hard-working, well-built footballer, he loved to roam from his inside-right position and when the Blues won the First Division title in 1938–39, he missed only one game. During the Second World War Bentham appeared in 216 Regional games for the club, netting 54 goals, and continued playing until 1949, having his last senior outing in a blue shirt on Christmas Day 1948 (a 0–0 draw with Manchester City). One pen-picture described him as being an 'honest 90-minute player who worked himself to a standstill fetching and carrying the ball'.

BENTLEY, JOHN
Outside-right: 1 app.
Born: Liverpool, 17 February 1942
Career: EVERTON (amateur, June 1957; professional, November 1959), Stockport County (May 1961–May 1963); later a successful businessman and now a Liverpool taxi driver

Reserve Jack Bentley's only first-team appearance for Everton was against Bolton in a home League game in February 1961, when he deputised for Billy Bingham. He netted six goals in 51 senior outings for Stockport.

BERNARD, MICHAEL PETER
Wing-half/defender: 161+10 apps, 8 goals
Born: Shrewsbury, 10 January 1948
Career: Stoke City (apprentice, April 1964; professional, January 1965), EVERTON (£140,000, April 1972), Oldham Athletic (July 1977; retired, knee injury, May 1979); became a Dee Valley publican; then Football in the Community Officer at Crewe Alexandra; later worked in the club's Commercial Department; now a lawnmower repairer and general maintenance gardener in Swindon

A hard-tackling and resourceful player, Mickey Bernard accumulated a fine record with Stoke, for whom he appeared in 177 games and scored 11 goals. Capped three times by England at Under-23 level, he helped the Potters win the League Cup in March 1972 and a month later moved to Goodison. He made his debut for Everton at Norwich the following August and played in 35 games in 1972–73, scoring his first goal for the club in a 4–1 defeat at West Brom. Linking up with Colin Harvey and Howard Kendall in midfield, Bernard produced some outstanding performances over the next five years, helping the Blues reach the 1977 League Cup final, playing in the first replay against Aston Villa.

BERRY, ARTHUR
Outside-right: 29 apps, 7 goals
Born: Liverpool, 3 January 1888 – *Died*: 15 March 1953
Career: Denstone School (rugby XV, 1904–5; captain, 1905–06); Wrexham (March 1907–March 1909, then December 1909), Wadham College/Oxford (Blue, 1908–09), Liverpool (April–October 1908), Oxford University (November 1908), Fulham (September 1909), EVERTON (August 1909), Wrexham (November 1911), Oxford City, Liverpool (October 1912), Wrexham (December 1912–April 1914), Northern Nomads (August 1914; retired October 1914, after being called to the bar, as a barrister, at Gray's Inn)
Capped once by England against Ireland in 1909 and 24 times as an amateur between 1908 and 1913, gaining Olympic gold medals with Great Britain in the 1908 and 1912 soccer tournaments, Arthur Berry was one of the most brilliant amateurs of his day. A direct, clever winger with thought and precision, one contemporary summed up his all-action style as 'a complete art without tinsel or gaudiness'. He was an FA Amateur Cup winner with Oxford in 1913 (his only club honour). His father, Edwin, was also on Everton's books for a short time. A practising solicitor, he later became a Liverpool director and was chairman at Anfield from 1904 to 1909.

BERRY, C.H.
Goalkeeper: 3 apps
Born: Warrington, *circa* 1883 – Deceased
Career: EVERTON (August 1908–May 1911)
An amateur, Berry deputised for Billy Scott in his three games, making his Everton debut at Bury in February 1909.

BERWICK, WILLIAM JOSEPH
Right-back: 1 app.
Born: Northampton, 1884 – Deceased
Career: Glossop (April 1910), EVERTON (August 1919–April 1920)
Bill Berwick played in one League game for Everton, as deputy for Jack Page against Bolton in November 1919 (3–3 draw). He scored seven goals in 25 League games for Glossop as an inside-right.

BEVERIDGE, ROBERT
Centre-forward: 4 apps
Born: Polmadie, Scotland, 1872 – *Died*: October 1901
Career: Maryhill Harp, Third Lanark, Nottingham Forest (July 1899), EVERTON (September 1900 until his sudden death)
Craggy Bob Beveridge had done well north of the border before Forest recruited him to lead their attack. He did a good job before being whisked away by Everton. He died suddenly at the age of 29 after only four games for the Blues.

BILEY, ALAN PAUL
Striker: 18+3 apps, 3 goals
Born: Leighton Buzzard, 26 February 1957
Career: Luton Town (apprentice, April 1973; professional, March 1975), Cambridge United (free, July 1975), Derby County (£350,000, January 1980), EVERTON (July 1981), Stoke City (loan, March–April 1982), Portsmouth (£100,000, August 1982), Brighton and Hove Albion (£45,000, March 1985), New York (May 1986), Cambridge United (n/c, November–December 1986), spells in Greece and Ireland; Ely Town (manager), Potton United (briefly); now runs his own gym and health club – Biley's in Biggleswade
A much-travelled striker, Alan Biley – positive and highly effective inside the box, especially in the lower divisions – netted over 160 goals in more than 400 matches, including a club record 82 for Cambridge. A Fourth Division championship winner in 1977 and Third Division winner six years later with Portsmouth, he had finished runner-up in that section with Cambridge under Ron Atkinson in 1978. He was 24 when he joined Everton – signed to replace Bob Latchford – but unfortunately injuries interrupted his stay at Goodison and he left after just one season on Merseyside. Biley scored on his debut for the Blues against Birmingham in August 1981.

BILIC, SLAVEN
Defender: 30+2 apps
Born: Croatia, 11 September 1968
Career: Karlsruhe/Germany, West Ham United (£1.3m, February 1996), EVERTON (£4.5m, July 1997; released February 2000)
A Croatian international (almost 50 caps won), Slaven Bilic, solid, well-built, 6 ft 2 in. tall and 13 st. 8 lb in weight, had excellent ball control and was Britain's most expensive defender when he joined Everton in 1997. Unfortunately, he suffered suspension after suspension in the worst season for red and yellow cards, being dismissed three times, all for tackles from behind, as well as receiving eight other cautions. He skippered the Blues at times and was named Croatia's 'Footballer of the Year' and 'Sports Personality of the Year' in 1998. Making his debut for the Blues in a 2–1 home Premiership defeat by Crystal Palace in August 1997, he then played for his country in the 1998 World Cup semi-final, getting French defender Lauren Blanc sent off!

BILLING, PETER GRAHAM

Defender: 5 apps

Born: Liverpool, 24 October 1964

Career: South Liverpool, EVERTON (January 1986), Crewe Alexandra (December 1986), Coventry City (June 1989), Port Vale (loan, February 1993; signed for £35,000, May 1993), Hartlepool United (free, August 1995), Crewe Alexandra (free, August 1996–May 1997)

A reserve at Goodison Park, blond-haired Peter Billing appeared in one League game for the Blues, against West Ham on the last day of 1985–86, replacing Derek Mountford prior to the FA Cup final with Liverpool. A composed defender, he appeared in over 200 League games during his career, helping Port Vale win the Autoglass Trophy in 1993.

BINGHAM, WILLIAM LAURENCE

Outside-right: 98 apps, 26 goals

Born: Belfast, 5 August 1931

Career: Glentoran (August 1949), Sunderland (£7,000, November 1950), Luton Town (£15,000, July 1958), EVERTON (£20,000, October 1960), Port Vale (£15,000, August 1963–April 1965); Southport (trainer/coach, July 1965; manager, December 1965–February 1968), Plymouth Argyle (manager, February 1968–March 1970), Northern Ireland (manager, 1968–August 1970), Linfield (manager, June 1970–May 1971), Greece (national coach, 1971–72), EVERTON (manager, May 1973–January 1977), PAOK Salonika/Greece (manager/coach, April–October 1977), Mansfield Town (manager, March 1978–July 1979), Northern Ireland (national manager, 1979–94), Blackpool (Director of Football, later vice-chairman)

Billy Bingham gained schoolboy and youth caps before going on to play for Northern Ireland on 56 occasions at senior level while also representing the Irish League as a Glentoran player. A fast raiding winger with good skills, he played his part in helping Everton win the First Division title in 1962–63, scoring five goals in 23 games. After leaving Goodison, he took his career tally of League appearances to 419 – 206 with Sunderland – netting 101 goals, an excellent return for a direct winger. He played for Luton in the 1959 FA Cup final defeat by Nottingham Forest and was forced to retire after breaking his leg with Port Vale in 1965.

Under a lot of pressure when he took the manager's job at Goodison, he did so with no illusions, pushing Everton up to seventh spot in the First Division. He signed Bob Latchford and Martin Dobson but sold Howard Kendall and Joe Royle, yet in 1974–75 got the Blues up into fourth place after they had been top at Easter and favourites to win the title. He was sacked when ironically the team lay 13th in the First Division. He played for Northern Ireland in the World Cup finals of 1958 and managed them in the finals of 1982 and 1986.

BIRCH, KENNETH JOSEPH
Wing-half: 45 apps, 1 goal
Born: Birkenhead, 31 December 1933
Career: Birkenhead Boys, Bebington Hawks, EVERTON (professional, August 1951; served in the Army, the Royal Tank Corps, for two years), Southampton (£6,000, March 1958), Chelmsford City (July 1959), Bangor City (August 1960), Benoni/Johannesburg (player–manager, January 1963–65)

Originally a schoolboy centre-forward, Ken Birch developed into a useful right-half who made his debut for the Blues against Sheffield United in April 1956, five years after joining the club (due to Army service). He played in the European Cup-Winners' Cup competition with Bangor.

BIRNIE, ALEXANDER
Outside-right: 3 apps
Born: Aberdeen, 11 January 1884 – Deceased
Career: West Ham United (1903), EVERTON (September 1905), Norwich City (August 1906), Southend United (season 1907–08), Bury (seasons 1908–11)

Signed as cover for Jack Sharp, Alex Birnie made his First Division debut for the Blues against his future club Bury in December 1905. He showed good pace at times and later did well with the Shakers, for whom he scored three goals in 86 League games.

BISHOP, IAN WILLIAM
Midfield: 0+1 app.
Born: Liverpool, 29 May 1965
Career: Merseyside schoolboy football, EVERTON (apprentice, June 1981; professional, May 1983), Crewe Alexandra (loan, March–April 1984), Carlisle United (£15,000, October 1984), Bournemouth (£35,000, July 1988), Manchester City (£465,000, August 1989), West Ham United (£500,000, December 1989), Manchester City (free, March 1998), Miami Fusion/USA (March 2001), Barry Town (August 2002), Rochdale (free, August 2002–January 2003); returned for a mini-spell in the USA; then Burscough (assistant manager, July 2003), Ratcliffe Borough (October 2003)

Ian Bishop's only League appearance for Everton was as a 'sub' against Manchester United in May 1984. He struggled hard and long to get into the first XI, but, after leaving Goodison, he did very well with West Ham. He amassed over 630 career appearances (43 goals) up to 2003. Capped by England 'B', he appeared in the Champions League qualifying games with Barry in 2002.

BLACK, WILLIAM
Right-half: 20 apps
Born: Flemington, Isle of Mull, 1883 – *Died:* Scotland
Career: Enfield Star, Dalziel Rovers, Queen's Park (amateur, August 1902), Celtic (September 1904), EVERTON (July 1905–May 1907)

Willie Black was a well-built, strong-tackling half-back who made 11 appearances for Celtic before joining Everton. He never established himself at Goodison, despite some plucky performances, and was released after two seasons. He made his League debut for the Blues against Newcastle in September 1905, deputising for Harry Makepeace.

BLAIR, JOHN ELLIOTT
Centre-forward: 6 apps, 3 goals
Born: Liverpool, 21 October 1898 – *Died*: Stafford, 1974
Career: Liverpool University, Northern Nomads, EVERTON (March 1920–April 1922), Oldham Athletic (August 1922), Northern Nomads (June 1925), Arsenal (briefly, April 1926), Ilford (August 1926), Northern Nomads (July 1927; retired May 1930); then Derbyshire Council District manager (August 1930–39)

An amateur throughout his career, John Blair, well built and of the 'dashing' sort, averaged a goal every two games for Everton, scoring twice on his League debut, a 4–0 home win over Derby in April 1920, when he stood in for Joe Peacock. He was injured frequently, probably due to the lack of full-time training, and broke his right ankle in April 1924 as an Oldham player. He won the FA Amateur Cup with Nomads in 1926.

BLOMQVIST, LARS JESPER
Winger: 12+6 apps, 1 goal
Born: Tavelsjo, Sweden, 5 February 1974
Career: Tavelsjo IK/Sweden (1990), Umea/Sweden (1992), IFK Gothenburg/Sweden (1993), AC Milan/Italy (1996), Parma/Italy (1997), Manchester United (£4.4m, July 1998), EVERTON (free, November 2001), Charlton Athletic (August 2002; retired June 2003)

A Swedish international, capped over 30 times, Jesper Blomqvist made 38 appearances during his time at Old Trafford. Despite injuries upsetting his rhythm in 2000–01, he nevertheless was a key member of the 1999 treble-winning side. He made his debut for the Blues against Manchester United on Boxing Day 2001 – eight years after being voted Sweden's 'Footballer of the Year' (1993).

BLYTHE, JOSEPH JOHN
Half-back: 35 apps, 1 goal
Born: Twidersmouth, 1877 – Deceased
Career: Delaval Villa (1890), Blyth (1895), Jarrow (August 1897), EVERTON (January 1899), West Ham United (August 1902), Millwall (May 1904), West Ham United (September 1906), Watford (December 1906–08)

A rugged, no-nonsense defender, strong in the tackle, Joe Blythe made an impressive start to his Everton career, playing his first game in February 1899 against Bolton, having been signed after impressing for Jarrow in the FA Cup against the Blues in an earlier game. He appeared in all three half-back positions for the club, always giving 100 per cent. In all he appeared in 60 senior matches for the Hammers.

BOCKING, WILLIAM
Right-back: 16 apps
Born: Stockport, 11 June 1905 – Deceased
Career: Stockport and District junior football, Hyde United, Stockport County (amateur, August 1923; professional, June 1924), EVERTON (£1,800, April 1931), Stockport County (£250, August 1934; retired May 1938)

Accomplished defender Bill Bocking occupied both full-back berths with authority and commitment, making his first-class debut for Stockport in 1925 against Crystal Palace and playing his last match, also for County, in March 1938. He amassed 396 appearances for the Hatters (six goals), skippering the side from 1928 to 1931 and again in 1934–35. During his three years at Goodison he managed only 16 games – due to the presence of Ben Williams and Warney Cresswell and then Billy Cook. Bocking played in three different divisions of the Football League in consecutive matches in 1931 – for Stockport against Wrexham (Division 3, N) on 18 April and then for Everton, his debut against Preston North End (Division 2) on 2 May and for the Blues against Birmingham (Division 1) on 29 August.

BOLTON, HUGH
Inside-right: 87 apps, 34 goals
Born: Port Glasgow, *circa* 1880 – Deceased
Career: Clydeville, Port Glasgow Athletic, Newcastle United (May 1905), EVERTON (January 1906), Bradford Park Avenue (December 1908), Greenock Morton (July 1910–12), Glentoran (to 1915)

Hugh Bolton was an Everton FA Cup winner in 1906 and finalist a year later – having made one appearance for Newcastle. An aggressive forward who could strike the ball hard and true and often placed it accurately, Bolton scored most of his goals for the Blues with low ground shots. He made his Everton debut against his former club, Newcastle, in January 1906 and then beat his former buddies in the Cup final as well.

BONE, JAMES
Inside-left: 2 apps
Born: Liverpool, *circa* 1880 – Deceased
Career: EVERTON (season 1901–02)

An unknown Everton reserve, Jack Bone made the first of his two appearances for the senior side against Blackburn Rovers in February 1902, deputising for Jimmy Settle in a 2–0 defeat.

BOOTH, THOMAS EDWARD
Half-back: 185 apps, 11 goals
Born: Pin Mill Brow, Ardwick, Manchester, 25 April 1874 – *Died*: 1939
Career: Hooley Hill FC, Ashton North End (August 1892), Rest of Lancashire, Blackburn Rovers (May 1896), EVERTON (April 1900–May 1908), Preston North End (briefly), Carlisle United (November 1908; retired 1910)

Tommy Booth was desperately unlucky to miss Everton's 1906 FA Cup final triumph over Newcastle through injury and was absent from the final again 12 months later, this time after losing his place to Jack Taylor. Capped twice by England – the first against Wales in March 1898, the second against Scotland in April 1903 – Booth was unspectacular but still a worthy and consistent defender, in essence a first-rate club man. He gave the Blues dedicated service after making his debut at Preston in September 1900. He scored 11 goals in 120 games for Blackburn.

BORROWS, BRIAN
Defender: 29 apps
Born: Liverpool, 20 December 1960
Career: EVERTON (associated schoolboy forms, April 1975; apprentice, April 1977; professional, April 1980), Bolton Wanderers (£10,000, March 1983), Coventry City (£80,000, June 1985), Bristol City (loan, September–October 1993), Swindon Town (free, September 1997; retired May 1999)
England 'B' international (capped against Czechoslovakia in 1990) Brian 'Bugsy' Borrows made his League debut against Stoke in February 1982 – seven years after joining Everton. He later appeared in almost 500 appearances for Coventry but missed the 1987 FA Cup final triumph after twisting his knee a week before the big event. A highly skilful and consistent performer, especially at Highfield Road, he played in over 700 games in his career and was voted 'Player of the Year' at Coventry in 1990 and Swindon in 1998.

BORTHWICK, JOHN B.
Centre-half: 25 apps
Born: Scotland, *circa* 1882 – Deceased
Career: Wemyss Violet FC, Lochgelly United, Hibernian, EVERTON (September 1907), Millwall Athletic (August 1911–May 1915)
Well-built defender, signed as cover for Booth and Taylor, Jack Borthwick made his League debut for the Blues against Sheffield Wednesday in April 1908. He remained loyal to the club, having his best spell in the first team between October 1909 and April 1910 when he made 19 appearances. His son, William Borthwick, who died in 2003, was Everton's youth-team coach immediately after the Second World War.

BOWMAN, ADAM
Inside/outside-left/centre-forward: 11 apps, 3 goals
Born: Forfar, 12 August 1868 – Deceased
Career: St Johnstone (1897), East Stirlingshire (1899), EVERTON (March 1902), Blackburn Rovers (March 1903), Brentford (July 1907), Leeds City (1908), Brentford, Portsmouth, Leith Athletic, Accrington Stanley (1914–15); did not figure after the First World War
Described in 1902 as being 'a tricky player, knowing how to seize any available opening, but is inclined to procrastinate', Adam Bowman's career spanned 18 years, during which time he served with nine different clubs. He played his first four League games for the Blues on the left-wing, making his debut in a 1–0

win at Small Heath in March 1902. He later moved inside and also played at centre-forward. He scored 44 goals in 104 starts for Blackburn.

BOYES, WALTER EDWARD
Inside-left/outside-left/left-half: 73 apps, 15 goals
Born: Kilamarsh, Sheffield, 5 January 1913 – *Died*: September 1960
Career: Sheffield Boys, Woodhouse Mills United, West Bromwich Albion (February 1931), EVERTON (£6,000, February 1938); guest for Aldershot, Brentford, Clapton Orient, Leeds United, Manchester United, Middlesbrough, Millwall, Newcastle United, Preston North End and Sunderland during the Second World War; Notts County (player–coach, June 1949), Scunthorpe United (player–trainer, 1950–53), Retford Town (player–manager, 1954), Hyde United (player–manager, 1958), Swansea Town (trainer, 1959; retired through illness, May 1960); also sports master at Oakwood Collegiate School, Sheffield (1952–58)
Standing a fraction under 5 ft 4 in. tall, Wally 'Titty' Boyes was a diminutive but well-built footballer who occupied three different positions for WBA before moving to Everton. He played predominantly on the left-wing for the Blues after replacing Doug Trentham, who had failed to establish himself in the side in place of Jackie Coulter. Always giving 100 per cent, he made his debut for the Blues in a 4–4 draw at Leeds in February 1938 and the following season netted four goals in 36 League outings when the League championship was won. Earlier he had scored for WBA in the 1935 FA Cup final defeat by Sheffield Wednesday. Boyes gained three full England caps (two with Everton) and also played in the Jubilee international (against Scotland in 1938). As a teenager he once scored 17 goals in a game that his team won 31–2. Boyes played with his former Everton team-mate Tommy Lawton at Notts County (1949–50).

BOYLE, DANIEL
Right-back/right-half: 7 apps
Born: *circa* 1875 – Deceased
Career: New Brighton Tower, EVERTON (August 1901), Dundee (May 1902)
Signed as cover for Wolstenholme, Danny Boyle remained at Everton for one season, making his debut at right-half against Manchester City in August 1901, starring in a 3–1 win.

BOYLE, RICHARD H.
Right-half/centre-half: 243 apps, 8 goals
Born: Dumbarton, 24 September 1869 – Deceased
Career: Dumbarton Episcopalians, Dumbarton Union (1888), Dumbarton (1890), EVERTON (August 1892), Dundee (May 1901)
A famous Scottish import, Dick Boyle, 5 ft 6in. tall, made an immediate impact at Goodison Park and after four years was appointed Everton captain. Strong in all aspects of defensive play, he led by example and was not just a stopper but could pass the ball with precision and authority and it was rare to see him hoof the ball downfield, hoping it would find a colleague! He could deliver a pin-point pass and,

with his awkward-looking gait, often surged upfield with great purpose. He made his League debut against Nottingham Forest in September 1892 and played his last game for the Blues against Derby County in April 1901. He was in Everton's beaten FA Cup final team of 1897.

BRACEWELL, PAUL WILLIAM

Midfield: 142+4 apps, 12 goals
Born: Heswall, Cheshire, 19 July 1962
Career: Stoke City (apprentice, July 1978; professional, February 1980), Sunderland (£225,000, July 1983), EVERTON (£250,000, May 1984), Sunderland (loan, August 1989; signed for £250,000, September 1989), Newcastle United (£250,000, June 1992), Sunderland (£50,000, player–coach, May 1995), Fulham (£75,000, player–coach, October 1997; retired as a player, May 1999; later coach/assistant manager, then manager, May 1999–July 2000), Halifax Town (manager), Walsall (assistant manager/coach, February 2004)

Paul Bracewell played in three losing FA Cup finals with Everton (1985, 1986, 1989) and a fourth with Sunderland (1992, against Liverpool). He made his first and last appearances for the Blues against Liverpool at Wembley – his debut came in the 1984 Charity Shield and his last was in the 1989 FA Cup final. Highly skilful, he gained three full and 13 Under-21 caps for England (1983–85), won the League title (1985), collected two First Division championship medals (1993, 1996), twice won promotion from the Second Division (1990, as runners-up, and 1999, as champions) and helped Everton win the European Cup-Winners' Cup (1985). A steadying influence on the game, Bracewell was a gritty, determined performer who had a simple yet efficient approach when it came to passing the ball, never looking hurried, always in control. Injuries certainly ruined his career at Goodison Park! He was the first signing made by Kevin Keegan when he took over as manager of Fulham, and appeared in 720 club games during his 21-year career (27 goals). Bracewell is one of the few players to have won titles with four different clubs.

BRADSHAW, FRANCIS

Inside/centre-forward: 74 apps, 21 goals
Born: Sheffield, 31 May 1884 – *Died*: Somerset, *circa* 1950
Career: Oxford St Sunday School, Sheffield Wednesday (amateur, April 1904; professional, September 1904), Northampton Town (July 1910), EVERTON (November 1911), Arsenal (June 1914; retired May 1923), Aberdare Athletic (manager, 1923–24); later worked and lived in Taunton

As a Sheffield Wednesday player, Frank Bradshaw gained an FA Cup-winner's medal in 1907 and one England cap in 1908. An ingenious forward, fast and dangerous with a powerful right-foot shot, he sustained several serious injuries during his career. He made his debut for Everton against Manchester City in November 1911 and played his last game against Oldham in April 1914. Converted into a wing-half and then full-back by Arsenal, he appeared in 142 games for the Gunners.

BRADSHAW, GEORGE FREDERICK
Goalkeeper: 3 apps
Born: Southport, 10 March 1913 – *Died*: 1989
Career: High Park Villa, Southport (amateur, August 1931), New Brighton (amateur, August 1932; professional, September 1933), EVERTON (November 1934), Arsenal (March 1935), Doncaster Rovers (May 1936), Bury (June 1938), Oldham Athletic (July 1950; retired July 1951)
George Bradshaw, whose anticipation and positioning was first class, made over 250 League appearances during his career, having his final outing for Oldham against Rotherham in August 1950. He made his debut for Everton against Aston Villa in February 1935, deputising for Ted Sagar.

BRADY, ALEC
Inside-right: 36 apps, 20 goals
Born: Cathcart, near Glasgow, Scotland, 1864 – *Died*: 28 April 1913
Career: Renton Thistle, Partick Thistle (1884), Burnley (August 1888), Sunderland (February 1889), EVERTON (November 1889), Celtic (August 1891), Sheffield Wednesday (with Jack Madden, August 1892; retired, injured, May 1899)
Alec Brady, who was regarded as one of the most scientific players in English football in the 1890s, scored twice on his League debut for Everton against Stoke in November 1889. He was also the first player to register a hat-trick for the Blues in the FA Cup, doing so against Derby in January 1890. A League championship-winner with Everton (1891), he later helped Celtic win the Scottish Cup (1892) and Sheffield Wednesday the FA Cup (1896). A fine inside-forward with the capacity for the inch-perfect pass, Brady was both tricky and fast, although many found it amusing to watch him run because he took such short steps. He never received the international recognition many thought he deserved. He played his last competitive game for the Owls against Stoke in January 1899, after netting 38 goals in 177 games for the Sheffield club.

BRAMWELL, JOHN
Full-back: 56 apps
Born: Ashton-in-Makerfield, 1 March 1937
Career: Wigan Athletic (April 1952), EVERTON (professional, April 1958), Luton Town (October 1960–May 1965)
A clean kicker with good positional sense, John Bramwell made his League debut for Everton at Burnley in September 1958 in place of Bryan Griffiths. He failed to hold down a regular place in the side the following season. After Tommy Jones had switched from centre-half to left-back, Bramwell moved to Luton, for whom he appeared in 187 League games.

BRANCH, PAUL MICHAEL
Forward: 17+27 apps, 3 goals
Born: Liverpool, 18 October 1978
Career: EVERTON (apprentice, April 1994; professional, October 1995),

Manchester City (loan, October–November 1998), Wolverhampton Wanderers (£500,000, November 1999), Reading (loan, March 2002), Hull City (loan, October–November 2002), Bradford City (free transfer, July 2003), Chester City (July 2004)

Capped by England at schoolboy, youth and Under-21 levels, Michael Branch was on the bench quite a lot during his Everton days. A life-long Blues' fan, he made his League debut as a substitute in a 2–0 defeat at Manchester United in February 1996 and later appeared in 79 games for Wolves. His elder brother, Graham, played for Tranmere, Bury, Wigan, Stockport and Burnley.

BRAND, ANDREW SCOUGAL

Goalkeeper: 2 apps
Born: Edinburgh, 8 November 1957
Career: EVERTON (apprentice, April 1974; professional, November 1975), Crewe Alexandra (loan, February–April 1977 and August 1978), Hereford United (May 1980), Wrexham (loan, November 1982), Witton Albion (August 1983), Blackpool (n/c, March–April 1984)

'Drew' Brand made his League debut for Everton in a 5–2 defeat at Leeds in November 1975 but had to wait 18 months before making his second appearance at senior level. He played in 54 League games for Hereford.

BRANNICK, JAMES

Inside-right: 3 apps, 2 goals
Born: Scotland, *circa* 1888 – Deceased
Career: EVERTON (April 1912), St Mirren (August 1914)

Reserve Jim Brannick spent two seasons at Goodison Park but failed to dislodge Frank Jeffers from the inside-right berth, despite netting twice in his three League games, including a fine goal on his debut against Blackburn on Boxing Day 1912.

BREARLEY, JOHN

Right-half/inside-right: 24 apps, 8 goals
Born: West Derby, Liverpool, October 1875 – Deceased
Career: Kettering Town, Notts County (August 1897), Chatham (May 1898), Millwall Athletic (July 1899), Notts County (May 1900), Middlesbrough (April 1901), EVERTON (May 1902), Tottenham Hotspur (May 1903), Crystal Palace (May 1907), Millwall Athletic (player–coach, September 1909–May 1911); later Berlin Victoria/Germany (coach, to 1915)

John Brearley, a player of all-round ability, was able to occupy at least five different outfield positions but always looked comfortable (and enjoyed) performing at inside-right, where he made his debut for Everton against WBA in September 1902. Signed for Spurs by his former colleague John Cameron, Brearley represented the Professionals of the South against the Amateurs of the South in an England trial at White Hart Lane in January 1905. He scored 24 goals in 133 games for the Londoners, having earlier netted 13 times in 51 games for Millwall, whom he helped win the Southern League District

Combination and reach the semi-final of the FA Cup in 1900. When working in Germany during the First World War, Brearley was then interned at Ruhleben prison camp along with several other sportsmen, most of them footballers, including his former manager Cameron.

BREWSTER, GEORGE
Centre-half: 68 apps, 5 goals
Born: Culsalmond, Aberdeenshire, 7 October 1893 – *Died*: 1963
Career: Aberdeen Mugiemoss, Aberdeen (May 1913), Falkirk (First World War guest), EVERTON (£1,500, January 1920), Wolverhampton Wanderers (November 1922), Lovells Athletic (February 1923), Wallasey United (June 1923), Brooklands Athletic/New York (coach, March 1924), Inverness (player–manager, August 1924–May 1926)

George 'Dod' Brewster was an influential, composed centre-half who was capped once by Scotland against England in 1921. Regarded as the proverbial 'sheet-anchor' in the Everton defence, 6 ft tall and weighing 13 st., he made his debut against Sheffield Wednesday in January 1920, taking over from Tom Fleetwood, who later moved to right-back. He had been immensely popular at Pittodrie, but the First World War severely disrupted his career and, in fact, after the hostilities he appeared in only 75 League games, having previously netted nine goals in 119 matches for the Dons.

BRIGGS, HENRY F.
Goalkeeper: 11 apps
Born: Lancashire, *circa* 1870 – Deceased
Career: Darwen (May 1893), EVERTON (April 1896; retired, injured, May 1897)

Harry Briggs spent just over a season with Everton, appearing in a third of the games. He made his debut against Stoke on the last day of the 1895–96 campaign, when he stood in for England international Jack Hillman.

BRINDLE, WILLIAM
Midfield: 2 apps
Born: Liverpool, 29 January 1950
Career: EVERTON (apprentice, April 1966; professional, August 1967), Barnsley (May 1970–April 1971)

Bill Brindle's League career amounted to two games (one with Everton, one as a 'sub' with Barnsley). A reserve midfielder, he made his debut for the Blues (in place of Howard Kendall) at Nottingham Forest when manager Harry Catterick fielded a weakened team just five days before the 1968 FA Cup semi-final with Leeds. His only other outing for the club was against Manchester City in a League Cup-tie at Maine Road in October 1969.

BRISCOE, WILLIAM HENRY
Inside-left: 4 apps
Born: Liverpool, *circa* 1865 – Deceased
Career: EVERTON (August 1886–May 1889)
Billy Briscoe – who appeared in all five forward-line positions for the Blues – scored 25 goals in 66 games during his first two seasons with Everton, appearing in the club's first-ever FA Cup-tie against Bolton in October 1887. Unfortunately, he failed to establish himself in the side when League football was introduced, making only three appearances in the initial campaign, his debut coming at Notts County in mid-October 1888.

BRITTON, CLIFFORD SAMUEL
Right-half: 242 apps, 3 goals
Born: Hanham, Bristol, 27 August 1909 – Deceased
Career: Hanham Athletic, Hanham United Methodists, Bristol St George, Bristol Rovers (amateur, April 1926; professional, August 1928), EVERTON (June 1930; retired October 1945); Burnley (manager, October 1945), EVERTON (manager, September 1948–February 1956), Preston North End (manager, August 1956; resigned April 1961), Hull City (manager, July 1961; general manager, November 1969; retired October 1971)
Cliff Britton was a member of Everton's Second Division championship and FA Cup-winning sides in 1931 and 1933 respectively. He won 21 caps for England, nine at full international level (1934–37) and 12 during wartime (1941–44), when he formed a tremendous middle-line with Stan Cullis (Wolves) and his own team-mate Joe Mercer. A right-half of great style and efficiency, polish and poise, he always wanted the ball and loved to drive forward, assisting his front men whenever possible. A real quality footballer, he actually began his career as a right-winger before developing into one of the finest half-backs in the game. He made only one appearance when Everton won the League title in 1939, having made his debut for the Blues against Tottenham Hotspur in October 1930, when he deputised for Lachlan McPherson.

BROAD, JAMES
Inside-forward: 21 apps, 8 goals
Born: Stalybridge, 10 November 1891 – *Died*: Chelmsford, 22 August 1963
Career: St Mark's (West Gorton), Stalybridge Celtic, Manchester City (November 1909), Oldham Athletic (August 1913); guest for Blackburn Rovers and Greenock Morton during the First World War; Millwall Athletic (£1,000, April 1919), Stoke (£2,000, June 1921), Sittingbourne, EVERTON (£1,400, November 1924), New Brighton (£200, December 1925), Watford (September 1926), Caernarvon Town (July 1927), Taunton Town (September 1928), Fleetwood Town (August 1931; retired November 1931), Chelmsford City (groundsman, December 1931); later coach with Coruña, Las Palmas and Barcelona (in Spain) and FC Geneva (Switzerland)
Jimmy Broad began as a goalkeeper before becoming one of the most dangerous

and gifted forwards in League football. Clever on the ball, a great finisher, he never gave less than 100 per cent and netted 32 goals in 39 games for Millwall in 1919–20 and was the Second Division's leading marksman in 1921–22 with Stoke. He never settled down at Goodison Park after a disappointing debut in a 3–0 defeat at Blackburn a week after joining the club. The son of the Manchester City trainer Jack Broad, he had two other footballing brothers: Wilf, who was also at Manchester City, and Tommy, who played for Oldham, Chesterfield, Bristol City, WBA, Stoke, Southampton, Manchester City and Rhyl.

BROMILOW, WILLIAM
Goalkeeper: 1 app.
Born: Liverpool, *circa* 1888 – Deceased
Career: EVERTON (August 1912), Oldham Athletic (July 1920), Wigan Borough (1921–23)
A reserve at Goodison Park, Bill Bromilow's only senior game for the Blues was against his future club, Oldham, in April 1913; they lost 3–2. He also played in six First World War games and later appeared in 33 League games for Wigan.

BROWELL, ANTHONY
Centre-half: 1 app.
Born: Walbottle, Northumberland, September 1888 – *Died*: Hull, 7 March 1964
Career: Newburn Juniors, Hull City (July 1907), EVERTON (February 1912), West Stanley (1913–24); returned to Hull, where he worked as a coal-miner and later for a local bus company
A very capable, solid, determined centre-half, 'Andy' Browell made over 100 first-class appearances for Hull City before following his brother Tom (q.v.) to Everton, a couple of months after the latter's transfer. His only start for the Blues was in place of the injured Tom Fleetwood against Manchester City in November 1912. He gave West Stanley dedicated service before, during and after the First World War. He had another brother, George, who also played for Hull and Grimsby.

BROWELL, THOMAS
Centre-forward: 60 apps, 37 goals
Born: Walbottle, Northumberland, 19 October 1892 – *Died*: 8 October 1955
Career: Newburn Grange (Tyneside), Hull City (£2, October 1910), EVERTON (£1,550, October 1911), Manchester City (£1,780, October 1913), Blackpool (£1,150, September 1926), Lytham FC (player–coach, June 1930), Morecambe (December 1933–May 1934); became a tram driver
Tom 'Boy' Browell – the youngest of three brothers – scored twice on his Everton debut against Manchester United in January 1912. Prior to that he had become one of the legendary Hull City 'Tigers', netting 32 goals in 48 games for the Humberside club. Full of pluck, he was a consistent scorer everywhere he went and claimed 223 goals in over 400 competitive matches at club level alone. Four of his 157 goals in 280 outings for Manchester City came against Everton in September 1925. Browell represented the Football League against the

Scottish League in 1920 and was an FA Cup winner with Manchester City in 1926. The three Browell brothers played together at Hull.

BROWN, ALEXANDER DEWAR
Full-back/Midfield: 210+43 apps, 11 goals
Born: Grangemouth, Scotland, 24 March 1939
Career: Partick Thistle (1957), EVERTON (£38,000, September 1963), Shrewsbury Town (free, May 1971), Southport (July 1972), Fleetwood Town (July 1973)
Sandy Brown (who came on as a substitute for Fred Pickering) was the first Everton substitute to score a goal, doing so against Liverpool in a League game in August 1966. A Scottish schoolboy international, he was a versatile player able to occupy a number of positions, producing his best form as a full-back. Signed as cover for Mick Meagan and Alex Parker, he made his debut for the Blues against Burnley in September 1964 (at left-back) before taking over the right-back berth. He unfortunately missed the 1966 FA Cup final triumph, having played in four earlier rounds. He was a Fourth Division championship winner with Southport (1973).

BROWN, WILLIAM
Outside-left/centre-forward: 6 apps, 2 goals
Born: Liverpool, *circa* 1865 – Deceased
Career: Stanley FC, EVERTON (October 1888–May 1889)
Billy Brown scored on his League debut for Everton against Bolton in November 1888. He was one of eight players used by the Blues in the left-wing position during that initial League season.

BROWN, WILLIAM
Right-half: 179 apps
Born: Cambuslang, 10 May 1897 – Deceased
Career: Flemington Hearts, Cambuslang Rangers, Partick Thistle, EVERTON (amateur, August 1913; professional, July 1914), Nottingham Forest (£200, May 1928), Liverpool Cables (player–coach, August 1930)
An engineer's fitter by trade, Willie Brown, a cultured, patient footballer, was part of a wonderfully effective Everton half-back line in the 1920s. The first 17-year-old to play for Everton (and the club's youngest before Tommy Lawton), he made his League debut against Manchester City in December 1914 and during the First World War made a further 22 appearances.

BUCK, HENRY STANLEY
Outside-right: 1 app.
Born: Birkenhead, *circa* 1883 – Deceased
Career: Tranmere Rovers, EVERTON (seasons 1907–09)
Reserve Harry Buck's only League outing for Everton was in a 3–0 defeat by Bradford City in April 1909.

BUCKLE, HERBERT EDWARD
Outside-right: 107 apps, 33 goals
Born: Southwark, London, 28 October 1924 – *Died*: 1990
Career: Royal Navy football, Manchester United (amateur, October 1945; professional, November 1945), EVERTON (November 1949), Exeter City (July 1955), Prestatyn FC (player–manager, summer 1957), Dolgellau (1961–62)

Ted Buckle, an inside-forward, could also play as a wing-half, but it was thought he was far too slight for the rigorous challenges in centre-field so Manchester United boss Matt Busby switched him to the wing. He scored on his League debut for the Reds against Charlton in January 1947, having earlier netted a hat-trick against Leeds when appearing in his first competitive wartime match in November 1945. His debut for Everton was against his former club (Manchester United) just after arriving on Merseyside, playing on the left-wing, but for his third game was switched to the right, and later had outings in both inside-forward positions.

BUCKLEY, MICHAEL JOHN
Midfield: 158 apps, 12 goals
Born: Manchester, 4 November 1953
Career: EVERTON (apprentice, April 1969; professional, June 1971), Sunderland (August 1978), Hartlepool United (August 1983), Carlisle United (September 1983), Middlesbrough (June 1984–May 1985)

As a teenager, Mick Buckley received offers from both Manchester clubs before joining Everton. Making excellent progress, he gained England youth recognition (playing in the 'Little' World Cup in Spain, 1972) and after adding one Under-23 cap to his collection, went on to accumulate a fine record as a midfielder, appearing in 314 League games for his five clubs (19 goals). He had to wait until March 1972 before making his debut for the Blues against Wolves, linking up with Howard Kendall and Henry Newton.

BURNETT, GEORGE GORDON
Goalkeeper: 54 apps
Born: Liverpool, 11 February 1920 – *Died*: 1985
Career: Litherland Boys' Club, Liverpool Schoolboys, EVERTON (amateur, May 1938; professional, September 1938), Oldham Athletic, Ellesmere Port (July 1955; retired May 1956); became a Chester licensee

George Burnett, cool and thoroughly capable, got few opportunities with Everton, where he was in the shadow of Ted Sagar. However, after leaving Goodison, he gave excellent service to Oldham, appearing in more than 100 competitive games, helping the Latics win the Third Division (N) title in 1953 when he missed only four League matches. He was between the posts when Everton beat Oldham 4–0 in 1954 to gain promotion to the top flight.

BURROWS, DAVID

Left-back: 23 apps
Born: Dudley, 25 October 1968
Career: St Martin's Junior and Alexandra High Schools (Tipton), West Bromwich District and West Midlands County Schools, Bustleholme Boys (West Bromwich), West Bromwich Albion (apprentice, April 1985; professional, October 1986), Liverpool (£625,000, October 1988), West Ham United (September 1993), EVERTON (deal involving Tony Cottee, September 1994), Coventry City (£1.1m, March 1995), Birmingham City (free, July 2000), Sheffield Wednesday (free, March 2002; retired May 2003); also Alexandra FC (Sunday team coach, 1987–88)

David Burrows made his League debut for WBA against Sheffield Wednesday in April 1986. He developed quickly, so much so that in 1988 Kenny Dalglish signed him for Liverpool. He went from strength to strength; gained three England 'B' caps and seven at Under-21 level and was rewarded with Charity Shield (1989), League Championship (1990) and FA Cup (1992) winner's medals while making almost 200 appearances during his time at Anfield. After his first start in a 'blue' shirt against Blackburn in the Premiership in September 1994, Burrows, who preferred the left-back position but could also occupy a central defensive berth, was unfortunately not the type of player for boss Joe Royle. He made 486 appearances at club level before retiring in 2003.

BURTON, ANDREW DOUGLAS

Outside- or inside-right: 12 apps, 4 goals
Born: Lochgelly, Scotland, 1884 – Deceased
Career: Thompson's Rovers (Lochgelly), Lochgelly Juniors, Motherwell (August 1903), Bristol City (July 1905), EVERTON (August 1911), Reading (February 1912–15)

Andrew Burton proved a great influence on the Bristol City team during the early 1900s. In his first season at Ashton Gate he won a Second Division championship medal; the following year he gained a Division One runner's-up medal and in 1909 helped City reach the FA Cup final, where they were beaten by Manchester United. In 1911, with City relegated, and having scored 51 goals in 216 games, he moved to Everton, making his debut for the Blues on the opening day of the season, netting once in a 2–2 home draw with Spurs. He failed to establish himself in the side and quickly switched his allegiance to Reading.

CADAMARTERI, DANIEL LEON

Forward: 60+61 apps, 15 goals
Born: Bradford, 12 October 1979
Career: EVERTON (trainee, April 1995; professional, October 1996), Fulham (loan, November–December 1999), Bradford City (free, February 2002), Leeds United (July 2004), Sheffield United (£50,000, September 2004)

Danny Cadamarteri, aged 17 years, 344 days, scored for Everton against Barnsley at Goodison Park in a Premiership game in September 1997, having made his debut as a 'sub' on the last day of the previous season against Chelsea. A powerful, positive, pacy striker with two good feet and an eye for goal, he was an FA Youth Cup winner in 1998 and played for England at both youth and Under-21 levels. A month into the 1998–99 season he scored five times in five games, including a memorable goal against Liverpool. He currently holds the record for most substitute appearances by an Everton player (61). He established a useful partnership with Ashley Ward at Bradford before injuries disrupted his performances.

CAHILL, TIMOTHY

Midfield: *apps *goals
Born: Sydney, Australia, 6 December 1979
Career: Sydney United/Australia (June 1996), Millwall (July 1997), EVERTON (£2m, July 2004)
Capped as a youth-team player by Western Samoa, Tim Cahill was recruited to boost the Blues' midfield, having appeared in almost 250 games for Millwall, helping the Lions reach the 2004 FA Cup final. A forceful, strong-running player with an eye for goal, he loves to arrive late inside the penalty area, and, besides packing a powerful right-foot shot, he is also a good header of the ball. He is looking to do well in the Premiership.
    * New signing for 2004–05.

CAIN, ROBERT

Full-back/wing-half: 10 apps
Born: Slamannan, Scotland, 13 February 1866 – Deceased
Career: Airdrieonians (1885), EVERTON (October 1889), Bootle (August 1890), Sheffield United (August 1892), Tottenham Hotspur (May 1898), Albion Rovers (July 1899), Small Heath/Birmingham (1900)
Bob Cain failed to make much of an impression with any of his first three clubs, including Everton, for whom he made his League debut in an 8–0 home win over Stoke in November 1889. He appeared in over 175 games for Sheffield United before adding a further 69 outings to his tally with Spurs.

CAIN, THOMAS

Goalkeeper: 12 apps
Born: Sunderland, October 1872 – *Died*: 1952
Career: Hebburn Argyle, Stoke (November 1893), EVERTON (April 1894), Southampton St Mary's (October 1895), Grimsby Town (£20, April 1896), Hebburn Argyle (October 1896), West Stanley (January 1897–May 1899)
Tom Cain, 6 ft tall and 12 st. in weight, was a reasonable keeper but weak under pressure. After 11 League appearances for Stoke, he joined Everton, for whom he made his debut in a 3–1 win at Bolton in October 1894. He had a nightmare baptism for Southampton, conceding seven goals at Clapton.

CALDWELL, JAMES HENRY
Goalkeeper: 36 apps
Born: Carronshore, near Falkirk, Scotland, 1886 – Deceased
Career: Carron Thistle, Dunipace FC (Stirlingshire), East Stirling (1905), Tottenham Hotspur (August 1908), Reading (November 1908), EVERTON (August 1912), Woolwich Arsenal (June 1913), Reading (July 1914); did not feature after the First World War
Signed to replace William Scott, Jimmy Caldwell made his debut for the Blues against his former club, Spurs, in September 1912. A safe handler of the ball with good reflexes, he held his position in the side until late in that season when fellow Scot Bill Hodge took over between the posts.

CAMERON, DANIEL PATRICK
Centre-half: 1 app.
Born: Dublin, Ireland, 16 June 1922
Career: Glencalm FC, Shelbourne United, EVERTON (July 1948), Sligo Rovers (September 1949–51)
A well-built defender who came to Goodison Park with a big reputation, Pat Cameron was one of three centre-halves used by Everton in the space of 11 days early in the 1948–49 season. He struggled in his only League game – a crushing 5–0 home defeat at the hands of Portsmouth in September 1948. He was never called upon again.

CAMERON, JOHN
Inside/centre-forward: 48 apps, 14 goals
Born: Ayr, Scotland, 13 April 1872 – *Died:* Glasgow, 20 April 1935
Career: Ayr Grammar School, Ayr Parkhouse, Queen's Park, EVERTON (September 1895), Tottenham Hotspur (May 1898; appointed player–manager, February 1899, reverting to amateur status, January 1906, resigning as manager in May 1907); Dresden FC/Germany (coach, 1907–08); Ayr United (manager, 1919); went into football journalism (1921) having been a columnist for various newspapers prior to the First World War
John Cameron was a very effective goal-maker and goalscorer who had done well in Scotland before joining Everton, for whom he made his senior debut in a 5–0 home League win over Sheffield United in October 1895. He occasionally produced some excellent displays for the Blues, but in 1898 chose to move to Spurs, where eventually he replaced Frank Brettell as manager. Cameron led the Spurs attack when they won the Southern League in 1900 and scored in the 1901 FA Cup final replay defeat of Sheffield United 12 months later. He notched 139 goals in 293 appearances for the Londoners and was a key figure when the Players' Union (the current PFA) was set up in 1907, the year he resigned as manager after differences of opinion with directors.

CAMPBELL, KEVIN JOSEPH
Striker: 135+22 apps, 51 goals
Born: Lambeth, London, 4 February 1970
Career: Arsenal (trainee, June 1986; professional, February 1988), Leyton Orient (loan, January–April 1989), Leicester City (loan, November–December 1989), Nottingham Forest (£3m, July 1995), Trabzonspor/Turkey (£2.5m, August 1998), EVERTON (£3m, March 1999)

Capped once by England 'B' and four times at Under-21 level, Kevin Campbell was Everton's top scorer three seasons running, 1998–99 to 2000–01, and again in 2002–03. He had done well at Highbury, making his League debut for the Gunners at Everton as an 18 year old in May 1988. He scored 59 goals in 228 games, helping Arsenal win the FA Youth Cup in 1988 and the League and FA Cup double in 1993, followed by European Cup-winner's Cup glory a year later. He then netted 35 times in 96 outings for Forest, whom he helped gain promotion to the Premiership before having a spell in Turkey. He returned to England and made his debut for Everton against Liverpool in April 1999 when the Reds won 3–2 at Anfield. A strong, purposeful player, who has suffered with injuries, Campbell made his 500th appearance in England for Everton against Arsenal in January 2004.

CAMPBELL, WILLIAM CECIL
Right-back/half-back/inside-left: 20 apps, 2 goals
Born: Scotland, 1865 – Deceased
Career: Bootle (1888), EVERTON (July 1890), Bootle (1892), EVERTON (briefly, 1896), Clyde (April 1896–98)

Versatile Bill 'Wattie' Campbell had to fight for first-team football with Everton owing to the form and the presence of Messrs Kirkwood, Parry, Robertson and others. He scored on his League debut in a 4–1 win at WBA in September 1890. (There was another inside-forward named W.C. Campbell around in the 1890s and some reference books have the respective records of these two players mixed up.)

CARSLEY, LEE KEVIN
Midfield: 51+9 apps, 6 goals
Born: Birmingham, 28 February 1974
Career: Derby County (apprentice, May 1990; professional, July 1992), Blackburn Rovers (£3.4m, March 1999), Coventry City (£2.5m, December 2000), EVERTON (£1.95m, February 2002)

Capped early in his career by the Republic of Ireland at Under-21 level, aggressive midfielder Lee Carsley has now won over 30 full caps while also accumulating more than 300 appearances (to 2004), including 166 for Derby. A dependable and committed player, Carsley gives nothing less than 100 per cent on the field.

CASKIE, JAMES
Outside-left: 5 apps, 1 goal
Born: Scotland, *circa* 1912 – Deceased
Career: St Johnstone, EVERTON (March 1939), Rangers (August 1945–May 1949)
Smart, attacking winger Jim Caskie gained eight wartime caps for Scotland (1939–44) after helping Everton win the League title in 1939, when he deputised late on for Wally Boyes. He netted five times in 39 outings for Rangers, helping them complete the League and League Cup double in 1947 and win the Scottish Cup the following season.

CASSIDY, JAMES
Outside-right: 2 apps
Born: Liverpool, *circa* 1865 – Deceased
Career: EVERTON (1887–88)
Jim Cassidy spent one season with Everton. He participated in two senior games – both in the FA Cup against Bolton in October 1887 – but was released before League football started the following September.

CATTERICK, HARRY
Centre-forward: 71 apps, 24 goals (plus a Second World War record of 71 apps and 55 goals)
Born: Darlington, 26 November 1919 – *Died*: Goodison Park, 9 March 1985
Career: Stockport County (amateur, May 1934), Cheadle Heath Nomads, EVERTON (professional, March 1937); guest for Manchester United during the Second World War; Crewe Alexandra (player–manager, December 1951; retired as a player, May 1952), Rochdale (manager, June 1953), Sheffield Wednesday (manager, August 1958), EVERTON (manager, April 1961; general manager, April 1973), Preston North End (manager, August 1975–May 1977)
Harry Catterick – one of the great football club managers of the post-Second World War era – reached the pinnacle of his success with Everton during the 1960s and 1970s. As a player at Goodison, he understudied Tommy Lawton, then Jock Dodds and his appearances were also limited owing to the war. When peacetime soccer returned, he broke his arm twice in a short space of time, but, despite some tempting offers, remained loyal to Everton until becoming player–manager of Crewe. He made his first-team debut for the Blues against Manchester City in a Western Regional League game in March 1940 and had to wait until August 1946 before his first League match, against Brentford, although he did play in two FA Cup matches against Preston seven months earlier. Catterick learned the managerial trade the hard way – in the lower divisions. He helped Sheffield Wednesday gain promotion from Division Two (1959), reach the FA Cup semi-final a year later and then finish runners-up to Spurs in the Football League in 1961. Frustrated by a lack of money to spend on new players, he left Hillsborough for Goodison, where he earned a reputation as being the 'silent gentleman of football'.

The Everton directors allowed him to buy and sell as he wished and in 1963 his efforts were rewarded when the Blues won the League title. He followed up with victory in the 1966 FA Cup final (against Sheffield Wednesday) but suffered defeat in the same competition two years later when WBA won in extra time. A second League title was secured in 1970.

Among the quality players he brought to Everton were Gordon West, Tony Kay, Ray Wilson, Fred Pickering, Alan Ball (for a record fee) and Howard Kendall, and he developed many more, including Colin Harvey, Jimmy Husband, Joe Royle, John Hurst and Tommy Wright.

After a couple of disappointing seasons, Catterick suffered with illness, including a mild heart attack (January 1972). This reduced his ability to carry on looking after the team and subsequently he became Everton's general manager (1973), but two years later returned to team management with Preston. He died shortly after watching Everton play Ipswich in an FA Cup-tie at Goodison Park.

CHADWICK, ALBERT
Left-back/left-half: 5 apps
Born: Church, Blackburn, *circa* 1868 – Deceased
Career: EVERTON (initially as a junior August 1886; professional, 1888), Accrington (1892–93)
A reserve with the Blues, Albert Chadwick made his League debut in a 4–1 defeat at WBA in December 1888 when he partnered George Dobson. His brother, Arthur Chadwick, was registered with Everton in 1902.

CHADWICK, EDGAR WALLACE
Inside-left: 300 apps, 110 goals
Born: Blackburn, 14 June 1869 – *Died*: Blackburn, 14 February 1942
Career: Rising Sun FC, St George's Mission, Little Dots FC/Blackburn (1884), Blackburn Olympic (1886), Blackburn Rovers (July 1887), EVERTON (August 1888), Burnley (May 1899), Southampton (August 1900), Liverpool (May 1902), Blackpool (May 1904), Glossop (May 1905), Darwen (July 1906; retired April 1908); later coached in Germany, The Hague and Haarlem sides (Holland), also the England Amateur team (from November 1908); later returned to Blackburn to work as a baker
One of the best-known players of his day, Edgar Chadwick, 5 ft 6 in. tall, was a master strategist and dribbler who was an ever-present in Everton's 1890–91 League championship-winning side. He also played in two of the Blues' losing FA Cup final teams (1893, 1897) and was a loser for the third time with Southampton in the 1902 final. One of only eight players to score over 100 goals for Everton, he made his debut for the club against Accrington in September 1888 (the first-ever League game). Capped seven times by England, Chadwick scored after just 30 seconds against Scotland in 1892. He also represented the Football League and the Football Alliance and made over 250 further appearances for his seven other clubs, helping Southampton win the Southern League in 1902. He was said to have been the first Englishman to coach abroad.

Chadwick's cousin, Arthur, played for Accrington, Burton Swifts, Southampton, Portsmouth, Northampton and Exeter and later managed Exeter, Reading and Southampton. Arthur also won two England caps. In December 1923 he applied for the manager's job at Blackpool, but, after being on the short list of three, he lost out to Major Frank Buckley.

CHADWICK, NICHOLAS GERALD
Striker: 4+12 apps, 4 goals
Born: Market Drayton, 26 October 1982
Career: EVERTON (apprentice, April 1998; professional, October 1999), Derby County (loan, February–March 2002), Millwall (loan, November 2003–May 2004)

A striker with a dominant presence up front, Nicky Chadwick's frst-team opportunities have been limited but he still found the net regularly for the reserves. A hernia operation interrupted his progress in 2002–03 after he had made his Premiership debut against Sunderland in December 2001, scoring his first goal in a 3–1 win over Bolton four months later (April Fools' Day). He was on the bench when Millwall beat Sunderland to reach the 2004 FA Cup final.

CHADWICK, THOMAS
Half-back/outside-left: 22 apps
Born: Blackburn, 2 March 1882 – *Died*: 1960
Career: Blackburn Rovers (August 1900), EVERTON (January 1902), Preston North End (August 1908–May 1909)

Recognised as a half-back, able to occupy all three positions across centre-field, Tom Chadwick was a well-built footballer who failed to make the first team at Blackburn, found it difficult to hold down a regular position with the Blues and made just nine League appearances for Preston. He made his debut for Everton at outside-left against his former club, Blackburn, two weeks after moving from Ewood Park.

CHADWICK, WILFRED
Inside/centre-forward: 109 apps, 55 goals
Born: Bury, 7 October 1900 – *Died*: Bury, 14 February 1973
Career: Bury (May 1917; professional, October 1918), Nelson (November 1920), Rossendale United (August 1921), EVERTON (February 1922), Leeds United (November 1925), Wolverhampton Wanderers (August 1926), Stoke City (£250, May 1929), Halifax Town (October 1930; retired May 1932)

Wilf Chadwick was a soccer nomad who served with eight different clubs at various levels during a 15-year career. Sprightly with good skills and a powerful right-foot shot, he scored 99 goals in 227 League games and also netted 35 goals in only 23 outings for Rossendale (in half a season). He struck twice on his League debut for Everton against Bradford City in March 1922 (won 2–0) and was the First Division's leading scorer in 1923–24.

CHEDGZOY, SAMUEL

Outside-right: 300 apps, 38 goals

Born: Ellesmere Port, Cheshire, 27 January 1890 – *Died*: Canada, 15 January 1967

Career: Burnell's Ironworks/Ellesmere Port (1908), EVERTON (professional, December 1910), New Bedford FC/USA (May 1926–May 1930); Carsteel FC/Montreal (1931–May 1940)

If a player enjoyed his football it was winger Sam Chedgzoy, swift and resourceful with a strong right-foot shot. He remained in the game, at various levels, for more than 30 years. He joined the Blues in 1910, made his League debut at Newcastle on Boxing Day of that year, gained a regular place in the first XI in 1914–15 when he won a League championship medal and during the First World War scored six times in 38 games. Chedgzoy was the player who forced the FA to change the law concerning corner-kicks! In April 1924, he deliberately chose to play the ball twice from a flag-kick in a League game at Spurs. He dribbled it along the bye-line, into the penalty area and then scored in a 5–2 win. A year later the embarrassed hierarchy changed the law whereby the ball had to be played by one player to another from a corner-kick. Chedgzoy came into his own after the First World War, gaining eight full caps for England between 1920 and 1925 before moving to Montreal as player–coach. He retired at the age of 50. His son, Sydney, was registered with Everton and went to play in America.

CLARK, ARCHIBALD WILLIAM

Right-half: 42 apps, 1 goal

Born: Shoreham, Kent, 4 April 1904 – *Died*: Sheffield, 14 January 1967

Career: Aylesford Paper Mills FC, Grays (Kent League), Brentford (March 1927), Arsenal (May 1927), Luton Town (£1,000, November 1928), EVERTON (May 1931), Tranmere Rovers (March 1936), Gillingham (manager, May 1939–June 1958), Sheffield United (chief scout, 1958; assistant manager, 1965–66)

A resourceful wing-half, Archie Clark gained a League championship medal in his first season (1931–32), appearing in 39 matches after making his debut for the Blues on the opening day of the campaign against Birmingham. He lost his place to Cliff Britton and had only two more League outings for the Blues. He did well as boss of Gillingham, guiding them to victory in the Kent League in 1945, the Southern League twice, in 1947 and 1949, and the Kent Senior Cup final, in 1947. He then saw the 'Gills' win a place in the Football League (1950) and spent 19 years in charge at Priestfield.

CLARK, CHARLES

Half-back: 7 apps, 1 goal

Born: Liverpool, *circa* 1881 – Deceased

Career: EVERTON (April 1901), Plymouth Argyle (September 1903), Crystal Palace (August 1909–May 1910)

Reserve to England international Sam Wolstenholme, Charlie Clark made his debut for Everton against Stoke in November 1901 and had his last outing against Sunderland in March 1903. He appeared in 189 games for Plymouth, featuring in the Pilgrims' first season in the Southern League (1903–04). He later had 32 games for Palace.

CLARKE, HAROLD
Outside-right: 12 apps, 2 goals
Born: Walsall, 1875 – Deceased
Career: Walsall (1892), EVERTON (April 1898), Portsmouth (August 1899), Burton United (1902–03)
Harry Clarke played on the right-wing for most of his career and scored on his League debut for Everton against Blackburn in September 1898 (won 2–1). He did very well for a time but then lost his way and was eventually transferred to Southern League side Portsmouth. (There were several players named H. Clark(e) around between 1890 and 1902, and it's likely that some reference books have got their respective records mixed up.)

CLARKE, PETER MICHAEL
Defender: 10+4 apps
Born: Southport, 3 January 1982
Career: EVERTON (trainee, April 1998; professional, January 1999), Blackpool (loan, August –October 2002), Port Vale (loan, February–April 2003) EVERTON (contract terminated May 2004)
A powerful, sharp-tackling centre-half, Peter Clarke's first appearance for Everton was as a 'sub' against Coventry (Premiership) in January 2001. After representing England at schoolboy level, he went on to skipper his country's Under-20 side in the 2002 Toulon Youth Tournament in France.

CLARKE, WAYNE
Striker: 54+22 apps, 22 goals
Born: Willenhall, 28 February 1961
Career: Wolverhampton Wanderers (apprentice, April 1976; professional, March 1978), Birmingham City (£80,000, August 1984), EVERTON (£500,000, March 1987), Leicester City (£500,000, July 1989), Manchester City (January 1990), Shrewsbury Town (loan), Stoke City (loan), Wolverhampton Wanderers (loan), Walsall (August 1992), Shrewsbury Town (July 1993), Telford United (player–manager, August 1995; resigned November 1996); later a postman in Telford
A former England schoolboy and youth international and West Midlands representative player, Wayne Clarke was a natural goal-poacher. Like his three brothers – Allan, Derek and Frank – he joined Wolves as a teenager and went on to net over 30 goals in more than 160 first-class matches for the Molineux club. He continued to pester defences, scoring 43 times in 105 outings for Birmingham before joining Everton, for whom he made his League debut against Watford in March 1987, hitting five crucial goals in the last ten games of that season. While at Goodison, he gained a League Championship medal (1987) and scored in the Charity Shield game against Coventry City. Clarke appeared in over 500 competitive games and scored more than 130 goals.

CLELAND, ALEXANDER

Right-back: 28+16 apps
Born: Glasgow, 10 December 1970
Career: Dundee United (juniors, 1986; professional, June 1987), Glasgow
  Rangers (January 1995), EVERTON (free, July 1998; retired June 2002)
A competent and tidy right-back, Alex Cleland represented Scotland at
schoolboy level before going on to gain 2 'B' and 11 Under-21 caps for his
country. He also appeared in 180 games for Dundee United and 134 for
Rangers, gaining three Premier League and two Scottish Cup-winner's medals
with the Ibrox Park club before moving to Goodison. He struggled with injuries
during his first season with Everton and was under treatment frequently,
starting only 28 matches in 4 years.

CLEMENTS, DAVID

Left-back/left-wing/right-half: 97+5 apps, 8 goals
Born: Larne, Northern Ireland, 15 September 1945
Career: Larne Grammar School, Portadown (amateur, 1961), Wolverhampton
  Wanderers (professional, January 1963), Coventry City (£1,500, July 1964),
  Sheffield Wednesday (£55,000, August 1971), EVERTON (£100,000,
  September 1973), New York Cosmos/NASL (May 1976)
Well-proportioned, strong and highly efficient, the versatile Dave Clements made
over 500 club and international appearances (391 in the Football League) in a 15-
year career. He never played in the first XI at Molineux but did well at Coventry,
helping the Sky Blues gain promotion as Second Division champions in 1967
with Wolves runners-up. He spent two useful seasons at Hillsborough before
joining Everton, for whom he made his debut against Wolves in September 1973.
A Northern Ireland amateur international, he went on to represent his country's
youth team before gaining three Under-23 and 48 full caps (21 with Coventry –
a club record he shared with Ronnie Rees of Wales but bettered since by Marcus
Hedman). Occasionally he skippered both Everton and his country. He was
appointed manager of Northern Ireland while an Everton player.

CLENNELL, JOSEPH

Inside-left: 74 apps, 33 goals
Born: New Silksworth, 18 February 1889 – *Died*: February 1965
Career: Silksworth United, Seaham Harbour FC, Blackpool (July 1910),
  Blackburn Rovers (£600, April 1911), EVERTON (£1,500, January 1914),
  Cardiff City (October 1921), Stoke (February 1925), Bristol Rovers
  (September 1926), Rochdale (March–October 1927), Ebbw Vale
  (player–manager, November 1927), Barry Town (player–manager–coach,
  August 1928), Distillery (manager from 1929), Bangor (player–manager),
  Great Harwood (player–manager), Accrington Stanley (coach, 1934–35)
A player with a terrific shot, Joe Clennell could also dribble through the
opposition in great style, although he did have the tendency to overdo the clever
stuff at times, much to the annoyance of his colleagues (and manager). Only a
little chap, difficult to knock off the ball, he was plagued by injuries during the

latter stages of his Goodison Park career and was allowed to move to Cardiff City in 1921. A League championship winner with the Blues in 1915 (scoring 15 goals in 36 games), he played in over 350 career games (309 in the League, 112 goals) and was often described as a 'little demon and a terror for his size'. He was killed in a car crash.

CLIFFORD, ROBERT
Right-back/half-back: 45 apps
Born: Rankinston, October 1883 – Deceased
Career: Rankinston, Trabbock, Bolton Wanderers (May 1903), EVERTON (November 1908), South Liverpool (March 1911), Fulham (October 1911–May 1912)
Bob Clifford made his League debut for Bolton at the age of 20 against Preston in January 1904. Originally a right-back, he switched to centre-half occasionally and appeared in 167 games for the Wanderers, helping them reach the FA Cup final in 1904 (beaten by Manchester City) and gain promotion from the Second Division a year later. He moved to Everton with 'Wattie' White in 1908 but made only ten appearances in his first season. He played at left-back and left-half for Fulham.

CLINTON, THOMAS JOSEPH
Full-back: 80 apps, 5 goals
Born: Dublin, Ireland, 13 April 1926
Career: Dundalk (1943), EVERTON (March 1948), Blackburn Rovers (April 1955), Tranmere Rovers (June 1956–April 1957)
Tom Clinton joined Everton in bizarre circumstances. Recommended to the club by an Irish scout, he was contacted by secretary Theo Kelly, who then travelled over to talk to the player at Dundalk station. As the train on which Clinton was boarded pulled out of the station, so Kelly handed the forms for him to sign through a carriage window and within seconds he was an Everton player. A rugged, strong-tackling full-back, Clinton, who made his League debut against Burnley in February 1949, had the misfortune to miss a penalty against Bolton in the 1953 FA Cup semi-final, a tie the Blues lost 4–3! He was capped three times by the Republic of Ireland (1951–53).

COCK, JOHN GILBERT
Centre-forward: 72 apps, 31 goals
Born: Hayle, Cornwall, 14 November 1893 – *Died*: Kensington, London, 19 April 1966
Career: West Kensington United (1908), Forest Gate (April 1910), Old Kingstonian (December 1912), Brentford (amateur, March 1914), Huddersfield Town (April 1914), Chelsea (£2,500, October 1919), EVERTON (January 1923), Plymouth Argyle (March 1925), Millwall (November 1927), Folkestone (July 1931), Walton FC/Surrey (October 1932), Millwall (manager, November 1944–August 1948); then a licensee in New Cross (London)
Perfectly proportioned, physical and dangerous, Jack Cock was a fine athlete,

fast with good skills, able to shoot with both feet and a fine header of the ball. He had already scored 56 goals in 117 League games (47 in 99 for Chelsea) before joining Everton, for whom he made his debut against Stoke in January 1923, scoring in a 4–0 win. Capped twice by England in 1919–20, he scored on his debut against Ireland and netted again in a 5–4 win over Scotland at Sheffield. He also played in one Victory international (1919) and represented the Football League. A classy dresser, he was often seen walking the street clad in sophisticated attire – and in 1930, when registered with Millwall, he was signed up by a London company to star in a major film. Two years earlier he helped the Lions gain promotion as Third Division (S) champions and then in 1945, as manager, led them to runners-up in the Third Division (S) Cup. Cock was awarded the Military Cross for his bravery in action during the First World War. He was born into a family of ten and one of his brothers, Don, played for Brentford, Fulham, Arsenal, Notts County, Wolves and Clapton Orient, and scored over 100 goals in almost 250 League games (1919–28). Another brother, Herbert, played for Brentford (1920).

COGGINS, WILLIAM HERBERT
Goalkeeper: 56 apps
Born: Bristol, 16 September 1901 – *Died*: West Town, Somerset, 7 July 1958
Career: Territorials, Whitehall FC, Victoria Albion, Bristol St George's, Bristol City (professional, September 1925), EVERTON (£2,000, March 1930), Queens Park Rangers (December 1935), Bath City (1936)
Bill Coggins, former blacksmith's apprentice, helped Victoria Albion win the Gloucestershire Senior Amateur Cup and the Bristol Suburban League, and also represented the Suburban League XI before signing for Bristol City. He appeared in 182 first-class games during his five seasons at Ashton Gate, gaining a Third Division (S) championship medal in 1927 as an ever-present. He made his debut for Everton against Grimsby in April 1930 when a 4–2 defeat virtually condemned the Blues to relegation. He was again an ever-present when the Second Division title was won the following season but lost his place to Ted Sagar soon afterwards. Coggins, who always gave a good account of himself between the posts, made only three appearances in two years with QPR.

COLEMAN, JOHN GEORGE
Inside-forward: 71 apps, 30 goals
Born: Kettering, 26 October 1881 – *Died*: 20 November 1940
Career: Kettering Town, Northampton Town (June 1901), Woolwich Arsenal (May 1902), EVERTON (February 1908), Sunderland (May 1910), Fulham (May 1911), Nottingham Forrest (June 1914), Tunbridge Wells Rangers (September 1920–May 1921); later coach in Holland (1927–28)
'Tim' Coleman, an England international against Ireland in February 1907, was a crafty inside-forward, usually found on the right, who was able to bring the best out of his colleagues with some deft ball control and precise passes. He netted 84 goals in 196 senior games for Arsenal, helping the Gunners gain

promotion to the First Division in 1904 before making his debut for Everton against his future club, Nottingham Forest, in February 1908. After an excellent 1908–09, when he scored 20 goals in a positive Blues' side, his form slumped and he was subsequently transferred to Sunderland. During his career, Coleman scored 186 goals in 404 League games.

COLIN, JURGEN

Defender: 0 apps
Born: Holland, 1981
Career: PSV Eindhoven/Holland; KRC Genk/Belgium (loan), NAC Breda/Holland (loan), EVERTON (loan, July 2004)
A strong, powerful defender, Jurgen Colin joined Everton on a season-long loan deal to add depth to David Moyes' senior squad.

COLLINS, HENRY

Goalkeeper: 3 apps
Born: Wynlaton, County Down, Ireland, 1876 – Deceased
Career: Birtley, Hebburn Argyle (1898), Burnley (May 1900), Queens Park Rangers (August 1901), EVERTON (August 1905–April 1906)
Smart, competent and clever, Harry Collins appeared in 33 senior games for Burnley and 121 for QPR before making his debut for Everton in a 6–2 home win over Notts County in October 1905, taking over from Billy Scott. He was called up only twice more before leaving the club.

COLLINS, JOHN

Left-back: 15 apps
Born: Scotland, *circa* 1870 – Deceased
Career: Cambuslang, EVERTON (August 1891–May 1893)
Jock Collins was a rugged, hard-tackling full-back who made his League debut for Everton against Darwen in September 1891. In the main he was regarded as a reserve to Earp, Howarth, Kelso and McLean.

COLLINS, JOHN ANGUS PAUL

Midfield: 59+5 apps, 4 goals
Born: Galashiels, Scotland, 31 January 1968
Career: Hutchison Vale Boys' Club, Hibernian (August 1984), Celtic (July 1990), AS Monaco (July 1996), EVERTON (£2.5m, August 1998), Fulham (£2m, July 2000)
A Scottish international, capped 58 times at senior level (12 goals scored) and on eight occasions by the Under-21s, having previously represented his country as a youth player, John Collins had already assembled a fine appearance record before being engaged by Everton. For Hibs, Celtic and Monaco, he had played in more than 440 League games and had netted 70 goals, helping the Bhoys win the Scottish Cup in 1995. A very skilful and committed performer who read the game well, he brought influence to those around him and made his debut for the Blues on the opening day of the 1998–99 Premiership campaign against Aston

Villa, missing a penalty in a 0–0 draw. His time at Goodison was generally disappointing and he failed to impose himself on the team, but after leaving the Blues he gained a First Division championship medal with Fulham (2001), playing with more purpose and determination.

COLLINS, ROBERT YOUNG
Inside-forward: 147 apps, 48 goals
Born: Govanhill, Glasgow, 16 February 1931
Career: Polmadie Hawthorn Juveniles, Glasgow Pollock, Celtic (professional, April 1948), EVERTON (£23,550, September 1958), Leeds United (£22,500, March 1962), Bury (February 1967), Morton (April 1969–April 1971), Ringwood City/Melbourne Australia (player–coach, May–September 1971), Oldham Athletic (1971); Hakoah/Sidney Australia (manager–coach, October 1971–May 1972), Oldham Athletic (player–coach, October 1972); Shamrock Rovers (briefly, October 1972); Oldham Athletic (player–assistant manager, January 1973; retired as a player, April 1973), Huddersfield Town (manager, July 1974–December 1975), Leeds United (youth-team coach, 1976–77), Hull City (coach, July 1977; manager, October 1977–February 1978), Blackpool (coach, March–May 1978), Barnsley (youth-team coach, 1980; manager, February 1984–June 1985), Guiseley (manager, November 1987–89)

Bobby Collins was described as a pocket general, a scheming inside-forward who could carve open a defence with one decisive pass or clever switch in play. His manager at Leeds, Don Revie, called him the 'teacher' on the field, as he was a real captain and leader. Before he moved to Everton (for a then record fee), Collins played in 273 games for Celtic and scored 54 goals including a hat-trick of penalties against Aberdeen in September 1953. He helped the Bhoys win the Scottish Cup in 1951, the League title in 1954 and two League Cups in 1957 and 1958 while also claiming a runners-up prize in the 1955 Cup final. He made his League debut for the Blues against Manchester City in September 1958 and played his last game in March 1962 against Wolves. He broke his thigh bone in a Fairs Cup match in Turin in 1965, but recovered and ended his playing days with over 800 appearances under his belt (clubs and country) with a League record of 154 goals in 639 games in Scotland and England. Voted 'Footballer of the Year' in 1965 when Leeds lost to Liverpool in the FA Cup final, having helped the Elland Road club win the Second Division title in 1964. A key member of Bury's promotion-winning side in 1968, he was in his 43rd year when he made his final League appearance for Oldham (as a substitute) against Rochdale in April 1973. Unfortunately, Collins failed as a manager, suffering relegation to the Fourth Division with Huddersfield (1975).

COMMON, EDWARD WINCHESTER
Full-back: 14 apps
Born: Seaton Delaval, County Durham, 25 January 1905 – Deceased
Career: Seaton Delaval, Blyth Spartans, EVERTON (August 1927), Preston North End (May 1933), Chester (June 1935–39); did not figure after the Second World War

Well-built defender Ted Common made 157 League appearances during his career, 142 with Chester. He deputised for Warney Cresswell in ten successive games in 1928–29, making his debut for Everton in a 2–1 win at Liverpool in early February. He was rewarded with a benefit match before departing.

CONNOLLY, JOHN

Outside-left: 114+4 apps, 15 goals
Born: Barrhead, Glasgow, 13 June 1950
Career: Barrhead High School, Glasgow United (1966), St Johnstone (amateur, January 1968; professional, August 1968), EVERTON (£75,000, March 1972), Birmingham City (£70,000, September 1976), Newcastle United (player-exchange deal, April 1978), Hibernian (September 1980), Gateshead (January 1982), Blyth Spartans (player–manager, November 1982), Gateshead (November 1983), Whitley Bay (manager, February–September 1984), Ayr United (part-time coach, 1995–96); Queen of the South (manager); worked for Vaux Breweries before becoming an advertising manager with *Golf Monthly* magazine; St Johnstone (manager, May 2004)
John Connolly – tall with excellent ball skills – loved to cut inside his full-back and have a crack at goal. Inventive and graceful with it, he scored 55 times and gained a Scottish League Cup runner's-up medal with St Johnstone (1970), but unfortunately suffered two broken legs as an Everton player, which resulted in long spells out of the game. He helped Hibs win the Scottish Second Division title in 1981 and appeared in one full (against Switzerland in 1973) and two Under-23 internationals for his country. His sons, Stuart and Graeme, both played for Ayr.

COOK, WILLIAM

Right-back: 249 apps, 6 goals
Born: Coleraine, 20 January 1909 – *Died*: 1993
Career: Port Glasgow Athletic Juniors, Celtic (professional, January 1928), EVERTON (£3,000, December 1932), Wrexham (April 1945), Ellesmere Port (briefly), Rhyl (player–manager, June 1946), Sunderland (coach, February 1948), Peruvian FA (coach, May 1952); coach in Norway; Wigan Athletic (manager, 1956–57), Norwich City (coach, 1957–60)
An Irish international, 15 caps won between 1932 and 1939, 12 as an Everton player, Billy Cook was noted for the power and accuracy of his 'long ball' and one programme editor wrote: 'He kicks like a horse and worries his way through.' Certainly a strong, willing defender, he was signed to take over from Ben Williams, having gained a Scottish Cup-winner's medal with Celtic in 1931, adding an FA Cup-winner's prize to his collection with the Blues two years later. He made his debut for Everton against WBA on New Year's Eve 1932 and played his last game for the club in March 1943 against Blackpool in the League (N). Besides his senior appearances for the Blues, Cook also played in 96 Second World War games. Five of his goals were penalties and the other was a rebound after another spot-kick had been saved. Described north of the border as being a 'grand and wholehearted player', Cook made 110 appearances for Celtic.

COOKE, HERBERT E.
Inside-forward: 9 apps, 3 goals
Born: Liverpool, *circa* 1882 – Deceased
Career: EVERTON (April 1905; retired, injured, May 1907, then trainer/coach for many years)
An inside-forward, Harry Cooke deputised for Jimmy Settle at Everton, making his League debut in a 3–2 defeat at Bolton in March 1906, and was reserve for that year's FA Cup final. After retiring, Cooke became one of the club's greatest-ever servants, acting as trainer and coach for many years, forming a wonderful relationship with Dixie Dean.

CORR, PETER JOSEPH
Outside-right: 24 apps, 2 goals
Born: Dundalk, 22 June 1923 – *Died*: 1999
Career: Dundalk (1939), Preston North End (April 1947), EVERTON (August 1948–November 1949), Bangor (Ireland)
Peter Corr made three League appearances for Preston before moving to Goodison Park, where he became one of six different players to don the number seven shirt in 1948–49, making his debut in a 1–0 League defeat at Stoke in September. Capped four times by the Republic of Ireland as an Everton player, including that famous 2–0 win over England on his home ground in 1949, he became surplus to requirements once Ted Buckle had arrived from Manchester United. (Corr was a relative of the famous Irish pop group The Corrs.)

CORRIN, THOMAS
Outside-left: 12 apps, 1 goal
Born: 1880 – Deceased
Career: EVERTON (August 1900), Portsmouth (season 1902–03), EVERTON (May 1903), Reading (August 1904), Plymouth Argyle (August 1905), Millwall Athletic (December 1907), Reading (April 1908–10)
Reserve to Joe Turner and then Harold Hardman during his spells at Goodison, Tom Corrin did far better in the Southern League after leaving Everton second time round, making 50 appearances for Plymouth. His senior debut for the Blues came at Sunderland in December 1900, while his last outing was against Sheffield United in January 1904.

COSTLEY, JAMES T.
Outside-left: 6 apps, 3 goals
Born: Liverpool, *circa* 1862 – Deceased
Career: Blackburn Olympic (1879), EVERTON (August 1886–May 1889)
Scorer of two goals on his League debut for Everton at Derby in October 1888, Jack Costley, a skilful winger and superb dribbler, had done very well during his first two seasons at the club, claiming 22 goals in 59 appearances. However, he failed to hold down a regular place in the side once the League had started. Scored the winning goal for Blackburn Olympic against Old Etonians in the 1883 FA Cup final.

COTTEE, ANTHONY RICHARD
Striker: 205+35 apps, 99 goals
Born: West Ham, London, 11 July 1965
Career: West Ham United (apprentice, July 1981; professional, September 1982), EVERTON (£2.3m, August 1988), West Ham United (September 1994), FC Selangor/Malaysia (March 1997), Leicester City (£500,000, August 1997), Birmingham City (loan, November–December 1997); Barnet (player–manager, October 2000), Millwall (free, March 2001; retired July 2001); later football reporter/summariser with Sky Sport

Tony Cottee, a pint-sized, live-wire striker and Everton's first £2m player, celebrated his debut for the club with a hat-trick in a 4–0 home League win over Newcastle in August 1988 and finished as Blues' top scorer on five occasions: 1988–89, 1989–90, 1990–91, 1992–93 and 1993–94. A real poacher, a snapper-up of the half-chance, he was a continual menace of opposing defenders and in a wonderful career netted 280 club and international goals (146 for the Hammers) in 725 matches – and he kept a personal record of how every one was scored. Capped seven times by England at senior level, he had eight games with the Under-21s and also represented his country's youth team. A League Cup winner with Leicester in 2000 – his only club honour – the following season, Cottee became only the second player to appear in all four divisions in the same season and, for the record, his first, 100th and 200th League goals were all scored against Tottenham.

COULTER, JOHN
Inside/outside-left: 58 apps, 24 goals
Born: Whiteabbey, County Antrim, Northern Ireland, 1912 – *Died*: Belfast, January 1981
Career: Carrickfergus (1928), Brantwood (1929), Dunmurry (1930), Cliftonville (1931), Belfast Celtic (1932), EVERTON (£3,000, February 1934), Grimsby Town (October 1937), Chelmsford City (June 1938), Chester (March 1939), Swansea Town (July 1939); did not play after the Second World War

Jackie Coulter played 11 times for Northern Ireland and twice for the Irish League. A very tricky, direct winger, his career was marred by a broken leg sustained playing for his country against Wales at Wrexham in 1935. Never quite the same player after that setback, he did, however, take his career appearance-tally past the 80 mark before the Second World War intervened. He made his League debut for Everton at inside-left against Portsmouth in April 1934 and replaced Jimmy Stein at outside-left.

COUPER, GEORGE
Outside-right: 4 apps, 1 goal
Born: Scotland, *circa* 1880 – Deceased
Career: Heart of Midlothian, EVERTON (March 1907–May 1908)

Signed as cover mainly for Jack Sharp and other forwards towards the end of 1906–07, when players were rested prior to the FA Cup final with Sheffield Wednesday, George Couper made his League debut for Everton in a 2–1 defeat at Blackburn 48 hours after joining.

COX, WALTER
Goalkeeper: 4 apps
Born: Scotland, *circa* 1863 – Deceased
Career: Hibernian (1886), Burnley (October 1888), EVERTON (February 1890), Nottingham Forest (July 1890–May 1891)
Walter Cox joined Everton after first-choice Bob Smalley had been injured. He conceded ten goals in his four League games and was released at the end of the season, following the return of Jack Angus. His debut for the Blues came in a 5–3 defeat at Accrington in February 1889. He did not appear for Forest.

COYLE, DARREN
Striker: 2 apps
Born: Belfast, Northern Ireland, 27 March 1965
Career: EVERTON (June 1984–May 1986)
Darren Coyle played in both the Screen Sport Super Cup semi-final encounters against Spurs in February–March 1986. A young reserve, he spent only two years at Goodison before his release.

COYNE
Inside-right: 2 apps, 1 goal
Born: Lincolnshire, *circa* 1864 – Deceased
Career: Gainsborough Trinity, EVERTON (September 1888–January 1889)
A reserve during his spell with the Blues, Coyne scored the winning goal on his League debut against Burnley in November 1888 (3–2).

CRELLEY, JOHN
Left-back: 127 apps
Born: Liverpool, 1882 – Deceased
Career: EVERTON (August 1900), Millwall Athletic (September 1901), EVERTON (August 1902), Exeter City (July 1908), St Helens Recreationalists (August 1910–May 1911)
Sturdy, clean-kicking full-back Jack Crelley partnered Walter Balmer in Everton's 1906 FA Cup-winning team against Newcastle, but missed out a year later when Bob Balmer was selected to partner his brother against Sheffield Wednesday. Crelley, who made his League debut for the Blues against Liverpool in January 1902, had just two outings with Millwall before returning to Goodison for a second spell. He later played in 52 games for Exeter.

CRESSWELL, WARNEFORD
Full-back: 306 apps, 1 goal
Born: South Shields, 5 November 1897 – *Died*: South Shields, 20 October 1973
Career: Stanhope Road School (South Shields), North Shields Athletic, guest for Heart of Midlothian and Hibernian during the First World War, South Shields (August 1919), Sunderland (£5,500, March 1922), EVERTON (£7,000, February 1927), Port Vale (manager/coach, May 1936), Northampton Town (manager, April 1937–September 1939), Dartford

(manager, 1939–40); was a licensee for many years after the Second World War

Warney Cresswell won three championship medals with Everton (First Division: 1928 and 1932; Second Division: 1931). He also helped the Blues win the FA Cup in 1933 at the age of 35 years, 175 days old – to became the oldest player to represent the club in a final. He was 37 when he appeared in his last game for the Blues against Bolton in September 1935 – having made his debut eight and a half years earlier, in a 6–2 defeat at Leicester (February 1927).

A defender of the highest quality, he perfected the art of retreating and jockeying an opponent instead of using the full-blooded first-time tackle which was the fashion during his time. Cresswell was, therefore, unorthodox in his ways but was rightly recognised as one of the most constructive full-backs in the game during the 1930s. He was capped seven times by England at senior level between 1921 and 1929, all at right-back, playing against Ireland on three occasions, Wales twice, France and Belgium, having earlier played for his country in a schoolboy international against Wales in 1911. He also represented the Football League on five occasions. His only goal for the Blues was scored against Manchester United (to no avail) in a 4–2 home defeat in April 1929. Cresswell was the first player to make 500 League appearances after the First World War.

CRITCHLEY, EDWARD
Outside/inside-right: 229 apps, 42 goals
Born: Ashton-under-Lyne, 31 December 1903 – Deceased
Career: Spring Gardens FC/Cheshire, Stockport Union Chapel, Cheadle (1919), Witton Albion (August 1920), Stalybridge Celtic (1921), Stockport County (£1,200, May 1922), EVERTON (December 1926), Preston North End (June 1934), Port Vale (in exchange for Jack Friar, December 1934), South Liverpool (May 1935)

Ted Critchley, a speedy, flamboyant right-winger who loved to get among the goals, won three championship medals with Everton (First Division: 1928 and 1932; Second Division: 1931). Besides averaging a goal every five games for the Blues, he laid on plenty more for Dixie Dean. Critchley succeeded Sam Chedgzoy in the forward-line and was a regular for five seasons before losing out to Albert Geldard. He came back and looked set to play in the 1933 FA Cup final (after impressing in the semis) but in the end had to sit and watch as Geldard helped beat Manchester City. He scored ten goals in 124 competitive games for Stockport and made 364 League appearances during his career.

CROMPTON, THOMAS
Centre-forward: 4 apps, 1 goal
Born: Liverpool, *circa* 1876 – Deceased
Career: EVERTON (season 1898–99)

Reserve Tom Crompton's four games for the Blues came in January 1899, scoring in his second outing against Preston after making his League debut in a 2–2 draw at Newcastle.

CROSSLEY, CHARLES ARTHUR
Inside-forward: 55 apps, 21 goals
Born: Hednesford, 1892 – *Died*: 1965
Career: Hednesford Town (1909), Walsall (August 1913), Sunderland (February 1914), EVERTON (August 1920), West Ham United (June 1922), Swindon Town (August 1923), Ebbw Vale (1924–25)

During his career, the broad-shouldered 'Chas' (Charlie) Crossley – small in stature with an unusual top-heavy build – made 146 League appearances and scored 48 goals. He had an excellent first season with Everton, top-scoring with 18 goals, but missed out on the first Wembley Cup final with the Hammers, despite playing in 16 games prior to the showdown with Bolton. Reserve to Charlie Buchan at Sunderland, he served on a minesweeper during the First World War.

CUMMINS, GEORGE PATRICK
Inside-forward: 29 apps
Born: Dublin, Ireland, 12 March 1931
Career: St Patrick's Athletic/Dublin (1948), EVERTON (trial, September 1950; signed November 1950), Luton Town (£8,000, August 1953), Cambridge City (£3,000, July 1961), Hull City (November 1962; retired April 1965)

George Cummins was a clever ball-player who gained 19 caps for the Republic of Ireland and was an FA Cup finalist with Luton in 1959. He manufactured countless goal chances during a career that spanned 17 years, amassing 260 appearances and scoring 29 goals. One of the first professional players to move to a non-League club for a sizeable fee, he made his League debut for Everton on Christmas Day 1951 in a 3–1 defeat at Doncaster.

CUNLIFFE, JAMES NATHANIEL
Inside-forward: 187 apps, 76 goals
Born: Blackrod, Lancashire, 5 July 1912 – *Died*: 1986
Career: Adlington FC, EVERTON (May 1930), Rochdale (September–November 1946)

Jimmy 'Nat' Cunliffe, a former apprentice plater, was always found in the forefront of his team's attack. A dangerous player, quick to pounce on anything loose, he achieved a fine scoring record in a 16-year career of competitive football and would surely have achieved greater fame if it hadn't been for the performances of Dixie Dean. After developing with the Blues' 'A' and Central League sides, he made a scoring senior debut against Aston Villa in March 1933 and, having stood in for the injured Dean, he gained a regular place in the side during 1933–34. Two-footed, he filled every forward position, except outside-left, and at times produced some outstanding performances. He was capped once by England against Belgium in Brussels, May 1936. His cousin, Arthur Cunliffe, played for Middlesbrough, Blackburn and Aston Villa.

CURRAN, EDWARD

Winger: 24+6 apps, 1 goal

Born: Hemsworth, Yorkshire, 20 March 1955

Career: Kinsley FC, Doncaster Rovers (trainee, April 1971; professional, July 1973), Nottingham Forest (£60,000, August 1975), Bury (loan, October 1977), Derby County (£50,000, November 1977), Southampton (£60,000, August 1978), Sheffield Wednesday (£100,000, March 1979), Sheffield United (tribunal set fee of £100,000, August 1982), EVERTON (loan, December 1982; signed permanently for £95,000, September 1983, contract cancelled May 1985), Huddersfield Town (July 1985), Panionios/Greece (1986), Hull City (October 1986), Sunderland (November 1986), Grantham Town (mid-1987), Grimsby Town (November 1987), Chesterfield (n/c, March–April 1988), Goole Town (player–manager, November 1989–90)

Journeyman 'Terry' Curran would drift in and out of a game and play moderately, but then in his next match he would perform like a world-beater – and that summed him up to a tee. He was also temperamental and occasionally produced something extra-special but was very disappointing at many of his 16 clubs, his best efforts coming at Sheffield Wednesday. During his senior career up to 1989, Curran appeared in over 460 games (412 in the League) and scored 72 goals. He made his debut for Everton against Birmingham in December 1982 and won a League championship medal in 1985.

DACOURT, OLIVIER

Midfield: 34+2 apps, 3 goals

Born: Montreuil-sous-Bois, France, 25 September 1974

Career: Thorvars FC (1991), RC Strasbourg (August 1992), EVERTON (£4m, August 1998), RC Lens/France (£6.5m, June 1999), Leeds United (£7.2m, July 2000), AS Roma/Italy (loan, January 2003; signed May 2003)

Prior to joining Everton, sharp and classy midfielder Olivier Dacourt made 127 League appearances for Strasbourg. He added steel and experience to the Blues' side before being lured away by Lens – and despite his departure, which certainly soured relationships with the Everton supporters, he was one of the few success stories in a disappointing 1998–99 season. After leaving Goodison, Dacourt won nine caps for France, having earlier represented his country's Under-21 side. He helped Roma reach the Italian Cup final in 2003 (beaten by AC Milan). His combative style resulted in 11 yellow cards and one red in his only season with Everton.

DANSKIN, JASON

Midfield: 1 app.

Born: Winsford, Cheshire, 28 December 1967

Career: EVERTON (apprentice, April 1984; professional, July 1985), Mansfield Town (March 1987–May 1988), Hartlepool United (loan, January–February 1988)

Jason Danskin had a relatively short career, making only 14 appearances for his three clubs – his only one for Everton, in May 1985, was against Luton, two months before he turned 'pro'.

DARCY, FRANCIS ANTHONY
Full-back: 8+9 apps
Born: Liverpool, 8 December 1946
Career: EVERTON (apprentice, April 1963; professional, August 1964), Tranmere Rovers (July 1972–May 1973)
Frank Darcy made his League debut for Everton in a 4–1 defeat at Leeds in April 1966. He remained loyal to the club and spent nine years at Goodison before leaving.

DARRACOTT, TERENCE MICHAEL
Full-back: 169+10 apps
Born: Liverpool, 6 December 1950
Career: EVERTON (apprentice, April 1967; professional, July 1968), Tulsa Roughnecks/NASL (February 1979), Wrexham (September 1979), Prescot (player–coach, February 1984), EVERTON (reserve-team coach, May 1984), Grimsby Town (assistant manager, November 1985), EVERTON (coaching staff, July 1986; assistant manager to November 1990), Manchester City (coach, February 1991–92)
A local lad, genuine to the last and a player who became a firm favourite with the Everton fans, Terry Darracott never really reached the heights he would have liked. Nevertheless, he was always totally committed and his presence certainly boosted morale within the camp, more so out on the field. He made his League debut against Arsenal in April 1968 (as an apprentice) and when he quit Wrexham in 1984, his appearance-tally in League action stood at 170. A League Cup finalist in 1977, he was offered the post of youth coach by Gordon Lee but turned it down to play in the NASL. Later Darracott was assistant to three Everton old boys: Mick Lyons (Grimsby), Colin Harvey (Goodison) and Peter Reid (Maine Road).

DAVIDSON, WILLIAM
Outside-left: 45 apps, 4 goals
Born: Glasgow, *circa* 1888 – Deceased
Career: Glasgow Old Boys, Queen's Park (amateur), Middlesbrough (August 1910), EVERTON (August 1911), St Mirren (June 1913–15); did not figure after the First World War
Bill Davidson made 19 appearances for Middlesbrough before spending two seasons with Everton, for whom he made his League debut against Spurs in September 1911 (2–2). A sprightly player, neat and tidy with good pace, he played in 29 games in his first season before losing out to Harold Uren.

DAVIE, GEORGE

Centre/inside-forward: 2 apps

Born: Renton, Dumbartonshire, Scotland, *circa* 1865 – Deceased

Career: EVERTON (September 1888), Sunderland (April 1889), Renton (1890), Royal Arsenal (October 1891–December 1892)

Signed to strengthen the attack for the first season of the Football League, George Davie made his debut for Everton in a 3–2 home win over Burnley in November 1888. He later made four FA Cup and 58 other senior appearances for Arsenal, whom he took to court in January 1893 for wrongful dismissal and loss of earnings. He lost the case.

DAVIES, ARTHUR LEONARD

Goalkeeper: 93 apps

Born: Wallasey, 3 January 1905 – *Died:* Plymouth, December 1939

Career: Harrowby FC (amateur, 1921), New Brighton (April 1924), Flint Town (May 1925), EVERTON (trial, July 1926; signed August 1926), Exeter City (£750, July 1930), Plymouth Argyle (1935), Southport (1937), Plymouth Argyle (1938–39); did not play after the Second World War

A gentleman both on and off the field, lanky Arthur Davies was an astute goalkeeper, confident and daring with a long reach. He had failed to make his mark at New Brighton and spent a season in Welsh football before joining Everton, for whom he made his League debut against Huddersfield in October 1926. He was an ever-present in 1928–29, but after relegation the following season and with Billy Coggins and Ted Sagar also at the club, he moved to Devon. He made 177 senior appearances for Exeter during his five years at St James's Park (124 consecutively from February 1931 to January 1934). When the Second World War halted domestic soccer in 1939, Davies had made over 300 appearances, 297 in the League, winning Inter-League honours.

DAVIES, JOHN WILLIAM

Left-half: 1 app.

Born: Holt, 14 November 1916 – *Died: circa* 1980

Career: Troedyrhiw, Ruthin Town, Chester (December 1934), Cardiff City (briefly, 1936) EVERTON (July 1937), Plymouth Argyle (February 1947), Bristol City (May 1948–May 1949)

A Welsh schoolboy international in 1930, Jack Davies, almost completely bald, made 18 League appearances for Chester but none with Cardiff before joining Everton, primarily as cover for Joe Mercer. Due to the Second World War (when he hardly ever played in this country), Davies had to wait until September 1946 before making his League debut as an emergency right-back in a 4–1 defeat at Blackburn – his only game for the Blues. He later made 33 League appearances for Plymouth and 30 for Bristol City.

DAVIES, JOSEPH

Outside-right: 8 apps, 2 goals

Born: Chirk, near Oswestry, 1870 – Deceased

Career: Chirk, EVERTON (November 1888), Chirk (May 1889)

Signed halfway through the first season of League football, Joe Davies made his senior debut for Everton in a 4–1 defeat at WBA in December 1888. He remained at the club for seven months. He is father of Stanley Davies (q.v.).

DAVIES, STANLEY CHARLES

Inside/centre-forward: 22 apps, 10 goals

Born: Chirk, near Oswestry, 24 April 1898 – *Died*: Birmingham, 17 January 1972

Career: Chirk Council Schools, Chirk schools representative, Chirk FC, Army Signals School (Dunstable), Manchester United (trial), Rochdale (January 1919), Preston North End (April 1919), EVERTON (£4,000, January 1921), West Bromwich Albion (£3,300, November 1921), Birmingham (£1,500, November 1927), Cardiff City (£1,000, August 1928), Rotherham United (player–manager, March 1929); Barnsley (August 1930), Manchester Central (October 1930), Dudley Town (1933), Chelmsford City (trainer, April 1938–May 1941), Shorts FC/Rochester (manager during the Second World War); later a West Bromwich licensee (1930s)

Stan Davies – a big, strong, forceful player (5 ft 10 in. tall, 12 st. 12 lb in weight) – appeared in six different positions for Wales, including that of goalkeeper against Scotland in 1922 – a clear indication of his tremendous versatility. He won 18 caps (plus one unofficial international) and netted five international goals while also touring Canada with the Welsh FA in 1930. Possessing a cracking shot, he could head a ball hard and true, and in a fine career netted over 100 goals in 250 games for his seven major clubs. He scored from the centre-forward position on his debut for Everton in a 3–0 home League win over Manchester City in February 1921 (playing in place of Bobby Parker) and during his time with WBA he netted 83 goals in 159 matches. As a manager, he took Shorts to two Kent Senior Cup final triumphs. When the First World War broke out, Davies, who was registered with the Volunteers in Aberystwyth, was immediately sent for training and by November 1914 found himself in France on the Western Front with the Royal Welsh Fusiliers. Wounded at Cambrai, on his discharge from hospital he joined the Army Signalling School in Dunstable and was later awarded the Military Medal and the Belgian Croix de Guerre. Davies' son, John, was a reporter with the *Daily Express* newspaper for many years, based in Birmingham and Bristol.

DAVIES, WILLIAM DAVID

Goalkeeper: 82 apps

Born: Ammanford, Wales, 1 April 1948

Career: Amman Valley Grammar School, Cardiff College of Education, Ammanford FC, Swansea City (August 1969), EVERTON (£20,000, December 1970), Swansea City (loan, February–March 1974), Wrexham

(£8,000, September 1977), Swansea City (July 1981), Tranmere Rovers (player–coach, June 1983; retired May 1984); returned briefly with Bangor City (European Cup-Winners' Cup, 1985); Wrexham (November 1985–May 1986 and February 1987); thereafter involved in a book/craft shop in Mold before continuing his teaching profession. He was also heard giving expert comment on soccer on the Welsh language S4C TV channel and radio programmes while managing the Welsh Under-15s team

Dai Davies, 6 ft 1 in. tall and 13 st. 3 lb in weight, was precisely the right size for a goalkeeper. He went on to gain 52 full and three Under-23 caps for Wales, conceding only 51 goals at senior level. A Welsh Amateur Cup winner with his college team prior to joining Ammanford, Davies made nine League appearances for Swansea before joining the champions Everton as cover and possible successor to Gordon West. He never entirely established himself at Goodison Park but he became a permanent fixture in the Welsh side, holding his position for eight years and topping Jack Kelsey's record of 41 caps when he faced Scotland in 1981. A commanding keeper who controlled his area well, he was loathe to bawl out instructions to his defenders and occasionally this let him down as he was prone to the odd slip here and there. A Third Division championship and Welsh Cup winner with Wrexham in 1978, he added a second Welsh Cup-winner's medal to his collection in 1986. He made 199 appearances for the Racecourse club. In August 1978 at the Cardiff National Eisteddfod, Davies became the first Welsh soccer player to be admitted to the Gorsedd Circle. He chose the bardic name 'Dai o'r cwm' (Dai of the Valley) after his native Amman Valley.

DAWSON, HAROLD

Outside-left: 5 apps
Born: Rossendale, *circa* 1884 – Deceased
Career: Rossendale United, EVERTON (August 1908), Blackpool (March 1909), Croydon Common (August 1911), Gillingham (1912–13)

A reserve at Goodison, Harry Dawson made his Everton debut in a 3–0 home defeat by Arsenal in September 1908. He later did well in the Southern League. (There was a Harold Dawson (goalkeeper) playing for West Ham in 1909–10 and some reference books have the records of the two players mixed up.)

DEAN, WILLIAM RALPH

Centre-forward: 433 apps, 383 goals
Born: Birkenhead, 22 January 1907 – *Died*: Liverpool, 1 March 1980
Career: Laird Street School (Birkenhead), Moreton Bible Class, Heswall FC, Pensby United, Tranmere Rovers (amateur, November 1923; professional, February 1925), EVERTON (March 1925), Notts County (March 1938), Sligo Rovers (January 1939), Hurst FC (May 1940; retired April 1941); later a licensee in Chester; gave up in 1962 through ill health; thereafter worked for Littlewoods Pools (Liverpool) until his retirement in January 1972

A football immortal, strong, dashing with a powerful right-foot shot and exceptional heading ability, 'Dixie' Dean was, without doubt, one of the greatest centre-forwards of his era. Blessed with unsurpassed goalscoring ability, he replaced Jimmy Broad to make his debut for the Blues against Arsenal at Highbury in March 1925 (lost 3–1) and notched his first goal on his home debut a week later when Aston Villa were defeated 2–0.

He was Everton's leading marksman on ten separate occasions, eight in succession: 1925 to 1933 and again in seasons 1934–35 and 1936–37. He suffered a life-threatening skull injury when he was involved in a motorcycling accident in 1926, from which he made a miraculous recovery, after surgeons had thought he would never be able to head a ball again!

Dean claimed his 100th goal for Everton in only his 105th game, while reaching the century mark in League football in just 104 outings (Divisions 1 and 2) with 60 coming in 1927–28 (a record never to be beaten). He netted in 12 consecutive League games (December 1930–February 1931) and claimed 37 hat-tricks (a record 34 in the League) with seven coming in 1927–28 and eight in 1931–32.

Dean also scored 28 FA Cup goals for the Blues (in 32 games) including nine in 1930–31 when the Blues reached the semi-finals. His goal tally also included 19 against Liverpool (two hat-tricks) and he also struck 18 times in 16 internationals for England (1927–32).

He gained three championship medals with the Blues (First Division: 1928 and 1932; Second Division: 1931) and scored when Everton beat Manchester City 3–0 to win the 1933 FA Cup final. At the end of his career he received a runner's-up medal when Sligo lost the 1939 FA of Ireland Cup final.

Dean had his right leg amputated in 1976 (after suffering pain for quite some time). He battled on, as always, before his death inside his beloved Goodison Park in 1980, just a few minutes after the final whistle of an Everton–Liverpool derby match. Thousands attended his funeral, paying tribute to a remarkable player. Dean was a greyhound enthusiast and won several races with the dogs he owned.

DEGN, PETER
Right wing-back: 1+4 apps
Born: Aarhus, Denmark, 6 April 1977
Career: Aarhus/Denmark, EVERTON (£20,000, February 1999), Brondby/Denmark (September 2000)
A Danish Under-21 international attacking right wing-back with good pace, Peter Degn made 76 League appearances for Aarhus before making his Premiership debut for the Blues as a substitute at Manchester United in March 1999 in front of 55,182 spectators. He never settled at Goodison Park.

DEL ALMEIDA (RODRIGO), JULIANO
Midfield: 0+4 apps
Born: Santos, Brazil, 7 August 1976
Career: Santos/Brazil (trial), Botafogo/Brazil (April 1999), EVERTON (loan, August–September 2002 and February–March 2003)
Left-sided midfielder Rodrigo scored 19 goals in 60 games for Botafogo but had

little to show for his broken-year loan spell at Goodison Park. He returned home to recuperate after making just four substitute appearances in the Premiership, his debut coming against Spurs in August 2002.

DEPLEDGE, RICHARD PERCY
Goalkeeper: 1 app.
Born: Wallasey, 1883 – Deceased
Career: EVERTON (junior, 1905; professional, August 1906–May 1908)
Reserve to Billy Scott, goalkeeper Dick Depledge's only League appearance for Everton came in a 3–0 home win over Stoke in March 1907.

DEWAR, JAMES
Left-back: 1 app.
Born: Liverpool, *circa* 1871 – Deceased
Career: EVERTON (season 1892–93)
Reserve left-back, Dewar's only League appearance for Everton (as stand-in for John Collins) was against Nottingham Forest in September 1892 (2–2).

DICK, ALEC
Right-back: 13 apps
Born: Scotland, *circa* 1865 – Deceased
Career: Kilmarnock, EVERTON (August 1886–April 1889)
Alec Dick made 77 first-team appearances for Everton before making 13 in the League and FA Cup (1887–89). He made his debut in the latter competition against Bolton in October 1887 and appeared in the Blues' first League game against Accrington on 8 September 1888. The first Scottish professional signed by Everton, he was a combative full-back who was suspended for a large part of that initial League campaign after striking an opponent at Notts County.

DICKINSON, W. ALFRED
Centre/inside-forward: 1 app.
Born: Saltney, 10 February 1914 – *Died*: 1998
Career: EVERTON (juniors, August 1930; professional, February 1931), Port Vale (September 1936), EVERTON (November 1936), Northampton Town (October 1937); guest for Chester and Wrexham during the Second World War; didn't play after 1945
Alf Dickinson's only League appearance for Everton was alongside Jimmy Cunliffe and Dixie Dean in a 5–1 defeat at Portsmouth in March 1935.

DILLY, THOMAS
Forward: 9 apps, 2 goals
Born: Arbroath, 12 November 1882 – *Died*: 1960
Career: Arbroath and Marwell Schools, Forfar County, Arbroath, Heart of Midlothian (1900), EVERTON (November 1902), West Bromwich Albion (March 1906), Derby County (£250, October 1907), Bradford Park Avenue

(June 1908), Walsall (August 1909), Shrewsbury Town (July 1910), Worcester City (September 1911), Kidderminster Harriers (April 1914), Cadbury Works FC (1918; retired May 1919)

Tommy Dilly could play at centre-forward and on both wings. Rather slim-looking, good on the ball, he loved to hug the touchline and did well in Scotland before making his League debut for Everton at Sunderland in November 1902. He left both Goodison Park and The Hawthorns unwittingly and was, in fact, the last Scotsman to play for WBA for 30 years. Dilly represented Forfar against Perthshire in 1899–1900 and won prizes in sprint races from 100 to 300 yards.

DIVERS, JOHN
Inside-right/outside-left: 32 apps, 11 goals
Born: Glasgow, 19 September 1873 – Deceased
Career: Glasgow Benburb, Hibernian (1890), Celtic (August 1893), EVERTON (April 1897), Celtic (November 1898), Hibernian (October 1901)

Jock Divers was a cunning footballer who delighted the fans with his subtle ball skills, a quality thought by a contemporary writer to have been enhanced at Parkhead by a master dribbler, Sandy McMahon. He was twice a League championship winner in his first spell with Celtic (1894, 1896) and, after returning, gained two Scottish Cup-winner's medals (1899, 1900) and was a beaten finalist (1901). He made his Everton debut on the left-wing against Derby in September 1897 and did well at Goodison before returning to Scotland. Capped once by his country against Wales in 1895 as well as representing the Scottish League, he netted 45 goals in 87 appearances for Celtic.

DOBSON, GEORGE
Left-half/right-back: 22 apps
Born: Bolton, Lancashire, 1862 – Deceased
Career: Bolton Wanderers (1884), EVERTON (March 1885; retired, injured, May 1889)

George Dobson, well built, strong and a clean kicker, made over 130 appearances for Everton before League football was introduced. He is said to have been Everton's first professional, ahead of George Farmer. In that initial 1888–89 season, he made 18 appearances, the first three in the left-half position.

DOBSON, JOHN MARTIN
Midfield: 190 apps, 29 goals
Born: Rishton, near Blackburn, 14 February 1948
Career: Clitheroe Grammar School, Lancashire Youths, Bolton Wanderers (apprentice, April 1963; professional, July 1966), Burnley (free, August 1967), EVERTON (£300,000, August 1974), Burnley (£100,000, August 1979), Bury (player–manager, March 1984–March 1989, retiring as a player, May 1986), Northwich Victoria (manager for 39 days, June–July 1991), Bristol Rovers (manager for 11 games, July–October 1991; left by mutual consent)

Martin Dobson was a great thinker but, surprisingly, perhaps due to the hefty price tag around his neck, he took quite a while to settle down at Goodison Park, despite a solid performance when making his debut in a 2–1 home League win over Arsenal in August 1974. He had been given a free by Bolton and almost quit the game, but his father persuaded him to continue and he went on to become an England international, gaining four caps, one at Under-23 level and representing the Football League (all as a Burnley player). He also helped the Clarets win the Second and Third Division titles (1973 and 1982 respectively) and as a manager guided Bury to promotion from Division Four (1985). After making his League debut at centre-forward against Wolves in September 1967, Dobson went on to appear in 499 games for Burnley, scoring 76 goals in two spells, surprising a lot of people when he returned there in 1979. During his career he amassed over 700 club appearances (661 in the League) and netted more than 100 goals. He was a League Cup finalist with Everton in 1977.

DODDS, EPHRAIM
Centre-forward: 58 apps, 37 goals
Born: Grangemouth, Stirlingshire, Scotland, 7 September 1915
Career: Medomsley Juniors, Huddersfield Town (amateur, June 1932; professional, September 1932), Sheffield United (free, May 1934), Blackpool (£10,000, March 1939), Shamrock Rovers (1946), EVERTON (November 1946), Lincoln City (£6,000, October 1948; retired September 1950 after being expelled from the Football League in June 1950 over his role as recruiting agent for the Bogota-based Marios Club, who were affiliated to the Colombian National League, but not FIFA); later a businessman in Blackpool

'Jock' Dodds had rare pace for such a big man (he peaked at 14 st. 2 lb) and certainly didn't lack enthusiasm, being a brilliant finisher, scoring a goal every 137 minutes for Everton alone. Prior to his move to Goodison, he netted 125 times for Sheffield United and 236 for Blackpool, including 223 in 159 during the Second World War matches when on leave from the RAF. Ironically in 1935–36 he had been the Second Division's joint top-scorer (34 goals) with the player he replaced at Bloomfield Road, Bob Finan. It is thought he was the first player to top 200 League goals after the war, doing so with Lincoln. Dodds, who once netted eight goals for Blackpool against Stockport and seven against Tranmere in Second World War football, was top scorer for the Imps in both his seasons at Sincil Bank. He won eight war caps for Scotland, grabbing a hat-trick in a 5–4 win over England in April 1942. He played for the Blades in the 1936 FA Cup final defeat by Arsenal and, before leaving for Blackpool, helped United gain promotion in 1939, scoring 17 goals in 29 games. Signed to replace Tommy Lawton, he made a scoring debut for Everton in a 3–3 home draw with Grimsby in November 1946. Before he joined Huddersfield, Dodds was a petrol delivery driver.

DOMINY, ARTHUR ALBERT

Forward: 33 apps, 13 goals

Born: South Stoneham, 11 February 1893 – *Died*: Mitcham, Surrey, 23 September 1974

Career: Weston Grove, Peartree Athletic, Bitterne Guild (September 1911), Woolston (July 1912), Southampton (March 1913), guest for Arsenal, Glasgow Rangers and Harland and Wolff FC during the First World War; EVERTON (May 1926), Gillingham (March 1928), Clapton Orient (May 1929), Newport/Isle of Wight (May 1931), Southampton (scout, late 1931, while licensee of the Mason's Arms in St Mary's Street), Itchen Sports (mid-1930s), Southampton (manager, June 1943–May 1946, then scout, 1946–50); later steward of the Saints' supporters' club

A boiler-maker by trade, 'Art' Dominy first came to prominence in 1911–12 when he scored over 50 goals in Hampshire County football. He was Southampton's leading marksman with 30 goals in 1913–14 (his first full season at The Dell), also finishing as the Southern League's top striker. Although a full England cap eluded him, he did appear in countless international trials and represented the Southern League against the Irish League. He skippered the Saints to promotion to the Second Division in 1922 and when he left for Everton his appearance-tally stood at 369 with 146 goals scored. He formed an alliance and friendship with Dixie Dean at Everton, for whom he made his senior debut in a 2–1 defeat at Tottenham in August 1926, scoring his first goal for the Blues in his second game four days later at Bury (lost 5–2). He had a good first season at Goodison (13 goals in 32 outings) but lost his place to Dick Forshaw. In 1934, Dominy turned down the manager's job of French club Le Havre, and during the Second World War helped run a sports stadium in Bournemouth His younger brother, Tom (a far better player), was with Southampton in 1914–15, but the First World War ended his career prematurely.

DONALDSON, JOHN McFARLANE

Left-half: 2 apps

Born: Glasgow, April 1884 – Deceased

Career: Stirlingshire (Juvenile Inter-County, 1901), EVERTON (April 1905), Preston North End (November 1907), Bradford Park Avenue (September 1908–April 1909)

A reserve for two-and-a-half seasons, Jack Donaldson, a carpenter by trade, made the first of his nine career League appearances for Everton against Sheffield United in February 1906, setting up one of Jack Sharp's hat-trick goals in a 3–2 win.

DONNACHIE, JOSEPH

Outside-right or left: 58 apps

Born: Kilwinning, Ayrshire, 1885 – Deceased

Career: Rutherglen Glencairn (1902), Albion Rovers (1903), Greenock Morton (March 1905), Newcastle United (June 1905), EVERTON (February 1906), Oldham Athletic (£250, October 1908), Rangers (£800, March 1919),

EVERTON (August 1919), Blackpool (June 1920), Chester (player–manager, season 1921–22); later licensee of the Mariner's Arms Inn, near the Sealand Road ground (Chester)

A Roman Catholic (one of the few to be associated with Rangers), Joe Donnachie was a Scottish international, capped three times in 1913–14 as an Oldham player. Bow-legged, stockily-built, he could occupy both flanks and regularly produced the goods with his dazzling footwork, startling acceleration and fiercely driven crosses from his wide position. Considered one of the finest wingers of his day, he was instrumental in making chances galore for his colleagues, and did just that on his debut for Everton against Notts County in February 1906, but none were taken. He was in and out of the Blues' side and made 39 appearances in his first spell at Goodison, but played in 16 of the first 24 League games when League football resumed in 1919. He was granted a benefit match: Oldham against Everton on New Year's Day 1914. A crowd of 14,500 saw the Latics win 2–0. Donnachie's son, Joe, was on Liverpool's books when he was killed in a Second World War flying accident.

DONOVAN, DONAL CHRISTOPHER
Half-back/full-back/inside-right: 187 apps, 2 goals
Born: Cork, Ireland, 23 December 1929
Career: Eire schoolboy football, Maymount Rovers/Cork, EVERTON (May 1949), Grimsby Town (£8,000, August 1958), Boston United (player–manager, May 1965–67)

Honoured at schoolboy level, full-back Don Donovan went on to gain five full caps for Eire and made over 400 League appearances for Everton and Grimsby. Very adaptable, he actually joined the Blues as a right-half, then switched to pivot before settling down at full-back, where he formed a fine partnership at Goodison with John Lindsay and then Eric Moore. He made his debut for the Blues against Sheffield Wednesday in August 1951 and took over the captaincy from his fellow countryman Peter Farrell before his last game at inside-right against Manchester City in April 1958. One of his two goals for the club was a stunning 35-yarder against League champions Manchester United in October 1956. The Blues won 5–2 to end the Busby Babes' 26-match unbeaten run. His son, Terry, played for Aston Villa, for whom he scored against Everton in January 1980.

DOUGAL, PETER GEORGE
Forward: 11 apps, 2 goals
Born: Denny, Stirlingshire, Scotland, 21 March 1909 – *Died*: 12 June 1974
Career: Denny Pace Thistle, Burnley (October 1926), Clyde (February 1929), Southampton (£1,000, September 1929), Arsenal (trial, September 1933; signed for £400, October 1933), EVERTON (August 1937), Bury (June 1938); guest for Manchester United during the Second World War; did not play after the hostilities

On his day, and in form, Peter Dougal was as good as Alex James! He had terrific on-the-ball skills, but unfortunately he tended to overdo the clever stuff and this exasperated his managers wherever he played. He had already appeared in over 70 first-class matches before joining Everton, for whom he made his League debut at Blackpool in September 1937 when he partnered Dixie Dean. He missed virtually the whole of the 1936–37 season through injury. When Dougal moved to Southampton in 1929, the fee was covered by the Saints' Supporters Club.

DOWNS, RICHARD JOHN W.

Full-back: 97 apps
Born: Middridge, 13 June 1886 – *Died*: 1949
Career: Crook Town, Shildon Athletic, Barnsley (May 1908), EVERTON (£3,000, March 1920), Brighton and Hove Albion (October 1923)

Renowned for his sliding tackle, 'Dickie' Downs scored ten goals in 274 League games for Barnsley before moving to Goodison Park. He skippered the Tykes for several seasons and was a vital member of two FA Cup final teams, gaining a runner's-up medal in 1910, and a winner's prize in 1912. After a successful international trial, he was rewarded with an England cap against Ireland in October 1920. He made his debut for the Blues against Manchester United in March 1920, partnering John Maconnachie. He held his place in the team until September 1922 before being replaced by David Raitt.

DOYLE, DANIEL

Full-back: 45 apps, 1 goal
Born: Paisley, Scotland, 16 September 1864 – *Died*: Scotland, 8 April 1918
Career: Rawyard Juniors, Slamannan Barnsmuir FC, Broxburn Shamrock (1882), Hibernian (1883), East Stirlingshire (1884), Newcastle East End (1886), Grimsby Town (1887), Bolton Wanderers (season 1888–89), EVERTON (August 1889), Celtic (April 1891–April 1899; then reserve-team player–coach to April 1904)

A League championship winner with Everton (1891) and Celtic (1893, 1894, 1896, 1898) as well as being a Scottish Cup winner with the Bhoys (1892) and a finalist (1893, 1894), Dan Doyle was among the greatest full-backs of his time. A big man, weighing over 13 st., he had perfect judgement, which atoned for a lack of speed. He was a powerful and accurate kicker, his clearances never more in evidence than in the unrivalled placing of his free-kicks. A mighty quick thinker, he was capped eight times by his country between 1892 and 1898, playing five times against England. He also represented the Scottish League XI and had three games for Glasgow against Sheffield in the annual challenge match. Celtic team-mate Willie Maley said: 'He was seen at his best when the tide was going against his side.' He made his League debut for Everton against Blackburn in September 1889 and later appeared in 123 matches for the Bhoys.

Doyle courted controversy during his time at Everton. He received a £200 signing-on fee in 1889 and was also paid by both Celtic and Bolton. In 1891 he broke his contract by moving to Celtic and was promptly sued for breach of contract by Everton in Glasgow High Court.

DUGDALE, GORDON
Left-back: 63 apps
Born: Liverpool, 21 February 1924 – *Died*: Anfield, Liverpool, May 1986
Career: Linacre School, Bootle Schoolboys, Lancashire Boys, EVERTON
(juniors, March 1945; served in the Royal Navy during the Second World
War; professional June 1947; retired with heart trouble, May 1950); later
director of South Liverpool FC (1952); stood as Conservative candidate for
Liverpool's Low Hill ward, but failed to unseat the Labour member
Gordon Dugdale was a brilliant left-back, a fine ball-winner, fast and deliberate
in everything he did, who looked more like an office clerk than a professional
footballer. Over 48,000 fans saw his Everton debut against Wolves in October
1947. He appeared in 23 games that season and 20 in each of the next two
before retiring with a recurring heart complaint, initially diagnosed when
serving in the Far East during the Second World War, having been a candidate
for England's 1950 World Cup squad.

DUNLOP, ALBERT
Goalkeeper: 231 apps
Born: Liverpool, 21 April 1932 – *Died*: 10 March 1990
Career: EVERTON (juniors, May 1947; professional, August 1949), Wrexham
(November 1963), Rhyl (April 1965)
A dependable, efficient and sometimes brave and daring player, Albert Dunlop
had to wait more than nine years before making his League debut for Everton
at Manchester United in October 1956 when over 43,000 fans saw the Blues
win 5–2. With Ted Sagar as first choice up to December 1949, Dunlop then saw
Burnett and O'Neill occupy the keeper's position before Sagar returned to the
fray. After that it was back to the reserves, with O'Neill and Harry Leyland
seemingly ahead of him before he finally established himself in the side during
1956–57. He was subsequently replaced by Gordon West and went on to play
in 21 games for Wrexham. In 1979 Dunlop was placed on probation for two
years after being found guilty of three charges of deception.

DUNN, JAMES
Inside-right: 155 apps, 49 goals
Born: Glasgow, 25 November 1900 – *Died*: 20 August 1963
Career: Glasgow St Anthony's, Edinburgh Hibernian (July 1920), EVERTON
(with Harry Ritchie, April 1928), Exeter City (May 1935), Runcorn
(player–coach, August 1936, retired May 1937)
Although frail-looking, Jimmy 'Ginger' Dunn was a soccer artiste, a clever,
tricky craftsman, hardworking with a terrific shot. Twice a Scottish Cup finalist
with Hibs (1923, 1924), he was one of Scotland's 'Wembley Wizards' who
hammered England 5–1 in 1928 and made his debut for Everton at Bolton in
August 1928. He scored 14 times in 28 games when the Second Division title
was won in 1931; a year later he netted ten more to help Everton clinch the First
Division championship and in 1933 struck the third goal in the FA Cup final
win over Manchester City. He won the last of his six caps as an Everton player

against Wales in 1929 and also represented the Scottish League. A self-taught footballer, Dunn collected memorabilia including pictures and programmes. One of his three sons (all footballers), Jimmy junior, won the FA Cup with Wolves in 1949, having made his League debut for the Molineux club against Everton at Goodison Park in October 1947.

DUNNE, RICHARD PATRICK
Defender: 65+7 apps
Born: Dublin, Ireland, 21 September 1979
Career: EVERTON (trainee, April 1995; professional, October 1996), Manchester City (£3m, October 2000)
Able to play at left-back or in central defence, Richard Dunne had his season with Everton in 1999–2000, when he played in 36 matches. Strong with great stamina, he became the youngest Blues player at 17 years, 107 days to appear in the FA Cup, when he lined up against Swindon in January 1997 (bettered since by Wayne Rooney). He followed up with his League bow against Sheffield Wednesday soon afterwards and later gained international recognition with the Republic of Ireland at youth, Under-21, 'B' and senior levels. An FA Youth Cup winner in 1998, he helped Manchester City win the League Division One title in 2002.

DURRANT, IAN
Midfield: 4+1 apps
Born: Glasgow, 29 October 1966
Career: Schoolboy football, Glasgow United, Rangers (professional, July 1984), EVERTON (loan, October–November 1994), Kilmarnock (free, June 1998; retired May 2002; joined coaching staff)
On his day, Ian Durrant was an exceptionally talented and naturally gifted midfielder, the playmaker in the Rangers side. He made his League debut in 1985 against Morton and by the time he joined Everton, had gained four Scottish League, a Scottish Cup and four League Cup-winner's medals while winning three youth, four Under-21 and 11 full caps. An Everton debutant as a 'sub' at Southampton in October 1994, he later took his Rangers stats to 45 goals in 348 appearances, collecting nine more caps.

EARP, MARTIN JOHN
Right–back: 10 apps
Born: Sherwood, Nottingham, 1872 – Deceased
Career: Sherwood Foresters, Nottingham Forest (September 1889), EVERTON (November 1891), Nottingham Forest (April 1892), Sheffield Wednesday (August 1893), Stockport County (May 1900)
Jack Earp, an amateur throughout his career, did not depend on football for a living. A fine player with deep conviction and strong principle, he loved the hurly-burly of the game and made 50 appearances in two spells with Forest, helping them win the Football Alliance in 1892 and gain entry to the Football League. Making his League debut for Everton against Darwen in November

1891, he never settled down at Goodison. An FA Cup winner with Wednesday in 1896, he scored eight goals in 174 games for the Owls and represented the Football League against the Irish League in 1898. Earp's brother, Frederick, also played for Forest (1878–85).

EASTHOPE, JOSEPH DONALD
Outside-left: 2 apps
Born: Liverpool, 16 September 1929 – *Died*: 1993
Career: Liverpool junior football, EVERTON (professional April 1950), Stockport County (June 1954–April 1955)
Reserve to Tommy Eglington, Joe Easthope made his League debut for Everton at Notts County in March 1953. He scored twice in ten games for Stockport.

EASTOE, PETER ROBERT
Inside-forward: 108+7 apps, 33 goals
Born: Dorden, Tamworth, 2 August 1953
Career: Glascote Highfield, Warton Hatters, Wolverhampton Wanderers (apprentice June 1970; professional, June 1971), Swindon Town (loan, November 1973, signed for £88,000, January 1974), Queens Park Rangers (March 1976), EVERTON (player-exchange deal involving Mick Walsh, March 1979), West Bromwich Albion (£250,000 deal involving Andy King, July 1982), Leicester City (October 1983), Huddersfield Town (loan, March 1984), Walsall (loan, August 1984), Leicester City (loan, October 1984), Wolverhampton Wanderers (loan, February 1985), Sporting Farense/Portugal (July 1985), Atherstone Town (August 1986), Bridgnorth Town (player–coach, 1989–90), Atherstone (again, 1990–91), Alvechurch (as manager, 1991–92), Nuneaton Borough (assistant manager, 1992–93), Bridgnorth Town (coach)
A capable goalscorer, Peter Eastoe's 15-year career took him all over the country and further. He netted over 100 goals (95 in 330 League games) and won eight England youth caps (1971–72). He made his League debut for Wolves against Manchester United in 1982, top-scored for Everton in 1980–81 and appeared in FA Cup semi-finals for both QPR and the Blues, for whom his debut came as a 'sub' at WBA in April 1979. He now lives near Stourbridge.

EASTON, WILLIAM CHARLES
Inside-forward: 15 apps, 3 goals
Born: Newcastle-upon-Tyne, 10 March 1906 – *Died*: circa 1982
Career: Blyth Catholic Young Men's Society, Eston FC, Blyth Spartans, West Stanley (trialist), Blyth Spartans, Rotherham County (March 1922; professional, April 1923), Montreal Maroons/Canada, Blyth Spartans, EVERTON (March 1927), Swansea Town (August 1929), Port Vale (May 1931), Aldershot (free, May 1933), Workington (1934–35)
Bill Easton, a brainy inside-forward, had a modest career, scoring 28 goals in 107 League games. He made his debut for Everton in a 0–0 draw against Portsmouth in March 1928 and netted his first goal for the club in his third

game at Sunderland. Easton sailed the Atlantic in the course of his occupation as shipyard worker, taking a job in Montreal.

EBBRELL, JOHN KEITH
Midfield: 253+12 apps, 19 goals
Born: Bromborough, 1 October 1969
Career: EVERTON (trainee, April 1986; professional, November 1986), Sheffield United (£1m, March 1997; retired, injured, May 1998)
A committed and technically adept midfielder, John Ebbrell skippered Everton in 1996 before loss of form and then injury led to him rejoining his former boss Howard Kendall at Bramall Lane. Capped by England at schoolboy, youth, 'B' and Under-21 levels at Goodison Park, he made his League debut as a 'sub' against Wimbledon in February 1989, having earlier played as a 17 year old against Charlton in the FMC in March 1987. A Charity Shield winner in 1995, he had the misfortune to break a rib on his debut for the Blades against Reading before an ankle injury ended his career.

ECCLES, GEORGE SAMUEL
Right-back: 60 apps
Born: Newcastle-under-Lyme, Staffs, 1874 – *Died*: Bolton, 18 December 1945
Career: Wolstanton Brotherhood FC, Stoke St Peter's, Titbury Town, Middleport, Port Vale (June 1893), Wolverhampton Wanderers (May 1896), EVERTON (January 1899), West Ham United (May 1902), Preston North End (July 1904), Bolton Wanderers (December 1904–May 1905)
George Eccles, a well-proportioned, strong-kicking right-back, played in over 150 games in his 12-year career. He made his League debut for Everton at Newcastle in January 1899 when deputising for George Molyneux. In 1895, as a Port Vale player, Eccles misread the timetable and selected a non-existent train that only ran on bank holidays, thus missing a game at Notts County. He also recovered from a fractured collarbone (against Rotherham).

EGLINGTON, THOMAS JOSEPH
Outside-left: 428 apps, 82 goals
Born: Dublin, Ireland, 5 January 1923 – *Died*: Dublin, Ireland, 18 February 2004
Career: Shamrock Rovers, EVERTON (£10,000, July 1946), Tranmere Rovers (June 1957–May 1961); later ran a butcher's shop in Dublin
Tommy Eglington, one of Everton's greatest players and servants, was signed with his colleague Peter Farrell. An out-and-out left-winger, he gave many right-backs a testing time. He made his League debut for the Blues in a 3–2 home win over Arsenal in September 1946 in front of 40,000 fans and four years later scored five goals against Doncaster in a home Second Division match – a record for an Everton winger. First choice from the time he arrived at the club until the day he left, Eglington had devastating speed and often left a defender for dead. He possessed a powerful shot and could deliver the sweetest of crosses for his forwards to race on to. Capped six times by Northern Ireland and 24 by

the Republic, he missed the most important international of his career when England were defeated 2–0 at Goodison Park in 1949. He helped Everton win promotion from the Second Division in 1954, scoring 11 goals while wearing his customary number 11 shirt.

ELLIOTT, JOHN
Left-half/utility forward: 15 apps, 1 goal
Born: Liverpool, *circa* 1879 – Deceased
Career: EVERTON (May 1890–May 1895; trainer at Goodison Park, early 1900s)
Versatile Jack Elliott could occupy a variety of positions but was mainly a reserve at Goodison. He made his League debut in a 3–1 defeat at Notts County in November 1890, deputising for Alex Latta on the right-wing, and scored his only goal for the club, in a 3–2 win at Wolves in March 1893 when he played on the opposite flank.

ELLIOTT, THOMAS
Inside-right: 2 apps, 1 goal
Born: Liverpool, 1922
Career: EVERTON (season 1945–46)
Reserve inside-right Tom Elliott made his debut for Everton against Sheffield United in November 1945 (FL North) and followed up with his FA Cup debut in the third-round, first-leg clash at Preston in the January, scoring in the second leg four days later.

EVANS, WILLIAM BYRON
Left-back: 2 apps
Born: Llanglos, Wales, *circa* 1899 – Deceased
Career: Welsh junior football, EVERTON (January 1920), Swansea Town (March 1920), Southend United (April 1921), Queens Park Rangers (August 1924–April 1925)
Reserve defender Bill Evans deputised for Louis Weller against Newcastle in January 1920 for his debut and at Oldham a month later. He made 65 League appearances for Southend.

FALDER, DAVID EDWARD JAMES
Centre-half: 30 apps
Born: Liverpool, 21 October 1922
Career: Wigan Athletic, EVERTON (December 1945–May 1951)
A well-built, physically strong defender, David Falder made his debut for Everton in December 1949 against Fulham, taking over at centre-half berth from Tommy Jones. He held his position until the early part of the following season, but then failed to get a look in following the introduction of the 'second' Tommy Jones.

FARLEY, ADAM JOHN
Defender: 0+1 app.
Born: Liverpool, 12 January 1980
Career: EVERTON (apprentice, April 1996; professional, February 1998; released, June 2000)
A tall, powerful defender and key member of Everton's successful FA youth side, Adam Farley's only game for the Blues was as a 'sub' in the Premiership game against Derby in February 1999.

FARMER, GEORGE
Utility forward/left-half: 31 apps, 1 goal
Born: Oswestry, 1863 – *Died:* West Derby, Liverpool, 4 May 1905
Career: Oswestry WS (1881), EVERTON (February 1885), Liverpool Caledonians (January 1890), Liverpool South End, Rock Ferry FC
George Farmer joined Everton just after George Dobson had been recruited from Bolton – thus being the second professional signed by the club. Only 5 ft 6in. tall, he was a clever, constructive player, noted as a 'fine passer' who was capable of 'beautiful work'. He was also adept with his in-swinging corner-kicks. He missed only one match during the first League season of 1888–89 and indeed was described as being 'one of the most skilful forwards in the League'. He later settled down at left-half, where his 'defensive tackling found full scope'. He was initially a skinner working in Oswestry and in 1884 helped the local club win the Welsh Cup for the first time and reach the final a year later. Capped twice by Wales against England and Scotland in 1885, he made his debut for Everton in March of that year against Crewe. When occupying six different positions, he scored 34 goals in 41 games the following season, struck 23 times in 1886–87 and notched another 15 goals in 1887–88. However, he registered only one in 1888–89 (against Aston Villa in October), although he did set up both when Accrington were defeated 2–1 in Everton's first-ever League game in September 1888. Farmer appeared in 164 first-team matches for the Blues (81 goals).

FARRALL, ALEC
Inside-left/left-half: 5 apps
Born: West Kirby, Cheshire, 3 March 1936
Career: Wirral Schools, EVERTON (professional, March 1953), Preston North End (May 1957), Gillingham (£5,000, July 1960), Lincoln City (May 1965), Watford (July 1966–May 1968)
Capped five times by England as a schoolboy – once in each of five consecutive seasons (1948–53) – Alec Farrall was a useful reserve who was handed his League debut against his future club Lincoln in April 1953 at inside-left. He later did well with Gillingham, helping them win the Fourth Division title (1964) and making over 200 appearances.

FARRELL, PETER DESMOND
Right-half: 453 apps
Born: Dublin, Ireland, 16 August 1922 – *Died:* 2001
Career: Shamrock Rovers (August 1939), EVERTON (£10,000, with Tommy Eglington, August 1946), Tranmere Rovers (player–manager, £2,500, October 1957, later manager to December 1960), Sligo Rovers (manager, February 1961), Holywell Town/Wales (manager, season 1961–62); then further football club management in Ireland while also running his own insurance business in Dublin
Capped 28 times by Northern Ireland and on seven occasions for Eire, wing-half Peter Farrell (playing out of position as an inside-forward) helped create history when he scored one of the goals in the Republic of Ireland's 2–0 win over England at Goodison Park in 1949. Adored by the Everton faithful, he was a sturdy, powerful and highly efficient right-half, who joined the Blues with Tommy Eglington – the best double-deal the club has ever made! Captaining the side for many years, he was first choice (injuries and international calls apart) for over a decade before moving to Tranmere. An Irish Cup winner in 1942, he helped Everton win promotion from the Second Division in 1954.

FARRELLY, GARETH
Midfield: 21+9 apps, 2 goals
Born: Dublin, Ireland, 28 August 1975
Career: Aston Villa (YTS, June 1991; professional, January 1992), Rotherham United (loan, March 1995), EVERTON (£700,000, July 1997), Bolton Wanderers (loan, November 1998; signed permanently December 1998), Rotherham United (loan, March–May 2003), Burnley (August 2003), Wigan Athletic (July 2004)
Gareth Farrelly made nine appearances for Villa before making his debut for Everton against Crystal Palace in August 1997. Then, on the last day of the following season, he scored one of the most important goals in the club's history against Coventry, the point from a 1–1 draw ensuring that the Blues retained their Premiership status. He developed his game considerably at Goodison and later established himself at Bolton, scoring in his first match with only his second touch of the ball at Sheffield United. Farrelly has represented the Republic of Ireland at senior (6 caps), 'B' (1), Under-21 (11), youth and schoolboy levels.

FAZACKERLEY, STANLEY
Inside/centre-forward: 57 apps, 21 goals
Born: Preston, 3 October 1891 – *Died:* 20 June 1946
Career: Lane End United (1906), Preston North End (professional, October 1909), Charleston FC/Boston (USA), Accrington Stanley (November 1911), Hull City (£50, August 1912), Sheffield United (£1,000, March 1913), EVERTON (record £4,000, November 1920), Wolverhampton Wanderers (November 1922), Kidderminster Harriers (1924–25), Derby County (August 1925; retired on medical advice, April 1926)
Stan Fazackerley was a big name in soccer immediately prior to and after the

First World War. He commanded hefty transfer fees in both eras when switching from Hull to Bramall Lane and then to Everton, the latter after insisting on a move. Tall and graceful, he was a clever footballer, an adroit dribbler and dangerous around goal with his power-packed shooting and direction. He always seemed to keep a cool head and often finished in style. In 1920, he toured South Africa with the FA, playing in two Test matches. He helped the Blades win the FA Cup in 1915 and was a Third Division (N) championship-winner with Wolves in 1924. Fazackerley scored 114 goals in 258 League appearances, his best efforts coming with the Blades. He made his debut for Everton against Bradford City in November 1920.

FELL, JAMES IRVING
Outside-left: 28 apps, 5 goals
Born: Cleethorpes, 4 January 1936
Career: Waltham FC (Grimsby), Grimsby Town (amateur, April 1951; professional, April 1954), EVERTON (£17,500, March 1961), Newcastle United (£3,000 plus George Heslop, March 1962), Walsall (£5,000, July 1963), Lincoln City (January 1964), Boston United (January 1966), Skegness Town (1969–70), Ross Group – official at the Grimsby Sports Centre (1970–72)
Jimmy Fell, tall and direct, had a long career, spanning some 20 years, during which time he appeared in 326 League games and scored 69 goals. He replaced Peter Kavanagh for his Everton debut in a 2–1 home defeat by Aston Villa in March 1961. After Derek Temple had established himself in the side he moved to Walsall. His son, James, also played for Grimsby.

FENG, LI WEI
Defender: 2 apps
Born: Jilin, China, 26 January 1978
Career: Shenzen Pingan/China, EVERTON (loan, August 2002–March 2003)
Already an established Chinese international with almost 60 caps to his credit, Li Wei Feng spent seven months of a 12-month loan spell with Everton – signed in a deal in conjunction with the club's sponsors. He made his Premiership debut at Southampton in September 2002.

FERGUSON, DUNCAN
Striker: 173+30 apps, 65 goals
Born: Stirling, 27 December 1971
Career: Carse Thistle (1988), Dundee United (February 1990), Glasgow Rangers (£4m, July 1993), EVERTON (£4.4m, October 1994), Newcastle United (£7m, November 1998), EVERTON (£3.75m, August 2000)
Duncan Ferguson was Everton's first £4m signing. The Goodison Park talisman had an excellent first spell on Merseyside (42 goals in 133 outings) before transferring to Newcastle. After returning he was continually struck down by injury but finally got over his worries in 2003–04 and produced some excellent performances. Strong in all aspects of forward play, especially powerful in the air, he causes defenders plenty of problems. He has represented Scotland at five

different levels – schoolboy, youth, Under-21, 'B' and senior – collecting seven caps in the latter category. He helped Rangers clinch the double in 1994 and a year later was an FA Cup winner with Everton, for whom he made his Premiership debut in October 1994 against Coventry.

FERGUSON, MICHAEL JOHN

Striker: 10+2 apps, 6 goals

Born: Newcastle-upon-Tyne, 3 October 1954

Career: Coventry City (apprentice, June 1970; professional, December 1971), EVERTON (£280,000, August 1981), Birmingham City (loan, November 1982; signed for £60,000, June 1983), Coventry City (loan, March–April 1984), Brighton and Hove Albion (£40,000, plus Mark Jones, September 1984), Wealdstone United (August 1987), Sunderland (youth-team manager; later football in the community officer at Roker Park, 1995–96); Newcastle United (football in the community officer, 1996–98), Leeds United (football in the community officer, 1998 onwards)

A powerfully built striker, good in the air, Mick Ferguson netted 54 goals in 128 League games for Coventry before transferring to Everton, where it was hoped he would link up with Alan Biley. Unfortunately, things didn't work out for manager Howard Kendall and after a dozen games and a loan spell with Birmingham, Ferguson joined the St Andrew's club for a reduced fee. He made his debut for Everton as a substitute at Southampton in September 1981, but his time at Goodison Park was affected by constant ankle problems – due to his size 7 feet for someone 6ft 3in. tall.

FERN, THOMAS EDWARD

Goalkeeper: 231 apps

Born: Measham, Leicestershire, 1 April 1886 – *Died*: Bootle, 21 March 1966

Career: Mafeking Rovers, Worksop Albion, Worksop Town (May 1905), Lincoln City (May 1909), EVERTON (£1,500, December 1913), Port Vale (June 1924), Colwyn Bay (August 1927)

A League championship winner with Everton in 1915 (36 appearances), well-built goalkeeper Tom Fern often performed splendidly, earning himself the nickname of 'Evergreen'. Discovered by Lincoln, he made 142 consecutive appearances for the Imps (from February 1910) before transferring to Everton. Always in the thick of the action, he was daring and courageous but unfortunately suffered niggling injuries in his last two seasons at Goodison. He amassed a career record of 433 League appearances.

FIELDING, ALFRED WALTER

Inside-forward: 410 apps, 54 goals

Born: Edmonton, London, 26 November 1919

Career: Charlton Athletic (amateur forms, 1937–38), Army service, Walthamstow Avenue (briefly), EVERTON (professional, September 1945), Southport (January 1959; retired May 1959)

When he scored in a 3–2 win at WBA in September 1958, Wally 'Nobby'

Fielding – also known as the 'Little Londoner' – became Everton's oldest-ever marksman at 38 years, 305 days. A brilliant ball-player who always had his sleeves down and buttoned at the wrist, he chose Everton ahead of Charlton after serving in the Army during the Second World War – and what a grand player he turned out to be! He grafted hard and long and often ran a game with cool authority, although he did score his fair share of goals himself while laying on plenty more for his colleagues. He made his League debut against Brentford in August 1946, having starred in 36 FL North and FA Cup games in 1945–46 and was a Second Division promotion-winner with the Blues in 1953. During his Army service he played in several representative matches and for England against Scotland in the Bolton Disaster fund game at Manchester in 1946. Fielding (born on the same day as Harry Catterick) is Everton's oldest ex-player, currently residing in south Devon.

FINNIS, HAROLD ALEXANDER
Defender: 1 app.
Born: Liverpool, 21 November 1920 – *Died*: 1991
Career: EVERTON (August 1940, professional June 1946; retired, injured, May 1947)
Reserve full-back, Harold Finnis made his only League appearance for Everton at Leeds in November 1946, having played in two first-class matches in the 1940–41 wartime season.

FLEETWOOD, THOMAS
Forward/half-back: 285 apps, 10 goals
Born: Toxteth Park, Liverpool, 6 December 1888 – Deceased
Career: Hindley Central, Rochdale, EVERTON (March 1911), Oldham Athletic (August 1922), Chester (September 1924–May 1925)
Tom Fleetwood – 13 years at Goodison Park – appeared in over 400 first-team games (121 in the First World War). Able to perform equally well at centre- or left-half, he was initially tried as a makeshift inside/centre-forward, but never looked comfortable in either of those two positions, despite scoring his first goal for Everton in a 1–0 win at Tottenham. After helping the Blues win the League title in 1915, he played some of his best football in the Lancashire Section during the First World War, starring in two competitive Victory internationals for England against Scotland in 1919. He also represented the Football League six times and made his senior debut for the Blues against Bradford City in April 1911, lining up at inside-right. He appeared at centre-half for the first time against Manchester United five months later. He was awarded a benefit match: Everton against Sheffield Wednesday (1921–22).

FLEMING, GEORGE
Utility-forward: 9 apps, 4 goals
Born: Liverpool, *circa* 1863 – Deceased
Career: EVERTON (August 1885–May 1889)
George Fleming made his debut for Everton against Bolton in the FA Cup in

October 1887 and followed up 11 months later by scoring twice when Accrington were defeated 2–1 on the opening day of the Football League competition, his first goal coming on the hour. A hard-running forward, able to occupy all five front-line positions, he produced his best form on the wing. He scored 45 goals in 82 games for the Blues before the start of League football.

FLEWITT, ALBERT WILLIAM
Inside-forward: 3 apps, 1 goal
Born: Beeston, Notts, 10 February 1872 – *Died*: 1943
Career: Stamford (1890), Mansfield Greenhalgh's FC (August 1892), Lincoln City (August 1893), EVERTON (August 1895), West Bromwich Albion (January 1896), Bedminster (June 1899–May 1900)
Albert Flewitt possessed a terrific shot, worked hard and at times produced a touch of elegance, but he failed to do the business with Everton, appearing in only three League games, his debut coming against Nottingham Forest in September 1985, scoring in a 6–2 win. Top marksman for the Imps in 1894–95 with 17 goals, he claimed 30 in 56 outings before joining Everton. A Football League representative in 1895 and 1896, he partnered Billy Bassett on the right-wing at WBA, for whom he scored a goal every four games. He fell foul of the Midland club's management and was suspended six times between August 1898 and March 1899 for breaches of club rules.

FORBES, FREDERICK JAMES
Forward: 14 apps, 4 goals
Born: Leith, Edinburgh, 5 August 1894 – Deceased
Career: Leith Athletic (1912), Heart of Midlothian (1914), EVERTON (August 1922), Plymouth Argyle (with Jack Cock, March 1925), Bristol Rovers (November 1929), Leith Athletic (May 1931), Northampton Town (August 1932), Airdrieonians (June 1933; retired May 1934); later ran his own business in Edinburgh
Direct with good pace and a few tricks, Fred Forbes could occupy any forward position. He did well with Hearts before making his debut for the Blues against Newcastle in September 1922. Injured in a 5–1 defeat by Liverpool in his seventh outing, he was out of the first team for six months, failing to hold down a regular place afterwards. He played in 165 games for Plymouth (53 goals) and made over 300 appearances at club level.

FORSHAW, RICHARD
Inside-right: 41 apps, 8 goals
Born: Preston, Lancashire, 20 August 1895 – Deceased
Career: St George's Church Lads' Brigade (Gateshead), Gateshead St Vincent's; Army (1914), guest for Middlesbrough and Nottingham Forest during First World War; Middlesbrough (briefly), Liverpool (June 1919), EVERTON (March 1927), Wolverhampton Wanderers (August 1929), Hednesford Town (August 1930), Rhyl Athletic (October 1930; retired May 1931)
The first player to win a League championship medal with both Merseyside

clubs, Dick Forshaw was a fine inside-forward, one of the most consistent performers of his day. An ever-present in successive campaigns when Liverpool took the title (1921–23), he played in 23 games in 1927–28, when Everton became champions. A scorer on his Blues' debut in a 7–3 defeat at Newcastle in March 1927, he partnered Ted Critchley on the right-wing and left Goodison after losing his place to Jimmy Dunn.

FREEMAN, BERTRAM CLEWLEY

Centre-forward: 94 apps, 67 goals

Born: Handsworth, Birmingham 10 October 1895 – *Died*: Birmingham, 11 August 1955

Career: Gower Street Council School (Aston), Gower Street Old Boys, Aston Manor, Aston Villa (April 1904), Woolwich Arsenal (November 1905), EVERTON (April 1908), Burnley (April 1911), Wigan Borough (September 1921–May 1922), Kettering Town (August 1923; retired August 1924)

Scorer of the 1914 FA Cup final-winning goal for Burnley and capped five times by England (1909–15), Bert Freeman was the first player to net over 30 League goals in a season for Everton, doing so in 1908–09 with a total of 38. He also recorded six hat-tricks for the Blues, for whom he made his senior debut against Liverpool in April 1908. Not a robust player, he was, in fact, a gifted, graceful footballer, an effective schemer who failed to make the breakthrough at Villa Park but then did extremely well after that while scoring 197 goals in 321 League games.

GABRIEL, JAMES

Wing-half: 303+1 apps, 36 goals

Born: Dundee, Scotland, 16 October 1940

Career: Lawside Academy, Tynecastle Boys' Club, Dundee North End, Dundee (1957), EVERTON (£30,000, March 1960), Southampton (£45,000, July 1967), Bournemouth (£20,000, July 1972), Swindon Town (loan, October–December 1973), Brentford (March 1974), Seattle Sounders (player–coach, June 1974; retired as a player April 1976), Argentina (coach, 1979), Phoenix (manager/coach, 1980), San Francisco Earthquakes/USA (coach, 1981), Washington State Youth Academy (coach/director); also USA National coach of Coaches; Bournemouth (assistant manager, March 1987), EVERTON (assistant manager, June 1990; caretaker-manager, October 1990; reserve-team coach, November 1990)

Everton's first £30,000 signing, blond wing-half Jimmy Gabriel was a hard-tackler who gave nothing away, always going in where it hurt and often coming up trumps. A solid performer, he produced many wholehearted displays and was instrumental when the League championship was won in 1962–63, scoring five goals in 40 games. A Scottish international, two caps won against Wales (1961) and Norway (1964), Gabriel also gained youth-team honours and played in six Under-23 matches. An FA Cup winner in 1966, he lost his place to Howard Kendall, having made his debut for Everton against Chelsea in March 1960, starring in a 6–1 win. He worked with Harry Redknapp in America and also at Bournemouth before returning as assistant to Colin Harvey at Everton. His father played for East Fife and Forfar.

GALT, JAMES HILL

Centre-half: 36 apps, 4 goals
Born: Ardrossan, Ayrshire, 11 August 1885 – *Died:* 17 November 1935
Career: Glasgow Rangers (January 1906), EVERTON (May 1914), Third Lanark (October 1920)
Jimmy Galt, 6 ft 1 in. tall, won two caps for Scotland in 1908 against Ireland and Wales as well as twice representing the Scottish League and playing four times for Glasgow against Sheffield. He helped Rangers win the Scottish League title three times in a row (1910–13) and the Scottish Cup (1909). Mainly a wing-half, he was switched to centre-half with immediate success by Everton and captained the Blues to League championship in his first season, making 32 appearances. A tough competitor, a player of method and commitment, he made one appearance during the First World War, scoring against Southport on Christmas Day 1915. Galt was a motor engineer by profession.

GANNON, MICHAEL JOHN

Defender: 3 apps
Born: Liverpool, 2 February 1943
Career: EVERTON (juniors, April 1958; professional, February 1960), Scunthorpe United (May 1962), Crewe Alexandra (October 1964–May 1970)
An Everton reserve for four years, Mick Gannon was restricted to just three appearances, making his debut against Sheffield United in March 1962, when he replaced Colin Green. He later appeared in 210 League games for Crewe.

GARDNER, THOMAS

Outside-right: 1 app.
Born: Liverpool, 17 March 1923
Career: South Liverpool, Liverpool (October 1946), EVERTON (June 1947–May 1948)
Tom Gardner failed to make Liverpool's first team and played once for Everton, partnering Eddie Wainwright in the home League game against Wolves in October 1947, when 46,000 fans saw the 1–1 draw.

GASCOIGNE, PAUL JOHN

Inside-forward/Midfield: 22+16 apps, 1 goal
Born: Gateshead, 27 May 1967
Career: Newcastle United (apprentice, June 1983; professional, May 1985), Tottenham Hotspur (£2m, July 1988), SS Lazio/Italy (£5.5m, July 1992), Glasgow Rangers (£4.3m, July 1995), Middlesbrough (£3.45m, March 1998), EVERTON (free, July 2000), Burnley (free, March 2002), Gansu

Tianma/China (January 2003), Wolverhampton Wanderers (trial, November–December 2003), Boston United (player–coach, July 2004)

Paul Gascoigne was a brilliant attacking midfielder with flair, ability, aggression and competitiveness as well as a useful scoring record. He made over 100 appearances for Newcastle, Spurs and Rangers and starred in almost 50 games for Lazio and Middlesbrough before moving to Everton, making his debut as a substitute against Leeds on the opening Saturday of the 2000–01 season, claiming his only goal for the Blues in a 2–2 draw at Bolton in November 2001. Capped 57 times by England, he also played in four 'B', 13 Under-21 and a handful of youth internationals. An FA Youth Cup winner with Newcastle (1985), FA Cup winner with Spurs (1991 – although his appearance in the final against Nottingham Forest was rather brief), he won two Scottish Premier League (1996, 1997), one Scottish Cup (1996) and the League Cup (1997) with Rangers. Always in the news, he had his hair dyed blond when he joined Rangers and thousands of youngsters followed suit. He also told a newspaper reporter: 'I've had 14 bookings this season, eight of which were my fault, but seven were disputable.' A great character – and a controversial one, too.

GAULD, JAMES

Inside-forward: 26 apps, 8 goals
Born: Aberdeen, 9 May 1929
Career: Aberdeen (part-time), Elgin City (1951–54), Waterford (August 1954), Charlton Athletic (£4,000, May 1955), EVERTON (£10,500, October 1956), Plymouth Argyle (£5,000, October 1957), Swindon Town (£6,000, August 1959), St Johnstone (August 1960), Mansfield Town (November 1960–March 1961)

Although the name of Jimmy Gauld will always be tarnished in football because of his role at the centre of a bribes scandal which shook the sport in the early 1960s, it's possible to consider his playing career in isolation from those latter, unsavoury events. A pretty useful inside-forward who often took the shortest route to goal, he scored over 70 goals in 200 games (70 in 183 League outings) over six years. He had his best spells at Charlton and Plymouth, but during his 12 months at Goodison Park he certainly made his mark, averaging a goal every three games. He made his Blues' debut in place of Harry Llewellyn in a 5–2 League win at Manchester United in October 1956. Capped by Scotland at schoolboy and youth-team levels, he twice represented the League of Ireland (1954–55) and was a Third Division championship winner with Plymouth (1959). In 1954–55, he scored 30 League goals for Waterford – the second-highest tally ever in FAI football. A broken leg suffered on Boxing Day 1960 effectively ended his career.

On 26 January 1965, Gauld, the ring-leader, plus nine players, including Everton's Tony Kay, were all sent to prison, serving sentences from 4 to 15 months. Gauld was also banned from football for life. In 1980 he resurfaced for a four-month period as a café-owner and bookshop manager at Torquay's railway station.

GAULT, WILLIAM ERNEST
Centre/inside-forward: 30 apps, 13 goals
Born: Wallsend, 20 September 1889 – *Died*: Liverpool, 1980
Career: Jarrow Caledonians, EVERTON (April 1912), Stockport County (season 1913–14), EVERTON (August 1917), Cardiff City (May 1920), Stockport County (December 1920), New Brighton (August 1922–May 1923)

Although Ernie Gault had two spells with Everton, there is no knowing what he might have achieved had the First World War not started when it did. Indeed, during the conflict, he scored 93 goals in 77 Regional games, while either side of the First World War he managed only 30 appearances (13 goals). He made his Everton debut in a 4–1 victory at Derby in mid-September 1912 and later returned to have his best League season in 1919–20, when he scored more than a goal every two games. Fast and direct, he loved to shoot on sight and always caused problems for defenders.

GEARY, FREDERICK
Centre-forward: 98 apps, 86 goals
Born: Hyson Green, Notts, 23 January 1868 – *Died*: 8 January 1955
Career: Balmoral FC/Nottingham, Notts Rangers (April 1886), Grimsby Town (June 1887), Notts Rangers (August 1888), Notts County (briefly), Notts Rangers (March 1889), EVERTON (July 1889), Liverpool (£60, May 1895; retired, injured, May 1899)

Fred Geary may well have been the first player to score a hat-trick for Everton in the FA Cup, doing so against Derby in January 1890. (Alec Brady and Alf Milward also hit trebles in the 11–2 win.) An ever-present and top marksman (20 goals) when the Blues won the League title in 1891, he also topped the scoring charts in 1889–90 and 1892–93. The first Everton player to claim 20 goals in a season (21 in 1889–90), he was quick with a lightning shot. He gained two England caps against Ireland 1890 and Scotland 1891, lining up alongside Edgar Chadwick and Alf Milward in the latter international at Blackburn. He also represented the Football League and was a Second Division championship winner with Liverpool in 1896. A teetotaller, he played for Lancashire at bowls.

GEE, CHARLES WILLIAM
Centre-half: 212 apps, 2 goals
Born: Reddish, near Stockport, 6 April 1909 – *Died*: 1981
Career: Reddish Green Wesleyans, Stockport County (December 1928), EVERTON (July 1930; retired, injured, May 1940)

A stylish player, sound and reliable on the ground and in the air, Charlie Gee was always in good heart, without a hint of temperament. The ideal link between defence and attack, he helped Everton win the Second and then First Division championships in successive seasons (1931, 1932) and was capped three times by England against Wales, Spain and Ireland (1931–36). He made his debut for the Blues against Bury (won 3–2) in place of the injured Tom Griffiths on New Year's

Day 1931 and had his last outing in a Second World War fixture against Fulham in May 1940. He was 12th man at the 1933 FA Cup final.

GEE, ELLIS

Outside-left: 32 apps
Born: Grassmoor, 1878 – Deceased
Career: Chesterfield Town (1896), EVERTON (March 1898), Notts County (April 1900), Reading (1907–08)

Having done well at Chesterfield, Ellis Gee was recruited by Everton as a replacement/deputy for Jackie Bell. He played in three of the last four games in 1897–98, making his debut in a 2–0 home win over Nottingham Forest in early April. The following season he made 18 appearances and 11 in 1899–1900 before Robert Gray took over on the left. Gee scored 21 goals in 214 League games for Notts County.

GELDARD, ALBERT

Outside-right: 180 apps, 37 goals
Born: Bradford, 11 April 1914 – *Died*: 1989
Career: Whetley Lane School (Bradford), Manningham Mills, Bradford Park Avenue (amateur, June 1928; professional, April 1930), EVERTON (November 1932), Bolton Wanderers (£4,500, July 1938; retired May 1947); returned to play for Darwen (November 1949–May 1950)

An England schoolboy international against Scotland and Wales in 1927 and Ireland a year later, Albert Geldard was only 15 years, 156 days old when he made his League debut for Bradford in September 1929. Then in 1933, aged 19 years, 18 days, he won the FA Cup with Everton. A class winger from an early age (he once scored 22 goals in one schoolboy match), Geldard was a slippery customer who possessed an exceptional turn of speed, could shoot with both feet and enjoyed taking on opponents, either on the outside or inside. He scored on his debut for the Blues against Middlesbrough and although not a prolific marksman, he had his best season in terms of goals in 1934–35, when he netted ten. Capped four times by England (1933–38), Geldard was a fine club cricketer and member of the Magic Circle – making him a magician both on and off the field!

GEMMILL, SCOT

Midfield: 89+21 apps, 5 goals
Born: Paisley, 2 January 1971
Career: Nottingham Forest (apprentice, April 1987; professional, January 1990), EVERTON (£250,000, March 1999), Preston North End (loan, March–May 2004), Leicester City (three-month contract, June 2004)

Scot Gemmill, a neat and tidy midfielder, made over 300 appearances for Nottingham Forest before moving to Everton. A Scottish international, capped 25 times at senior level, on four occasions by the Under-21s and twice by the 'B' team, he was a Zenith Data Systems Cup winner in 1992 and a First Division championship winner in 1998.

GERRARD, PAUL WILLIAM
Goalkeeper: 98+1 apps
Born: Heywood, Lancs, 22 January 1973
Career: Oldham Athletic (apprentice, April 1989; professional, November 1991), EVERTON (£1m, July 1996), Oxford United (loan, December 1998–January 1999), Ipswich Town (loan, November–December 2002), Sheffield United (loan, July–September 2003), Nottingham Forest (loan, March–May 2004); EVERTON (contract expired, June 2004), Nottingham Forest (June 2004)

Capped 18 times by England at Under-21 level, Paul Gerrard made 136 appearances for the Latics. A fine shot-stopper, he was initially recruited as cover for Neville Southall, but Thomas Myhre kept him out and although he gained a regular first-team place eventually, after a spate of injuries, he was seeking pastures new in 2004.

GIBSON, ARCHIBALD
Centre-half: 5 apps
Born: Scotland, *circa* 1866 – Deceased
Career: EVERTON (July 1886–May 1888)

Craggy Scot Archie Gibson, who could man several positions, was primarily Everton's regular centre-half for two seasons and during that time appeared in 74 first-team matches, scoring 17 goals, including one against Oakfield in the final of the Liverpool Cup in April 1887, which the Blues won 5–0. He also played in Everton's first FA Cup-tie against Bolton in October 1887 but was not retained once League football was introduced the following season.

GIBSON, DAVID JAMES A.
Outside-right: 3 apps
Born: Runcorn, 18 March 1931
Career: EVERTON (amateur, June 1947; professional, August 1950), Swindon Town (November 1954–May 1957)

A reserve at Goodison, Dave Gibson made his debut in a 1–0 win at Derby in April 1951. His two other senior outings came eight months later. He appeared in over 70 matches for Swindon.

GIDMAN, JOHN
Full-back: 78 apps, 3 goals
Born: Liverpool, 10 January 1954
Career: Merseyside schoolboy football, Liverpool (apprentice, June 1969), Aston Villa (professional, August 1971), EVERTON (£650,000, October 1979), Manchester United (£450,000, August 1981), Manchester City (free, October 1986), Stoke City (August 1988), Darlington (player/assistant manager, February–May 1989), Kings Lynn (manager, early 1990s); now café/bar owner in Spain

Attack-minded John Gidman had an excellent career. After failing to make the breakthrough at Anfield, he took time to establish himself in the first XI with

Villa but once in, he stayed and appeared in 243 games (nine goals), winning England caps at full, 'B' and Under-23 levels, having earlier represented his country as a youth player. He helped Villa win the FA Youth Cup (1972) and the League Cup (1977, against Everton) but missed the 1975 League Cup final win over Norwich with an eye injury following a firework accident on Bonfire Night 1974. He was also sent off in the Nou Camp Stadium playing for Villa against Barcelona in the UEFA Cup in 1978. He quickly settled into his stride at Goodison, making an impressive debut against Manchester United in October 1979. He held his position, injuries apart, until leaving for Old Trafford, duly collecting an FA Cup-winner's medal when United beat Everton in the 1983 final. Gidman made 432 League appearances in total.

GILLICK, TORRANCE
Outside-right/left: 133 apps, 44 goals
Born: Airdrie, 19 May 1915 – *Died*: 16 December 1972
Career: Airdrie schoolboy football, Peterhill FC (1931), Glasgow Rangers (professional, May 1933), EVERTON (£8,000, December 1935); guest for Airdrieonians and Glasgow Rangers during the Second World War; Glasgow Rangers (November 1945), Partick Thistle (August 1951; retired May 1952); later manager of a scrap-metal company in Lanarkshire

After winning the double with Rangers in 1934–35, Torry Gillick was a League championship winner with Everton in 1938–39, before returning to Ibrox. He then helped Rangers win the League title three times more (1946–47, 1948–49, 1949–50) and twice lift the Scottish Cup (1947, 1948). A goal-scoring winger, solid and chunky with good close control and a stinging shot, he was capped five times by Scotland (1936–39), played three times for the Scottish League and also appeared in three Second World War internationals against England (1941–43). He occupied all five forward positions during his first spell with Rangers. He made his debut for Everton against Leeds in December 1935.

GINOLA, DAVID DESIRÉ MARC
Winger/Midfield: 4+3 apps
Born: Gossin, near Toulon, France, 25 January 1967
Career: FC Toulon/France (1985), Racing Club de Paris/France (1988), Brent (1990), Paris St Germain/France (1992), Newcastle United (£2.5m, July 1995), Tottenham Hotspur (£2m, July 1997), Aston Villa (£3m, August 2000), EVERTON (free, February 2002; retired May 2002); coach in France (2002–03); also film star and TV personality

David Ginola was on £40,000 per week when he joined Aston Villa – making him the highest-paid player in the Midland club's history. A French League title-winner with PSG in 1994 when he was also named both France's 'Player of the Year' and the 'Players' Player of the Year', he appeared in over 200 games in his homeland (25 goals) and won international recognition.

He then netted seven times in 76 senior outings for Newcastle, appeared in 127 matches for Spurs (21 goals) and made 41 appearances, 22 as a 'sub' (five goals) for Villa before joining Everton, for whom he made his debut against

Arsenal in February 2002. Blessed with tremendous on-the-ball skill, he had a wonderful body-swerve, a stunning right-foot shot and a great deal of charisma. He was voted both the FWA and PFA 'Player of the Year' in 1999, being regarded at the time as one of the greatest wingers (left side) in England. A celebrity both on and off the field, Ginola unfortunately fell out with the management of the French national team in the mid-1990s and after attempting to settle his differences, failed to get a recall and subsequently missed out on World Cup and European Championship glory. He gained 17 caps – his first in 1990 as a 'sub' against Albania and his last in September 1995 against Azerbaijan.

Ginola was found guilty of misconduct by the FA and fined £22,000 with a two-match suspension during his time with Villa. His book *El Magnifique* was a best-seller in 2000.

GLAZZARD, JAMES
Centre-forward: 3 apps
Born: Normanton, 23 April 1923 – *Died*: 1996
Career: Altofts Colliery, Huddersfield Town (amateur, July 1943; professional, October 1943), EVERTON (£4,000, September 1956), Mansfield Town (December 1956; retired September 1957)
Known as 'Gentleman Jim' during his time with Huddersfield, Glazzard was a fine marksman who scored 153 goals in 321 outings for the Terriers (plus another 33 in 98 Second World War games). His impeccable character and ability to find the back of the net made him a huge favourite with the supporters. He was instrumental to the Terriers when promotion was gained to the First Division in 1952–53, bagging 30 goals, four in one match, all headers from left-wing crosses, when Everton were belted 8–2 in April. The following season he grabbed another 29 goals when the Terriers finished third in the top flight. Capped by England 'B' against Germany in March 1954, unfortunately his best years were over when he moved to Goodison Park, making the first of his three League appearances against Wolves in September 1956.

GLOVER, GERARD JOHN
Wing-half: 2+1 apps
Born: Liverpool, 27 September 1948
Career: EVERTON (amateur, April 1964; professional, August 1964), Mansfield Town (September 1967–May 1968)
Gerry Glover, an England schoolboy and youth international, was the first substitute used by Everton in a Merseyside derby, replacing Brian Labone in September 1965. He had made his senior debut the previous April against Sunderland, at left-half in a 1–1 draw.

GODFREY, BRIAN CAMERON
Inside-forward/midfielder: 1 app.
Born: Flint, Wales, 1 May 1940
Career: Flint Alexandra (1955–56), Wrexham (trial), Chester (junior), Tranmere

Rovers (junior), EVERTON (amateur, June 1957; professional, May 1958), Scunthorpe United (June 1960), Preston North End (October 1963), Aston Villa (deal involving Brian Greenhalgh, September 1967), Bristol Rovers (deal involving Ray Graydon, May 1971), Newport County (June 1973), Portland Timbers/NASL (March 1975–May 1976), Bath City (manager, June 1976–December 1978), Exeter City (manager, January 1979–June 1983), Weymouth (manager, 1983–87), Gloucester City (manager, 1987–89 and from February 1992–94); later Cinderford Town (manager, 1998–2000); played for Aston Villa Old Boys until he was 55

Brian Godfrey's only game for Everton was on the left-wing at Fulham in January 1960. After leaving Goodison his career developed fast and he went from strength to strength, amassing over 600 appearances for clubs and country (scoring 125 goals). A Welsh international, capped three times at senior level and once by the Under-23s, Godfrey lined up for Aston Villa in the 1971 League Cup final – one of 160 appearances for the Midland club (25 goals). A gritty, hard-working player, he was bitterly disappointed to be left out of Preston's 1964 FA Cup final team against West Ham. A qualified FA coach, he guided Bath City to the Southern League title in 1978, Exeter to the FA Cup quarter-finals in 1981, saw Weymouth finish fifth in the Conference in 1986 and steered Gloucester to the Midland League, Southern Division title in 1989.

When Godfrey was manager of Exeter, he saw his side beaten 5–1 at Millwall in 1982. As a punishment to his players he kept them in London overnight and the next day made them take on Millwall's reserve side – and they even lost that game 1–0!

GOLDIE, HUGH

Right-half: 19 apps, 1 goal
Born: Dalry, Scotland, *circa* 1870 – Deceased
Career: St Mirren (1892), EVERTON, (September 1895), Celtic (July 1897), Dundee (March 1899), New Brompton (1900)

Tough-tackling Hugh Goldie had his best spell with Everton between October 1895 and February 1896 when he occupied the right-half berth with confidence. He made his debut in a 3–2 home win over Bury two weeks after joining and scored his only goal in a 3–0 win over Small Heath in February 1896. He made 27 appearances for Celtic, gaining a League championship medal in 1898.

GOODLASS, RONALD

Forward: 47+4 apps, 2 goals
Born: Liverpool, 6 September 1963
Career: EVERTON (apprentice, September 1968; professional, July 1971), NAC Breda/Holland (£75,000, October 1977), Den Haag/Holland (£80,000, September 1979), Fulham (£30,000, September 1980), Scunthorpe United (March 1982), Hong Kong, Tranmere Rovers (December 1983–August 1984), Barrow (1984–85)

An avid Everton fan and an England schoolboy international, Ronnie Goodlass realised his lifetime ambition when he joined the club in 1968. He made his senior debut against Manchester United in December 1975 and two years later appeared in both the FA Cup and League Cup finals, sadly finishing up a loser each time against Liverpool and Aston Villa respectively. Unfortunately he had the tendency to drift in and out of the game far too often and this led to him being dropped several times and when Dave Thomas arrived at Goodison, Goodlass departed. He scored four goals in his 87 outings in League football.

GORDON, PATRICK

Outside-right: 23 apps, 5 goals
Born: Glasgow, Scotland, *circa* 1865 – Deceased
Career: Renton (1887), EVERTON (September 1890), Liverpool (July 1893), Blackburn Rovers (October 1894–May 1895)
Speedy Paddy Gordon was equally effective at inside-right, the position he occupied when Everton lost to Wolves in the 1893 FA Cup final. A reserve at Renton, he became a major force in Scottish football, understudying several international forwards. He made his Everton debut against Bolton in October 1890 and was a Second Division championship winner with Liverpool in 1894.

GOUDIE

Centre-forward: 5 apps, 1 goal
Born: Scotland, *circa* 1865 – Deceased
Career: EVERTON (August 1887–May 1888)
Goudie scored three goals in 13 first-team appearances for Everton as injury plagued him for a long period between January and May 1888. He scored twice on his debut in a 9–0 friendly win over Bury and a month later (October 1887) played in the Blues' first-ever FA Cup-tie against Bolton.

GOUGH, CHARLES RICHARD

Defender: 41+1 apps, 1 goal
Born: Stockholm, Sweden, 5 April 1962
Career: Wits University/South Africa, Southern Transvaal/South Africa, Charlton Athletic (trial, 1978), Dundee United (apprentice, June 1979; professional, March 1980), Tottenham Hotspur (£750,000, August 1986), Glasgow Rangers (£1.5m, October 1987), Kansas City/USA (loan, May 1997), San Jose Clash/USA (loan, May 1998), Nottingham Forest (free, March 1999), EVERTON (free, June 1999), Northern Spirit/Australia (July 2001; retired March 2002)
The oldest post-Second World War outfield player to don an Everton jersey, centre-half Richard Gough was 39 years, 24 days old when he made his last appearance for the Blues against Bradford City in April 2001. The son of a Scottish mother and a former footballer (Charlie), Gough represented South Africa as a schoolboy. He failed to impress Charlton but quickly established himself with Dundee United, for whom he made over 250 appearances, gaining international recognition for Scotland at Under-21 (5 caps) and senior level (eventually winning 61 caps). He played 65 times for Spurs, collecting a loser's

medal in the 1987 FA Cup final and during his 11 years at Ibrox amassed 427 appearances (34 goals), collecting medals galore. He was a Scottish League winner on ten occasions between 1983 and 1997 (the first with Dundee United). He also gained five League Cup and three Scottish Cup-winner's medals (all with Rangers). He made his Everton debut against Manchester United in August 1999 (1–1 draw), but after one good season on Merseyside, the second was blighted by injury. In 1987 a Scottish brewery presented Gough with an award to 'honour the performance of the Scottish-born player', though he was actually born in Sweden!

GOURLAY, JAMES WALTER
Inside/centre-forward/wing-half: 58 apps, 9 goals
Born: Annbank, near Glasgow, *circa* 1884 – Deceased
Career: Port Glasgow, EVERTON (March 1910), Greenock Morton (May 1913)
Jim Gourlay had already made his mark in Scotland before joining Everton. A strong, purposeful player, he scored on his debut for the Blues in a 2–2 home draw with Chelsea in March 1910 and in 1911–12 helped the team finish runners-up in the First Division. (Some reference books name him as Gorlay.)

GRACIE, THOMAS
Centre/inside-forward: 13 apps, 1 goal
Born: Glasgow, 12 June 1889 – *Died:* Glasgow, 23 October 1915
Career: Glasgow junior football, Greenock Morton, EVERTON (March 1911), Liverpool (February 1912 with Billy Lacey, in exchange for Harold Uren), Heart of Midlothian (April 1914); did not feature after the First World War
A Scottish League representative, Tom Gracie performed mostly as an inside-left, although in 1912 one newspaper reporter said that he 'played wonderfully well for Morton and [was] selected as reserve centre-forward for Scotland'. Unfortunately he had a thin time at Everton, scoring one goal against Nottingham Forest in his third game after making his debut against Blackburn in April 1911. He netted five times in 32 games for Liverpool. He was only 26 when he died serving as a corporal with the Royal Scots.

GRAHAM, ROBERT
Inside-right: 3 apps
Born: Glasgow, *circa* 1879 – Deceased
Career: Third Lanark, Fulham (July 1904), Third Lanark (August 1905), EVERTON (January 1907), Bolton Wanderers (February 1908–May 1909)
Highly intelligent with a powerful right-foot shot, Bob Graham played his best football with Third Lanark, with whom he gained a Scottish Cup runner's-up medal. He never settled down at Goodison Park, making his debut against Bolton in March 1907.

GRANT, ANTHONY JAMES

Midfield: 54+25 apps, 3 goals
Born: Liverpool, 14 November 1974
Career: EVERTON (apprentice, April 1991; professional, July 1993), Swindon Town (loan, January–February 1996), Tranmere Rovers (loan, September–October 1999), Manchester City (£450,000, December 1999), West Bromwich Albion (loan, December 2000), Burnley (£250,000, October 2001)

A useful ball-winner and neat passer, Tony Grant made his debut for Everton as a 'sub' at Newcastle in February 1995. An England Under-21 international, he failed to hold down a regular place at Maine Road but did well at Turf Moor, reaching the milestone of 200 career appearances in 2003.

GRANT, JOHN ALBERT

Wing-half: 133 apps, 11 goals
Born: Gateshead, 8 September 1924
Career: High Spennymoor Athletic, EVERTON (December 1942), Rochdale (May 1956), Southport (January 1959–May 1960)

Jackie Grant, initially an inside-forward, took over from Joe Mercer and scored six goals in 92 appearances for Everton during the Second World War before making his League debut against Wolves in October 1946. A regular in the side for just one season, 1950–51, when he was an ever-present, he lined up in seven different positions for the Blues, becoming an integral part of the Central League side, leading them to numerous successes. Signed by Harry Catterick for Rochdale, he made over 100 appearances for the Spotland club.

GRAVESEN, THOMAS

Midfield: 122+10 apps, 7 goals
Born: Vejle, Denmark, 11 March 1976
Career: Vejle BK/Denmark (professional August 1993), SV Hamburg/Germany (July 1997), EVERTON (£2.5m, August 2000)

A Danish international, who has also played in six Under-21 games, technically gifted Thomas Gravesen, with his shaven head, has given some impressive displays in Everton's midfield, although at times he has failed to produce the goods. He certainly has everything a manager requires – aggression, work-rate, passing skills and shooting power – but often remains an enigma because of his too many off days. He made his League debut against Charlton in August 2000 and reached the milestone of 100 Premiership appearances in 2003, having made 58 for Vejle and 74 for Hamburg. He played for Denmark in Euro 2004 and now has almost 50 senior caps to his credit.

GRAY, ANDREW MULLEN

Striker: 61+7 apps, 22 goals
Born: Gorbals, Glasgow, 30 November 1955
Career: Clydebank Strollers, Dundee United (amateur, 1970; professional, May 1973), Aston Villa (£110,000, September 1975), Wolverhampton Wanderers

(£1.15m, September 1979), EVERTON (£250,000, November 1983), Aston Villa (£150,000, July 1985), Notts County (loan, August 1987), West Bromwich Albion (£25,000, September 1987), Glasgow Rangers (September 1988), Cheltenham Town (August 1989), Aston Villa (assistant manager/coach, July 1991–June 1992); now Sky TV soccer analyst/pundit

Andy Gray became the most expensive footballer in Britain when Wolves bought him in 1979. A colourful figure wherever he played, he was brave, determined, totally committed, a tremendous header of the ball, who scored most of his goals from crosses. He made almost 80 appearances for Dundee United, gaining a Scottish Cup runner's-up medal in 1974. Villa signed him for a record fee and two years later he played in the two drawn games of the 1977 League Cup final against Everton and was voted PFA 'Player of the Year' and 'Young Player of the Year'.

Gray scored 45 goals in 162 appearances for Wolves, including the winner against Nottingham Forest in the 1980 League Cup final. He then did the business with Everton, hitting a goal every three games following his debut against Forest in November 1983 when he replaced Graeme Sharp.

During his time at Goodison, Gray collected winner's medals in three competitions: the FA Cup (when he scored in the 1984 final against Watford), League championship and European Cup-Winners' Cup (when he netted against Rapid Vienna in Rotterdam). Villa re-signed Gray as a stop-gap and after assisting Notts County and WBA, he joined Rangers, gaining both the League Cup and Premier title. His job done, Gray played for Cheltenham before going back to Villa as assistant to Ron Atkinson. Capped 20 times by Scotland, he also won Under-23, youth and schoolboy honours and scored over 200 goals in more than 600 club matches.

Gray is one of only three players so far to score in three competitive finals – doing so in the FA Cup (for Everton in 1984), the League Cup (for Wolves in 1980) and the European Cup-Winners' Cup (for Everton in 1985). He appeared in a major final with five different clubs: Dundee United, Villa, Wolves, Everton and Rangers.

GRAY, ROBERT

Outside-left: 21 apps, 1 goal
Born: Scotland, *circa* 1876 – Deceased
Career: Partick Thistle, EVERTON (November 1899), Southampton (May 1901–March 1902)

Bob Gray was signed by Everton to take over from the injured Ellis Gee. He made his debut in a 3–0 home League win over Derby in December 1899 and scored his only goal in a 2–1 win at Manchester City a fortnight later. He failed to establish himself at The Dell.

GREEN, ROBERT COLIN

Full-back: 18 apps, 1 goal
Born: Brynteg, near Wrexham, 10 February 1942
Career: Wrexham District Schools, Wrexham (trialist, May 1957), EVERTON

(amateur, July 1957; professional, February 1959), Birmingham City (£15,000, December 1962), Wrexham (loan, January 1971), Tamworth (June 1971), Rhyl (August 1972; retired May 1974); worked in the garage business and was also a sales rep for a Wrexham veterinary medicine company

Colin Green made his League debut at the age of 17 for Everton at Blackpool in September 1960, having a fine game against Stanley Matthews in a 4–1 win (he almost joined Wrexham on leaving school). A bad knee seriously restricted his appearances for the Blues and he eventually moved to Birmingham, the deal being set up while Green was playing for the Welsh Under-21 side in Aberdeen. A cool, unflappable defender, he gained the first of his 15 full caps in 1965 against Italy. In 1966 a broken leg sidelined him for five months and then after recovering from a serious chest infection, he fought back to make 271 senior appearances for the St Andrew's club.

GREENHALGH, NORMAN

Wing-half/left-back: 115 apps, 1 goal
Born: Bolton, 10 August 1914 – *Died*: 1995
Career: Bolton Wanderers (amateur, May 1931; professional, September 1933), New Brighton (October 1935), EVERTON (£800, January 1938), Bangor City (free, May 1949; retired June 1950); later a licensee

Norman 'Rollicker' Greenhalgh, an ever-present in Everton's League championship-winning season of 1938–39, was one of the few defenders feared by Stanley Matthews. A rugged defender, strong and confident, he could also play up front and even in goal in an emergency. After failing at Bolton, he broke into League football with New Brighton and then formed a redoubtable full-back partnership with Billy Cook at Everton, for whom he made his senior debut against his former club, Bolton, in January 1938. His last outing came in a 6–0 defeat at Chelsea in September 1948. Greenhalgh missed out on full international honours but did represent England in wartime against Scotland in December 1939 and played once for the Football League.

GRENYER, ALAN

Left-half: 148 apps, 9 goals
Born: North Shields, Northumberland, 31 August 1892 – *Died*: June 1953
Career: Collingwood, North Shields, North Shields Athletic, EVERTON (November 1910), South Shields (November 1924; retired May 1929)

Alan Grenyer helped Everton win the League championship in 1915; four years later he represented England against Wales in a Victory international and shared the left-half position at Goodison Park from 1912 to 1915 with Harry Makepeace. Initially a forward, it was in the left-half berth where he played most of his senior football. An expert at heading and noted for judicious and accurate distribution, he made his League debut against Nottingham Forest in April 1911 (won 2–1) and during the First World War played in 119 Regional games for Everton (three goals).

GRIFFITHS, BRYAN
Full-back: 2 apps
Born: Liverpool, 27 November 1938
Career: EVERTON (amateur, April 1954; professional, March 1956), Southport (June 1960–May 1963)
A competent reserve full-back, Bryan Griffiths made his League debut for Everton against PNE at Deepdale in September 1958. He later played in 117 Division Three (N) games for Southport.

GRIFFITHS, PHILIP HENRY
Outside-right: 8 apps, 3 goals
Born: Tylorstown, Glamorgan, Wales, 25 October 1905 – *Died*: Bucknall, Stoke-on-Trent, 14 May 1978
Career: Tylorstown, Watts Town, Stoke City (trialist, during the second half of the 1925–26 season), Port Vale (trialist, July 1926; signed August 1926), EVERTON (£6,000, May 1931), West Bromwich Albion (May 1933), Cardiff City (June 1934), Folkestone (August 1935–39); Port Vale (August 1939; retired May 1940; became 'A' team coach; pressed into service in 1944–45, continued as a player until May 1946)
A prolific marksman from the centre-forward position for Watts Town (79 goals scored in 1925–26), Phil Griffiths was switched to the right-wing by Port Vale, who snatched him from under the noses of their neighbours, Stoke. He did well with the Valiants (32 goals in 85 League games), helping them win the Third Division (N) title in 1930. During his two seasons with Everton he occupied both wing positions and the centre-forward berth, making his Blues' debut against Birmingham in August 1931. He failed to break into the first XI at WBA and had 13 outings for Cardiff. Griffiths, capped as a junior in 1929, gained one senior cap against Scotland in 1932.

GRIFFITHS, THOMAS PERCIVAL
Centre-half: 79 apps, 9 goals
Born: Moss, near Wrexham, 21 February 1906 – *Died*: Moss, 25 December 1981
Career: Ffrith Valley, Wrexham District Schools, Wrexham Boys' Club, Wrexham (amateur, December 1922; professional, March 1924), EVERTON (£2,000, December 1926), Bolton Wanderers (December 1931), Middlesbrough (£6,500, March 1933), Aston Villa (£5,000, November 1935), Wrexham (player–coach, August 1938; retired February 1939 with rheumatism; had two spells as coach in the 1950s; later director of club); also Wales trainer; then licensee of the Turf and Hand Hotels and Red Lion pub in Marchwiel; he played the cello in several major concerts and was a cabinet-maker by trade
Tom Griffiths began as a centre-forward but much to his indignation was switched to centre-half when chosen to represent his local schools. He did well but reverted back to the attack within a week! Then the former Wales full-back Tom Matthias saw Griffiths net eight goals in a match and immediately introduced him to Wrexham. Playing first as an amateur, he turned professional

at the age of 18 and after a few outings as right-half, he settled down at pivot. He won both inter-League and junior international caps for Wales and joined Everton after scoring twice in 36 League games for Wrexham. His first game for the Blues was a nightmare, a 6–2 defeat at Leicester in February 1927. But the following Saturday he lined up for Wales in his first international, his opponent none other than club colleague Dixie Dean of England! A stylish defender, Griffiths was a fine header of the ball and wasted very little time in clearing his lines. He took over from Fred Keenor, the Cardiff skipper, in the Welsh side and went on to lead his country, gaining 21 caps, his last in 1937 against Northern Ireland. He made 53 appearances for Bolton and 67 for Villa before returning to Wrexham. Griffiths was at centre-half when Arsenal's Ted Drake fired seven goals past Villa in a League game in 1935.

GRUNDY, HARRY

Outside-left: 2 apps
Born: Oswestry, *circa* 1881 – Deceased
Career: Chirk, Neston, EVERTON (July 1905), Reading (March 1906), Lincoln City (April 1908–May 1910)

Reserve to Harold Hardman during his short spell at Goodison Park, Harry Grundy's debut for Everton came at Middlesbrough in December 1905. He helped Lincoln win the Midland League title in 1909, scoring six goals in 36 games. Later played at centre-half.

HAMILTON, BRYAN

Midfield: 47+7 apps, 5 goals
Born: Belfast, 21 December 1946
Career: Linfield, Ipswich Town (£15,000, August 1971), EVERTON (£40,000, November 1975), Millwall (£12,000, July 1977), Swindon Town (£20,000, November 1978), Tranmere Rovers (player–manager, October 1980–February 1985; retired as a player, November 1983), Wigan Athletic (manager, 1985–June 1986), Leicester City (manager, June 1986; sacked December 1987), Wigan Athletic (chief executive, March 1988; manager, March 1989–March 1993); Norwich City (manager, April 2000–January 2001); now a radio/TV summariser

Bryan Hamilton, a terrier-like midfielder, began his career on £6 per week with Linfield. He went on to gain two Under-21 and 50 full caps for Northern Ireland, appearing in his first full international in 1968, and later skippered his country. He played in most of Everton's games during the second half of 1975–76 but was not a regular in the side after that, although he did collect a League Cup runner's-up medal in 1977. He made his debut for Everton against Leeds in November 1975 and went on to amass over 400 appearances at club level during his career. As a manager his only success was to guide Wigan to victory in the FRT final of 1985. He also reached the northern final of the Autoglass Trophy in 1993, beaten by Stockport, having steered Tranmere through several crisis periods. He suffered relegation with Leicester. He also kept Wigan in the Third Division four years running – a minor miracle.

HAMILTON, HERBERT HAROLD
Right-back: 1 app.
Born: Wallasey, 27 March 1906 – *Died*: 1951
Career: New Brighton Baptists, Harrowby FC, Poulton Rovers, New Brighton (amateur, December 1923), EVERTON (October 1924), Preston North End (May 1927), Chesterfield (£250, June 1931), Tranmere Rovers (May 1937), Accrington Stanley (November 1938), Bangor City (briefly, 1939), Marine (season 1939–40)
'Duke' Hamilton joined Everton as an 18 year old, having made only one appearance for New Brighton. Initially reserve to Jock McDonald and then Warney Cresswell, his only League outing for the Blues was against Spurs in January 1927. He appeared in 275 League games after leaving Everton, 192 with Chesterfield, whom he helped win the Third Division (N) title in 1936. He won the same division with Tranmere in 1938.

HAMMOND, HENRY
Left-back: 1 app.
Born: Liverpool, *circa* 1865 – Deceased
Career: EVERTON (season 1889–90)
Harry Hammond's only League outing for Everton came in the 5–1 win over WBA in March 1890, when he took over from Danny Doyle, who was switched to centre-forward.

HAMPSON, ALAN
Inside-forward: 1 app.
Born: Prescot, 31 December 1927
Career: EVERTON (juniors, 1945; professional, August 1949), Halifax Town (November 1952), Bradford City (July 1956), Prescot Cables (July 1957)
Enforced National Service took out two of Alan Hampson's seven years at Goodison, where, in the main, he was a reserve forward. His only League appearance for Everton was at inside-left in the 1–1 home draw with Bolton in October 1950. He scored 32 goals in 121 League games for Halifax.

HANNAH, ANDREW BOYD
Right-back: 44 apps
Born: Renton, Dunbartonshire, 17 September 1864 – *Died*: Scotland, June 1940
Career: Renton (August 1883), West Bromwich Albion (briefly, September–October 1888), Renton (November 1888), EVERTON (August 1889), Renton (July 1891), Liverpool (July 1892), Rob Roy FC (October 1895; retired May 1897)
A noted Victorian footballer, Andrew Hannah was the first player to captain both Everton and Liverpool. He also appeared in three Scottish Cup finals with Renton, gaining winner's medals in 1885 and 1888, and collecting a full international cap against Wales, also in 1888. Formidable, physically strong with a biting tackle, like most full-backs of his time, he could 'punt' the ball long distances upfield, his clearances usually being made with thought and accuracy.

Partnering Dan Doyle in the Everton side, they were described as the finest full-backs in the country, both winning League championship medals in 1891, with Hannah later adding a Second Division championship medal to his collection with Liverpool (1893). A well-respected and highly efficient athlete, Hannah won prizes at the Highland Games.

HANNAH, JOHN

Left-back: 1 app.
Born: Scotland, *circa* 1880 – Deceased
Career: Celtic, EVERTON (1905)
Reserve at both Celtic and Everton, Jock Hannah's only League appearance for the Blues was against Bury on Boxing Day 1905, when he deputised for Jack Crelley in a 2–1 defeat.

HARBURN, PETER ARTHUR PATRICK

Centre-forward: 4 apps, 1 goal
Born: Shoreditch, 18 June 1931
Career: Portsmouth (amateur), Brighton and Hove Albion (professional, February 1956), EVERTON (August 1958), Scunthorpe United (January 1959), Workington (October 1959–May 1961)
Scorer of 61 goals in 126 League games for Brighton, Peter Harburn was recruited as a possible partner to either Dave Hickson or Eddie Thomas, or both. With Hickson sidelined, he played in the opening four games (all lost) of 1958–59, making his debut at Leicester and scoring against PNE. When Hickson returned, Harburn reverted to the reserves, where he remained until his transfer. He netted eight goals in 20 League games for Scunthorpe and 23 in 67 outings for Workington.

HARDMAN, HAROLD PAYNE

Outside-left: 156 apps, 29 goals
Born: Kirkmanshulme, Manchester, 4 April 1882 – *Died*: Sale, Cheshire, 9 June 1965
Career: South Shore High School (Blackpool), South Shore Choristers FC, Blackpool (amateur, July 1900), EVERTON (amateur, May 1903), Manchester United (amateur, August 1908), Bradford City (amateur, January 1909), Stoke (amateur, February 1910), Manchester United (amateur, September 1913; retired as a player 1915); Manchester United (director, 1912, while still with Stoke; continued to serve on the board at Old Trafford until 1951; then chairman until 1965); served on the committees of the FA, the Lancashire County FA and the Central League
Dashing outside-left Harold Hardman – an amateur throughout his career – was an Olympic Games gold medal winner in 1908 when England beat Denmark 2–0 in the final. He gained four full caps plus 20 at amateur level. He helped Everton win the FA Cup in 1906 and finish runners-up a year later, and he scored on his debut against Blackburn in September 1903. Associated with Manchester United for over 50 years, Hardman was a remarkable man. A

qualified solicitor, he was able to withstand the rigours of professional football without the benefit of full-time training. In later years, still working as a solicitor and doing his duty as chairman of Manchester United, this tiny, bird-like figure was a regular at the 'other' Old Trafford, watching cricket.

HARDY, HENRY J.

Goalkeeper: 45 apps
Born: Stockport, 14 January 1895 – Deceased
Career: Alderley Edge (August 1912), Stockport County (August 1920), EVERTON (October 1925), Bury (July 1928–April 1930)

Harry Hardy made 207 League appearances for Stockport before moving to Goodison as a replacement for Alf Harland – this after the Blues had utilised three different goalkeepers during the first seven weeks of 1925–26. Very capable, with safe hands, he made his debut for Everton in a 4–1 defeat at Arsenal soon after joining and left soon after Ted Taylor had arrived from Huddersfield. He made almost 300 appearances during his career.

HARGREAVES, FRANK

Inside-forward: 9 apps, 2 goals
Born: Ashton-under-Lyne, Lancashire, 17 November 1902 – *Died*: Ashton-under-Lyne, September 1987
Career: Ashton Boys, Droylsden United, Manchester North End, Oldham Athletic (October 1923), EVERTON (£750, May 1924), Oldham Athletic (£250, May 1925), Rochdale (August 1930), Bournemouth and Boscombe Athletic (July 1931), Watford (October 1931), Oldham Athletic (March 1932; second-team trainer, August 1933, then first-team trainer, 1936–48); later a licensee in Ashton

Slight of build and essentially an 'artistic' type of player, Frank Hargreaves possessed fine dribbling skills and was an exponent of the defence-splitting pass, often drilling the ball up to 40 yards along the ground to a colleague. Never at his best on heavy pitches, his goalscoring achievements let him down, although he did net 25 times in 104 second XI games for Oldham. Scorer of 22 goals in 126 League appearances, his Everton debut was at Birmingham in August 1924.

HARLAND, ALFRED

Goalkeeper: 70 apps
Born: Crookstown, Northern Ireland, *circa* 1894 – Deceased
Career: Linfield, EVERTON (October 1922), Runcorn (May 1926)

A Northern Ireland international (two caps gained), Alf Harland was signed following an injury to Tom Fern. He did well and kept his place in the side for almost four months before Fern returned. Harland then served in the reserves until being recalled to the senior ranks in January 1924. The following season he made 29 appearances but then lost his place, first to Jack Kendall and then to Harry Hardy.

HARPER, ALAN
Defender/Midfield: 198+43 apps, 5 goals
Born: Liverpool, 1 November 1960
Career: Liverpool (apprentice, April 1976; professional, April 1978), EVERTON (£100,000, June 1983), Sheffield Wednesday (£275,000, July 1988), Manchester City (£150,000, December 1989), EVERTON (£200,000, August 1991), Luton Town (free, September 1993), Burnley (free, August 1994), Cardiff City (free, November 1995–February 1996)

An England youth international (capped with Liverpool), Alan Harper was twice a League championship winner with Everton (1985, 1987), appeared in the 1984 League Cup and in two Charity Shield games at Wembley (1986, 1987). During an excellent career, he amassed 440 League appearances, 178 with Everton. An adaptable footballer, able to play in a variety of positions, he made his debut for the Blues against Stoke City at Goodison Park in August 1983, and had his best season, in terms of appearances, in 1986–87, when he made 44.

HARPER, JOSEPH MONTGOMERY
Forward: 48+3 apps, 14 goals
Born: Greenock, Scotland, 11 January 1948
Career: Larkfield BC, Morton (August 1963), Huddersfield Town (£30,000, March 1967), Morton (£15,000, August 1968), Aberdeen (£40,000, October 1969), EVERTON (£180,000, December 1972), Hibernian (£120,000, January 1974), Aberdeen (£40,000, June 1976), Peterhead (player–coach, August 1981; player–manager, September 1981)

A direct, sturdy, irrepressible little outside-right or centre-forward, composed and quick in thought, Joe Harper scored regularly throughout his career, doing so from all angles and from long distances, mainly with his right foot. A youth international, he was capped by Scotland on four occasions at senior level (1973–76), represented the Scottish League and also played twice at Under-23 level. When he was transferred to Everton, the fee involved was a record received by a Scottish club, and when he moved to Hibs two years later it was a record paid by a Scottish club for an English-based player. Harper missed a penalty on his debut for the Blues against Spurs in December 1972, but was still a winner (3–1). He scored for Aberdeen in their 1970 Scottish Cup final win over Celtic, gained a League Cup-winner's medal with the Dons in 1977 and collected two runner's-up medals in the same competition: 1975 with Hibs and 1979 with the Dons. He also finished on the losing side in the 1978 Scottish Cup final.

HARRIS, ALBERT EDWARD
Goalkeeper: 5 apps
Born: Bootle, 21 November 1931
Career: Maghull, EVERTON (January 1955), Tranmere Rovers (May 1957), Southport (July 1960–May 1965)

Reserve to Jimmy O'Neill and then Albert Dunlop, Albert Harris made his debut for Everton at Aston Villa in March 1956 (lost 2–0). He appeared in 159 League games for Southport and kept goal when they crashed 11–0 at Oldham on Boxing Day 1962.

HARRIS, BRIAN
Left-half: 360 apps, 29 goals
Born: Bebington, 16 March 1935
Career: Port Sunlight FC, EVERTON (£10, professional, January 1954), Cardiff City (£10,000, October 1966), Newport County (player–coach, July 1971; assistant manager, 1972; player–manager, January 1974–March 1975), Chepstow (1975–76, while also working as a licensee); Cardiff City (assistant manager, December 1978–May 1980); Ipswich Town (coach, 1980–81); then licensee before running his own promotions business in Chepstow

Making his League debut for the Blues as a right-winger at Burnley in August 1955 (the same time as Jimmy Harris, q.v.), Brian Harris went on to occupy a variety of positions before settling down at left-half, from where he produced some excellent displays. He eventually lost his place to Tony Kay during Everton's championship-winning season of 1962–63, although he did qualify for a medal, having been a regular for six years. He started in the club's 1966 FA Cup final win over Sheffield Wednesday and spent 13 years at Goodison Park. He made 544 League appearances during his career and played in Europe with both Everton and Cardiff. He resigned as manager of Newport after a disagreement over financial restraints.

HARRIS, JAMES
Forward: 207 apps, 72 goals
Born: Birkenhead, 18 August 1933
Career: Birkenhead Schools, EVERTON (amateur, 1949; professional, September 1951), Birmingham City (£20,000, December 1960), Oldham Athletic (July 1964), Tranmere Rovers (August 1966), Rhyl Athletic (October 1966; retired May 1967); steward of the Prenton Golf Club (Birkenhead)

Jimmy Harris – a sharp, fleet-footed forward whose greatest asset was his appetite for hard work – was a member of the district's successful schoolboy team. He made his Everton debut against Burnley in August 1955 when he took over the centre-forward berth from Dave Hickson. Honoured by England at Under-23 level and later by the Football League, Harris switched to the right-wing in 1957 and a year later (October 1958) scored a hat-trick to no avail in a 10–4 League defeat at Spurs. Harris continued to score regularly during his three and a half years at St Andrew's, amassing 53 goals in 115 appearances, helping the Blues reach the 1961 Inter-Cities Fairs Cup final (against AS Roma) and win the League Cup two years later.

HARRIS, JOSEPH ANTHONY
Outside-right: 14 apps, 4 goals
Born: Liverpool, 20 December 1926
Career: EVERTON (junior, 1947; professional, July 1950), Bangor City (May 1953)
Although he served Everton for six years, winger Joe Harris was mainly a reserve to Wally Fielding and Tony McNamara. He appeared in 13 successive games in 1952, after his debut against Sheffield Wednesday in March 1951.

HARRIS, VALENTINE
Versatile: 214 apps, 2 goals
Born: Dublin Bay, *circa* 1885 – Deceased
Career: Dublin Shelbourne, West Bromwich Albion (amateur, May 1904), Dublin Shelbourne (January 1908), EVERTON (March 1908), Dublin Shelbourne (August 1914); did not play after the First World War
Val Harris was a most consistent and highly effective player. Already an established international by the time he moved to Everton, having collected the first of 20 caps as a centre-forward, it was in the right-half position where he excelled best and was regarded as one of the League's finest players in 1910. Nevertheless, he still turned out in six different berths for the Blues, making his League debut at Woolwich Arsenal in April 1908.

HARRISON, GEORGE
Outside-left: 190 apps, 17 goals
Born: Church Gresley, 18 July 1892 – *Died*: Derby, 12 March 1939
Career: Gresley Rovers, Leicester Fosse (February 1911), EVERTON (with Bob Thompson, April 1913), Preston North End (December 1923), Blackpool (November 1931); later a licensee in Preston, then in Church Gresley until his death
Well-built and strong-limbed, George Harrison's stamina was almost as remarkable as his touchline skill. He scored nine goals in 60 first-team appearances for Leicester before joining Everton, jointly with Bob Thompson. A fine crosser of the ball, he helped the Blues win the League title in 1915 and gained two full England caps, lining up against Belgium and Ireland in 1921. He made his debut for Everton against Liverpool in September 1913.

HART, HUNTER
Half-back: 301 apps, 5 goals
Born: Glasgow, 11 March 1895 – Deceased
Career: Airdrieonians (professional, August 1919), EVERTON (£4,000, January 1922; retired as a player, February 1930, later club coach)
Hunter Hart, who lost an eye in a childhood accident, was a stylish player, able to occupy all three half-back positions. He made his Everton debut at Bolton 24 hours after joining from Airdrie, was a member of the League championship-winning side in 1927–28, missing only one game, and for a short time skippered

the side. Totally committed, strong in the tackle, he played in a struggling team when he first joined the Blues, who were again in trouble when he retired.

HARTFORD, RICHARD ASA

Inside-forward: 98 apps, 7 goals
Born: Clydebank, Scotland, 24 October 1950
Career: Fairfley Primary and Clydebank High Schools, Dunbartonshire Boys, Drumchapel Amateurs, West Bromwich Albion (apprentice, April 1966; professional, October 1967), Leeds United (for 24 hours, November 1971), West Bromwich Albion (November 1971), Manchester City (£225,000, August 1974), Nottingham Forest (July 1979), EVERTON (record fee of £500,000, August 1979), Manchester City (October 1981), Fort Lauderdale Sun/NASL, May 1984), Wolverhampton Wanderers (trial, August 1984), Norwich City (September 1984), Norway (coach, May 1985), Bolton Wanderers (July 1985), Stockport County (player–manager, June 1987), Oldham Athletic (March 1989), Shrewsbury Town (coach, July 1989; manager, July 1990; sacked January 1991), Boston United (March 1991), Blackburn Rovers (coach), Stoke City (coach/assistant manager, 1993–94), Manchester City (coach, assistant manager, later reserve-team manager; also coach at School of Excellence, 1997–2001)

Asa Hartford made his League debut for WBA as a 17 year old. He developed quickly and became a midfield dynamo – a player who darted here, there and everywhere, seeking to create chances for his colleagues. Full of energy, he was always buzzing around in centre-field, and during his career amassed over 800 appearances. In 1971 he was rejected by Leeds on medical advice when doctors diagnosed a 'hole in the heart'. Three years later the same Asa Hartford was sold to Manchester City for almost a quarter of a million pounds. After a spell with Nottingham Forest, Everton paid £500,000 for him and he spent two useful years at Goodison Park, making his debut against Aston Villa in September 1979. A Scottish international at youth, Under-21, Under-23 and senior levels (gaining 50 caps in the latter category), Hartford was a loser with WBA in the 1970 League Cup final before collecting winner's medals in the same competition with Manchester City (1976) and Norwich (1985), scoring with a deflected shot in the latter. In 1986 he was a loser in the FRT final for Bolton against Bristol City. (He was christened Asa after the celebrated American singing star Al (Asa) Jolson.)

HARTILL, WILLIAM JOHN

Centre-forward: 5 apps, 1 goal
Born: Wolverhampton, 18 July 1905 – *Died*: Walsall, 12 August 1980
Career: Wolverhampton Schools, Army (Royal Horse Artillery), Wolverhampton Wanderers (August 1928), EVERTON (July 1935), Liverpool (January 1936), Bristol Rovers (March 1936; retired May 1938); later a Wolverhampton licensee
Nicknamed 'Artillery Billy', Hartill fired home 170 goals in 234 appearances for Wolves, helping them win the Second Division championship in 1932. Prior to

that, he had netted 70 times in two seasons for the RHA (his Army unit) and the British Army Select XI, making his League debut in 1928. A scorer in his first game for Everton against Portsmouth in September 1935, he never settled down at Goodison or at Anfield and retired with over 200 goals to his name in more than 360 senior appearances. He represented the Football League (Midland XI) in 1935.

HARTLEY, ABRAHAM

Forward: 61 apps, 28 goals

Born: Dumbarton, 8 February 1872 – *Died*: Southampton dockyard, 9 October 1909

Career: Artizan Thistle (Dumbarton), Dumbarton, EVERTON (December 1892), Liverpool (December 1897), Southampton (May 1898), Woolwich Arsenal (July 1899), Burnley (December 1899; retired May 1900); later employed by the South West Railway. He collapsed and died outside the pay office on the dockside at Southampton

Abraham Hartley, the son of a tailor and one of three brothers who all assisted Dumbarton, was generally regarded as a 'useful' centre-forward, although he could occupy both inside-forward positions and right-back. A scorer on his League debut for Everton in a 4–2 win at Wolves in March 1893, he was never a regular in the side and had his best spell in the first team during his last season, having gained an FA Cup runner's-up medal in 1897. He helped Southampton win the Southern League title in his first season at The Dell. Hartley had the habit of placing a rolled-up cigarette behind one ear prior to kick-off and then smoking it at half-time – if he hadn't lost it.

HARVEY, JAMES COLIN

Inside-forward/wing-half: 382+5 apps, 24 goals

Born: Liverpool, 16 November 1944

Career: EVERTON (apprentice, April 1960; professional, October 1962), Sheffield Wednesday (£70,000, September 1974; retired through injury, March 1976); EVERTON (youth-team coach, July 1976; reserve-team coach, then first-team coach, August 1983; manager, June 1987, sacked October 1990; returned to club as assistant to manager Howard Kendall, November 1990–December 1993); then coach; retired from football May 2003 after serving the Blues for over 40 years

Colin Harvey made his debut for Everton in the European Cup against Inter Milan in September 1963 and, with Brian Labone, jointly holds the record for most 'European' appearances for the Blues (19). After establishing himself in the first team as an inside-forward, he was an FA Cup winner in 1966, a runner-up in the same competition two years later and the recipient of a League championship medal in 1970, when he appeared in 35 games, playing superbly in midfield with Alan Ball and Howard Kendall.

Nicknamed the 'White Pele', Harvey possessed fine ball control, his accurate, defence-splitting passes being the main feature of his game. He gave Everton excellent service for 14 years (as a player), during which time he was capped once by England against Malta in February 1971, and also played in five Under-23 internationals. After announcing his retirement, Harvey returned to Goodison and lengthened his association with Everton to over 40 years.

HAUGHEY, WILLIAM
Inside-forward: 4 apps, 1 goal
Born: Glasgow, 20 December 1932
Career: Larkhall Thistle, EVERTON (June 1956), Falkirk (June 1958)
During his time at Goodison, reserve Bill Haughey played in just four First Division games, making a scoring debut against Manchester City at Maine Road in April 1957 (won 4–2).

HEARD, TIMOTHY PATRICK
Defender: 10+1 apps
Born: Hull, 17 March 1960
Career: Hull and Humberside District Schools, EVERTON (apprentice, June 1976; professional, March 1978), Aston Villa (£150,000 plus John Gidman, October 1979), Sheffield Wednesday (£60,000, January 1983), Newcastle United (September 1984), Middlesbrough (August 1985), Hull City (March 1986), Rotherham United (July 1988), Cardiff City (August 1989), Hull City (n/c, August–October 1992)
England youth international Pat Heard failed to make the breakthrough at Goodison Park. He made his League debut against Wolves (as a substitute) in February 1979 and after leaving Everton became a useful 'stand-in' during Aston Villa's League Championship-winning season of 1980–81. A defender with the 'right attitude', he scored twice in 26 outings for Villa, having earlier collected an FA Youth Cup loser's medal with Everton (1977). During his career Heard made over 300 senior appearances (293 in the League).

HEATH, ADRIAN PAUL
Forward: 278+29 apps, 94 goals
Born: Stoke-on-Trent, 17 January 1961
Career: Stoke City (apprentice, June 1977; professional, January 1979), EVERTON (£700,000, January 1982), Español/Spain (August 1988 to July 1989), Aston Villa (£360,000, August 1989), Manchester City (February 1990), Stoke City (March 1992), Burnley (August 1992), Sheffield United (December 1995), Burnley (n/c, March 1996; then manager, late March 1996–97); Sheffield United (assistant manager/coach), Sunderland (coach/scout, 2000–03); Coventry City (assistant manager, 2004–05)
Capped eight times by England at Under-21 level and once by the 'B' team, Adrian Heath was a sharp-shooting, nippy, all-action striker with good close control, who scored 120 goals in 525 League games in England alone. Known as 'Inchy' due to his size, he was a record signing by Everton and certainly played his best football at Goodison. He made his debut for the Blues against Southampton in January 1982 and secured his first goal at Brighton the

following month. He won two League championship medals (1985, 1987), an FA Cup-winner's medal (1984), a European Cup-Winners' Cup medal (1985) and starred in four Charity Shield triumphs, plus one shared with Liverpool when he scored (1986). In December 1984 he was on the fringe of the England team, but an injury, suffered in a challenge with Sheffield Wednesday's Brian Marwood, ended his chances. He never settled down at Villa, no goals in 12 outings, and he also failed as manager at Turf Moor.

HEDLEY, JOHN ROBERT
Left-back: 61 apps
Born: Willington Quay, 11 December 1923 – *Died*: 1985
Career: North Shields, EVERTON (April 1945), Sunderland (August 1950), Gateshead (July 1959–May 1960)
Jack Hedley was a solid, tough-tackling defender who had his best season in 1948–49, when he appeared in 25 first-class matches, mainly as partner to George Saunders. He made his debut for the Blues against Tranmere in May 1945, but had to wait over two years before making his League bow against Aston Villa in September 1947. Hedley later appeared in 269 League games for Sunderland. In May 1950, along with his Everton team-mate Bill Higgins, Hedley flew to Colombia, hoping to sign for the Marios club. He declined the offer.

HENDERSON, WILLIAM
Right-back: 17 apps
Born: Broxburn, summer 1878 – Deceased
Career: Broxburn Athletic, EVERTON (November 1896), Reading (January 1897), Southampton (June 1901), EVERTON (May 1902), Reading (August 1904), Clapton Orient (August 1906), New Brompton (1908–09)
A capable defender who tackled strongly, Bill Henderson spent half of his career playing in the Southern League. When selected, he did reasonably well at Everton second-time round after failing to make an appearance in his first spell. His debut for the Blues was against Newcastle in September 1902.

HESLOP, GEORGE WILSON
Centre-half: 11 apps
Born: Wallsend, 1 July 1940
Career: Dudley Welfare, Newcastle United (February 1959), EVERTON (part-exchange for Jimmy Fell, March 1962), Manchester City (£25,000, September 1965), Cape Town/South Africa (loan, season 1971–72), Bury (August 1972–May 1973), Northwich Victoria (manager, November 1977), Bury (coach, June 1978–June 1980); later licensee of the Hyde Road Hotel, the original home of the Ardwick/Manchester City FC
A tall, well-built blond defender, George Heslop made his League debut for Newcastle in an 8–2 win over Everton in November 1959. His first appearance for the Blues followed in April 1963 against Birmingham City. Signed as cover for Brian Labone, he never really got a look-in at Goodison Park and after

joining Manchester City collected winner's medals for the Second Division (1966), the First Division (1968) and both the League Cup and European Cup-Winners' Cup (1970).

HIBBERT, ANTHONY JAMES
Midfield: 63+8 apps
Born: Liverpool, 20 February 1981
Career: EVERTON (apprentice, April 1997; professional, July 1998)
A regular at the heart of midfield in Everton's FA Youth Cup-winning side of 1998 and their championship-winning reserve side in 2001, Tony Hibbert developed into a tigerish and sharp-tackling right-back, who made his Premiership debut at West Ham in March 2001. Injury kept him out of the England Under-21 team but he did have an excellent 2002–03 season.

HICKSON, DAVID
Centre-forward: 243 apps, 111 goals
Born: Ellesmere Port, Cheshire, 30 October 1929
Career: Ellesmere Port (1944), EVERTON (amateur, 1947; professional, May 1949), Aston Villa (£17,500, September 1955), Huddersfield Town (£16,000, November 1955), EVERTON (£6,500, July 1957), Liverpool (£10,500, November 1959), Cambridge City (July 1961), Bury (£1,000 paid to Liverpool, January 1962), Tranmere Rovers (July 1962, two-month trial, signed permanently, September 1962), Ballymena (player–manager, July 1964), Ellesmere Port (February 1965; player–manager, March 1965), Northwich Victoria (1966), Winsford United (September 1967), Fleetwood Town, Ellesmere Port Town (manager, 1973–74); later employed as a Liverpool bookmaker; now working as Everton's stadium guide and match-day host
Dave Hickson was a colourful, dashing centre-forward, brilliant in the air. Often in the headlines (more so due to brushes with authority), he was a quiet, unassuming man off the field, even shy, but a lion on it! He scored 71 goals for Everton before moving to Villa Park as a replacement for Dave Walsh, but he failed to settle down in the Midlands and was transferred to Huddersfield. Hickson then returned to Goodison, where he took his goal-tally past the century mark. He then netted 37 times in 60 outings for Liverpool and on quitting League soccer in 1964, he had a record of 182 goals in 404 League games, with 200 scored in all competitions. He made his debut for Everton (first time round) at Leeds in September 1951 and his 'second' debut followed six years later against Wolves in August 1957. Hickson netted 16 goals in 18 FA Cup games for Everton (third behind Dixie Dean's 32 and Graeme Sharp's 20).

HIGGINS, MARCUS
Left-half: 6 apps
Born: Liverpool, *circa* 1862 – Deceased
Career: EVERTON (July 1880–May 1889); later a publican who also posted telegram reports of other League games

Long-serving half-back, 'Mike' Higgins appeared in 178 matches and scored 36 goals while occupying eight different positions during his time with Everton. He made his debut in October 1880 against Darwen and was a Liverpool Cup winner in 1884, 1886 and 1887. He also played in Everton's first-ever FA Cup-tie against Bolton in October 1987 and his only League game was against Aston Villa in September 1888. Totally reliable, very consistent, he loved his football.

HIGGINS, MARK NICHOLAS
Defender: 179+4 apps, 6 goals
Born: Buxton, 29 September 1958
Career: North West Derbyshire Schools, EVERTON (apprentice 1975; professional, August 1976; retired, injured, serious pelvic disorder, May 1984), Manchester United (£60,000, insurance compensation, December 1985); Bury (loan, January 1987, signed for £10,000 February 1987), Stoke City (£150,000, September 1988), Burnley (trial 1990; retired 1991 with back injury)

Mark Higgins announced his retirement owing to a groin injury in 1984, but defied doctor's orders and returned to the game and played on until 1991, amassing 260 League appearances. After turning down several clubs as a teenager, and playing in the 1977 FA Youth Cup final, he established himself in the Everton side in 1977–78, taking over from Ken McNaught. He did superbly well at the heart of defence until suffering a pelvic injury in a Milk Cup-tie with West Ham in December 1983. He had made his League debut at left-back for the Blues against Manchester City, in October 1976. His father, John Higgins, made over 200 appearances for Bolton and gained an FA Cup-winner's medal in 1958.

HIGGINS, WILLIAM CHARLES
Forward: 49 apps, 9 goals
Born: Birkenhead, 28 February 1924 – *Died*: 1981
Career: Tranmere Rovers (amateur), EVERTON (March 1946), Marios Bogota/Colombia (May 1950)

After four useful seasons at Goodison Park, Bill Higgins – along with other League players, including Everton colleague Jack Hedley (q.v.), England's Neil Franklin (Stoke) and Charlie Mitten (Manchester United) – flew to Colombia to play football outside FIFA jurisdiction. Higgins signed for the Marios club with coaching a side-line, but never played in England again. He made his debut for the Blues at Sheffield Wednesday soon after signing, replacing Harry Catterick in a 0–0 draw.

HIGHAM, NORMAN
Inside-forward: 14 apps, 6 goals
Born: Chorley, 14 February 1912 – Deceased
Career: Chorley, EVERTON (amateur, May 1929; professional, February 1931), Middlesbrough (March 1936), Southampton (May 1939); did not play after the Second World War

Well-built Norman Higham spent most of his time in Everton's reserves. He made his League debut against Manchester City in February 1934 and had a decent run in the side during the second half of that season before Alex Stevenson took over at inside-left. He scored ten goals in 50 games for Middlesbrough.

HILL, MATTHEW JAMES

Inside-forward: 7 apps, 1 goal
Born: Carrickfergus, Northern Ireland, 31 October 1935
Career: Carrickfergus YMCA, Carrick Rangers, Linfield (1953), Newcastle
  United (June 1957, in part-exchange deal involving Jackie Milburn),
  Norwich City (£3,000, July 1958), EVERTON (£25,000, August 1963), Port
  Vale (£5,000, October 1965), Derry City (player–manager, February 1968),
  Linfield (manager, August 1971–May 1972); out of the game; Carrick Rovers
  (manager, November 1988–May 1991); later ran a sports shop in
  Carrickfergus

A skilful player, Jimmy 'Tiger' Hill was honoured by Northern Ireland at amateur, 'B' and senior levels, gaining a total of seven full caps (1959–63). After failing at Newcastle, he was a key member of the Norwich team that reached the 1959 FA Cup semi-final and won the League Cup in 1962. He netted 66 goals in almost 200 appearances for the Canaries before transferring to Everton, for whom he made his debut at Bolton in September 1963. Unfortunately, injuries plagued him at Goodison Park.

HILL, PERCY

Full-back: 16 apps
Born: Hampshire, *circa* 1884 – Deceased
Career: Southampton (1904), EVERTON (September 1905), Manchester City
  (November 1906), Airdrieonians (November 1909), Swindon Town
  (1910–11)

Percy Hill, a strongly built defender, was reserve at Southampton before making his League debut for Everton in a 5–2 home win over Wolves in December 1905. Deputising for Robert Balmer after that, he later appeared in 48 matches for Manchester City.

HILLMAN, JOHN

Goalkeeper: 38 apps
Born: Tavistock, 30 October 1870 – *Died*: 1955
Career: Tavistock intermediate football, Burnley (October 1891), EVERTON
  (February 1895), Dundee (July 1896), Burnley (March 1898), Manchester
  City (January 1902), Millwall Athletic (January 1907; retired April 1908
  with elbow injury); returned as Burnley trainer after the First World War;
  remained in town and ran a sweet shop for a number of years

An England international, capped against Ireland in February 1899 (a 13–2 win), Jack Hillman, 6 ft tall, 16 st. in weight, was second only to the enormous Billy 'fatty' Foulke of Sheffield United. Naturally gifted, he mastered every phase of the goalkeeping art. An impeccable performer, he amassed 326 League appearances during his career, helping Manchester City win the Second Division title in 1903 and the FA Cup a year later. Prior to that, he had done well with Everton, who secured him following injury to Tom Cain and gambles with Bill Sutton and Dick Williams. He missed only one game in 1895–96 before moving to Dundee.

HILLS, JOHN DAVID
Defender/Midfield: 1+2 apps
Born: Blackpool, 21 April 1978
Career: Blackpool (apprentice, May 1994; professional, October 1995), EVERTON (£90,000, November 1995), Swansea City (loan, January–March 1997; loan August–September 1997), Blackpool (£75,000, January 1998), Gillingham (July 2003)
John Hills joined Everton after just three games for Blackpool. After his Premiership debut as a substitute against Wimbledon in December 1996, he failed to oust Earl Barrett from the right-back position and following loan spells at The Vetch Field, he returned to Bloomfield Road. He made almost 200 more appearances for the Seasiders, helping them win the LDV Trophy in 2002.

HINCHCLIFFE, ANDREW GEORGE
Defender: 211+5 apps, 11 goals
Born: Manchester, 5 February 1969
Career: Manchester City (apprentice, April 1985; professional, February 1986), EVERTON (£800,000, plus Neil Pointon, July 1990), Sheffield Wednesday (£2.85m, January 1998; retired, injured, March 2002; moved into coaching)
After making more than 450 appearances for his three League clubs and winning seven full England caps, plus others at Under-21 and youth-team levels, Andy Hinchcliffe's career was ended by an Achilles injury in 2002. He spent five years at Maine Road before joining the Blues, for whom he made his debut against Leeds in August 1990, taking over at left-back from Neil Pointon, who moved to City. He played in half of Everton's games in his first season at Goodison Park and 23 in the next, injury interrupting his progress. After that he became an established member of defence while also playing occasionally on the left side of midfield.

HODGE, MARTIN JOHN
Goalkeeper: 31 apps
Born: Southport, 4 February 1959
Career: Plymouth Argyle (apprentice, September 1975; professional, February 1977), EVERTON (£135,000, July 1979), Preston North End (loan, December 1981–March 1982), Oldham Athletic (loan, July–August 1982), Gillingham (loan, January 1983), Preston North End (loan, February–April 1983), Sheffield Wednesday (£50,000, August 1983), Leicester City (£200,000, August 1988), Hartlepool United (August 1991), Rochdale (July 1993), Plymouth Argyle (August 1994–May 1995)

Martin Hodge made his first real impact at Hillsborough, having failed to establish himself at Goodison Park. He made his senior debut for Everton against Leeds in September 1979, replacing George Wood, but then Jim McDonagh arrived on the scene, followed by Jim Arnold and then Neville Southall, and as a result Hodge moved on. He made 520 League appearances overall.

HODGE, WILLIAM
Goalkeeper: 10 apps
Born: Kilwinning, Scotland, *circa* 1885 – Deceased
Career: EVERTON (March 1912–December 1913)
Bill Hodge deputised for Jimmy Caldwell and then Frank Mitchell during his Everton days, leaving after Tom Fern had been signed from Lincoln.

HOLBEM, WALTER
Full-back: 18 apps
Born: Sheffield, *circa* 1885 – Deceased
Career: Heeley Friends FC, Sheffield Wednesday (September 1906), EVERTON (September 1911), St Mirren (March 1913), Preston North End (January 1914); did not play competitively after the First World War
Wally Holbem made 89 appearances for Sheffield Wednesday before moving to Everton as cover for John Maconnachie and Willie Stevenson. He made his debut at Newcastle soon after joining.

HOLD, OSCAR
Inside/centre-forward: 22 apps, 5 goals
Born: Carlton, near Barnsley, Yorkshire, 19 October 1918
Career: Denaby United, Barnsley (August 1937), Aldershot (April 1939); guest for Barnsley, Bradford City, Burnley, Chelsea and Derby County during the Second World War; Norwich City (March 1946), Notts County (October 1948), Chelmsford City (August 1949), EVERTON (February 1950), Queens Park Rangers (February 1952), Wisbech Town (February 1957; player–manager, February 1960); March Town (player–manager), Cambridge City (player–manager), Gainsborough Trinity (player–manager), Wisbech Town (player–manager), Doncaster Rovers (manager, 1963–64); Fenerbahce/Turkey (coach, 1965–66), Ankara FC/Turkey (coach, 1966–67); later coach in Nigeria
In his career, Oscar Hold scored 36 goals in 104 League games. A 1940s write-up described him as being 'a forceful type and can keep at it with rare zest'. He scored on his League debut for Notts County in a 9–0 win over Exeter and his first appearance for Everton was at centre-forward in place of Harry Catterick at Stoke in March 1950 (lost 1–0).

HOLMES, PAUL
Defender: 26+2 apps
Born: Stocksbridge, 18 February 1968
Career: Doncaster Rovers (apprentice, June 1984; professional, February 1986),

Torquay United (£8,000, August 1988), Birmingham City (£40,000, June 1992), EVERTON (£100,000, March 1993), West Bromwich Albion (£80,000, January 1996), Torquay United (free, November 1999; retired May 2003)

Paul Holmes, who turned down Liverpool as a teenager, could occupy several positions. Always assured, he lacked consistency with his crossing and, due to the presence of Andy Hinchcliffe, Alan Harper and Matt Jackson, had few opportunities at Goodison. He made his debut for the Blues in March 1993 against Ipswich, had a decent spell with WBA (115 appearances) and in 2003 reached the milestone of 500 career appearances. His father, Albert Holmes, made 470 League appearances for Chesterfield (1961–76).

HOLT, JOHN

Centre-half: 252 apps, 4 goals

Born: Church, Blackburn, 10 April 1865 – Deceased

Career: King's Own Blackburn, Blackpool St John's, Church FC, Blackpool (briefly), Bootle (1887), EVERTON (August 1888), Reading (August 1898)

Despite being a relatively small man at 5 ft 5 in, Johnny Holt was one of the best centre-halves in the country during the 1890s as well as being one of the great characters in the game. A pocket dynamo with boundless energy, he could outjump the tallest opponent but was a temperamental player, known for his petty and crafty fouls performed on the blind side of the referee. A League championship winner (1891) and twice an FA Cup runner-up with Everton (1893, 1897), he won ten England caps (1890–1900). Nicknamed the 'Little Everton Devil', he made his debut for the Blues against Accrington on 8 September 1888, the club's first League game (won 2–1).

HORNE, BARRY

Midfield: 144+7 apps, 3 goals

Born: St Asaph, Denbighshire, 18 May 1962

Career: Flint Town United, Rhyl (August 1983), Wrexham (free, June 1984), Portsmouth (£60,000, July 1987), Southampton (£700,000, March 1999), EVERTON (£675,000, July 1992), Birmingham City (£250,000, June 1996), Huddersfield Town (October 1997), Sheffield Wednesday (March 2000), Kidderminster Harriers (August 2000); also chairman of the PFA; Walsall (March 2001), Belper Town (July 2001); now media pundit

Barry Horne made full use of the opportunity when Rhyl took him on in 1983. Wrexham quickly spotted his talent and he became a star at The Racecourse Ground, earning selection to the full Welsh squad. Frustrated at Wrexham's lack of success, he was signed by Alan Ball for newly promoted Portsmouth in 1987, having scored 16 goals in 136 League games for the Welsh club. Surprisingly used as a defender at Fratton Park, it was as a hard-working, efficient and totally committed midfielder that he performed best. One of manager Joe Royle's 'Dogs of War' with Ebbrell and Parkinson, he helped Southampton stave off relegation before moving to Everton. He continued to perform well with the Blues, scoring on his debut against Sheffield Wednesday in August 1992. His most memorable goal, however, was the 30-yard lob against Wimbledon on the final day of 1993–94, when the Blues won 3–2 to stay in the Premiership. Capped 59 times by Wales, Horne was a Welsh Cup winner with Wrexham (1986) and both an FA Cup and Charity Shield winner with Everton (1995). He gained his BSc in 1983 and added a Masters degree in engineering the following year.

HOTTIGER, MARC

Full-back: 14+1 apps, 1 goal
Born: Lausanne, Switzerland, 7 November 1967
Career: FC Sion/Switzerland, Newcastle United (£520,000, August 1994), EVERTON (£700,000, March 1996), Lausanne/Switzerland (May 1997)

An attack-minded full-back, Marc Hottiger made over 50 appearances for Newcastle before being recruited by Blues' manager Joe Royle following an injury to Earl Barrett. His Everton debut was against Coventry in March 1996 and in the close season he featured in two of Switzerland's three European championship matches. However, when Barrett returned the following season, Hottiger spent a frustrating time on Merseyside, making only a handful of appearances, way below the figure required for him to receive a Department of Employment work permit. With two years still remaining on his contract, he left the club. He was capped 65 times by Switzerland.

HOUGHTON, HAROLD

Inside-forward: 1 app.
Born: Liverpool, 26 August 1906 – *Died*: Liverpool, 3 February 1986
Career: Anfield SC, EVERTON (junior, July 1921; professional, August 1923), Exeter City (£350, July 1928), Norwich City (£1,000, March 1934), Bristol Rovers (November 1935), South Liverpool (September 1937–September 1939); he did not feature after the Second World War

Harold 'Happy' Houghton was a quiet man off the field but an inspirational schemer on it. His best days were, without doubt, spent with Exeter, for whom he scored 83 goals in 223 appearances. An England schoolboy international, he joined Everton at the age of 17 and his only senior outing came when Dixie Dean was absent, allowing him to play in the 0–0 draw with Portsmouth in March 1928. Exeter paid out a record fee for his services and he repaid the money ten times over with some majestic performances. He toured Canada with the FA in 1931 and a year later turned down a £3,000 move to Spurs. In 1934 he moved to Norwich.

HOUSTON, JOHN

Outside-right/centre-forward: 28 apps, 2 goals
Born: Belfast, Northern Ireland, *circa* 1888 – Deceased
Career: Linfield, EVERTON (February 1913), Linfield (March 1915); did not play after the First World War

An Irish international, capped six times (1912–14), winning three with both Linfield and Everton, Jack Houston was already a highly rated footballer before moving to Goodison Park. He made his debut at centre-forward for the Blues against Liverpool in February 1913 and scored his first goal for the club the following October in a 4–1 League defeat at Newcastle, by which time he was playing on the right-wing. He lost his place in the Everton attack to Sam Chedgzoy and made only one appearance during 1914–15.

HOWARTH, HORACE ROBERT
Inside-forward: 8 apps, 2 goals
Born: Liverpool, *circa* 1889 – Deceased
Career: EVERTON (May 1914–May 1920)
Reserve Bob Howarth's six-year association with Everton was savaged by the conflict of the First World War. During the hostilities he made only two appearances before making seven more, all in the League during March–April 1920. His First Division debut was in the 1–1 draw at Sheffield United in March 1915 when he partnered George Harrison on the left-wing. He scored in the next two matches, the return fixture with the Blades and against Derby.

HOWARTH, ROBERT HENRY
Full-back: 68 apps
Born: Preston, 1865 – *Died*: 20 August 1938
Career: Preston North End, EVERTON (November 1891), Preston North End (May 1894); later became a solicitor, admitted in 1908; he practised in Preston
An England international, capped five times (1887–94), Bob Howarth was an immaculate right-back, cool and collected, who possessed a sure and timely tackle. He made over 50 appearances in total for Preston, was a double-winner in 1889 (having been an FA Cup loser 12 months earlier) and he also helped the Lillywhites win the League again in 1890. He played for Everton in the 1893 FA Cup final after making his debut for the Blues against Blackburn in December 1891.

HUGHES, DARREN JOHN
Left-back/Midfield: 3 apps
Born: Prescot, 6 October 1965
Career: EVERTON (apprentice, April 1982; professional, October 1983), Shrewsbury Town (June 1985), Brighton and Hove Albion (September 1986), Port Vale (loan, September 1987; signed for £5,000 later that same month; released, February 1994; reinstated November 1994); Northampton Town (January 1995), Exeter City (November 1995–May 1998)
A speedy left-back, Darren Hughes never got a chance at Goodison Park owing to the presence of John Bailey and Pat Van den Hauwe. He made his debut against Wolves in December 1983 and the following year gained an FA Youth Cup-winner's medal, scoring in the final at Stoke City. He played in 386 matches after leaving Everton, 222 for Port Vale, whom he helped win promotion from the Third Division in 1989. Hughes underwent two hernia operations in 1990–91 and then, after regaining fitness, suffered a ruptured

thigh muscle (July 1992). This twice required surgery and after failing to recover he was released. However, he took Port Vale to an industrial tribunal, claiming unfair dismissal. In August 1994 the Potteries club agreed to give him six weeks to prove his 'fitness and ability'. He quit after three months, feeling he was being strung along.

HUGHES, EDWARD

Half-back: 8 apps
Born: Rhiwabon, Clwyd, Wales, 1876 – *Died*: USA, *circa* 1940
Career: Formby (August 1894), EVERTON (July 1896), Tottenham Hotspur (July 1899), Clyde (August 1908–10); emigrated to Springfield, Massachusetts, USA

Ted Hughes made his Everton debut at left-half against Notts County in December 1898 and although a reserve, he was rated good enough to play for Wales, winning two caps, the first against Ireland in March 1899, the second against Scotland soon afterwards. A hard-working, brainy and fearless competitor, particularly skilful at heading, he was also regarded as a 'stopper' when performing at the heart of the defence. Hughes was secured by ex-Evertonian John Cameron for Spurs and went on to appear in over 300 matches for the Londoners, gaaining an FA Cup-winner's medal in 1901.

HUGHES, LESLIE MARK

Forward: 16+3 apps, 1 goal
Born: Wrexham, 1 November 1963
Career: Ysgol Rhiwabon, Rhos Aelwyd Boys (Under-16s), Wrexham Schoolboys, Manchester United (apprentice, June 1980; professional, November 1980), Barcelona/Spain (£2.5m, August 1986), Bayern Munich/Germany (loan, 1987), Manchester United (£1.5m, July 1988), Chelsea (£1.5m, July 1995), Southampton (£650,000, 1998), EVERTON (free, March 2000), Blackburn Rovers (free, October 2000); Welsh national team manager (2000–04); Blackburn Rovers (manager, September 2004)

Mark 'Sparky' Hughes scored a goal every three games for Manchester United – 162 in 473 outings. He helped the Reds win the FA Cup on three occasions (1985, 1990, 1994), the European Cup-Winners' Cup (1991), the League Cup (1992), two Premier League Championships (1993, 1994), the Super Cup (1991) and the Charity Shield twice (1993, 1994). After leaving Old Trafford, he added another FA Cup-winner's medal to his collection with Chelsea (1997), also helping the London club win the Cup-Winners' Cup and League Cup in 1998. His winning of four FA Cup medals established a new record. Capped 72 times by Wales, whom he also represented at schoolboy, youth and Under-21 levels (gaining five caps in the latter category), in his prime Hughes was one of the best 'leaders of the attack' in the game. Able to hold the ball up and then lay it off to a colleague, he had strength, skill, used his head thoughtfully and possessed a powerful right-foot shot.

Voted PFA 'Player of the Year' in 1989 and 1991, he is one of only three players – Andy Gray and Peter Osgood are the others – to score in the final of the FA Cup, League Cup and European Cup-Winners' Cup – his two goals seeing off Barcelona in the latter in 1991.

He helped Blackburn regain their Premiership status in 2001 and in February 2002 played his part in a League Cup final win over Spurs. In all major competitions for clubs and country, Hughes appeared in more than 750 games, scoring 230 goals. He made his debut for Everton in the 0–0 draw with Coventry in March 2000 – as his career slowly wound down. He has since done a good job as the Welsh team manager.

HUGHES, STEPHEN JOHN
Midfield: 30+3 apps, 2 goals
Born: Reading, 18 September 1976
Career: Arsenal (apprentice, April 1993; professional, July 1995), Fulham (loan, July 1999), EVERTON (£500,000, March 2000), Watford (free, July 2001)
Capped by England at schoolboy, youth and Under-21 levels, Stephen Hughes made 77 appearances for Arsenal, helping them win the FA Youth Cup in 1994 and both the Premiership and Charity Shield four years later. A left-footed player, he moved to Everton as part of manager Walter Smith's rebuilding schedule and made his debut on the left of midfield against Chelsea in March 2000. He played in the last 11 Premiership games of that season and 22 in the following campaign before switching to Watford, having been replaced by Mark Pembridge.

HUMPHREYS, GERALD
Forward: 12 apps, 2 goals
Born: Llandudno, Wales, 14 January 1948
Career: EVERTON (apprentice, April 1961; professional, September 1963), Crystal Palace (June 1970), Crewe Alexandra (January 1972–May 1976)
Gerry Humphreys, the stepson of John Humphreys (q.v.), was only six when his father died. He then followed in his adopted dad's footsteps, spending nine years at Goodison Park. His debut was against Leeds in April 1966. After his spell with Palace he scored 30 goals in 193 League outings for Crewe. Humphreys, honoured by Wales as a schoolboy, won five Under-23 caps as an Everton player.

HUMPHREYS, JOHN VAUGHAN
Centre-half: 61 apps
Born: Llandudno, 28 October 1920 – *Died*: Llandudno, 14 September 1954
Career: Friars School (Bangor), Loughborough College XI, University Athletic Union XI, Llandudno Town (1937); served as a bombardier in France during the Second World War; EVERTON (amateur, August 1942; professional, April 1943–May 1951)
The son of a schoolmaster, Jack Humphreys scored 12 goals in one school match as a centre-forward but as he grew in size he switched to centre-half. He attended an education course at Loughborough University and almost became a teacher, qualifying in PE, athletics and games, but chose football instead and played for Wales against Northern Ireland in 1947. A powerful defender,

Humphreys was unfortunate to be a contemporary of Tommy Jones at Goodison, managing over 100 appearances, 50 during the war. He made his League debut against Bolton in October 1946, having earlier played in two FA Cup games against PNE nine months earlier. In 1950 he turned down a move to the Marios club in Colombia along with his team-mate Jack Hedley, but Bill Higgins (q.v.) did move to Bogota. Humphreys was also a useful cricketer.

HUNT, ROGER PATRICK

Inside-forward/Midfield: 14+2 apps, 3 goals
Born: Swindon, 17 March 1943
Career: Wiltshire Boys, Swindon Town (initially on amateur forms, May 1958; professional, March 1960), Wolverhampton Wanderers (September 1965), EVERTON (£80,000, September 1967), Coventry City (£70,000, March 1968), Doncaster Rovers (loan, January–March 1973), Bristol City (December 1973–May 1974); later licensee of the Full Pitcher pub, Ledbury, and also worked as a window cleaner

After starting out with Swindon, 'Ernie' Hunt joined Wolves and was all set to make his debut at Southampton, but just before the game chose not to play because he wasn't quite up to it! Wolves lost 9–3 . . . good choice! Hunt scored 35 goals in 82 games for the Molineux club, helping them gain promotion from the Second Division before transferring to Everton, for whom he played his first game at Fulham in September 1967. He never settled down at Goodison and left after six months. With Coventry, Hunt was involved in that famous 'donkey kick' incident when Willie Carr flicked the ball up for him to score against Everton in October 1970 (this innovative manoeuvre was later outlawed by the FA). Hunt retired with 165 goals in 467 League game to his credit. He also won three England Under-23 caps.

HUREL, ELI

Inside/centre-forward: 5 apps, 1 goal
Born: Jersey, 10 April 1915
Career: St Helier, EVERTON (April 1936), Northampton Town (May 1938–September 1939); did not play after the Second World War

The first Channel Islander to sign as a League professional, Eli Hural made his debut for Everton at Bolton in September 1936 and scored his first goal a fortnight later against Huddersfield. He started off well enough but then lost his way and after a period in the reserves moved to Northampton.

HURST, JOHN W.

Defender: 388+14 apps, 34 goals
Born: Blackpool, 6 February 1947
Career: EVERTON (juniors, September 1962; professional, October 1964), Oldham Athletic (June 1976–May 1981)

An ever-present when Everton won the League championship in 1970, John Hurst was also an FA Youth Cup winner with the Blues in 1965 and during his 14 years with the club amassed over 400 appearances. The sort of player a manager dreams about, he was a dedicated club-man who gave nothing less than 100 per cent. An England schoolboy international, he was initially a striker but was quickly converted into a defender where he performed with great commitment, and was seldom ruffled while possessing a timely tackle. He gained nine Under-23 caps and recovered from a bout of hepatitis to play in the 1968 FA Cup final. He was Everton's first-ever League substitute when he came off the bench for his debut against Stoke in August 1965. He played his last game against Middlesbrough in April 1976.

HUSBAND, JAMES
Forward: 191+8 apps, 55 goals
Born: Newcastle, 15 October 1947
Career: Shields FC, EVERTON (apprentice, April 1963; professional, October 1964), Luton Town (November 1973–May 1978), Everton FC (Bedfordshire side, 1984–85)
An FA Youth Cup winner in 1965, Jimmy 'Skippy' Husband played in the FA Cup final three years later and helped Everton take the League title in 1970, scoring six times in 30 appearances, including goals in decisive wins over Leeds and West Ham at home and Newcastle away. A likeable Geordie, he was unorthodox and unpredictable, yet in his day was a wonderful player who netted some cracking goals. He made his debut for the Blues at Fulham in April 1965 and as an 18-year-old played in the Fairs Cup second-round clash against Ujpesti Dozsa of Hungary. He was capped by England at Under-23 level.

HUTCHISON, DONALD
Midfield: 81+8 apps, 11 goals
Born: Gateshead, 9 May 1971
Career: Hartlepool United (trainee, June 1987; professional, March 1990), Liverpool (£175,000, November 1990), West Ham United (£1.5m, August 1994), Sheffield United (£1.2m, January 1996), EVERTON (£1m in part-exchange deal involving Jon O'Connor, February 1998), Sunderland (£2.5m, July 2000), West Ham United (£5m, August 2001)
An attacking midfielder (and occasional striker), Don Hutchison took time to settle down at Anfield and also at Upton Park, but was immediately into his stride at Bramall Lane, where his strength and creative ideas were an enormous benefit to the side. Although short on pace and with a relatively poor scoring-record, he has produced some fine performances over the years, but unfortunately suffered long-term injuries at both Everton and West Ham (second time round), being out of action with a torn cruciate ligament for ten months from February 2002. He made his debut for the Blues against Newcastle in February 1998 and netted his first goal for the club in a 2–0 win over Leeds a fortnight later. So far 'Hutch' has gained one 'B' and 25 full caps for Scotland, scoring on his debut against Germany in April 1999. He has now made over 400 appearances at club level (to 2004).

IRVINE, JAMES ALAN
Winger: 69+10 apps, 6 goals
Born: Glasgow, 12 July 1958
Career: Queen's Park (amateur, 1975), EVERTON (May 1981), Crystal Palace (August 1984), Dundee United (June 1987), Blackburn Rovers (October 1989–May 1992)

Scorer of 31 goals in 335 League games for his five clubs, Alan Irvine suffered a lot with injuries, especially in Scotland, robbing him of representative honours. After waiting seven months for his Everton debut against Aston Villa in December 1981, he kept his place in the side for the remainder of that season. He was then hurt but returned for a decent spell in the first team between October 1983 and March 1984 before damaging a knee. He played his best football with Palace, for whom he netted 14 times in 125 games.

IRVINE, ROBERT
Inside/centre-forward: 214 apps, 57 goals
Born: Lisburn, near Belfast, 29 April 1900 – *Died*: Ireland, 1979
Career: Dunrummy (Belfast), EVERTON (September 1921), Portsmouth (March 1928), Connah's Quay (August 1929), Derry City (September 1930), Watford (May 1933–April 1935)

Bobby Irvine was a magical dribbler, a ball-controller well above the ordinary. Brave and determined, he thrilled the crowds week after week. A huge favourite with the Goodison fans, he scored a goal every four games for Everton, including 11 in his first season, making his debut against Liverpool in November 1921. He won 11 full caps for Northern Ireland during his time on Merseyside, playing in teams that twice beat England (1923, 1927). He helped the Blues win the League in 1928 but did not receive a medal as he appeared in only nine games. On his departure it was written of him: 'There is no man who takes harder knocks and squeals less than Irvine.' Sadly injury robbed him of a place in Pompey's FA Cup final side of 1929 and he made only 35 starts for the club. He won the last of his 15 caps with Derry – almost a decade after gaining his first.

IZATT
Outside-left: 5 apps
Born: Scotland, *circa* 1864 – Deceased
Career: EVERTON (September–December 1887)

Nippy left-winger Izatt scored twice for Everton, both in an 8–0 friendly win over Haydock St James in November 1887 – a month after making his debut in the club's first-ever FA Cup-tie against Bolton.

JACK, JAMES ROSS
Forward: 1 app., 1 goal
Born: Avoch, Ross-shire, Scotland, 21 March 1959
Career: Ross County, EVERTON (apprentice, April 1976; professional, February 1977), Cardiff City (loan, October 1979), Norwich City (£20,000,

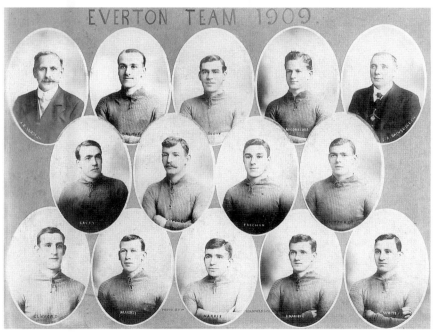

TOP INSET: Edgar Chadwick — scorer of 110 goals in 300 appearances for the Blues

TOP: 1906 FA Cup winners — defeated Newcastle United 1—0 in the final

ABOVE: First Division runners-up in 1909 behind Newcastle United

TOP LEFT: Sam Chedgzoy — 300 games for Everton, 8 caps for England

TOP RIGHT: Stan Fazackerley — scored 21 goals in 2 seasons

ABOVE: The team finished seventh in the First Division in 1923–24

TOP LEFT: Dixie Dean — one of the game's greatest-ever goalscorers

ABOVE LEFT: FA Cup winners in 1932–33. The team defeated
Manchester City 3–0 in the Wembley final.

RIGHT: Charlie Gee — appeared in over 200 games for the Blues in 9 years

LEFT: Torrance Gillick — League championship winner in 1938–39

MIDDLE: Ted Sagar — appeared in almost 500 games for
Everton, whom he served for over 24 years

RIGHT: Stan Bentham — missed just one match when the League title was won in 1938–39

LEFT: Joe Mercer, a superb wing-half who also played for and managed England

MIDDLE: Tommy 'G' Jones — Welsh international, capped 17 times

RIGHT: Tommy Lawton, who scored 70 goals in only 95 games for the Blues

TOP: The 1953–54 team that regained First Division status
under manager and former Everton player Cliff Britton

ABOVE LEFT: Peter Farrell — scored for the Republic of Ireland at
Goodison Park in 1949 (© Albert Marrion Photography)

ABOVE RIGHT: Albert Dunlop — made his debut for Everton
in front of more than 50,000 fans

TOP LEFT: Dave Hickson — robust centre-forward who had two spells at Goodison Park

TOP RIGHT: Jimmy O'Neill, the Irish international goalkeeper who spent 11 years at the club

LEFT: Billy Bingham — winger who later managed Everton and Northern Ireland

ABOVE: Alex Young, 'the Golden Vision'

RIGHT: Bobby Collins — Scotland
international who scored a
hat-trick of penalties

December 1979), Lincoln City (£15,000, August 1983), Dundee (July 1985), Dunfermline Athletic (October 1987), Kilmarnock (£50,000, July 1991), Sligo Rovers (loan, January–March 1993), Montrose (March 1993), Ayr United (October 1993)

Ross Jack was never given a chance by Everton, although he did score in his only game, a 2–1 win at Middlesbrough in March 1979, being the only Everton player to achieve this feat since the Second World War. After netting 16 goals in 60 outings for Lincoln, he was top scorer for Dunfermline in three successive seasons, helping them win the Second Division title in 1989.

JACKSON, GEORGE

Full-back: 79 apps
Born: Liverpool, 14 January 1911 – Deceased
Career: Arnott Street School, Walton Parish Church FC, EVERTON (May 1932), Liverpool Marine (loan, 1933–34), Caenarvon Town (May 1947–May 1949)

George 'Stonewall' Jackson spent 15 years at Goodison Park. Unfortunately the Second World War took a hefty chunk out of his career, although he did appear in over 200 Regional matches during the hostilities, occupying every position including goalkeeper against Burnley in January 1941 (won 3–2). But it was at right-back where he performed best, being a tough tackler with good speed, fine positional sense and a cool temperament. An FA Amateur Cup finalist with Marine, he made his League debut against Wolves in February 1935 and played his last game for the club against Blackpool in April 1947.

JACKSON, MATTHEW ALAN

Defender: 159+6 apps, 6 goals
Born: Leeds, 19 October 1971
Career: Luton Town (apprentice, April 1988; professional, July 1990), Preston North End (loan, March–April 1991), EVERTON (£600,000, October 1991), Charlton Athletic (loan, March–May 1996), Queens Park Rangers (loan, August–September 1996), Birmingham City (loan, October–December 1996), Norwich City (£450,000, December 1996), Wigan Athletic (free, October 2001)

Matt Jackson has produced scores of competitive and authoritative performances during his career. An England schoolboy international, he added ten Under-21 caps to his collection while establishing himself in Everton's first team, having made his League debut for Preston against Crewe in March 1991. He moved to Goodison seven months later and made his first appearance at right-back against Aston Villa in October 1991. He played alongside a variety of defenders during five years spent on Merseyside, gaining an FA Cup-winner's medal in 1995 after scoring the winning goal against Bristol City in the fourth round and the opening goal against Spurs in the semi-final. A Second Division championship winner with Wigan in 2003, he has now made over 500 club appearances.

129

JACKSON, THOMAS
Midfield: 34+4 apps
Born: Belfast, 3 November 1946
Career: Glentoran (1965), EVERTON (£10,000, February 1968), Nottingham Forest (£150,000, player-exchange deal involving Henry Newton, October 1970), Manchester United (£75,000, June 1975), Waterford (free, player–manager, July 1978); later Glentoran (manager, 1988–91); now lives in Glengormley (Belfast)

Tommy Jackson won 35 caps for Northern Ireland (six during his time at Everton), collecting his first against Israel in September 1968. He also played at Under-23 level and after leaving Everton skippered Manchester United's second XI in his first season, being unable to get into the first team. He strove hard to establish himself in Everton's side but when included he performed with aggression and a fair amount of skill. He made his Football League debut against his future club, Nottingham Forest, in April 1968 and then helped Everton beat Leeds in the FA Cup semi-final. During his career Jackson made only 132 League appearances (six goals). He won Irish League championship and Irish Cup runner's-up medals with Glentoran, and, as a manager, guided the same club to four trophy successes in 1989–90.

JAMIESON, JAMES
Left-half: 15 apps
Born: Lockerbie, Scotland, 3 November 1867 – Deceased
Career: EVERTON (September 1889), Sheffield Wednesday (June 1893–May 1899)

Never a first-team regular with Everton, Jack Jamieson made his League debut at centre-forward in a 3–0 home win over Derby in March 1891. After that he played most of his football at left-half and had his best period in 1892–93 when he made 14 successive appearances at wing-back following the departure of Hope Robertson. He made 135 appearances for Wednesday.

JARDINE, DAVID
Goalkeeper: 37 apps
Born: Liverpool, *circa* 1865 – Deceased
Career: Bootle (1886), EVERTON (November 1890), Nelson (May 1894)

Signed to replace Jack Angus, David Jardine had an impressive League debut for Everton, helping them defeat Blackburn 3–1 in November 1890. He retained his place in the side (injuries apart) until Dick Williams replaced him.

JEFFERIS, FRANK
Winger/inside-forward: 137 apps, 25 goals
Born: Fordingbridge, Hampshire, 3 July 1884 – *Died*: New Cross ground, London, 21 May 1938
Career: Fordingbridge Turks, Southampton (trial, March 1905; signed for £5, April 1905), EVERTON (£1,500, March 1911), Preston North End (January 1920, player–coach July 1922), Southport (player–coach, June

1923), Preston North End (reserve-team coach, October 1925), Southport (coach, May 1926; played twice in 1927 in an emergency), Millwall (trainer, May 1936 until his death)

A League championship winner with Everton in 1915 (four goals in 18 appearances), Frank Jefferis was a fast-moving forward who scored two hat-tricks as a Southampton trialist. He went on to net 48 goals in 184 outings for Saints. He settled in quickly at Goodison after his debut at Blackburn in April 1911 and the following year gained two England caps, against Wales and Scotland. He played for Preston in their defeat by Huddersfield in the 1922 FA Cup final. Jefferis received a benefit: Southampton against Manchester City in October 1910.

JEFFERS, FRANCIS

Striker: 51+31 apps, 22 goals

Born: Liverpool, 25 January 1981

Career: EVERTON (apprentice, April 1997; professional, February 1998), Arsenal (£8m, June 2001), EVERTON (on loan, September 2003–May 2004), Charlton Athletic (£2.6m, August 2004)

The second 16-year-old to play League football for Everton, Franny Jeffers was just one month short of his seventeenth birthday when he made his debut as a substitute at Manchester United in front of 55,000 fans in December 1997. He developed fast and made 13 appearances the following season (four goals) and 20 (eight goals) in 1999–2000. He was in and out of the side through injury and suspension the following year before his transfer to Highbury. He returned to Goodison for a second time after helping the Gunners win the Premiership title, netting twice in six games, one against Everton on the last day. Capped by England at four different levels – schoolboy, youth and Under-21 (13) – he scored on his full debut against Australia. Jeffers holds the record with Alan Shearer for most goals at Under-21 level (13) including a hat-trick against Macedonia in October 2002. He scored when Everton won the FA Youth Cup in 1998.

JENKINS, IAIN

Defender: 3+2 apps

Born: Prescot, 24 November 1972

Career: EVERTON (apprentice, April 1989; professional, June 1991), Bradford City (loan, December 1992–January 1993), Chester City (August 1993), Dundee United (March 1998), Shrewsbury Town (July 2000), Chester (2003–04)

Reserve Iain Jenkins made his League debut for Everton at left-back at QPR in May 1991 and appeared in over 200 games for Chester, helping them regain their League status in 2004. He's also won international honours for Northern Ireland at both full and 'B' team levels.

JEVONS, PHILIP

Striker: 3+6 apps

Born: Liverpool, 1 August 1979

Career: EVERTON (apprentice, April 1996; professional, November 1997),

Grimsby Town (£150,000, July 2001), Hull City (loan, September–November 2002), Yeovil Town (July 2004)
Strong and pacy, Phil Jevons played in Everton's intermediate and reserve teams with Franny Jeffers and Danny Cadmarteri, gaining a Youth Cup-winner's medal in 1998. He made his League debut against Bradford City in April 2000, assisting in two goals. Unable to gain regular first-team football at Goodison, he scored a famous winner for Grimsby against the holders, Liverpool, in a Worthington Cup-tie at Anfield in 2001.

JOHNSON, ALBERT
Outside-right: 9 apps
Born: Weaverham, 15 July 1920
Career: Prescot Church Institute, EVERTON (May 1939), Chesterfield (September 1948–April 1949)
Reserve right-winger Bert Johnson played four games for Everton during the Second World War before making his League debut against Derby in December 1946, deputising for John McIlhatton. He scored once in 19 League outings for Chesterfield.

JOHNSON, DAVID EDWARD
Forward: 91+12 apps, 20 goals
Born: Liverpool, 23 October 1951
Career: EVERTON (apprentice, April 1967; professional, April 1969), Ipswich Town (November 1972), Liverpool (£200,000, August 1976), EVERTON (August 1982), Barnsley (loan, February–March 1984), Manchester City (March 1984), Tulsa Roughnecks/NASL (June–September 1984), Preston North End (n/c, October 1984–March 1985)
David Johnson scored on his Youth Cup, Central League, Football League, FA Cup, League Cup and European debuts for Everton. He also netted in his first Merseyside derby (which was also the fastest), did likewise for England and also for Ipswich. A colourful character, sharp and positive, he netted 110 goals in 409 League games over 14 years, following his debut for the Blues against Burnley in January 1971. He did well in his first spell at Goodison and after doing likewise at Portman Road, Bob Paisley recruited him to take over from John Toshack at Anfield. He helped the Reds win three League titles (1977, 1979, 1980), the European Cup (1981) and reach the FA Cup final (1977), netting 55 goals in almost 150 outings in the process.

Eyebrows were then raised when Johnson (30) was re-signed by Everton boss Howard Kendall to boost a goal-shy attack. Unfortunately his second stint was nothing short of a disaster – only five goals in almost 50 games – the great touch with which he had been renowned was sadly missing. In his day he had the tendency of lying dormant during the course of a game, but then would burst into life and score or set up a vital goal. He won eight full caps for England.

JOHNSON, THOMAS
Striker: 0+2 apps
Born: Newcastle-upon-Tyne, 15 January 1971
Career: Notts County (apprentice, June 1987; professional, January 1989), Derby County (£1.3m, March 1992), Aston Villa (£1.45m, January 1995), Celtic (£2.4m, March 1997), EVERTON (loan, September–October 1999), Sheffield Wednesday (free, September 2001), Kilmarnock (free, December 2001), Gillingham (free, August 2002)

Tommy Johnson scored 57 goals in 149 games for Notts County and 41 in 129 outings for Derby. He continued to hit the target with Aston Villa (17 in 71 appearances) before losing his way under Brian Little. Capped seven times by England at Under-21 level, Johnson was sidelined for six months with a serious knee injury with Celtic in 1999. Regaining match fitness, he played for Everton, making his debut against Leeds in October 1999. He then returned to have a useful season with Celtic under Martin O'Neill, gaining a League Cup-winner's medal in 2000 while later winning the League and Cup double in 2001. Five years earlier he had been a League Cup winner with Aston Villa.

JOHNSON, THOMAS CLARK FISHER
Inside-left/centre-forward: 64 apps, 159 goals
Born: Dalton-in-Furness, near Barrow, 19 August 1901 – *Died*: 29 January 1973
Career: Dalton Athletic, Dalton Casuals, Manchester City (amateur, May 1918; professional, February 1919), EVERTON (£6,000, March 1930), Liverpool (March 1934), Darwen (August 1936; retired May 1937)

Tommy 'Tosh' Johnson, one-time apprentice riveter in a shipyard, scored 22 goals and missed only one game when Everton won the League in 1931–32. Forming a lethal partnership with Dixie Dean, between them they netted over 200 goals in more than 300 games, including 180 in three seasons: 1931–34. A third of those goals (67) came in 1931–32 when Johnson played splendidly, as he had done a year earlier when the Second Division title was won. In 1933 he helped the Blues win the FA Cup (against his former club) and between May 1926 and October 1932 he scored five times in five international wins for England (5–3 against Belgium, 6–0 against Wales, 7–1 against Spain, 3–0 against Scotland and 1–0 against Ireland). He also represented the Football League.

The perfect foil for any centre-forward, Johnson was an FA Cup runner-up and Second Division championship winner with Manchester City in 1926 and 1928 respectively. He is City's record scorer in a season with 28 goals in 1928–29, including a five-timer against Everton in September, making him the only player so far to achieve that feat against the Blues. He also holds City's record in terms of aggregate goals scored – 158 in the League and 166 overall. He finished with 222 League goals to his credit (in 511 games). He made his debut for Everton at Newcastle in March 1930.

JOHNSTON, LESLIE
Inside-left: 8 apps, 1 goal
Born: Liverpool, *circa* 1890 – Deceased
Career: EVERTON (seasons 1913–15); did not appear after the First World War
Reserve Les Johnston made his League debut for Everton in a 4–1 defeat at Sheffield United in October 1913 and netted his only goal in a 4–1 reverse at Tottenham six weeks later.

JOHNSTON, MAURICE JOHN GIBLIN
Striker: 32+7 apps, 10 goals
Born: Glasgow, 30 April 1963
Career: Partick Thistle (1980), Watford (November 1983), Celtic (September 1984), Nantes/France (June 1987), Glasgow Rangers (July 1989), EVERTON (November 1991), Heart of Midlothian (March 1993); later played in the USA
'Mo' Johnston scored 71 goals in 127 games for Celtic and 46 in 100 for Rangers before playing for Watford against Everton in the 1984 FA Cup final. He helped the Bhoys win the Scottish League title in 1986 and 'Gers likewise in successive seasons (1989, 1991) while also lifting the Scottish League Cup in 1991, having collected a runner's-up prize in the same competition a year earlier.

Positive and aggressive, always eager and willing to shoot at goal, he gained 38 full and three Under-21 caps for his country, and although never at his best in England, he produced the goods north of the border. Linking up with Tony Cottee in attack, he made his League debut for Everton in a 1–0 home win over Notts County soon after signing and struck seven goals in 23 outings in his first season but struggled with his form and fitness after that and eventually returned to Scotland.

JOLIFFE, CHARLES JAMES
Goalkeeper: 7 apps
Born: Liverpool, *circa* 1861 – Deceased
Career: EVERTON (November 1883–August 1890)
Charlie Joliffe, tall and lean, was first choice for Everton for two years (October 1885–October 1887). He then lost his place to Bob Smalley but remained loyal to the club for another three years before moving on. He appeared in 100 games for the Blues, making his senior debut against Bolton in the FA Cup in October 1887, Everton's first game in this competition. The following season he conceded eight goals in four League matches.

JONES, DAVID RONALD
Full-back: 95+8 apps, 2 goals
Born: Liverpool, 17 August 1956
Career: EVERTON (apprentice, July 1972; professional, May 1974), Coventry City (£275,000, June 1979), FC Seiko/Japan (May 1982), Preston North End (August 1983–May 1985); Southport (manager, 1986), Mossley

(manager, 1988), Morecambe (manager 1989), Stockport County (chief scout, 1990; then assistant manager and manager, March 1995), Southampton (manager, July 1997–December 1999), Wolverhampton Wanderers (manager, January 2001)

Five years a professional at Goodison Park, Dave Jones had to work hard and long to get first-team football, owing to the presence of Terry Darracott and Steve Seargeant. He eventually established himself at left-back in 1976–77 but had the misfortune to miss the League Cup final second replay defeat by Aston Villa, having played in the initial game at Wembley. With the arrival of Mike Pejic, he moved over in the right before transferring to Coventry. He made his League debut as a substitute against Leicester in November 1976. As a manager, Jones did well at Stockport, leading the Edgeley Park side to the League Cup semi-finals and promotion from Division Two in 1997. He then did a sound job at Southampton before being replaced by Glenn Hoddle after a long drawn-out court case. Subsequently cleared of all charges made against him, Jones then took Wolves into the Premiership and out again in 2003 and 2004.

JONES, GARY KENNETH
Forward: 90+8 apps, 15 goals
Born: Whiston, Liverpool, 5 January 1951
Career: EVERTON (apprentice, June 1966; professional, October 1968), Birmingham City (£110,000, July 1976), Fort Lauderdale Strikers/NASL (1978–79); later licensee of the Albert pub (Liverpool)

An aggressive winger, never afraid to run at defenders, Gary Jones was plagued by inconsistency throughout his career and his goal-tally was a poor reward for a player whose primary function was that of an attacker! He made his League debut for Everton against Coventry in April 1971 and had his best run in the first team during the second half of 1974–75, when he occupied both flanks. He struggled at times during his spell with Birmingham.

JONES, GEORGE WILFRED
Outside-right: 36 apps, 2 goals
Born: Crook, 28 June 1895 – *Died*: 1970
Career: Crook Town, Gwersylt, EVERTON (professional, September 1919), Wigan Borough (January 1923), Middlesbrough (September 1925), Southport (April 1926), Yeovil and Petters United (1928–29), Great Harwood (1929–31)

A smart fast-raiding winger who appeared in over 200 competitive games as a professional, George Jones made his League debut for Everton in a 4–1 home win over Bradford in November 1919. He had a decent first season before losing his way and his place to Sam Chedgzoy.

JONES, JOHN EDWARD
Full-back: 108 apps
Born: Bromborough, 3 July 1913 – *Died*: 1995
Career: Ellesmere Port, EVERTON (professional, March 1932), Sunderland
(December 1945; retired May 1947)
Strong and resilient, Jack Jones made over 150 appearances for Everton, 50 during the Second World War. He developed steadily and made his League debut in April 1934 against Leeds, eventually establishing himself in the left-back position in 1935–36, partnering Billy Cook in half of the matches.

JONES, PHILIP ANDREW
Right-back: 0+1 app.
Born: Liverpool, 1 December 1969
Career: EVERTON (apprentice, April 1986; professional, June 1989), Blackpool (loan, March–April 1990), Wigan Athletic (January 1991), Bury (n/c, August–October 1993)
Reserve initially to Gary Stevens, Phil Jones's only appearance for Everton was as a substitute against Southampton in February 1988. He later had 86 League outings for Wigan.

JONES, ROBERT H.
Goalkeeper: 3 apps
Born: Liverpool, 9 January 1902 – *Died*: Great Harwood, near Blackburn, 1989
Career: Ferndale, EVERTON (professional, April 1924), Southport (May 1926), Bolton Wanderers (October 1929), Cardiff City (free, July 1937), Southport (player/ assistant trainer, July 1939; then trainer, 1950–58)
Tall, thin and serious but very effective, Bob Jones took over from Kendall for games against Manchester City, Arsenal and Aston Villa in November 1924. He later gave Bolton superb service after taking over from the legendary Dick Pym, appearing in 244 games and helping the Wanderers gain promotion from the Second Division in 1935. For many years before becoming a footballer, Jones worked as a cabin boy on a liner out of Liverpool docks.

JONES, ROBERT SAMUEL
Defender: 7 apps, 1 goal
Born: Wrexham, 1868 – *Died*: Salford, Manchester, 25 May 1939
Career: Challenger Boys (Wrexham), Wrexham Grosvenor, EVERTON (December 1887), Ardwick/Manchester City (June 1894; retired, injured, October 1895); later a labourer in the dockyard
Rob Jones played at centre-half in Everton's first-ever League game against Accrington in September 1888, having made his debut for the club the previous January (against Notts Rangers). A burly, reliable reserve, he played in a Welsh international trial in 1894 and won a full cap against Ireland that same year. He made 18 League appearances for Manchester City before breaking his leg in March 1895 in a Manchester Cup-tie against Bolton.

JONES, THOMAS

Centre-forward: 15 apps, 5 goals
Born: Prescot, 1885 – Deceased
Career: Bootle, EVERTON (September 1905), Birmingham (September 1910),
   Southport Central (May 1912); did not feature after the First World War
Tommy 'Prescot' Jones was a classy forward who found his career hampered by
Scottish international Sandy Young at Everton, although when chosen he never
let the club down, making a scoring League debut against Derby in April 1906.
He later netted 12 times in 31 outings for Birmingham.

JONES, THOMAS EDWIN

Centre-half: 411 apps, 14 goals
Born: Liverpool, 11 April 1930
Career: England and Liverpool County FA, EVERTON (amateur, 1945;
   professional, January 1948; retired May 1962); later coached Montreal FC
   (Italy); later in private business (1970s)
Tommy Jones was Everton's first-choice centre-half throughout the 1950s.
Initially a full-back, he developed into an outstanding, cool, calculated defender,
a 'stopper' of the highest quality who made his League debut against Arsenal in
September 1950, following excellent progress in the reserves. He gained youth
honours for his country, played for an England XI against the British Army and
captained the FA side on tour to Ghana and Nigeria in the summer of 1958. He
was forced to retire in 1962 after smashing his kneecap in a reserve game against
Burnley.

JONES, THOMAS GEORGE

Centre-half: 175 apps, 5 goals
Born: Connah's Quay, Flintshire, 12 October 1917 – *Died*: Bangor, 3 January
   2004
Career: Connah's Quay Council School, Flint and District Schools, Llanerch
   Celtic, Wrexham (amateur, November 1932; professional, October 1934),
   EVERTON (£3,000, March 1936), Pwllheli and District (player–manager,
   April 1950–May 1956), Bangor City (manager, June 1956–May 1967), Rhyl
   FC (manager, 1967–68); then a soccer journalist for the north Wales edition
   of the Liverpool *Daily Post*; later ran his own newsagent's business in Bangor
Tommy Jones was the linchpin of the Everton defence during their League
championship-winning season of 1938–39. Six ft 1 in. tall and 13 st. in
weight, he was quite brilliant in the air as well as being able to use his long
legs to good advantage when making a tackle. A deliberate, concise, steady
sort of defender, who always gave encouragement to his colleagues around
him, 'TG' or 'Gentleman Tom', as he was known, wasn't a battering-ram of a
centre-half, who smashed through centre-forwards; he was a thoughtful,
intelligent player, regarded in some quarters as a 'footballing scientist'. A
Welsh schoolboy international, he went on to win 17 full caps for his country
(1938–50) while also appearing in 11 Wartime/Victory internationals
(1939–46). He made his Everton debut at Leeds in October 1936 (lost 3–0)

137

and during the Second World War appeared in a further 132 matches for the club (41 goals).

Jones, who succeeded Peter Farrell as captain at Goodison Park, may well have moved to Italy in 1948 but a deal with AS Roma collapsed at the eleventh hour. Later, Jones upset the Everton board by publicly expressing his concern at the way the club was being run.

As manager, he won the Welsh Cup with Bangor (1961) and the following season took his team to Highbury to play AC Napoli, only going out of the European Cup-Winners' Cup after a replay.

Dixie Dean said of Tommy Jones: 'He was the best all-round player I've ever seen. He had everything. No coach could ever coach him or teach him anything. He was neater than John Charles, for instance, and could get himself out of trouble just by running towards the ball and then letting it run between his legs, knowing his team-mate would be in a position to take it.'

JORDAN, WILLIAM CHARLES
Centre-forward: 2 apps
Born: Langley, Worcestershire, December 1885 – *Died*: Belbroughton, Worcestershire, December 1949
Career: Langley and District Junior and Infants Schools, Five Ways Grammar School (Birmingham), Birmingham City Technical School, St John's College (Oxford), Oxford University, Liverpool (reserves), Langley Church FC, Langley Victoria, Langley St Michael's (1903), West Bromwich Albion (November 1904–April 1909), EVERTON (September 1911), Wolverhampton Wanderers (July 1912; retired January 1913); a graduate in Natural Science at Oxford University and, ordained in 1907, he was curate at St Clement's Church, Nechells, Birmingham (1911–12) and thereafter devoted most of his time to the church, conducting several Sportsman's Services up and down the country, choosing to 'appear' on the soccer field whenever he could. Served the Church of Wales, on the Isle of Man, at Slaidburn (West Riding of Yorkshire), in Darlington and also in Belbroughton; also a director of Darlington FC (1936–39)

Billy Jordan was a brilliant amateur centre-forward, a player with precision and thought, speed and deadly marksmanship. An England amateur international, he scored six goals against France in 1907 when making his debut for his country and claimed a hat-trick for WBA on his League debut against Gainsborough in February 1907. Having his Everton baptism at Manchester United in September 1911, his second game a week later was at home to Liverpool. He played for WBA against Everton in the 1907 FA Cup semi-final.

JULISSON, ALBERT LAURENCE
Centre-forward: 10 apps, 1 goal
Born: Blyth, County Durham, 20 February 1920
Career: Dundee, Portsmouth (March 1948), EVERTON (September 1948), Berwick Rangers (August 1951)
Signed after failing to establish himself at Portsmouth, Bert Julisson made all

his senior appearances for Everton over a period of four months when manager Cliff Britton was trying to sort out the centre-forward position. He made his debut in a 5–0 home defeat at the hands of Birmingham and scored his only goal in his second game against Stoke (won 2–1).

KANCHELSKIS, ANDREI

Winger: 60 apps, 22 goals
Born: Kirovograd, Ukraine, 23 January 1969
Career: Dinamo Kiev/Ukraine, Shakhtar Donetsk/Ukraine, Manchester United (n/c March 1991; signed for £650,000, May 1991), EVERTON (£5m, August 1995), Fiorentina/Italy (£8m, early 1997), Glasgow Rangers (£5.5m, 1998), Manchester City (loan, early 2001), Al Hilal/Saudi Arabia (February to May 2003), Brighton and Hove Albion (trial, August 2003; n/c, September 2003); Dynamo Moscow/Russia (March 2004)

Fast, tricky and direct, Andrei Kanchelskis accumulated a fine scoring record with Manchester United (36 goals in 161 games). He helped the Reds win the Super Cup, the League Cup, the Premiership (twice), the FA Cup and Charity Shield (twice) before transferring to Everton, for whom he made his debut in a 2–0 home win over Southampton in September 1995. He had an excellent first season, finishing up as top scorer with 16 goals.

He struggled at times in Italy before winning two League, two Scottish Cup and League Cup-winner's medals with Rangers, for whom he netted 20 goals in 114 outings. The recipient of 59 full caps – 36 for Russia (five goals), 6 with the CIS and 17 with the USSR (three goals), he made over 450 appearances at club level (90 goals scored) and is the only player to have appeared in a Manchester, Liverpool and 'Old Firm' derby. He was Everton's first £5m player and became the world's most expensive winger when sold to Fiorentina in 1997.

KAVANAGH, PETER JOHN

Outside-left: 6 apps
Born: Ilford, 3 November 1938
Career: Dagenham (1954), Fulham (professional, October 1956), Romford (August 1957), EVERTON (February–June 1961), Dagenham

After failing to make a breakthrough at Fulham, Peter Kavanagh had a useful spell with Romford, before signing a contract with Everton. Unfortunately, he didn't make the most of his opportunity and was released after four months, having made his League debut against Chelsea in February 1961, becoming the team's seventh left-winger that season.

KAY, ANTHONY HERBERT

Wing-half: 57 apps, 4 goals
Born: Attercliffe, Sheffield, May 1937
Career: Sheffield junior football, Sheffield Wednesday (professional, May 1954), EVERTON (£60,000, December 1962; suspended April 1965); later lived and worked in Spain

Everton's first £60,000 signing, red-haired Tony Kay was a tenacious footballer who contested every 50–50 ball with total commitment. He helped the Owls gain promotion to the First Division in 1959 and four years later was a League championship winner with Everton, appearing in 19 games and scoring one goal. He had made his senior debut for the Blues at left-half against Leicester in February 1963 (in place of Brian Harris) and netted his first goal six weeks later in a 4–3 defeat at Arsenal.

His career was cut short when, in 1965, he was at the centre of one of football's greatest-ever scandals. He, along with several other players, was banned for life, and sent to prison after the infamous soccer bribes trial arising from the fixing of the result of a League match involving Sheffield Wednesday and Ipswich. At the time his career was in full flight and, having already gained an England call-up (against Switzerland, 1963), he would have collected more caps but for that stupid misdemeanour.

KEARSLAKE, JOSEPH G.

Outside-right/centre-forward: 1 app., 1 goal
Born: Southampton, *circa* 1895 – Deceased
Career: EVERTON (June 1919), Wigan Borough (July 1920), Stockport County (July 1921–April 1923)
Deputising for Ernie Gault, reserve Joe Kearslake scored in his only League game for Everton – in a 4–1 defeat at Oldham in February 1920. He netted twice in 15 games for Stockport. (Some reference books have this player listed as Kerslake.)

KEARTON, JASON BRETT

Goalkeeper: 5+3 apps
Born: Ipswich, Australia, 9 July 1969
Career: Brisbane Lions/Australia, EVERTON (October 1988), Stoke City (loan, August–November 1991), Blackpool (loan, January–March 1992), Notts County (loan, January–March 1995), Crewe Alexandra (October 1996), Brisbane Lions (August 2001)
Signed as cover for Neville Southall, blond Jason Kearton was given very little chance to show his worth by Everton, owing to the consistency and form of his Welsh international counterpart. He made his League debut on loan with Stoke and also assisted Blackpool, making his first appearance for the Blues as a substitute against QPR in December 1993. An FA Cup winner with Everton in 1995, he was Crewe's 'Player of the Year' in 2000 and made over 200 appearances under manager Dario Gradi at Gresty Road before returning to Australia.

KEELEY, GLENN MATTHEW

Defender: 1 app.
Born: Basildon, Essex, 1 September 1954
Career: Ipswich Town (apprentice, July 1970; professional, August 1972), Newcastle United (£70,000, June 1974), Blackburn Rovers (£30,000, August 1976), Birmingham City (loan, August 1982), EVERTON (loan,

October 1982), Oldham Athletic (£15,000, August 1987), Colchester United (loan, February–March 1988), Bolton Wanderers (September 1988–May 1989), Chorley (August 1990), Clitheroe (1991–92); later a pub licensee in Leyland

Glenn Keeley had the misfortune to get sent off on his Everton debut against Liverpool in November 1982. During his career he appeared in over 450 League games (370 for Blackburn), won England youth honours, the FA Youth Cup (1973), played in the 1976 League Cup final (for Newcastle against Manchester City) and in 1980 helped Blackburn rise from the Third Division. His brother, Andy Keeley, played for Sheffield United and Spurs.

KEELEY, JOHN JAMES
Inside-forward: 7 apps, 3 goals
Born: Liverpool, 16 October 1936
Career: EVERTON (junior, April 1952; professional, May 1954), Accrington Stanley (July 1959), Southport (December 1959–April 1960)

Jack Keeley scored his only League goal for Everton on his debut in a 5–1 win at Bolton on Boxing Day 1957. He also netted twice in a third-round FA Cup game against Sunderland a week later. He was reserve to John Parker and Wally Fielding at Goodison Park.

KEELEY, SAMUEL
Centre-forward: 1 app.
Born: Scotland, *circa* 1874 – Deceased
Career: Dundee, EVERTON (trial, April 1897), Dundee (May 1897)

Sam Keeley's only League game for Everton was at Stoke two days after arriving. He deputised for Lawrie Bell.

KELLY, JEREMIAH
Right/centre-half: 83 apps, 1 goal
Born: Hamilton, Scotland, 1900 – Deceased
Career: Hamilton Welfare, Ayr United (1921), EVERTON (February 1927), Celtic (October 1929), Carlisle United (November 1929), Rennes University Club/France (1931–32)

Jerry Kelly had a fine 1927–28 season, missing only two games as Everton captured the League title for the third time. Tall and strong, he was a positive tackler, with sound positional sense, who was nurtured along at Ayr but failed to make inroads with Celtic, quickly moving to Carlisle, for whom he appeared in 32 League games. He made his debut for the Blues at Liverpool in February 1927 and netted his only goal for the club in a 4–1 home win over Burnley ten months later.

KELSO, ROBERT
Right-half/full-back: 103 apps, 5 goals
Born: Renton, Dumbartonshire, 1 October 1865 – *Died*: 10 August 1942
Career: Renton, Newcastle West End (July 1888), Preston North End (1889),

141

EVERTON (January 1889), Preston North End (May 1889), EVERTON (May 1891), Dundee (May 1896)

Bob Kelso made the successful switch from wing-half to full-back as an Everton player. Difficult to circumvent, he caught the eye with his powerful and timely tackling, always clearing the ball well while specialising in long-range dipping shots at goal. He made his debut for Everton against his future club Preston in January 1889, was in the 1893 FA Cup final side and gained seven caps for Scotland between 1885 and 1898. He also played for the Scottish League and Dumbartonshire in representative matches. His uncle, Tom Kelso, a Scottish international, played for Manchester City and Rangers.

KENDALL, HOWARD

Wing-half: 273+3 apps, 29 goals

Born: Ryton-on-Tyne, 22 May 1946 (the same day as George Best)

Career: Ryton and District Schools, Preston North End (apprentice, June 1961; professional, May 1963), EVERTON (£80,000, March 1967), Birmingham City (£350,000 deal involving Bob Latchford and Archie Styles, March 1974), Stoke City (£40,000, August 1977), Blackburn Rovers (player–manager, July 1979–May 1981), EVERTON (n/c, player–manager, May 1981), Atletico Bilbao/Spain (coach, June 1987), Manchester City (manager, December 1989), EVERTON (manager, November 1990–December 1993), FC Xanti/Greece (manager, May–November 1994), Notts County (manager, January–April 1995), Sheffield United (manager, December 1995–June 1997), EVERTON (manager, June 1997–May 1998); then scout for and coach to several clubs

Howard Kendall's uncle, Harry Taylor, played for Newcastle but it was his father who inspired him to become a footballer. He was selected to play for England against Wales in a schoolboy international in 1961, did well and almost immediately was signed as an apprentice by Preston. In 1964, after skippering England youngsters to victory in the Little World Cup, he became the youngest player since 1879 to appear in an FA Cup final, aged 17 years, 345 days (for Preston against West Ham). His game got better and better, and after more than 100 League outings for the Deepdale club he joined Everton. He quickly gained the first of six Under-23 caps (against Wales) but that elusive senior cap always eluded him, despite him being regarded as one of the finest attacking midfielders in the country during the 1969–72 period. In 1968 he collected a second runner's-up medal when Everton lost in the FA Cup final, but in 1970 he was a key performer when the First Division championship came to Goodison Park, Kendall forming a terrific partnership in midfield with Alan Ball and Colin Harvey. Moving to St Andrew's in 1974 as part of a complicated deal involving Bob Latchford, he had three-and-a-half excellent seasons with Birmingham, who entrusted him with the captaincy. After a decent spell with Stoke, he spent two seasons as player–manager at Ewood Park, helping Rovers win the Third Division title before returning to Goodison Park. He brought a great deal of success to Everton – two League championships (1985, 1987), an FA Cup final triumph (1984), two runners-up prizes (1985, 1986), European

Cup-Winners' Cup glory (1985) and a hat-trick of Charity Shield successes (1984–86). After spells in Spain and at Maine Road (no joy), he surprisingly returned to Everton for a third time and after serving in Greece, at Meadow Lane and Bramall Lane, he was taken on a fourth time (third as manager) in 1997. Kendall, who is still regarded as a great hero by Everton fans, appeared in 613 games and scored 65 goals, making his 600th appearance as player–manager of Blackburn in March 1981.

KENDALL, JOHN WILLIAM

Goalkeeper: 23 apps
Born: Broughton, Brigg, 9 October 1905 – *Died*: October 1961
Career: Broughton Rangers (North Lindsey League), Lincoln City (March 1922), EVERTON (£1,250, April 1924), Preston North End (May 1927), Lincoln City (July 1928), Sheffield United (£1,125, March 1930), Peterborough United (July 1934; retired May 1938)

When registered with Lincoln, Jack Kendall was described as one of the best goalkeepers in the Northern Section, summed up at the time as being 'a cool, fearless player, has a keen eye and possesses an enormous reach who on his day was capable of the most brilliant saves imaginable'. He became a goalkeeper by accident, standing between the posts for his school team after the regular number one had failed to turn up. He did well, saved two penalties and was snapped up by Lincoln shortly afterwards. Kendall made 117 appearances for the Imps prior to his transfer to Everton, for whom he made his debut against Spurs at Goodison Park 48 hours after joining. He started 1924–25 as first choice but then lost his place to Harland and after that struggled to get into the first team. He made 220 League appearances during his career. Before becoming a footballer he worked as a labourer on Lord Yarborough's estate at Broughton.

KENNEDY, ANDREW LYND

Left-back: 1 app.
Born: Belfast, 1 September 1895 – *Died*: 21 December 1963
Career: Belfast Celtic Juniors, Glentoran, Crystal Palace (September 1920), Arsenal (August 1922), EVERTON (January 1928), Tranmere Rovers (June 1930–August 1932); worked for south Liverpool schools up to the Second World War

Andy Kennedy made 129 appearances for Arsenal. He played for the Gunners against Cardiff in the 1927 FA Cup final and gained two full caps for Ireland in 1923–24. A well-built and well-proportioned defender, he was signed as cover for Jack O'Donnell by Everton and made his only start against Burnley in November 1929.

KENNEDY, FRED

Inside/outside-left: 35 apps, 11 goals
Born: Bury, October 1902 – *Died*: Failsworth, Lancashire, November 1963
Career: Rossendale United (1920), Manchester United (May 1923), EVERTON (£2,000, March 1925), Middlesbrough (May 1927), Reading

(May 1929), Oldham Athletic (November 1930), Rossendale United (September 1931), Northwich Victoria (December 1931), Racing Club de Paris/France (September 1932), Blackburn Rovers (August 1933), Racing Club de Paris/France (June 1934), Stockport County (July 1937–September 1939); did not play after the Second World War

A lightweight forward, with good skills, Fred Kennedy made over 175 appearances during a varied career, gaining League and Cup-winner's medals with the Paris club. He made his Everton debut at inside-left against Notts County in March 1925 and scored his first goal three days later at Arsenal. He had a decent first half to the 1925–26 season but then lost his way – especially after Jack O'Donnell had switched from full-back. He was awarded the Humane Society's Medal (for saving a young woman from drowning). He was also a champion crown green bowler.

KENNY, WILLIAM AIDAN, SENIOR
Midfield: 10+2 apps
Born: 23 October 1951
Career: EVERTON (apprentice, April 1967; professional, July 1969), Tranmere
    Rovers (March 1975–May 1977), Barrow (August 1977)
Bill Kenny had to work long and hard to get into the first XI at Goodison Park, owing to the form of Alan Ball, Colin Harvey, Tommy Jackson, Howard Kendall and others. He made his League debut at Nottingham Forest in March 1971 and played his last game against QPR in September 1974. His son, William Aidan Kenny junior (q.v.), also played for Everton.

KENNY, WILLIAM AIDAN, JUNIOR
Midfield: 22+1 apps, 1 goal
Born: Liverpool, 19 September 1973
Career: EVERTON (apprentice, April 1990; professional, June 1992), Oldham
    Athletic (August 1994–March 1995)
An England Under-21 international (one cap), Bill Kenny made his debut for Everton against Coventry in October 1992 and netted his only goal in a 2–1 defeat at Chelsea in March 1993. Released at the end of the following season (due to well-documented off-the-field problems), he was then signed by ex-Everton star Joe Royle for Oldham.

KENT, JAMES
Left-back: 1 app.
Born: Liverpool, *circa* 1869 – Deceased
Career: EVERTON (season 1891–92)
A reserve at Everton, Jack Kent's only League outing was at Darwen in November 1891, when he deputised for Duncan McLean.

KENYON, ROGER NORTON

Defender: 291+17 apps, 9 goals
Born: Blackpool, 4 January 1949
Career: EVERTON (apprentice, April 1964; professional, September 1966), Vancouver Whitecaps/NASL (February 1979), Bristol City (October 1979–April 1980)

A reliable and consistent defender, Roger Kenyon sat on the bench and watched Everton lose the 1968 FA Cup final, but two years later he made up for that disappointment by helping the Blues win the League championship, playing in the last eight matches. He made his debut as a 'sub' against Arsenal in November 1967 and in 1974 his career was severely disrupted by a car accident. In fact, during his time at Goodison he suffered a series of niggling injuries but fought back on each occasion and went on to serve Everton for 15 years, making over 300 appearances. Named as an England 'sub' for the European Championship encounters against West Germany, Cyprus and Wales in 1975, unfortunately he never represented his country. In 1979 he helped the Whitecaps win the Super Bowl.

KEOWN, MARTIN RAYMOND

Defender: 121+5 apps
Born: Oxford, 24 July 1966
Career: Arsenal (apprentice, June 1982; professional, February 1984), Brighton and Hove Albion (loan, February 1985), Aston Villa (£200,000, June 1986), EVERTON (£750,000, August 1989), Arsenal (£2m, February 1993), Leicester City (free transfer, July 2004)

Aston Villa did good business in the transfer market when they sold Martin Keown to Everton in 1989, making a profit of £550,000. Strong in the tackle, dominant in the air, a defender of the highest quality, he went on to greater things, appearing in over 120 games for the Blues, for whom he made his League debut as a substitute against Sheffield Wednesday in August 1989. He failed to score for Everton but did find the net for England against Czechoslovakia in Prague in March 1992 (2–2 draw).

After returning to Highbury, he became an established England defender, going on to win 43 caps to go with those he gained at youth (four), Under-21 (eight) and 'B' team levels. He helped the Gunners win three Premiership titles, the FA Cup on three occasions and the Charity Shield (also three times), and was part of the London club's double-winning side in 1998. On his release by Arsenal (after a testimonial game), Keown's record, at club level, was impressive: 750 appearances and 14 goals.

KERR, JASPER

Full-back: 21 apps, 1 goal
Born: Burnbank, Scotland, 1 January 1903 – Deceased
Career: Larkhall Thistle, Bathgate (1922), EVERTON (August 1924), Preston North End (March 1927), New Brighton (November 1933), Lancaster Town (1934–35)

A reserve for most of his seven years at Goodison, Jasper Kerr made his League debut at left-back as partner to Doug Livingstone at Blackburn in December 1924. He had his best spell in the side halfway through 1926–27, playing in 18 senior games.

KEYS

Centre-forward: 1 app.
Born: *circa* 1865 – Deceased
Career: EVERTON (August 1888–March 1889)
Unknown forward who made just one League appearance for the Blues, taking over as leader of the attack from Bill Lewis at Aston Villa in September 1888.

KIDD, BRIAN

Forward: 51 apps, 19 goals
Born: Collyhurst, Manchester, 29 May 1949
Career: St Patrick's School (Collyhurst), Manchester Boys, Manchester United (apprentice, August 1964; professional, June 1966), Arsenal (£110,000, August 1974), Manchester City (£100,000, July 1976), EVERTON (£150,000, March 1979), Bolton Wanderers (£110,000, May 1980), Atlanta Chiefs/NASL (loan, April–August 1981), Fort Lauderdale Strikers (January–February 1982), Minnesota Strikers/NASL (May 1984), Barrow (manager, August 1984), Swindon Town (assistant manager, April 1985), Preston North End (assistant manager briefly, then manager, January–March 1986), Manchester United (junior coach/director of School of Excellence, May 1988; youth development officer, October 1990; assistant manager, 1995), Blackburn Rovers (manager, December 1998–November 1999), Leeds United (director of football, 2000; then assistant manager/coach); also on England coaching staff
Brian Kidd, who attended the same school as Nobby Stiles, where his headmaster was another ex-Manchester United player, Laurence Cassidy, made his League debut in August 1967 against Everton. At the end of that season he celebrated his 19th birthday by scoring in United's European Cup final win over Benfica. A very effective striker, hard-working with an appetite for the game, Kidd represented England at youth, Under-23 and senior levels, winning two full caps as a Manchester United player. He also played for the Football League. With 126 League goals to his name, he made his Everton debut against Bolton in April 1979. He had a decent spell at Goodison Park but had the misfortune to become only the third player ever to be sent off in an FA Cup semi-final when dismissed against West Ham in 1980. He retired in 1984 with 461 League appearances to his credit (151 goals). As a manager, he was sacked by Blackburn with two and a half years of his contract remaining and later did well as Alex Ferguson's aide at Old Trafford.

KILBANE, KEVIN DANIEL

Left-wing/forward: 29+4 apps, 4 goals
Born: Preston, 1 February 1977
Career: Preston North End (apprentice, April 1993; professional, July 1995),

West Bromwich Albion (record, £1m, June 1997), Sunderland (£2.5m, December 1999), EVERTON (£2m, September 2003)

After leaving WBA, well-built, fast-raiding left-winger Kevin Kilbane went on to establish himself in the Republic of Ireland team, playing his part in a successful 2002 World Cup in the Far East. Impressive at times, especially when running at defenders, his long strides, individual skill and strength brush aside many a challenge. He does, however, have the tendency at times to hold on to the ball too long. Nevertheless, he has scored some cracking goals over the years, several from distance. Relegated with Sunderland, he returned to the top flight with Everton, for whom he made his debut against Newcastle United at Goodison Park in September 2003. Kilbane has now played in more than 50 full internationals for Eire, having previously won 11 caps at Under-21 level.

KING, ANDREW EDWARD
Midfield: 243+4 apps, 67 goals
Born: Luton, 14 August 1956
Career: Luton and Dunstable Schools, Bedfordshire Boys, Stopsley Youths, Tottenham Hotspur (trialist, August–September 1971), Luton Town (apprentice, August 1972; professional, July 1974), EVERTON (£35,000, March 1976), Queens Park Rangers (£425,000, September 1980), West Bromwich Albion (£400,000, September 1981), EVERTON (£225,000 plus Peter Eastoe, July 1982), SC Cambuur/Holland (July 1984), Wolverhampton Wanderers (January 1985), FC Orebro/Sweden (loan, April–August 1985), Luton Town (December 1985), Aldershot (August 1986), Aylesbury United (1988), Waterford (player–manager, 1988–89), Cobh Ramblers (1989), Southport (August 1989), Luton Town (commercial manager), Sunderland (scout, late 1990s), Grimsby Town (assistant manager, 1997), Swindon Town (coach 1998, then manager, October 2000–May 2001; returned as Swindon manager, January 2002)

An England Under-21 international (two caps won), Andy King had two spells with Everton, the first undoubtedly his best. An all-action, aggressive and totally committed midfielder, he played in the 1977 League Cup final and in three losing FA Cup semi-finals. He top-scored for the Blues in 1978–79 with 12 goals and is currently in the top ten of League Cup marksmen for the Merseysiders and is the only Everton player to appear in the 1977 and 1984 League Cup finals.

He made his debut for the Blues against Middlesbrough in April 1976 and five and a half years later played his first game for WBA against Everton. He also appeared in two semi-finals with the Baggies, losing them both in 1982. In 1987 he helped Aldershot gain promotion from the Fourth Division while pushing his career appearance-tally past the 450 mark (112 goals). As a manager, he took Swindon into the Second Division play-offs in 2004.

KING, FRANCIS OLIVER
Goalkeeper: 14 apps
Born: Alnwick, 13 March 1917
Career: Blyth Spartans (1932), EVERTON (October 1933), Derby County

(£200, July 1937–October 1938); did not figure after the Second World War
Frank King made his League debut for Everton against Middlesbrough in April
1935 when he deputised for Ted Sagar. He continued to understudy the
England international until his departure to Derby.

KING, JOHN ALLEN
Wing-half: 49 apps, 1 goal
Born: Marylebone, London, 15 April 1938
Career: EVERTON (amateur, June 1953; professional, March 1956),
   Bournemouth (July 1960), Tranmere Rovers (February 1961), Port Vale (July
   1968), Wigan Athletic (June 1971, later coach), Tranmere Rovers (coach,
   1973; manager, May 1975–September 1980), Rochdale (coach, October
   1980), Northwich Victoria (manager until May 1985), Caernarfon Town
   (manager, July 1985), Tranmere Rovers (manager, April 1987–May 1996;
   then a director at Prenton Park)
Johnny King made his Everton debut against Preston in October 1957 while
still a teenager. He spent seven years at Goodison, having his best spell in the
side during 1959–60 with a run of 27 successive outings at right-half. A
tenacious defender, he loved his football and played with chickenpox for Port
Vale against Swansea in October 1969, helping the Valiants gain promotion
from the Fourth Division that season. He made over 250 appearances as a player
with Tranmere, helping them win promotion in 1967 before working wonders
as their manager. First, in 1976, he took Rovers into the Third Division, steered
them to runners-up spot in Division Four (1989) and promotion again two years
later after beating Bolton in the play-off final. A Leyland DAF Cup winner in
1990 and runner-up in the same competition the following season, he saw
Rovers lose 4–3 to Swindon in the 1993 First Division play-offs. At non-
League level he led Northwich to victory in the FA Trophy final of 1984, having
finished second the year before. All told, King spent 25 years with Tranmere (as
a player, coach, manager and director).

KIRBY, GEORGE C.R.
Centre-forward: 27 apps, 9 goals
Born: Liverpool, 20 December 1933 – *Died*: 24 March 2000
Career: Longwen Juniors, EVERTON (amateur, April 1949; professional, June
   1952), Sheffield Wednesday (March 1959), Plymouth Argyle (January
   1960), Southampton (£17,000, September 1962), Coventry City (£12,000,
   March 1964), Swansea Town (October 1964), Walsall (May 1965), New York
   Generals/USA (June 1967), Brentford (October 1968–May 1969),
   Worcester City (manager, June 1969), Halifax Town (manager, July
   1970–August 1971), Watford (manager, August 1971–May 1973),
   Akranes/Iceland (coach/manager, mid-1970s), Halifax Town (manager,
   November 1978–June 1981); also coach in Kuwait, Indonesia and Saudi
   Arabia; later an insurance broker in England
George Kirby, regarded by Leeds and England centre-half Jack Charlton as the
hardest player he ever faced, was a bustling, robust 6 ft tall centre-forward,

strong and fearless who gave defenders plenty to think about throughout his nomadic career. He entered League football in April 1956 – seven years after joining Everton – making his debut against Sheffield United. He netted his first goal for the Blues against Wolves the following September. After averaging a goal every three games he moved to Hillsborough and thereafter roamed the country, scoring for virtually every club he served. He eventually retired with a League record of 119 goals in 309 games, having had his best set of figures with Plymouth (38 strikes in 93 outings). He scored a hat-trick in just four minutes for Southampton against Middlesbrough in November 1962.

KIRKWOOD, DAVID

Right-half/inside-right/outside-right: 38 apps, 2 goals
Born: Liverpool, *circa* 1868 – Deceased
Career: EVERTON (September 1889), Broxburn (July 1891), EVERTON (October 1891), Liverpool Caledonian (March 1892)
David Kirkwood, strong and athletic, had two spells with Everton, making his League debut against Bolton in September 1889. Preferring the right-half position, he actually filled four different roles for the Blues, playing his final game in a 5–1 defeat at Wolves in November 1891.

KIRSOPP, WILLIAM HENRY JAMES

Inside-right: 63 apps, 29 goals
Born: Liverpool, 21 April 1892 – *Died*: 1978
Career: Wallasey Borough, EVERTON (April 1914), Bury (£400, May 1921), Grimsby Town (£50, September 1922), New Brighton (June 1923), Crystal Palace (trialist, July–August 1924; retired, injured, September 1924)
A League championship-winner with Everton in 1915 (claiming nine goals in 16 outings), inside-right Bill Kirsopp was a skilful footballer with an eye for the scoring opportunity. During his career he netted 32 times in 98 League games and played for New Brighton in their first League campaign of 1923–24.

KIRWAN, JOHN H.

Outside-left: 26 apps, 5 goals
Born: Wicklow, Ireland, 1879 – *Died*: 9 January 1959
Career: Southport, EVERTON (July 1898), Tottenham Hotspur (July 1899), Chelsea (May 1905), Clyde (May 1908), Leyton (July 1909), Holland (coach, September 1910), Livorno/Italy (coach, 1923–24)
Choosing Everton instead of Blackburn and replacing John Cameron (sold to Spurs), John Kirwan, an out-and-out winger with good pace and neat skills, made his League debut for the Blues at Preston in September 1898. He had a fine season at Goodison before teaming up with Cameron at White Hart Lane, helping Spurs win the Southern League title in 1900. An FA Cup winner the following year, he gained 17 full caps for Ireland, the first against Wales in February 1900, the last against Scotland in 1909.

KITCHEN, GEORGE WILLIAM
Goalkeeper: 90 apps
Born: Fairfield, Derbyshire, April 1876 – *Died*: Hampshire, *circa* 1965
Career: Buxton, Stockport County (August 1897), EVERTON (August 1901),
West Ham United (August 1905), Southampton (October 1912), Boscombe
FC (May 1914–April 1915); did not play after the First World War; became
golf professional at Bournemouth Golf Club (1912), having taken up the
sport as an Everton player; later a doorman at Lee Green Working Men's
Club
A former England trialist, George Kitchen, at 6 ft 1 in. tall and 13 st. in weight,
was the perfect build for a goalkeeper. He instilled confidence in his defence and
took over between the posts from Willie Muir at Goodison Park, making his
Everton debut against Bury in October 1901. He made 205 appearances for
West Ham, scoring six penalties, the first on his debut against Swindon.

LABONE, BRIAN
Centre-half: 534 apps, 2 goals
Born: Liverpool, 23 January 1940
Career: Liverpool Collegiate School, EVERTON (amateur, June 1955;
professional, July 1957; retired June 1972); insurance business; EVERTON
(Commercial Department, mid-1970s)
Brian Labone was described by his manager Harry Catterick as 'the last of the
Corinthians'. A dominant figure at the heart of the Everton defence for many
years, being strong, aggressive and powerful in the air, he was an automatic
choice from 1959 to 1970, appearing in over 530 games. He gained two League
championship medals in 1963 (40 games) and 1970 (34 outings), collected an
FA Cup-winner's medal (1966) and a runner's-up prize (1968). He made his
League debut against Birmingham in March 1958, replacing Tommy Jones, and
gained a regular place in the side a year later. Capped 26 times by England
(1962–70), Labone also played in seven Under-23 internationals and was a
member of the 1970 World Cup squad. One of the Blues' finest-ever defenders,
his appearance-tally is the best by an outfield player and the second highest for
the club behind Neville Southall. He made 19 European appearances for
Everton, sharing that record with Colin Harvey.

LACEY, WILLIAM
Half-back/forward: 40 apps, 11 goals
Born: Wexford, Ireland, 24 September 1889 – *Died*: 30 May 1969
Career: Shelbourne, EVERTON (February 1909), Liverpool (February 1912
together with Tom Gracie for Harold Uren), New Brighton (June 1924),
Shelbourne (May 1925), Cork Bohemians (1927; retired 1931)
Bill Lacey was a great footballing character and, as someone once wrote, 'a
rounded, lovable personality whose jutting chin was the delight of the
cartoonists'. His career spanned 20 years, during which time he appeared in over
350 games for both Liverpool clubs and in Ireland. The first player to be capped
at full international level with both Liverpool clubs, he won 23 caps in all

between 1909 and 1925 – the first ten with Everton. Able to play in any forward position, he made his debut as leader of the Blues' attack against Bradford City in April 1909. He netted 18 goals in 229 games for Liverpool.

LANGLEY, KEVIN JAMES
Midfield: 22+1 apps, 3 goals
Born: St Helens, 24 May 1964
Career: Wigan Athletic (apprentice, June 1980; professional, May 1982), EVERTON (£100,000, July 1986), Manchester City (£150,000, August 1987), Chester City (loan, January–February 1988), Birmingham City (March 1988), Wigan Athletic (£50,000, September 1990), Halifax Town (August 1994), Bangor City

The career of Kevin Langley, a tall, elegant and hard-working midfielder, spanned 14 years and in that time he amassed over 400 appearances. He played in the Charity Shield game for Everton against Liverpool (1–1) a few weeks after collecting a runner's-up medal with Wigan in the final of the FRT at Wembley. He later helped Bangor win the League of Wales title (1995). Langley earned a high reputation at Springfield Park before moving to Goodison, making his League debut for the Blues against Nottingham Forest a week after that Charity Shield clash. He was perhaps a shade out of his depth in the First Division.

LATCHFORD, ROBERT DENNIS
Centre-forward: 286+3 apps, 138 goals
Born: King's Heath, Birmingham, 18 January 1951
Career: Brandwood School (King's Heath), Birmingham and Warwickshire County Schools, Birmingham City (apprentice, May 1966; professional, August 1968), EVERTON (£350,000 in a deal involving Howard Kendall and Archie Styles, February 1974), Swansea City (£125,000, July 1981), NAC Breda/Holland (free, July 1984), Coventry City (December 1984), Lincoln City (July 1985), Newport County (loan, January–May 1986), Merthyr Tydfil (August 1986); director of Alvechurch; Birmingham City (community office, late 1990s; then coach 1999–2000); now lives in Austria

Bob Latchford was a swashbuckling striker, the main target man for Birmingham for four years before joining Everton. A huge favourite with the fans wherever he played, he initially partnered Trevor Francis and Bob Hatton at Birmingham before doing the business up front at Everton. Strong, powerful, a sound header of the ball, he could shoot with both feet and scored some cracking goals during his career, including 84 for Birmingham. He helped the Midland club finish runners-up in the Youth Cup final, reach the semi-finals of the FA Cup (1975) and win promotion to the First Division.

Taking over from Joe Royle, Latchford scored seven times in his first 13 games for Everton, but failed to find the net on his debut against West Ham in February 1974. In 1977–78, he was presented with a cheque for £10,000 by a national newspaper after becoming the first player to score 30 goals in Division One for six years, clinching the money with a brace in the last match of the season against Chelsea. He became Everton's highest post-war scorer, finishing as the club's top marksman five seasons running (1974–79).

He enjoyed mixed fortunes at Swansea but still managed to tuck away 32 goals in 1982–83. With Merthyr he gained a Welsh Cup-winner's medal (1987) and during an excellent career Latchford – regarded as one of Everton's greatest heroes – netted over 280 goals in more than 650 appearances. Capped 12 times by England at senior level, he also played in six Under-23 and four youth internationals and represented the Football League once. Latchford's brothers, Dave (Birmingham) and Peter (WBA and Celtic) were both goalkeepers.

LATTA, ALEX
Outside-right: 148 apps, 70 goals
Born: Dumbarton, 1 September 1867 – *Died*: 25 August 1928
Career: Dumbarton Athletic (1882), EVERTON (August 1889; retired May 1896); later ran his own yacht-making business and worked for 20 years as manager of a boat-building yard
A non-smoker and teetotaller, Alex Latta was a tall, clever winger with pace and strong shot. His combination play with Alec Brady was one of the outstanding features of Everton's performances during their League championship-winning season of 1890–91. Capped twice by Scotland (against England and Wales), he also played for the Blues in the 1893 FA Cup final and made his debut against Blackburn in September 1889. He scored six hat-tricks for Everton.

LAVERICK, ROBERT
Outside-left: 23 apps, 6 goals
Born: Castle Eden, County Durham, 11 June 1938
Career: Chelsea (amateur, June 1953; professional, June 1955), EVERTON (February 1959), Brighton and Hove Albion (June 1960), Coventry City (July 1962–April 1963)
After entering League football with Chelsea, England youth international Bobby Laverick enhanced his career with Everton, for whom he made a scoring debut in a 3–3 draw with WBA in February 1959. Leaving Goodison after the arrival of Tommy Ring, he registered 20 goals in 63 League outings for Brighton.

LAWSON, DAVID
Goalkeeper: 152 apps
Born: Wallsend, 22 December 1947
Career: Newcastle United (apprentice, April 1964; professional, April 1966), Shrewsbury Town (trialist), Bradford Park Avenue (October 1967), Huddersfield Town (May 1969), EVERTON (June 1972), Luton Town (October 1978), Stockport County (March 1979–May 1981); now a postmaster
In his 17-year career David Lawson amassed over 300 appearances, making 124

and 106 in the League for Everton and Stockport respectively. Agile, a fine shot-stopper, he failed to make the grade at Newcastle, spent a season and a half with Bradford and then did extremely well at Leeds Road before a record transfer fee for a goalkeeper took him to Goodison, where he eventually took over from Gordon West. He made his Blues' debut at Norwich in August 1972 and held his place for two seasons before giving way to Dai Davies, only to bounce back in the late 1970s. A League Cup runner-up in 1977, Lawson moved on after George Wood had kept him out of the side in 1977–78.

LAWTON, THOMAS

Centre-forward: 95 apps, 70 goals
Born: Bolton, 6 October 1919 – *Died*: Nottingham, November 1996
Career: Tonge Moor Council, Castle Hill and Foulds Road Schools (Bolton), Bolton and Lancashire Boys, Bolton Wanderers (amateur), Sheffield Wednesday (amateur), Hayes Athletic, Rossendale United, Burnley (amateur, May 1935; professional, October 1936), EVERTON (£6,500, December 1936), Chelsea (£11,000, November 1945), Notts County (£20,000, November 1947), Brentford (March 1952), Arsenal (£10,000 plus James Robertson, September 1953), Kettering Town (£1,000, player–manager, February 1956), Notts County (manager, May 1957–July 1958); Kettering Town (manager, November 1963–April 1964; then director), Notts County (coach and chief scout, October 1968–April 1970); later a publican in Lowdham, Notts; lived in Nottingham until his death

Having notched 570 goals in three seasons of Burnley schools football, Tommy Lawton became the youngest-ever player to score a League hat-trick when at the age of 17 years, 4 days he netted three times for Burnley against Spurs in October 1936 – this being only his fifth game for the Clarets. Then, as an Everton player, he was 17 years, 362 days old when he hit the target against Liverpool in October 1937 – and to this day remains as the youngest 'derby' scorer. The following season (1938–39) he finished up as the Blues' top marksman with 34 goals in 38 games when the League title was won.

Ideally built for a centre-forward, Lawton was a master in the air, brilliant on the ground, a constant threat to defenders and was universally regarded (by players, managers and coaches alike) as one of the greatest of his era – despite suffering from flat feet.

His extraordinary promise as a youngster was completely realised as he went on to score 232 goals in 390 League games up to 1956.

He was 17 years, 130 days old (the youngest prior to Wayne Rooney) when he made his Everton debut in a 7–2 away defeat at Wolves in February 1937. He went on to register a magnificent record for the Blues: 222 goals in 209 first-team matches, including 152 in 114 Second World War fixtures. He also claimed 22 goals in 23 outings for England, including two four-timers against Holland and Portugal in 1946 and 1947 respectively, and he struck 24 times in 23 wartime internationals. He represented the Football League on three occasions and was a Third Division (S) winner with Notts County in 1950. Lawton had a testimonial match at Goodison Park in November 1972. His

£20,000 transfer fee from Chelsea to Notts County was a record for a Third Division club.

LEE, JOHN
Left-back: 2 apps
Born: *circa* 1880 – Deceased
Career: EVERTON (season 1902–03)
Reserve Jack Lee made the first of his two appearances for the Blues at left flank against WBA in September 1902, when he partnered Walter Balmer in a 2–1 defeat.

LEEDER, FREDERICK
Left-back: 1 app.
Born: Seaton Delaval, 15 September 1936
Career: Seaton Delaval, EVERTON (professional, March 1955), Darlington (July 1958), Southport (July 1960–May 1962)
Fred Leeder was reserve at Everton and, owing to the form of Jimmy Lindsay, was given just one game, at Chelsea in January 1958. He later made 21 and 63 League appearances for Darlington and Southport respectively.

LELLO, CYRIL FRANK
Inside-left/wing-half: 254 apps, 9 goals
Born: Ludlow, 24 February 1920
Career: Shrewsbury Town, EVERTON (September 1947), Rochdale (November 1956–April 1957)
Cyril Lello commenced his serious football career with Shrewsbury in the Birmingham and District League. After moving to Goodison Park, he bided his time in the reserves before making his League debut (at inside-left) three days ahead of his 28th birthday against Wolves in February 1948. During the second half of the following season he established himself at left-half, holding his place for 18 months. However, he didn't get a first-team call at all in 1950–51, as Peter Farrell and Jackie Grant bedded themselves in the wing-half positions. However, he remained loyal to the club and reclaimed his place in the side in 1952, going on to amass over 250 appearances before departing. Lello could 'kill' a ball dead; he placed his passes with precision and was a terrier for work.

LEWIS, GWYNFOR
Centre-forward: 10 apps, 6 goals
Born: Bangor, Wales, 22 April 1931 – *Died*: 1992
Career: EVERTON (juniors, May 1946; professional, May 1948), Rochdale (June 1956), Chesterfield (February 1957–May 1961)
Gwyn Lewis spent ten years with Everton, although his National Service accounted for one-fifth of that time. Acting in the main as reserve to at least half-a-dozen other potential goalscoring forwards, he was a fine marksman who never let the side down. He made his League debut against Bury in March 1952 and scored twice in his second game a year later against Notts County. After

leaving Goodison, he netted 11 goals in 27 League outings for Rochdale and 58 in 123 starts for Chesterfield.

LEWIS, THOMAS HEWITT
Left-half: 1 app.
Born: Ellesmere Port, 11 October 1909 – Deceased
Career: EVERTON (June 1927), Wrexham (June 1930), Bradford Park Avenue (June 1933), Blackpool (December 1938); did not play after the Second World War

After just one League game for Everton – at left-half against Newcastle on the last day of the 1928–29 season – Tom Lewis went on to give both Wrexham and Bradford superb service. Switching to outside-left, he hit 48 goals in 123 games in three seasons for Wrexham, gaining a Welsh Cup-winner's medal in 1931 and then netted 69 goals in 200 games for Park Avenue. His son, Kevin, played for Liverpool and scored in the Merseyside 'derby' in September 1962.

LEWIS, WILLIAM
Centre-forward: 3 apps, 1 goal
Born: Bangor, Wales, 1864 – *Died*: Manchester 1935
Career: Bangor Rovers, Bangor (1882), EVERTON (August 1888), Bangor (January–October 1889), Crewe Alexandra (November 1889), Chester (December 1892), Manchester City (September 1896), Chester (September 1897–May 1898); later licensee of the Duke of York (Chester)

Bill Lewis played in Everton's first-ever League game against Accrington on 8 September 1888. A stonemason and the first professional footballer produced by Bangor, he was known as 'Billy Cae Top' and invariably took the honours in the annual athletics competitions. He signed for Everton in anticipation of making it big time in the Football League. That didn't happen and after three outings he returned to Bangor, who, during the 1880s, were regarded as one of the best clubs in Wales and indeed were the first to win the Welsh Cup (1889). He was chosen to play for Wales against England in 1885 – the first of 27 appearances he made for his country up to 1898 (12 goals scored). In fact, he held the record for most Welsh caps gained for a number of years, finally overhauled by Billy Meredith, whom he played alongside at Manchester City. The FAW assessment of Lewis in 1891 described as him as being 'a speedy forward and very clever – does not use sufficient judgment'. Lewis also represented the Northern Welsh FA (against Liverpool in 1884) and appeared for his country in two unofficial Test matches against the Canadian tourists in 1891.

LEYFIELD, CHARLES
Winger: 38 apps, 13 goals
Born: Chester, 30 October 1911 – *Died*: 1982
Career: Chester junior football, EVERTON (April 1934), Sheffield United (£2,500, July 1937), Doncaster Rovers (October 1938); did not play after the Second World War

Sturdy, two-footed, Charlie Leyfield was a useful asset to the Everton forward-line, scoring on his debut from the right flank against Leicester in August 1934. He then netted in his next two outings, and was the last Everton player to score in his first three senior games for the club. He switched to the right wing the following season, holding his place in the side until replaced by Torry Gillick.

LEYLAND, HARRY KENNETH

Goalkeeper: 40 apps
Born: Liverpool, 12 May 1930
Career: EVERTON (amateur, June 1946; professional, August 1950), Blackburn Rovers (August 1956), Tranmere Rovers (March 1961–May 1967), Wigan Athletic (player–manager, July 1967–May 1968)

After being released by Everton, Harry Leyland was all set to join Ron Saunders at Tonbridge. But out of the blue, on the eve of the 1956–57 campaign, Blackburn manager Johnny Carey swooped to sign him as a replacement for Reg Elvy. Small and stocky, Leyland made his debut for the Blues in September 1951 against Leicester, taking over from Ted Sagar. He held his place for a while before Jimmy O'Neill took over, leaving Leyland to ponder his future. He came back for a decent spell during the first half of 1953–54 but then languished in the reserves until his departure. He made 188 appearances for Blackburn, helping them gain promotion to the First Division in 1958 and finish FA Cup runners-up two years later. He made a further 180 League appearances for Tranmere.

LIEVESLEY, WALTER

Centre-half: 5 apps
Born: Haydock, *circa* 1888 – Deceased
Career: Haydock Colliery, EVERTON (August 1919), Reading (May 1920)

A post-First World War signing by Everton, Walter Lievesley spent only one season at Goodison Park, deputising for Tom Fleetwood and Louis Weller. He made his debut against Sheffield United in March 1920. (Some reference books spell this player's surname as Leivesley.)

LILL, MICHAEL JAMES

Winger: 34 apps, 12 goals
Born: Barking, 3 August 1936
Career: Storey Athletic, Wolverhampton Wanderers (professional, June 1954), Everton (February 1960), Plymouth Argyle (June 1962), Portsmouth (March 1963–May 1965), Guildford (1965–66), Germiston Callies/South Africa (1967–68)

Micky Lill, an England youth international, was brought up with three of the country's finest wingers at Wolves – Norman Deeley, Johnny Hancocks and Jimmy Mullen. He learnt an awful lot from those England internationals but was limited to just 30 League outings during his six years at Molineux. Fast and direct with a strong right-foot shot, he made his debut for Everton at Arsenal in February 1960 but with Billy Bingham and Derek Temple around, his opportunities for first-team football were limited. He made a further 60 League appearances while serving with Plymouth and Portsmouth and helped Germiston Callies escape relegation by scoring 13 goals in 13 games. He is still living and working in South Africa, employed as a physical education teacher at a state school near Johannesburg.

LIMPAR, ANDERS ERIK
Winger: 64+18 apps, 6 goals
Born: Sweden, 24 August 1965
Career: Cremonese/Italy, Arsenal (£1m, July 1990), EVERTON (£1.6m, March 1994), Birmingham City (£100,000, January–May 1997); now a football agent

After making over 100 appearances for Arsenal and gaining a League championship medal, Swedish international Anders Limpar joined Everton and quickly added FA Cup and Charity Shield winner's medals to his collection. Capped 69 times by his country, including appearances in the 1994 World Cup finals, he was a crowd-pleasing winger with dash and skill. Equally at home on either flank, he was always willing to take on a defender and packed a powerful shot, mainly with his right foot. He made his debut for the Blues against Spurs in March 1994 and spent almost three years at Goodison, moving on after manager Joe Royle had decided to play with one winger (Andrei Kanchelskis).

LINDEROTH, TOBIAS
Midfield: 33+13 apps, 1 goal
Born: Marseilles, France, 21 April 1979
Career: Hasselholm/Sweden (1995), Elfsborg/Sweden (April 1996), Stabaek FC/Norway (August 1999), EVERTON (£2.5m, February 2002), FC Copenhagen/Denmark (£1.3m, August 2004)

A steady, technically sound central midfielder, Tobias Linderoth had already won 22 Under-21 and 24 full caps for Sweden (due to his Swedish parentage) before joining Everton, for whom he made his debut as a substitute against Ipswich in February 2002. He then went with his country to the 2002 World Cup finals (adding another cap to his collection) but struggled with injuries throughout 2002–03, which restricted his first-team outings to just six. He made 125 League appearances in Scandinavian football before moving to Goodison Park. Now a senior member of the Swedish national team, he played in Euro 2004 and has over 30 full caps to his name. His father played for Sweden in the 1978 World Cup finals in Argentina.

LINDLEY, WILLIAM MAURICE
Half-back: 54 apps
Born: Keighley, 5 December 1915 – *Died*: 1994
Career: Keighley Town, EVERTON (amateur, 1934; professional, March 1936), Swindon Town (August 1951; retired March 1952)

Owing to the Second World War, centre-half Maurice Lindley had to wait 13 years before making his League debut for Everton against Derby in September 1947. In the late 1930s he had been reserve to Cliff Britton, Charlie Gee, Tommy Jones and Joe Mercer and then during the hostilities made 39 first-team appearances, mainly as a centre-half, his favoured position. Owing to a tedious knee injury, he failed to get a game with Swindon and retired at the age of 36.

LINDSAY, JOHN SMITH
Full-back: 115 apps, 2 goals
Born: Auchinleck, 8 August 1924
Career: Glasgow Rangers, EVERTON (March 1951), Worcester City (briefly, 1955), Bury (May 1956–April 1957)
A well-built, strong-kicking full-back never afraid to rough it with his opponents, Jock Lindsay made 22 appearances for Rangers before moving to Everton, initially as cover for George Rankin, whom he replaced in the first team on a regular basis at the start of 1951–52. He held his place in the Blues' defence for three years before fracturing his leg in 1954 and being replaced by Don Donovan, who was switched from right to left to let in Eric Moore. Lindsay made his debut for the Blues in a 3–0 defeat at Manchester United in March 1951.

LINDSAY, WILLIAM ARCHIBALD
Full-back: 9 apps
Born: Stockton-on-Tees, 10 December 1872 – *Died*: 27 February 1933
Career: Stockton St John's (1888), Stockton Town (1888), EVERTON (September 1893), Grimsby Town (May 1894), Newcastle United (February 1898), Luton Town (May 1900), Watford (September 1903), Luton Town (April 1907), Hitchin Town (September 1907–May 1909)
Bill Lindsay failed to establish himself at Goodison Park. A big kicking, tenacious defender, reliable and honest, difficult to circumvent, he was once described as being 'one of the most powerful backs of his day and [it is] questionable if there had ever been a faster defender of his build'. He made his debut for Everton against Sheffield Wednesday in November 1893 and, as captain, made 106 appearances for Grimsby. His younger brother, James Lindsay, was an FA Cup winner with Bury.

LINEKER, GARY, OBE
Striker: 57 apps, 40 goals
Born: Leicester, 30 November 1960
Career: Leicester City (apprentice, July 1977; professional, December 1978), EVERTON (£800,000 plus £250,000 from any subsequent transfer, June 1985), CF Barcelona/Spain (£2.75m, July 1986), Tottenham Hotspur (£1.2m, June 1989), Grampas 8 Nagoya/Japan (£946,000, November 1991; retired April 1994); now BBC sports presenter
Gary Lineker was technically Everton's first seven-figure signing, having already scored 103 goals in 216 matches for Leicester, whom he helped win promotion

from the Second Division in 1983. A darting striker, keen, alert, with an eye for goal, he won the first of his subsequent 80 England caps in 1984 (at Leicester) and went on to net 48 international goals, just one short of Bobby Charlton's all-time record.

Signed by Howard Kendall, he spent just the one season at Goodison Park, netting 40 goals, 30 in the League – a tremendous return as Everton finished runners-up in the League. His efforts at Wembley in the FA Cup final, however, were secondary as Liverpool won 3–1. He made his debut for Everton in the Charity Shield victory over Manchester United and his League baptism followed, away at his former club Leicester (lost 3–1). At the end of that season he was voted both the PFA and the FWA 'Player of the Year'.

After being snapped up by Terry Venables, Lineker did the business in Spain, helping Barcelona win the Spanish Cup in 1988 and the European Cup-Winners' Cup the following season when he played on the wing for coach Johan Cruyff. This followed some lacklustre performances for his country in the European Championships when he struggled to shake off a bout of hepatitis. In 1989, Venables, by now in charge at White Hart Lane, enticed Lineker to Spurs, and he quickly regained full fitness and his appetite for goals! He netted 80 in 138 competitive matches for the London club and collected an FA Cup-winner's medal in 1991 despite missing a penalty in the final against Nottingham Forest. Awarded the OBE in the 1992 New Year's Honours List, he did very well in Japan before announcing his retirement at the age of 33. Lineker, a fine cricketer and member of the MCC, scored a century for Leicestershire's 2nd XI.

LIVINGSTONE, ARCHIBALD

Inside-forward: 4 apps, 2 goals
Born: Pencaitland, Lothian, 15 November 1915 – *Died*: 16 August 1961
Career: Ormiston Primrose, Dundee (1933), Newcastle United (£35, March
    1935); guest for Rochdale (1939–42), Leeds United (1941–42), York City
    (1942–43), Liverpool (1942–43), Wrexham (1942–45), Middlesbrough
    (1942–45), Accrington Stanley (1944–45), Brentford (1944–45), Fulham
    (1944–45); EVERTON (May 1946), Southport (June 1947), Glenavon
    (player–manager, July 1948), Worksop, Dundee (retired 1952)
Archie Livingstone, a highly talented footballer, could occupy both inside forward positions as well as centre-forward. Small in stature, he was a tricky customer, possessed an exciting body swerve, which he used to good effect, and was not afraid to battle it out with the many robust defenders he came up against. Unfortunately, his best football was played away from Goodison Park, for he failed to settle on Merseyside. He made his debut for Everton against Aston Villa in September 1946 and during his career appeared in only 83 League games. When guesting for Wrexham he scored seven goals in one Regional match against Tranmere.

LIVINGSTONE, DUGALD
Full-back: 100 apps
Born: Alexandria, Dumbarton, Scotland, 25 February 1898 – *Died*: Marlow, Bucks, 15 January 1981
Career: Celtic (1915), EVERTON (April 1921), Plymouth Argyle (February 1926), Aberdeen (August 1927), Tranmere Rovers (June 1930), Jersey (briefly, 1933; retired same year), Exeter City (trainer, 1935), Sheffield United (trainer 1936), Sparta Rotterdam/Holland (manager, 1949), Republic of Ireland (national manager, 1951), Belgium (national manager, 1953), Newcastle United (manager, December 1954–January 1956), Fulham (manager, January 1956–May 1958), Chesterfield (manager, May 1958–59)
Duggie Livingstone was an unflappable, happy-go-lucky character who failed to establish himself at Celtic but went on to appear in over 300 matches for his other four clubs, including 81 for Aberdeen and 88 for Tranmere. Cool and calculated, a lack of speed let him down on occasions and probably prevented him from representing Scotland. He made his League debut for Everton against Manchester United in September 1921 and played his last game for the club against Liverpool in February 1926. As a manager, his best efforts came at Newcastle, whom he led to FA Cup glory in 1955. He left St James's Park after a furious row with the chairman and directors.

Prior to that, he was a highly respected trainer at Bramall Lane, serving the Blades for 13 years, did reasonably well with the Republic of Ireland and took Belgium to the 1954 World Cup finals. He left Fulham after they had lost to Manchester United in the FA Cup semi-final replay. He was a football supporter right up until his death.

LLEWELLYN, HERBERT ARTHUR
Centre-forward: 11 apps, 2 goals
Born: Golborne, 5 February 1939
Career: EVERTON (amateur, April 1954; professional, May 1956), Crewe Alexandra (£3,000, July 1958), Port Vale (£7,000, November 1960), Northampton Town (£7,000, February 1963), Walsall (February 1964), Wigan Athletic (1965–66)
England youth international Bert Llewellyn was only 17 years, 200 days old when he scored on his League debut for Everton against Blackpool in August 1956. After leaving Goodison, he developed into a bustling centre-forward, always creating problems in and around the penalty area. During his career he netted over 120 goals, 50 for Port Vale.

LOCHHEAD, ALEXANDER
Wing-half: 6 apps
Born: Johnstone, Renfrewshire, Scotland, 12 May 1866 – Deceased
Career: Arthurlie, Third Lanark, EVERTON (March 1891), Third Lanark (December 1891)
A worthy member of Third Lanark's Scottish Cup-winning side of 1899, appreciative of demands in both defence and attack, dour wing-half Alex

Lochhead made the first of his six League appearances for the Blues against Burnley in March 1891, replacing David Kirkwood.

LODGE, PAUL
Midfield: 31+4 apps
Born: Liverpool, 13 February 1961
Career: EVERTON (apprentice, April 1977; professional, February 1979), Wigan Athletic (loan, August–September 1982), Rotherham United (loan, January 1983), Preston North End (February 1983), Bolton Wanderers (July 1984), Port Vale (loan, November–December 1984), Stockport County (March–May 1985), Southport (1986)

Paul Lodge, a 'playmaker' on the left of midfield, made over 100 senior appearances during his career. He looked the part at times with Everton, for whom he made his League debut as a substitute against Aston Villa in February 1981. However, with so much talent around, he moved on accordingly.

LOWE, HENRY
Right-back: 5 apps
Born: Skelmersdale, 18 February 1907 – *Died*: Skelmersdale 1975
Career: Skelmersdale Mission, Southport (April 1927), EVERTON (August 1929), Preston North End (December 1932), Swindon Town (March 1939), Skelmersdale United; later returned to the shoe trade

Signed as cover for Ben Williams, Harry Lowe worked in a boot and shoe factory while developing his football. After two excellent seasons with Southport (75 appearances), he made his debut for Everton against Oldham in December 1930, setting up one of Dixie Dean's four goals in a thrilling 6–4 win. A cool, methodical player, he possessed a strong kick and gave opposing forwards little or no room in which to move. He remained loyal to the club for over three years before making 182 League appearances for Preston, helping the Lillywhites gain promotion to the First Division in 1934 and reach the FA Cup final in 1937.

LYONS, MICHAEL
Defender: 434+26 apps, 39 goals
Born: Croxteth, Liverpool, 8 December 1951
Career: EVERTON (apprentice, April 1968; professional, July 1969), Sheffield Wednesday (August 1982), Grimsby Town (player–coach, November 1985; sacked July 1987), EVERTON (reserve-team coach, July 1987–November 1990), Wigan Athletic (first-team coach, 1991)

Mike Lyons – 'Mr Everton' to the supporters – gave the club wonderful service for over 14 years, during which time he amassed 460 appearances, 389 in the First Division. He never gave less than 100 per cent and some said he would have run through a brick wall if need be, such was his determination and willpower as a player. After being groomed in the forward-line for the youth and reserve sides, he was then demoted to the 'A' team when David Johnson appeared on the scene. It was during this period that coach Tommy Casey switched him to the defence. He never looked back, making his League debut against Nottingham Forest in March 1971, when he donned the number six shirt and played alongside Brian Labone at the back. His career blossomed as the games rolled by. He remained first choice for the next ten years, playing in the 1977 League Cup final and in two FA Cup semi-finals. He eventually severed his ties at Goodison Park in 1982 by moving to Hillsborough, subsequently helping Wednesday gain promotion to the First Division. He was dismissed from his post as Everton's reserve-team coach when Howard Kendall returned to the club as manager. Lyons gained international honours for England at 'B' and Under-23 levels, collecting five caps in the latter category.

MACONNACHIE, JOHN SMITH
Left-back: 270 apps, 7 goals
Born: Aberdeen, 8 May 1888 – Deceased
Career: Hibernian, EVERTON (April 1907), Swindon Town (August 1920)
A cool and polished defender, John Maconnachie made his debut for Everton at centre-half against Preston at Goodison Park in September 1907 and immediately the fans knew they had got a class act. He slowly but surely established himself in the side and settled down at left-back, from where he produced some outstanding performances. An ever-present in 1908–09, he helped the Blues win the League title in 1915 and spent 20 years with the club, making 29 appearances during the First World War. One of the most skilful defenders ever to don an Everton shirt, Maconnachie was a confident footballer, unruffled with an authoritative approach to the game, often playing his way out of trouble rather than giving the ball an almighty heave-to downfield.

McBAIN, NEIL
Half-back: 103 apps, 1 goal
Born: Campbeltown, Argyllshire, 15 November 1895 – *Died*: 13 May 1974
Career: Campbeltown Academicals, Hamilton Academical (trial), Ayr United (July 1914), guest for Portsmouth and Southampton during the First World War, Manchester United (£5,000, November 1921), EVERTON (£4,000, January 1923), St Johnstone (£1,000, July 1926), Liverpool (March 1928), Watford (November 1928; player–manager, May 1929; manager, July 1931–May 1937), Ayr United (manager, 1937–38), Luton Town (manager, June 1938–June 1939), New Brighton (secretary–manager, June 1946), Leyton Orient (assistant manager, February 1948; manager, April 1948–May 1949), Estudiantes de la Plata/Argentina (coach, August 1949), Ayr United (manager, 1955–56), Watford (manager, August 1956–February 1959), Ayr United (manager, January 1963–May 1964); also scout for Mansfield Town, Watford, EVERTON and Chelsea
Neil McBain had toured Canada and the USA with Scotland in 1921 and had appeared in 43 games for Manchester United before transferring to Everton. He made his debut for the Blues against Chelsea in February 1923 just 48 hours after signing and did exceptionally well with the club. Strong in the air and decisive and combative on the ground, he won his first full cap (against England) while at Old

Trafford but after playing out of position as a forward, he left to join Everton, with whom he collected two more caps. On 15 March 1947, as New Brighton's secretary–manager, McBain came out of retirement to assist his club in an emergency, appearing in goal in a Third Division (N) game against Hartlepools, aged 51 years, four months – a League record, which still stands today. He made his senior debut 32 years earlier for Ayr and played throughout both world wars. McBain was also a fine billiards player who achieved a record break of 157.

McBRIDE, BRIAN
Striker: 7+1 apps, 4 goals
Born: Arlington Heights, USA, 19 June 1972
Career: St Louis University/USA (1989), VfL Wolfsburg/Germany (August 1994), Columbus Crew/USA (September 1996), Preston North End (loan, September–November 2000), EVERTON (loan, February–March 2003), Fulham (January 2004)
Everton boss David Moyes signed USA international Brian McBride (over 70 caps gained at 2004) on a three-month loan deal, having previously recruited him while boss at Preston. He made an immediate impact, scoring on his debut at Spurs and then netting twice on his home debut shortly afterwards against Sunderland. Honest, full of commitment and endeavour, unfortunately he failed to agree on a permanent move to Everton (with Major League Soccer, who own his contract) and went back to the States, only to return to England and score again on his debut for Fulham against Spurs.

McBRIDE, JOSEPH
Winger/Midfield: 70 apps, 11 goals
Born: Glasgow, 17 August 1960
Career: EVERTON (apprentice, September 1976; professional, August 1978), Rotherham United (August 1982), Oldham Athletic (£45,000, September 1983), Hibernian (£20,000, January 1985)
A Scottish schoolboy international, Joe McBride was on the losing side for Everton in the 1977 Youth Cup final. A player with a fine footballing pedigree (his father, Joe McBride, twice capped by Scotland, played for Celtic, Clyde, Dunfermline, Hibs, Kilmarnock, Luton, Motherwell and Partick), he was a willing competitor, whose career in England realised 138 League appearances and 26 goals. He scored on his debut for Everton against Bolton in December 1979 and two years later gained an Under-21 cap against Denmark.

McCALL, ANDREW STUART MURRAY
Midfield: 134+7 apps, 10 goals
Born: Leeds, 10 June 1964
Career: Bradford City (apprentice, July 1980; professional, June 1982), EVERTON (£850,000, June 1988), Glasgow Rangers (£1.2m, August 1991), Bradford City (free, June 1998), Sheffield United (free, July 2002; upgraded to player–coach, May 2003)
Stuart McCall was the first substitute to score twice in an FA Cup final – for

Everton against Liverpool in 1989. Ian Rush equalled this feat in the same game, which the Reds won 3–2.

Energetic, inspirational, a 100 per cent grafter to the last and a great leader, McCall never admits defeat and reached the career milestone of 700 League appearances (north and south of the border) in 2003 while passing the 900 mark in all competitive matches (club and country). A Third Division championship-winner with Bradford in 1985 before joining Everton, for whom he made his debut in a 4–0 win over Newcastle in August 1988, linking up with Pat Nevin and Peter Reid in midfield. After leaving Goodison, he gained five League, three Scottish Cup and two League Cup-winner's medals with Rangers while making over 250 appearances. After returning to Yorkshire with Bradford, he then helped Sheffield United reach both the FA Cup and League Cup semi-finals and Division One play-off final in his first season at Bramall Lane. Capped 40 times by Scotland, McCall also played in two Under-21 internationals. His father, Andy McCall, played for Blackpool, Leeds and WBA.

McCAMBRIDGE, JAMES

Forward: 1 app.
Born: Larne, Northern Ireland, 6 September 1905 – Deceased
Career: Larne, Ballymena, EVERTON (September 1930), Cardiff City (December 1930), Ballymena, Bristol Rovers (August 1933), Exeter City (September 1935), Sheffield Wednesday (September 1936), Hartlepool United (January 1937), Cheltenham Town (1938–39); did not play after the Second World War

Jim McCambridge's only League game for Everton was at Bradford City in September 1930 when he deputised for Dixie Dean in a 3–0 win. A joiner by trade, his stay at Goodison Park was short-lived but after leaving he went on to become an opportunist whose goal return was quite exceptional. He netted consistently for the remainder of his career, including hauls of 50 in 95 games for Cardiff and 23 in 58 starts for Bristol Rovers. Twice capped by Northern Ireland while at Ninian Park, he played in every position except goal.

McCANN, GAVIN PETER

Midfield: 5+6 apps
Born: Blackpool, 10 January 1978
Career: EVERTON (apprentice, June 1992; professional, July 1995), Sunderland (£500,000, November 1998), Aston Villa (£2.25m, July 2003)

An England international, capped once against Spain in 2001, attacking midfielder Gavin McCann was never able to hold down a place in Everton's first team after making his debut as a substitute against Newcastle in September 1997. Just over a year later, he moved to Sunderland, for whom he made 135 appearances prior to his transfer to Villa Park, becoming manager David O'Leary's first major signing for the Birmingham-based club.

McCLURE, JOSEPH HENRY
Half-back: 34 apps, 1 goal
Born: Cockermouth, 3 November 1907 – *Died*: 1973
Career: Workington, Preston North End (briefly in 1926), Workington (seasons 1927–29), Wallsend (July 1929), EVERTON (November 1929), Brentford (June 1933), Exeter City (August 1934), Nuneaton Town (player–manager, August 1935–39)
Joe McClure was 22 when he joined Everton after failing to make the grade at Preston. He made his debut for the Blues in a 4–0 defeat at Sheffield Wednesday on Boxing Day 1929 when he deputised for Tom Griffiths, and although mainly a reserve, he returned to have a decent run in the side at right-half during the second half of 1930–31. Indeed, he helped the Blues win the Second Division title, appearing in 15 League games and scoring his only goal for the club in a 4–2 win at Bradford.

McCORMICK, HENRY
Outside-left: 4 apps
Born: Coleraine, Northern Ireland, 10 January 1924
Career: Coleraine (1942), Derby County (October 1946), EVERTON (July 1948), Coleraine (September 1949)
A League of Ireland representative during the Second World War, Harry McCormick appeared in 11 League games in three years of English football, making his Everton debut in place of Tommy Eglington at home to Portsmouth in September 1948, when the visitors won 5–0.

McDERMOTT, THOMAS
Inside-forward: 71 apps, 19 goals
Born: Bridgetown, Scotland, 12 January 1878 – *Died*: 1961
Career: Cambuslang Hibs, Dundee, Celtic (September 1901), EVERTON (July 1903), Chelsea (October 1905), Dundee (August 1906), Bradford City (1907), Gainsborough Trinity, Kilmarnock, Bradford City (briefly, 1908), Dundee Hibernian (1909), Anfield Royal (1910), St Helens Recreationalists (1911), Wirral Railway (1912), Vale of Leven (1913), Broxburn (1914) Shamrock (1915–16), Clyde (1917)
A scheming inside-forward with plenty of ability, Tommy McDermott's play suffered from inconsistency. He had produced some good performances at Celtic before moving to Goodison Park, where he immediately established himself in the first team after making his debut in a 3–1 League win over Blackburn in September 1903.

He netted seven goals in 30 games that season, helping the Blues reach third place in the table. He followed up with another seven goals in 1904–05, when Everton finished second and reached the FA Cup semi-final. He lost his place in the forward-line during the early stages of 1905–06 and later toured the UK, playing on until he was almost 40.

McDONAGH, JAMES MARTIN

Goalkeeper: 48 apps
Born: Rotherham, 6 October 1952
Career: Rotherham United (apprentice, April 1969; professional, October 1970), Bolton Wanderers (£10,000, August 1976), EVERTON (£25,000, July 1980), Bolton Wanderers (£90,000 plus Mike Walsh, August 1981), Notts County (£50,000, July 1983), Birmingham City (loan, September 1984), Gillingham (loan, March 1985), Sunderland (loan, August–September 1985), Wichita Wings/USA (October 1985), Scarborough (free, November 1987), Huddersfield Town (loan, February–March 1988), Charlton Athletic (free, March–May 1988), Galway United (player–manager, July 1988), Derry City (manager, to May 1989), Spalding United (September 1989), Grantham Town (February 1990), Telford United (player–reserve-team manager, August 1990), Arnold Town (1993–94), Ilkeston Veterans (1994–95); now works for an insurance company

Honoured by England as a youth, 'Seamus' McDonagh went on to gain 24 full caps for the Republic of Ireland while also amassing 471 League appearances, including 242 for Bolton (helping them win the Second Division title in 1978) and 121 for Rotherham. Big and burly and a fine shot-stopper, he made his debut for Everton in a 3–1 defeat at Sunderland in August 1980 (after taking over from George Wood) and kept his place throughout that campaign before returning to Bolton.

McDONALD, ALEXANDER

Forward: 23 apps, 6 goals
Born: Greenock, Scotland, 12 April 1878 – Deceased
Career: Jarrow, EVERTON (February 1900), Southampton (May 1901), West Ham United (December 1901), Portsmouth (March 1902), Wellingborough (July 1903), Luton Town (August 1905), Croydon Common (1907), Luton Town (1910–11)

A first-rate marksman, Alex McDonald made his League debut as a 21-year-old for Everton against Blackburn in March 1900 and scored his first goal in 'English' football two weeks later in a 4–1 home win over Glossop. He held his place in the forward-line for nine months before slipping into the reserves and eventually leaving for Southampton, for whom he made an explosive start, netting five goals in five games. He later did well in the Southern League.

McDONALD, JOHN

Full-back: 224 apps
Born: Dykeland, Scotland, 4 January 1896 – Deceased
Career: Motherwell (1913), Airdrieonians (August 1919), EVERTON (£2,200, April 1920), New Brighton (£750, August 1927), Connah's Quay (August 1931–May 1939)

Jock McDonald captained Everton from August 1921 and was an inspirational leader, making over 220 appearances. He represented the Scottish League against the Football League in April 1919 before making his debut for the

Blues at left-back in the 3–3 draw with Bradford in August 1920. Injuries apart, he held his position in the side until halfway through 1926–27, when Warney Cresswell and Jack O'Donnell became the regular full-backs. Although he lost his speed as he got older, his experience, strategy and skill took him through four years at New Brighton, during which time he made a further 160 appearances.

McDONALD, NEIL RAYMOND
Right-back/Midfield: 109+15 apps, 7 goals
Born: Willington Quay, near North Shields, 2 November 1965
Career: Wallsend Boys' Club, Carlisle United (January 1980), Newcastle United (£10,000, August 1982), EVERTON (£525,000, July 1988), Oldham Athletic (£500,000, September 1991), Bolton Wanderers (free, August 1994), Preston North End (£40,000, November 1995; retired March 1997 to become youth-team coach)

When lining up against Barnsley in September 1982, Neil McDonald became Newcastle's youngest-ever League debutant, aged 16 years, 326 days. He went on to appear in 208 games for the Geordies before joining Everton, playing his first game for the Merseysiders at right-back in a 4–0 win over his former club, Newcastle, in August 1988. At times he played very well, being considered at one stage as a possible full England international, having previously represented his country as a schoolboy and youth-team player, and later capped five times by at Under-21 level. He helped Oldham gain promotion from Division Two in 1984, Preston win the Third Division title in 1996 and Everton reach the 1989 FA Cup final. He made over 400 club appearances.

McFADDEN, JAMES
Winger: 15+12 apps
Born: Glasgow, 14 April 1983
Career: Motherwell (from 1999), EVERTON (£1.25m, September 2003)

An impish winger, fast and clever, James McFadden moved to Goodison Park after having an excellent season with Motherwell (13 goals in 30 League games) and had also gained four caps for Scotland (later adding more to his tally with the Blues). He made his debut for the Blues against Middlesbrough, as a substitute, in September 2003.

McFARLANE, ROBERT
Goalkeeper: 9 apps
Born: Greenock, Scotland, 1875 – Deceased
Career: Greenock Rosebery, Morton (August 1894), Third Lanark (September 1896), EVERTON (July 1897), East Stirlingshire (March 1898), Bristol St George's, New Brompton (August 1900), Grimsby Town (£20, December 1900), Celtic (May 1901), Middlesbrough (May 1902), Aberdeen (1904–08)

Capped by Scotland against Wales in 1896 and also a Scottish League representative against the Football League, 'Rab' McFarlane was famous as a character as well as for his unorthodox goalkeeping techniques, relishing an exchange of quips involving any spectator within his range. Taking over from Charlie Menham, he made his debut for Everton against Bolton on the opening day of the 1897–98 season but after just nine outings was replaced by Willie Muir. He helped Grimsby win the Second Division title (1901) and Celtic the Scottish crown a year later. He appeared in 123 games for Aberdeen.

McGOURTY, JOHN

Inside-right: 15 apps, 2 goals
Born: Addiewell, Midlothian, Scotland, 10 July 1912 – Deceased
Career: Fauldshaw St John's (amateur), Partick Thistle (1929), EVERTON (April 1932), Hamilton Academical (August 1934), Waterford (loan, 1936), Ipswich Town (June 1938–February 1939); did not feature after the Second World War

Over 51,000 fans witnessed John McGourty's debut for Everton at Arsenal in September 1932 when he deputised for the injured Jimmy Dunn. A clever, thrustful inside-forward, he had 14 outings that season before languishing in the reserves prior to his move to Hamilton. Ipswich cancelled his contract after just one game.

McILHATTON, JOHN

Outside-right: 58 apps, 2 goals
Born: Ardrossan, Scotland, 3 January 1921 – *Died*: Scotland, 1954
Career: Albion Rovers, EVERTON (April 1946), Dundee (September 1948–50)

John McIlhatton played his first game for Everton on the last day of the 1945–46 transitional season against Bury and then made his first appearance in the top flight against Brentford at Goodison Park the following August. He impressed during that initial post-Second World War campaign when playing wide of Wally Fielding, Eddie Wainwright and Alex Stevenson. Decidedly quick, he could deliver a fine cross and caused defenders plenty of problems. He suffered with injuries during the second half of 1947–48 and again the following season, prompting a move back to Scotland. He was forced to retire early and died aged 33.

McINNES, THOMAS

Inside-forward: 47 apps, 18 goals
Born: Glasgow, 22 March 1870 – Deceased
Career: Cowlars FC (1888–89), Notts County (September 1889), Third Lanark (August 1893), EVERTON (May 1894), Luton Town (July 1895), Bedford Queen's Engineers

A Scottish international, capped against Ireland in 1899, Tom McInnes also represented Glasgow in an Inter-City match. An attack-minded inside-forward, able to play on the wing if required, he made a scoring debut for Everton against Sheffield Wednesday in September 1894 (won 3–1) and was on the scoresheet seven times in his first nine matches, finishing the season with ten goals. Injuries upset his rhythm the following year and he was eventually replaced by Taylor. Earlier he had done well with Notts County (20 goals in 73 League outings) and scored over 70 times in more than 250 appearances during his career. (There was another Thomas McInness around at the same time as the Everton player. Also born in 1870, he served with Clyde, Nottingham Forest, Third Lanark and Lincoln and some reference books have the two players' records mixed up.)

McINTOSH, JAMES McLAREN
Winger/centre-forward: 59 apps, 19 goals
Born: Dumfries, Scotland, 5 April 1918
Career: Droylsden, Blackpool (professional, May 1935), Preston North End (November 1937), Blackpool (May 1946), EVERTON (March 1949), Distillery (May 1952)

Jim McIntosh was a very useful forward who made his League debut for Blackpool as a 17-year-old winger in September 1935. He then appeared in over 100 games for PNE, 83 during the Second World War, and after returning to Bloomfield Road helped the Seasiders reach the 1948 FA Cup final. Sadly, he missed the showdown with Manchester United owing to injury. His first game in the blue of Everton was against his former club, Blackpool, in March 1949, when he scored and made two more goals for Eddie Wainwright, in a 5–0 victory at Goodison Park. He also found the net from the centre-forward position in his last outing for the club against Aston Villa in April 1951.

McKENZIE, DUNCAN
Inside-forward: 61+1 apps, 21 goals
Born: Grimsby, 10 June 1950
Career: Nottingham Forest (junior, July 1965; apprentice, July 1967; professional, June 1968), Mansfield Town (loan, March 1970 and February 1973), Leeds United (£240,000, August 1974), RSC Anderlecht/Belgium (£200,000, June 1976), EVERTON (£200,000, December 1976), Chelsea (£165,000, September 1978), Blackburn Rovers (£80,000 March 1981), Tulsa Roughnecks/NASL (player-exchange deal involving Viv Busby, June 1981), Chicago Sting/NASL (May 1982), Bulowa/Hong Kong (June 1983); EVERTON (community officer); later columnist for the *Today* newspaper; now an accomplished after-dinner speaker, living in Newton-le-Willows while also running his own delicatessen business

Duncan McKenzie was the first player signed by Everton from a non-British club. During a nomadic career, which saw him serve with ten different clubs worldwide, he scored over 150 goals, 112 in 330 League games. He made his debut for Forest against Sunderland in September 1969 and kicked his last ball with Bulowa in 1983. Blessed with heaps of natural skill, he had flair and huge reserves of energy, although often doubtful commitment. He topped the Second Division scoring charts in 1973–74 and sat on the England bench as a substitute for the Home Internationals that same season but never represented his country. He did well at Elland Road (27 goals in 66 League games) and after his spell in Belgium, returned 'home' to make his debut for the Blues alongside Bob Latchford against Coventry in December 1976. He played in both the 1977 League Cup final replays but missed the decider at Old Trafford. He also helped the Blues reach that season's FA Cup semi-final. He never acclimatised to a Chelsea side of limited ability but still scored some stunning goals, as he did throughout his career.

McKINNON, ALEX
Centre-half/outside-right: 6 apps, 4 goals
Born: Edinburgh, 1865 – Deceased
Career: Hibernian, EVERTON (September–December 1888), Hibernian
Jock McKinnon made his debut for the Blues at centre-half against Notts County in September 1888 – the club's second League game. During October and November of that year he made five successive appearances on the right-wing and scored four goals, including Everton's first-ever League hat-trick in a 6–2 home win over Derby. He left the club suddenly.

McLAUGHLIN, JOHN IAN
Full-back: 70+2 apps, 1 goal
Born: Stirling, 3 January 1948
Career: Falkirk (1965), EVERTON (October 1971; contract cancelled, April 1976)
John McLaughlin, a tough, resolute defender, had done well in Scotland before moving to Everton, signed by Harry Catterick, initially to take over from Peter Scott but was then switched to the opposite flank when Keith Newton was injured. He made his debut for the Blues against Leeds and performed with aggression and commitment before having his contract cancelled.

McLAUGHLIN, WILLIAM JAMES
Inside-forward: 15 apps, 5 goals
Born: Glasgow, 1881 – Deceased
Career: Hamilton Academical, EVERTON (October 1904), Plymouth Argyle (August 1906), Preston North End (October 1907–January 1908)
Willie McLaughlin was initially signed as cover for Tom McDermott and Jimmy Settle and in his first season at Goodison scored three times in three League games, making his debut against Stoke in December 1904. He remained second choice throughout the next campaign before moving to Plymouth, for whom he played mostly on the left-wing, making 40 appearances.

McLEAN, DUNCAN
Full-back/wing-half: 26 apps
Born: Dumbarton, 12 September 1869 – Deceased
Career: Renton Union, Renton FC (1888), EVERTON (October 1890), Liverpool (1892), Edinburgh St Bernard's (May 1895–May 1899)
A very sound and steadying influence on the defence, Duncan McLean tipped the scales at 13 st. 8 lb to complement a handy height of 5 ft 11 in. He had done the business in Scotland with the top club at the time, Renton, and made his League debut for Everton at Notts County in November 1890. After switching across Stanley Park, he was a key player in Liverpool's Second Division

championship-winning side of 1894 and later skippered St Bernard's, with whom he won two caps for Scotland against Wales (1896) and Ireland (1897).

McLEOD, KEVIN ANDREW
Left-winger: 1+6 apps
Born: Liverpool, 12 September 1980
Career: EVERTON (apprentice, April 1997; professional, September 1998), Queens Park Rangers (loan, March–May 2003)
A direct, pacy and robust left-winger, Kevin McLeod was booked in his second senior outing in the Premiership versus Arsenal, having made his debut against Ipswich in September 2000. He made five substitute appearances for the Blues during his first Premiership season. He appeared for QPR in the 2003 play-off final.

McMAHON, STEPHEN
Midfield: 119+1 apps, 14 goals
Born: Liverpool, 20 August 1961
Career: EVERTON (apprentice, June 1977; professional, August 1979), Aston Villa (£300,000, May 1983), Liverpool (£350,000, September 1985), Manchester City (December 1991), Swindon Town (player–manager, November 1994–October 1999), Blackpool (manager, January 2000–May 2004)
An aggressive, hard-tackling, totally committed central midfielder, Steve McMahon made his debut for Everton against Sunderland on the opening day of the 1980–81 League programme, after developing his game for three seasons in the youth and reserve teams. His best season at Goodison was his last when he made 42 appearances and scored five goals. After switching to Liverpool (from Aston Villa), he gained medals galore – three League championships (1986, 1988, 1990), two FA Cup wins (1988, 1989), a European Super Cup success (1989) and three Charity Shield victories (1986, 1988, 1989). He won 17 caps for England, played in six Under-21 and two 'B' internationals and was in his country's 1990 World Cup squad. McMahon had 91 outings for Villa (seven goals), starred in 277 matches for Liverpool (50 goals), played 90 times (one goal) for Manchester City and made 51 appearances for Swindon. McMahon, who played for Villa against Everton in the two-legged League Cup semi-final of 1984, is one of only a handful of players to have skippered both Everton and Liverpool. McMahon and his brother John (now Tranmere coach) were together as players at Goodison Park while Steve's son, Stephen junior, joined Blackpool in 2002.

McMILLAN, JAMES A.
Inside-left: 7 apps, 5 goals
Born: 1870 – Deceased
Career: EVERTON (February 1892–April 1895)
An unknown inside-forward, Jim McMillan scored twice for Everton in a 4–0 win over Nottingham Forest in September 1893, having made his debut against Wolves in March 1893.

McNAMARA, ANTHONY
Outside-right: 113 apps, 22 goals
Born: Liverpool, 3 October 1929
Career: Merseyside schools and amateur football, EVERTON (amateur, July 1947; professional, May 1950), Liverpool (£4,000, December 1957), Crewe Alexandra (July 1958), Bury (September 1958–April 1959), Runcorn (1959–60)

The principal part of Tony McNamara's career was the seven years he spent at Goodison Park. A heavily built winger, yet described as an 'elegant footballer', he took over the number seven shirt from Ted Buckle, making his debut in a 2–1 home win over Leeds in September 1951. Buckle returned to the right-wing and after that, with other players taking over the same position, McNamara's outings were limited. Indeed, he played in just four games when the Blues gained promotion in 1954. He scored 27 goals in 144 League appearances during his career, appearing in all four divisions of the Football League in the space of 12 months (1957, 1958).

McNAUGHT, KENNETH
Central-defender: 84+2 apps, 3 goals
Born: Kirkcaldy, Fife, Scotland, 17 January 1955
Career: EVERTON (apprentice, July 1970; professional, May 1972), Aston Villa (£200,000, July 1977), West Bromwich Albion (£125,000, August 1983), Manchester City (loan, December 1984–January 1985), Sheffield United (£10,000, July 1985; retired May 1986); Dunfermline Athletic (coach, 1986–87), Swansea City (assistant manager, 1987–88), Vale of Earn/Scotland (manager, 1988–89); later worked in the Pro's Shop at the Gleneagles golf course

Ken McNaught gained both youth and amateur international honours for Scotland before appearing in 86 games for Everton, making his League debut against Leicester in January 1975 when he partnered Roger Kenyon in the centre of the defence. An excellent pivot, commanding in the air, positive and sure in the tackle, he was the backbone of Ron Saunders's and Tony Barton's defences during his time with Aston Villa, for whom he scored 13 goals in 260 appearances, gaining League championship, European Cup and Super Cup-winner's medals. A WBA debutant in a 4–3 defeat at Villa in August 1983, he made 356 League appearances during his career. McNaught's father, Willie McNaught, was a Scottish international.

McPHERSON, LACHLAN
Wing-half/inside-forward: 31 apps, 1 goal
Born: Cambuslang, Scotland, 1 July 1900 – Deceased
Career: Cambuslang Rangers, Notts County (May 1921), Swansea Town (June 1924), EVERTON (£5,000, January 1930), New Brighton (August 1933), Hereford United (player–coach, July 1935); did not figure after the Second World War

'Lachy' McPherson learned his football at the same school as Scottish international Andy Wilson. He played 33 games for Notts County before scoring 29 goals in 199 League games for Swansea. He made 11 appearances in his first season with Everton, occupying both wing-half positions, making his debut against Liverpool when 52,600 fans witnessed the 3–3 draw. The following season he helped the Blues win the Second Division title and reach the FA Cup semi-final. He became surplus to requirements (following the emergence of Archie Clark) and switched to New Brighton, ending his senior career with over 350 club appearances to his name. In 1934–35, he had the misfortune to suffer several injuries both on and off the field, being involved, as a pedestrian, in a road accident, damaging both his ankles.

MADAR, MICKAEL RAMOND

Striker: 17+3 apps, 6 goals
Born: Paris, France, 8 May 1968
Career: Paris FC/France, Laval/France, Socheaux/France, Cannes/France, AS
    Monaco/France, Deportivo La Coruña/Spain (1996), EVERTON (free,
    December 1997), Paris St Germain/France (December 1998), Creteil
    FC/France (August 2001; retired May 2003)
The thrice-capped French striker Mickael Madar, 6 ft 1 in. tall and over 12 st. in weight, made a significant impact in the Premiership after being lured to Goodison Park by manager Howard Kendall halfway through the 1997–98 season. However, when Walter Smith replaced Kendall in the hot seat, Madar's career with Everton was over and after 12 months with the club he returned 'home'. Not typical of the majority of European strikers, he was good in the air and led the line with strength and intelligence, but was temperamental in the extreme! He scored on his debut for the Blues against Crystal Palace in January 1998 (won 3–1).

MAGNER, EDWARD

Centre-forward: 9 apps, 3 goals
Born: Newcastle-upon-Tyne, 1 January 1891 – *Died*: 1948
Career: Expansion FC, Gainsborough Trinity (August 1909), EVERTON
    (December 1910), St Mirren (January 1912); did not figure after the First
    World War
Basically a reserve wherever he played, Ted Magner was with Everton for a year, during which time he scored a goal every third game, including one on his debut against Preston in January 1911.

MAHER, AIDEN

Outside-left: 1 app.
Born: Liverpool, 1 December 1946
Career: EVERTON (apprentice, April 1962; professional, December 1964),
    Plymouth Argyle (October 1968), Tranmere Rovers (June 1971–May 1972)
An England schoolboy international, Aiden Maher looked to have a bright future ahead of him but never fulfilled his early promise. His only game for Everton was against the subsequent First Division champions Manchester

City in November 1967. He scored three times in 64 League outings for Plymouth.

MAKEPEACE, JOSEPH WILLIAM HENRY

Right-half: 336 apps, 23 goals
Born: Middlesbrough, 22 August 1882 – *Died*: Bebington, December 1952
Career: Liverpool schoolboy football, EVERTON (professional, April 1902; retired May 1915; later coach at Goodison Park)

An FA Cup and League championship winner with Everton in 1906 and 1915 respectively, Harry Makepeace also performed in the 1907 losing FA Cup final. He gained four England caps (1904–12 – three against Scotland, one against Wales), represented the Football League (1901), helped Lancashire win four County cricket titles (1926, 1927, 1928 and 1930) and in 1920–21 played in four Test matches against Australia, scoring 117 in Melbourne.

One of England's finest all-round sportsmen, he made his League debut for Everton against Bury in February 1903, having had his first senior game a week earlier against Manchester United in the FA Cup, lining up in both matches at inside-left. He was, however, quickly switched to half-back, where he performed with class and authority, his fierce tackling being the main feature of his game. He remained at Goodison Park for over 20 years (as a player and coach).

MALEY, WILLIAM

Left-half/inside-right: 2 apps
Born: Newry, County Down, Ireland, April 1868 – *Died*: 2 April 1958
Career: Cathcart FC, Celtic (amateur, May 1888; match secretary, 1890–91; player-secretary/professional, 1893), Ardwick (February 1896), Celtic (March 1896), EVERTON (January–April 1897), Celtic (May 1897; retired July 1897; then secretary–manager to February 1940); President of the Scottish League (1921–24)

The son of a Scotsman, Willie Maley gained two international caps for Scotland, against England and Ireland in 1893. He also represented the Scottish League (as a Celtic player) and played for Glasgow against Sheffield in the Inter-City challenge match. He appeared in 97 games for Celtic before retiring to become the club's first successful manager, leading the Bhoys to 16 Scottish League titles and 14 Scottish Cup final victories, having as a player gained three League championship medals and one Cup winning medal himself. A big man, he gave himself without stint to all phases of a game and was never ruffled. He was fast and was a noted athlete in both the 100 yards and one mile races. He helped Everton out in two games, making his debut against Sheffield United on New Year's Day 1897.

MARSDEN, JOSEPH THOMAS

Right-back: 1 app.
Born: Darwen, 1868 – *Died*: Darwen, 18 January 1897
Career: Darwen, EVERTON (July 1891; retired, due to ill-health, April 1892)

A lightly built but astonishingly dexterous player, Joe Marsden's judgement was of a high order. He only made one appearance for Everton, in a 4–0 defeat at WBA on the opening Saturday of the 1891–92 season. As a Darwen player, he was capped once by England, in a 6–1 win over Ireland at Molineux, March 1891.

MARSHALL, CLIFFORD

Winger: 7 apps
Born: Liverpool, 4 November 1955
Career: EVERTON (apprentice, April 1971; professional, November 1973), Southport (September 1976–April 1977)
Reserve to Gary Jones on Everton's right, Cliff Marshall made only seven appearances in five years at Goodison Park, his League debut coming as a substitute against Leicester in January 1975.

MARSHALL, IAN PAUL

Defender/forward: 17+7 apps, 2 goals
Born: Oxford, 20 March 1966
Career: EVERTON (apprentice, April 1982; professional, March 1984), Oldham Athletic (£100,000, March 1988), Ipswich Town (£750,000, August 1993), Leicester City (£875,000, August 1996), Bolton Wanderers (free, August 2000), Blackpool (free, November 2001; retired June 2002)
In a fine career, Ian Marshall made 495 appearances and scored 113 goals while occupying eight different positions. A versatile performer, he manned defence, midfield and performed admirably as an out and out striker, hence his fine goal-tally. After developing in the youth and reserve teams at Goodison Park, he made his League debut in Everton's defence against WBA in August 1985. He was a Second Division championship winner with Joe Royle's Oldham (1991) and a League Cup winner with Leicester (2000).

MARTIN, GEORGE SCOTT

Inside-forward: 86 apps, 32 goals
Born: Bothwell, Lanarkshire, 14 July 1899 – *Died*: 1972
Career: Cadzow St Anne's (Motherwell), Bo'ness, Hamilton Academical (1920–21), Bathgate (loan), Hull City (October 1922), EVERTON (March 1928), Middlesbrough (May 1932), Luton Town (August 1933; retired May 1937; coach, 1937–39; manager, August 1939–May 1947), Newcastle United (manager, May 1947–December 1950), Aston Villa (manager, December 1950–August 1953); into business in Liverpool; Luton Town (chief scout, 1959–1960; then caretaker-manager, February 1965–November 1966)
A quiet, stylish player, fast over short distances, powerful when required, George Martin occupied all five forward positions and scored 56 goals in 204 League games. A plumber by trade, he had his best years with Everton, whom he helped win the Second Division title in 1931, netting seven times in 15 outings, having made his debut for the Blues at Leicester in March 1928.

In his first spell as Luton's manager he found many good young players and then built the club up after the Second World War. A smart and elegant man, he guided Newcastle back into the First Division in 1948 but had a tough time with the board at Villa Park and quit football to go into business. He was a talented sculptor and fine singer who made several records in the 1950s.

MARTYN, ANTONY NIGEL

Goalkeeper: 39+1 apps
Born: St Austell, Cornwall, 11 August 1966
Career: St Blazey (Cornwall), Bristol Rovers (free, August 1987), Crystal Palace (£1m, November 1989), Leeds United (£2.25m, July 1996) EVERTON (nominal fee, July 2003)

A former England international, winning 23 senior caps, plus six for the 'B' team and 11 for the Under-21s, Nigel Martyn made 124 appearances for Bristol Rovers before becoming the first £1m goalkeeper when he joined Crystal Palace. He helped the Eagles reach the 1990 FA Cup final, collecting a runner's-up medal after a replay. An FMC-winner in 1991 (against Everton) he played in 349 games during his time at Selhurst Park before taking over from John Lukic at Leeds. For six years he performed splendidly for the Yorkshire club, amassing 272 appearances. After languishing in the reserves for a year, he returned to the Premiership with Everton, for whom he made his debut at Middlesbrough, as a substitute, in September 2003. He produced some excellent displays for the Blues and performed as good as any Premiership goalkeeper during the latter stages of 2003–04.

MATERAZZI, MARCO

Defender: 32+1 apps, 2 goals
Born: Perugia, Italy, 19 August 1973
Career: FCS Messina/Italy, Tor di Quinto/Italy, Marsale/Italy, Trapani/Italy, Perugia/Italy, Carpi/Italy, Perugia/Italy, EVERTON (£2.8m, July 1998), Perugia/Italy (£3m, July 1999), Inter Milan/Italy (August 2002)

Marco Materazzi, a huge, powerful defender, 6 ft 4 in. tall and over 14 st. in weight, delighted the Everton fans with classy ball skills and excellent passing ability. Unfortunately, he tried on occasions to be far too clever and also he had a fiery temper, being sent off three times and was shown countless yellow cards. He made his debut in the 0–0 draw against Aston Villa in August 1998 and scored his first goal for the Blues with a clever back-heel against Huddersfield in a League Cup-tie. Prior to joining Everton, he made over 100 appearances in Italy and in 2003 played in the Champions League semi-final for Inter Milan. He played for Italy in Euro 2004.

MAXWELL, ALLAN

Inside-right/centre-forward: 50 apps, 16 goals
Born: Glasgow, 1870 – Deceased
Career: Cambuslang Rangers (1888), EVERTON (October 1891), Darwen (November 1893), Stoke (February 1896), St Bernard's/Edinburgh (May 1897)

An alert and clever forward, Allan Maxwell was injured on his League debut for

Everton, in a 4–0 defeat at Preston in October 1891. He regained full fitness and went on to serve the Blues splendidly over the next two years, performing well alongside Edgar Chadwick and Fred Geary in 1892–93. He joined Stoke for a set of wrought-iron gates after scoring 22 goals in 60 League games for Darwen.

MAYERS, DEREK

Outside-right: 19 apps, 7 goals
Born: Liverpool, 24 January 1935
Career: EVERTON (amateur, April 1950; professional, August 1952), Preston North End (May 1957), Leeds United (June 1961), Bury (July 1962), Wrexham (October 1963–April 1964)

A reserve during his time at Goodison Park, Derek Mayers had to wait until October 1953 before making his League debut in a 1–0 defeat at Brentford, when Ted Buckle switched over to the left. His second outing followed two years later at Bolton and he scored the first two of his seven goals in a 5–1 home win over Huddersfield in November 1955. He played in the same forward-line as Tom Finney at Preston and Billy Bremner and Don Revie at Leeds.

MAYSON, THOMAS F.

Inside-left: 1 app., 1 goal
Born: Whitehaven, 8 December 1886 – *Died*: 1972
Career: Whitehaven Chapel, Northern Alliance Football, Burnley (December 1907), Grimsby Town (£350, October 1911); guest for Leeds City during the First World War; EVERTON (July 1919), Pontypridd (£350, July 1920), Wolverhampton Wanderers (August 1921), Aberdare Athletic (May 1922; retired April 1926); Queens Park Rangers (trainer, August 1926–May 1933)

A class forward with loads of skill, Tom Mayson scored in his only game for Everton against Chelsea in September 1919 – after recovering from a fractured right leg playing for Grimsby against Nottingham Forest in April 1913. He was a Welsh Cup winner with Pontypridd in 1921.

MEAGAN, MICHAEL KEVIN

Left-back: 179 apps, 1 goal
Born: Dublin, Ireland, 29 May 1934
Career: Rathfarnham (1950), Johnville Juniors (1951), EVERTON (professional, September 1952), Huddersfield Town (£40,000, player-exchange deal involving Ramon Wilson, July 1964), Halifax Town (July 1968–May 1969); Drogheda (coach), Shamrock Rovers (coach), Bray (coach); later worked in a Dublin hospital

An Eire schoolboy international inside-forward, Mick Meagan developed into a fine wing-half before making his mark as a full-back, helping Everton win the League title in 1962–63, making 32 appearances as partner to Alex Parker. Taking over from Peter Farrell, he made his debut for the Blues at left-half against Wolves in August 1957 and his last outing was against West Ham in April 1964. Valued at £15,000 when he moved to Huddersfield in the deal involving future England World Cup winner Ray Wilson, Meagan was capped

17 occasions at senior level, played in one 'B' international and captained his country and Halifax.

MEEHAN, PETER

Full-back: 28 apps

Born: Broxburn, Scotland, 28 February 1872 – *Died*: Broxburn, 1915

Career: Broxburn Shamrock, Hibernian (February 1892), Sunderland (June 1893), Glasgow Celtic (May 1895), EVERTON (January 1897), Southampton (£200, August 1898), Manchester City (September 1900), Barrow (June 1901), Clyde (August 1903), Broxburn Athletic (September 1904–June 1906)

Originally employed in the Linlithgowshire coalmines, Peter Meehan made 44 League appearances for Sunderland but none for Celtic before enjoying a brief sojourn at Goodison Park. He made his debut for the Blues against Bury in a second-round FA Cup-tie in February 1897 and followed up with his first League outing against the same team a fortnight later, deputising for Scottish international David Storrier. He helped Southampton win the Southern League title (1899) and his final game for the Saints was in the FA Cup final a year later.

MEGSON, GARY JOHN

Midfield: 23+2 apps, 3 goals

Born: Manchester, 2 May 1959

Career: Frampton Rangers, Parkway Juniors, Mangotsfield United, Plymouth Argyle (apprentice, August 1975; professional, May 1977), EVERTON (loan, November 1979; signed for £250,000, December 1979), Sheffield Wednesday (£130,000, August 1981), Nottingham Forest (£170,000, August 1984), Newcastle United (£110,000, November 1984), Sheffield Wednesday (loan, December 1985; signed for £65,000, January 1986), Manchester City (£250,000, January 1989), Norwich City (July 1992, player/assistant manager, January 1994), Lincoln City (n/c, July 1995), Bradford City (assistant manager/coach, August 1995), Shrewsbury Town (n/c, September–October 1995), Norwich City (manager, December 1995–June 1996), Blackpool (manager, July 1996–June 1997), Stockport County (manager, July 1997), Stoke City (manager, August–November 1999), West Bromwich Albion (manager, March 2000)

The son of Don Megson, the former Sheffield Wednesday left-back who played in the 1966 FA Cup final against Everton, Gary Megson was a hard-working, aggressive midfielder who made 588 appearances and scored 50 goals in a 20-year playing career. He had his best spell with Sheffield Wednesday (233 League outings) and his worst with Nottingham Forest (no games). The first player to join Everton on loan, he made his debut against Wolves in February 1980, teaming up in midfield with Asa Hartford. After disappointing in 1980–81, when he was handicapped by a spate of injuries, Megson moved to Hillsborough. He played in three losing FA Cup semi-finals (1980, 1983, 1986) and twice took WBA into the Premiership (2002, 2004).

MEIKLEJOHN, GEORGE
Centre-half: 1 app.
Born: Scotland, *circa* 1873 – Deceased
Career: EVERTON (March–April 1897)
Unknown defender who played in one League game for Everton, in a 4–1 defeat at Preston in April 1897.

MENHAM, CHARLES GEORGE GORDON
Goalkeeper: 3 apps
Born: Bromley, Kent, 28 August 1896 – *Died:* 1979
Career: Northern Nomads, EVERTON (September–November 1925), Northern Nomads, Bradford City (1927–28), Northern Nomads
An amateur throughout his career, Charlie Menham had a nightmare debut for Everton, being on the wrong end of a 7–3 defeat at Sunderland in October 1925. His other two outings ended in victories.

MENHAM, ROBERT WILLIAM
Goalkeeper: 23 apps
Born: North Shields, 1871 – *Died:* 1949
Career: Luton Town. EVERTON (1896), Wigan County, Swindon Town
A relation of Charlie Menham (q.v.), Bob Menham kept goal for Everton during the second half of 1896–97 and lined up against Aston Villa in the FA Cup semi-final. Recruited from Luton following an injury to Harry Briggs, he was a tall man, courageous with a safe pair of hands.

MERCER, JOSEPH, OBE
Half-back: 184 apps, 2 goals
Born: Ellesmere Port, Cheshire, 9 August 1914 – *Died:* Merseyside, August 1990
Career: Ellesmere Port and Cheshire Schools, Elton Green FC, Shell Mex FC, Runcorn, Ellesmere Port Town, Bolton Wanderers (trial), EVERTON (amateur, August 1931; professional, September 1932); guest for Aldershot during the Second World War; Arsenal (£7,000, November 1946–54); Sheffield United (manager, August 1955), Aston Villa (manager, December 1958–July 1964), Manchester City (manager, July 1965–October 1971, then general manager to June 1972), Coventry City (general manager, June 1972–June 1975; director at Highfield Road, April 1975–July 1981); England caretaker-manager, May 1974
Genial Joe Mercer retired twice as a player – in May 1953 and June 1954 – the second time after suffering a double fracture of his leg in a League game against Liverpool at Highbury. Bandy-legged, he was an outstanding wing-half with a biting tackle and a never-say-die attitude. From April 1933 to April 1954, he appeared in over 450 games for Everton and Arsenal and won six full and 27 wartime caps for England, also representing the Football League. He was part of a tremendous international half-back line, comprising Cliff Brittan and the redoubtable Stan Cullis. Mercer gained three League championship medals, the

first with Everton in 1938–39 and two with the Gunners in 1947–48 and 1952–53. He also skippered the Londoners to victory in the 1950 FA Cup against Liverpool and collected a runner's-up prize in the same competition two years later. He was voted 'Footballer of the Year' in 1950.

Eventually retiring in 1954 – shortly before his 40th birthday – Mercer spent a year or so out of the game, running a grocery shop in the Wirral. He moved back into football as manager at Bramall Lane before taking over at Villa Park. He introduced several youngsters into the game, calling them 'Mercer's Minnows'. He took Villa to the Second Division title and League Cup success in 1960 and 1961 respectively, and saw them finish runners-up in the latter competition in 1963. Mercer stayed out of the game for a short while (his wife and friends thought the pressure would kill him) before reappearing as manager of Manchester City. With Malcolm Allison as his assistant, he revitalised the Maine Road club, guiding City to the Second Division championship (1967), First Division glory (1968), an FA Cup triumph (1969), League Cup final success (1970), victory in the European Cup-Winners' Cup final (1971) and a Charity Shield win (1968).

He managed England for a handful of games in 1974, between the respective reigns of Sir Alf Ramsey and Don Revie. He brought a smile back to the faces of the players and, indeed, the fans with some positive results. He lived in retirement in Birkenhead and watched Tranmere quite regularly until his death at the age of 76. A wonderful man, his father was centre-half for Nottingham Forest and Tranmere (1910–22).

MESTON, SAMUEL WILLIAM
Forward: 1 app.
Born: Southampton, 30 May 1902 – *Died*: Woolston, Southampton, 12 October 1953
Career: St Bernard's, Scholing Athletic (August 1921), Southampton (January 1922), Gillingham (August 1926), EVERTON (March 1928), Tranmere Rovers (July 1929), Newport/Isle of Wight (July 1931–May 1933); later a bookie's runner in Southampton

The son of a former Southampton player by the same name, Sam Meston was a coppersmith by trade and was just beginning to establish himself in the Southampton side when he broke his right leg against Bristol City in October 1923, an injury that kept him out for a year. He was never the same again and after a spell with Gillingham he surprisingly joined Everton, for whom he made just one League appearance, deputising for Ted Critchley on the right-wing in a 3–1 win at Sheffield United in April 1928. He died of a heart attack, aged 51.

MEUNIER, JAMES BROWN
Full-back: 5 apps
Born: Poynton, Stockport, 1885 – *Died*: 30 September 1957
Career: Heaton Chapel, Stockport County (amateur, 1903), Manchester City (July 1904), Southport Central (June 1906), Canadian football (September 1906–March 1907), EVERTON (£50, October 1908), Lincoln City (June

1912), Coventry City (July–November 1914), Hyde United (June 1919), Macclesfield (December 1919–May 1920)

Jim Meunier was a strong, physical defender who skippered Everton's reserve side to two Lancashire Combination championships during his stay at Goodison Park. Recruited after being out of the game following his return from Canada, the first of his appearances was a joyous occasion – a 6–1 home League win over Blackburn in November 1910.

MICHAELS, WILLIAM
Outside-right: 3 apps
Born: *circa* 1884 – Deceased
Career: EVERTON (season 1909–10)
A registered player with Everton for one season, Bill Michaels made his League debut on the right-wing in place of Jack Sharp in a 2–1 home defeat of Sheffield United in October 1909.

MILLER, HENRY JAMES
Inside-forward: 2 apps
Born: Preston, *circa* 1900 – Deceased
Career: Fleetwood, Leyland, EVERTON (August 1922), Preston North End (August 1924), Lancaster Town (June 1925)
Harry Miller was a reserve at both Goodison Park and Deepdale. He made his League debut for Everton against Nottingham Forest in October 1922 in place of Bobby Irvine.

MILLER, JAMES
Outside-right: 8 apps, 1 goal
Born: Tynemouth, 1889 – Deceased
Career: Wallsend Park Villa, Newcastle United (£25, May 1912), Grimsby Town (£50, April. 1913), EVERTON (August 1919), Coventry City (December 1919), Preston North End (January 1920), Pontypridd (May 1920), Darlington (1921), Chesterfield (May 1922), Bournemouth and Boscombe Athletic (June 1923), Swansea Town (August 1924), Luton Town (May 1925–June 1926)
Jimmy Miller's main characteristics were his speed (he was a champion sprinter), crossing of the ball on the run and his powerful shooting. A soccer journeyman, 5 ft 6 in. tall, he served with 11 major clubs in 14 years (it would have been more, had the First World War not interrupted his career). He made 141 League appearances in all, scoring eight goals. His debut for Everton came in a 3–2 home defeat by Chelsea in August 1919 and his only goal for the club arrived three games later in a 2–0 win over Bradford. He was a Third Division (S) title-winner with Swansea in 1925.

MILLER, WILLIAM RENNIE
Inside-forward: 13 apps, 2 goals
Born: Camelon, Scotland, 19 January 1910 – Deceased
Career: Bainsford Primary and Camelon Council Schools, Alva Albion Rovers

(1925), Partick Thistle (April 1929), EVERTON (£3,000, July 1935), Burnley (October 1936), Tranmere Rovers (November 1938), Falkirk (season 1939–40)

A tireless player with great stamina and willpower, Bill Miller (known as 'Golden Miller') scored over 20 goals in more than 100 senior appearances south of the border, including 19 in 77 games for Burnley. He joined Everton after six years with Partick and made his Blues' debut in a 4–0 home win over Derby in August 1935, setting up Dixie Dean's goal. He lost his place in January 1936, when Alex Stevenson returned after injury halfway through the season and after a long spell in the reserves moved to Burnley.

MILLIGAN, GEORGE HARRY
Half-back: 1 app.
Born: Failsworth, Lancashire, August 1917 – *Died*: Rhyl, November 1983
Career: Manchester North End, Oldham Athletic (amateur, March 1935; professional, May 1935), EVERTON (£3,150, May 1938); guest for Chelsea, Crystal Palace, Reading and York City during the Second World War; EVERTON (scout, 1940s), later Rhyl Athletic (director and manager); played cricket for Woodhouses CC

George Milligan was a talented junior footballer and avid Oldham fan. He developed into a fine left-half and made over 80 appearances for the Latics but managed only one for Everton, in a 4–2 defeat at Bolton in October 1938. As a cricketer, he scored 320 runs in four consecutive innings for Woodhouses and also had trials with Lancashire, hitting 70 against a Manchester public school's XI.

MILLIGAN, JAMIE
Midfield: 0+4 apps
Born: Blackpool, 3 January 1980
Career: EVERTON (apprentice, April 1996; professional, July 1997), Blackpool (free, March 2001)

An England Under-18 international, slightly built midfielder Jamie Milligan was unable to establish himself in Everton's first XI and left Goodison Park on transfer deadline day, 2001. An FA Youth Cup-winner in 1998, he was used as a substitute in four Premiership games by the Blues, making his debut at Arsenal in November 1998. He was a LDV Vans Trophy winner with Blackpool (2002).

MILLIGAN, MICHAEL JOSEPH
Midfield: 21+3 apps, 2 goals
Born: Manchester, 20 February 1967
Career: Manchester City (trial), Oldham Athletic (apprentice, December 1984; professional, March 1985), EVERTON (August 1990), Oldham Athletic (July 1991), Norwich City (March 1994), Blackpool (July 2000; retired May 2001)

A grant from the European Social Fund and Greater Manchester Council launched Mike Milligan's professional career with Oldham in 1985, the Latics becoming the first sports club to apply under the scheme. A hard-working, tenacious midfielder, Milligan qualified through parentage to play for the Republic of Ireland, and gained caps at four different levels: full (one), 'B' (two), Under-21 (one) and Under-23 (one). He made 162 League appearances in his first spell with Oldham, playing in the Premiership under former Everton striker Joe Royle. He played in 117 games in his second stint before joining Norwich. In between times he served Everton for one season, making his debut against Leeds at Goodison Park in August 1990. Continuing to play with total commitment until retiring in 2001, Milligan accumulated 530 senior appearances at club level, including 446 in the Football League.

MILLINGTON, THOMAS
Outside-right: 14 apps
Born: Wrexham, 12 January 1906 – Deceased
Career: Wrexham (trial), Oswestry Town, Wrexham (August 1924), EVERTON (March 1925), Gillingham (March 1928), Oswestry Town (1929), Crewe Alexandra (1930), Yeovil and Petters United, Tottenham Hotspur (briefly, 1932), Oswestry Town (1932–33)

An efficient outside-right who played his best football with Gillingham and Crewe, making 398 appearances in the competition for both clubs. He also did well in his spells with Oswestry. During his three-year stay at Goodison Park he was basically reserve to Sam Chedgzoy, making his League debut against Birmingham in September 1926. After 11 more starts (out of 12 games) up to mid-December, Ted Critchley arrived on the scene and Millington dropped into the second XI.

MILWARD, ALFRED
Outside-left: 224 apps, 96 goals
Born: Great Marlow, Bucks, 12 September 1870 – *Died*: Winchester, 1 June 1941
Career: Sir William Borlase's Grammar school/Marlow; Old Borlasians, Marlow AFC (1886), EVERTON (May 1888), New Brighton Tower (£200, May 1897), Southampton (free, May 1899), New Brompton (July 1901), Southampton Cambridge (July 1903; retired 1905); later licensee of the Diamond Jubilee pub, Orchard Lane, Southampton; also a qualified referee, officiating in Southampton FA fixtures (1909–10)

The son of a Marlow tradesman, Alf Milward reached the peak of his career with Everton, being an ever-present in the Blues' 1890–91 League championship-winning side. He later helped Southampton reach the 1900 FA Cup final and win the Southern League title a year later, having twice been an FA Cup runner-up with the Blues (1893, 1897). A well-built, hard-working and technically clever winger, he was determined and contested every ball. He played at full stretch for the duration of the game and had the knack of delivering a cross-field pass to perfection from up to 40 yards but was more renowned for his shooting powers from wide positions. He gained four England caps (two against Wales, two against Scotland: 1891–97), hit three international goals and scored 40 times in 63 games for Saints.

MIMMS, ROBERT ANDREW

Goalkeeper: 33 apps
Born: York, 12 October 1963
Career: Halifax Town (apprentice, April 1980; professional, August 1981), Rotherham United (£15,000, November 1981), EVERTON (£150,000, June 1985), Notts County (loan, March–April 1986), Sunderland (loan, December 1986), Blackburn Rovers (loan, January 1987), Manchester City (loan, September–October 1987), Tottenham Hotspur (£325,000, February 1988), Aberdeen (loan, February–March 1990), Blackburn Rovers (free, December 1990), Crystal Palace (n/c, August 1996), Preston North End (free, September 1996), Rotherham United (free, August 1997), York City (free, player–coach, August 1998), Mansfield Town (free, player–coach, March 2000–May 2001; retired May 2002), Wolverhampton Wanderers (goalkeeping coach, 2003)

Bobby Mimms was a League championship and Charity Shield winner with Everton in 1987, helped Blackburn win the Premiership in 1995 and gained five England Under-21 caps – his only honours in a wonderful career that spanned 21 years, during which time he accumulated 507 appearances (437 League). One of soccer's top-line nomads, he served 14 different clubs and played under possibly the same number of managers! A consistent performer, he was second choice at Goodison Park (behind Neville Southall) for quite some time and, in fact, was loaned out on four separate occasions. He made his debut for the Blues at Manchester City in October 1985 (1–1 draw) and played his last game for the club at Newcastle two years later (also 1–1).

MITCHELL, FRANK WILLIAM G.

Goalkeeper: 24 apps
Born: Elgin, Morayshire, Scotland, 25 May 1890 – Deceased
Career: Milngarvie Alexander, Maryhill FC, Motherwell, EVERTON (August 1913), Liverpool (July 1920), Tranmere Rovers (June 1923–May 1925), Blue Circle FC (1925–26)

At Motherwell, Frank Mitchell had to vie with Scottish League star Colin Hampton for the goalkeeping spot; at Goodison Park he had to contend with in-form Tommy Fern and at Anfield he had the great Elisha Scott ahead of him. Nevertheless, he still managed to play in over 50 League games north and south of the border (plus 99 for the Blues during the First World War) before going on to claim a regular first-team spot at Tranmere (60 outings). An efficient custodian, he helped Everton win the Lancashire Section Principal Tournament (1919), having made his Blues' debut against Burnley in September 1913.

MOFFAT, ANDREW NAYSMITH

Centre-forward: 1 app.
Born: Rosewell, Scotland, 5 September 1900 – *Died*: 1990
Career: Glencraig Rovers (1915), Kinglassie United, Glencraig Celtic, Lochgelly United, East Fife, EVERTON (March 1920), East Fife (May 1920),

Wrexham (October 1922), East Fife (March 1923), Lochgelly United, Dunfermline Athletic, Lochgelly United

Except for eight months when he served with Everton and Wrexham, Andrew Moffatt spent all his career playing in Scotland, mainly with East Fife and Lochgelly United. His only outing for the Blues was in a 1–0 win at Oldham in April 1920. He scored once in nine games for Wrexham.

MOFFAT, HAROLD

Outside-right: 3 apps

Born: Camerton, 1900 – Deceased

Career: Arsenal (1923), Guildford United, Luton Town (April 1925), EVERTON (September 1926), Oldham Athletic (May 1927), Walsall (May 1928), Queens Park Rangers (July 1929–May 1930)

After failing with Arsenal and playing non-League football with Guildford, stocky winger Harry Moffat made 33 League appearances for Luton before joining Everton, for whom he made his debut against WBA a week after arriving. He later faced Arsenal and Hull in the FA Cup before appearing in 41 League games for Walsall and 15 for QPR.

(Some reference books list Moffat as Moffatt.)

MOLYNEUX, GEORGE M.

Full-back: 45 apps

Born: Liverpool, August 1875 – *Died*: Rochford, Essex, 14 April 1942

Career: Third Grenadiers, South Shore (Blackpool), Kirkdale (August 1894), EVERTON (March 1896), Wigan County (June 1897), EVERTON (May 1898), Southampton (free, May 1900), Portsmouth (May 1905), Southend United (May 1906; player–manager, August 1910), Colchester Town (1912–14)

England international full-back George Molyneux (four caps gained: 1902–03) had all-round ability, being strong in the tackle, quick over short distances and one of the best exponents in the art of heading around the turn of the century. A model professional, he made his debut for Everton in the left-back position against Blackburn in September 1898 but was injured a year later and took four months to recover. In the meantime the Blues installed George Eccles at full-back and as a result Molyneux moved to Southampton, with whom he won three Southern League championships (1901, 1903 and 1904), played in the 1902 FA Cup final and in the ill-fated Ibrox Park disaster game (against Scotland).

MOORE, ERIC

Full-back: 184 apps

Born: Haydock, 16 July 1926 – *Died*: August 2004

Career: EVERTON (amateur, 1947; professional, February 1949), Tranmere Rovers (free, July 1957; retired June 1958); later an Atherton publican

Eric Moore had his fair share of ups and down during his time with Everton. After making excellent progress with the second XI when he was used as a centre-forward and right-half, he was converted into a full-back and made his League debut in December 1949 against Middlesbrough, taking over from George Saunders. From that point on he was a regular for the best part of 18 months, but was then laid up with a knee injury that lingered on for quite some time. He finally regained his fitness and missed only one game in two seasons, but in 1956–57 was given just one League outing before asking for a transfer.

MOORE, JOE-MAX
Striker: 27+37 apps, 10 goals
Born: Tulsa, USA, 23 February 1971
Career: New England Revolution/USA (April 1996), EVERTON (December 1999), New England Revolution/USA (free, January 2003)
Joe-Max Moore gained his 100th cap and netted his 24th goal for his country while at Goodison Park, thus becoming the only player ever to represent the club with a century of international appearances to his name. A small, lively striker, with an eye for goal and an impeccable attitude, he also represented the States at Under-21 level and starred in the 2002 World Cup finals in Korea and Japan. He had netted 37 times in 77 games for the 'Revolution' before making his Premiership debut as a substitute for Everton in a 5–0 home win over Sunderland on Boxing Day 1999. He then became frustrated at not being a regular in the Blues and returned to America after three years on Merseyside.

MOORE, NEIL
Defender: 4+2 apps
Born: Liverpool, 21 September 1972
Career: EVERTON (apprentice, April 1989; professional, June 1991), Blackpool (on loan, September–October 1994), Oldham Athletic (loan, February–March 1995), Carlisle United (loan, August–September 1995), Rotherham United (loan, March–May 1996), Norwich City (January 1997), Burnley (August 1997), Macclesfield Town (free, December 1999), Telford United (free, March 2000), Mansfield Town (free, July 2002), Southport (loan, December 2002–May 2003); contract then paid up by Mansfield (June 2003)
Competing with several good defenders, Neil Moore struggled to get first-team football and after eight years at Goodison Park he switched to Norwich. He made his debut for Everton as a substitute against Rotherham in a League Cup-tie in October 1992 and followed up with his Premiership debut, also as a substitute, at Sheffield United in May 1993. He appeared in over 60 games for the Canaries.

MORRIS
Centre-forward: 1 app.
Born: *circa* 1865 – Deceased
Career: EVERTON (season 1888–89)
An unknown forward, Morris's only outing for Everton was in the 0–0 draw at Stoke in December 1888.

MORRISSEY, JOHN JOSEPH, SENIOR
Outside-left: 312+2 apps, 50 goals
Born: Liverpool, 18 April 1940
Career: Liverpool Schools, Liverpool (professional, April 1957), EVERTON (£10,000, August 1962), Oldham Athletic (May 1972; retired, injured, January 1973)

Mainly an outside-left with pace, neat skills and strong shot, Johnny Morrissey scored six goals in 36 games for Liverpool before switching to Everton. In his first season with the Blues he gained a League championship medal, appearing in 28 matches as partner to Roy Vernon, making his debut for the club in the third game against Sheffield Wednesday. In his ninth outing he netted a hat-trick in a 4–2 win over WBA. An FA Cup winner in 1966, he collected his second League championship medal four years later and went on to serve Everton for a decade. An England schoolboy international, Morrissey also played for the Football League (1969). His son, John Morrissey, also played for Everton (q.v.).

MORRISSEY, JOHN JOSEPH, JUNIOR
Outside-left: 1+2 apps
Born: Liverpool, 8 March 1965
Career: EVERTON (apprentice, April 1981; professional, March 1983), Wolverhampton Wanderers (August 1985), Tranmere Rovers (£8,000, October 1985; retired June 1999)

An outside-left like his father, Johnny Morrissey made his debut for Everton as a 'sub' against Slovan Bratislava in the European Cup-Winners' Cup in November 1984. An England youth international, he didn't get much of a chance at Goodison Park and after struggling with Wolves, he finally did the business with Tranmere. He scored over 60 goals in more than 600 appearances in almost 14 years at Prenton Park, being rewarded with a testimonial match against Everton in July 1999.

MORTON, HAROLD
Goalkeeper: 29 apps
Born: Oldham, 7 January 1909 – *Died*: *circa* 1975
Career: Chadderton School, Middleton Road Primitives, Oldham Boys, Bury (trial), Bolton Wanderers (trial), Royal Welsh Fusiliers (1928–30), Aston Villa (trial, professional, September 1930), EVERTON (March 1937), Burnley (May 1939; retired during the Second World War)

Harry Morton, an ex-fireman and Rugby League full-back, was spotted by Aston Villa playing in the Army and, when demobbed, was invited down to Birmingham for a trial. He impressed, was offered a professional contract within a week and then made his debut in unusual circumstances against Manchester City in November 1930. He was sitting in the stand awaiting kick-off when he was called down to the dressing-room after Fred Biddlestone had been injured during the pre-match warm-up. He never looked back and made 207 appearances for Villa before joining Everton, after Ted Sagar had been injured.

One of the smallest keepers in the game, he commanded his area well, was brave and daring and played his first game for the Blues at WBA in March 1937 and his last against Wolves away in February 1939, when the Blues lost 7–0. Arsenal's Ted Drake also put seven goals past Morton in a League match at Villa Park in 1935.

MOUNTFIELD, DEREK
Defender: 147+7 apps, 25+ goals
Born: Liverpool, 2 November 1962
Career: Tranmere Rovers (junior, June 1978; professional, November 1980), EVERTON (£30,000, June 1982), Aston Villa (£450,000, June 1988), Wolverhampton Wanderers (£150,000, November 1991), Carlisle United (free, May 1994), Northampton Town (loan, October 1995), Walsall (November 1995, player–coach July 1997), Bromsgrove Rovers (September 1998), Scarborough (caretaker-manager, January–April 1999), Ballymena (manager), Workington (player–coach, 1999–2000)

Nurtured to play at full-back or centre-half, Derek Mountfield made only 29 appearances for Tranmere before entering the First Division with Everton. After making his debut at Birmingham in April 1983 (deputising for Mark Higgins), Mountfield subsequently partnered Kevin Ratcliffe and won two League championship medals (1985, 1987), the FA Cup (1984) and the European Cup-Winners' Cup (1985). He also played in two losing FA Cup finals (1985, 1986) and represented England once at both Under-21 and 'B' team levels. Mountfield scored 17 goals in 120 games for Villa and took his tally of club appearances beyond the 600 mark before joining Bromsgrove.

MOUNTFORD, HARRY WASHINGTON
Forward: 25 apps, 5 goals
Born: Hanley, Stoke-on-Trent, 1884 – Deceased
Career: Hanley Swifts, Burslem Port Vale (amateur, August 1903), EVERTON (April 1907), Burnley (August 1911), Third Lanark (November 1913); did not figure after the First World War

Versatile, keen and aggressive, Harry Mountford hit 30 goals in 103 appearances for Port Vale before leaving, as the club was struggling financially. He scored his debut for Everton against Nottingham Forest in November 1907 but thereafter had to fight for his place in the first team.

MUIR, WILLIAM
Goalkeeper: 137 apps
Born: Ayr, Scotland, 22 September 1877 – Deceased
Career: Glenbuck Athletic, Third Lanark, Kilmarnock (January 1897), EVERTON (April 1897), Dundee (May 1902), Bradford City (1907), Heart of Midlothian (1908–11), Dundee Hibernians, Dumbarton; did not play after the First World War

A Scottish international, capped against Ireland in 1907, Willie Muir's career see-sawed north and south of the border. He appeared in more than 300 games in all, half of them with Everton and Bradford City. Described as being an 'estimable custodian who believed in soundness and safety rather than playing for every applause', he made his debut for the Blues against WBA in November 1897, taking over from Rab McFarlane. Holding his position until October 1901, he was replaced by George Kitchen. Later, he helped Bradford City win the Second Division title (1908) and twice represented the Scottish League.

MURRAY
Wing-half: 2 apps
Born: Scotland, *circa* 1865 – Deceased
Career: EVERTON (August–December 1887)
Murray, who was recruited with Izatt, played in eight first-team matches and was in the starting line-up for the Blues' initial FA Cup-tie against Bolton in October 1887.

MURRAY, DAVID B.
Full-back: 2 apps
Born: Glasgow, 1882 – *Died*: 1915
Career: Glasgow Rangers, EVERTON (September 1903), Liverpool (May 1904), Hull City (November 1905), Leeds City (December 1905), Mexborough Town (August 1909), Burslem Port Vale (briefly)
A reserve with Rangers, David Murray (the first foreigner to play for Everton) could occupy both full-back positions, doing so with some authority. Deputising for Jack Crelley, his two League outings for Everton were against Sheffield Wednesday and Sunderland in November 1903. A League championship winner with Liverpool (1905), he scored 7 goals in 85 games for Leeds.

MURRAY, DAVID JAMES
Inside-forward/half-back: 3 apps, 1 goal
Born: Wynberg, South Africa, 1902 – Deceased
Career: Clyde (Cape Town) and Wynberg/South Africa, EVERTON (August 1925), Bristol City (October 1926), Bristol Rovers (1926), Swindon Town (March 1930), Rochdale (1931–32), Bangor City (1932–33)
One of several South Africans to come to England, Dave Murray was a versatile footballer who occupied six different positions in a varied career. He scored on his League debut for Everton from inside-right against Cardiff in September 1925 and kept his place for the next game before having his third and last outing at centre-forward 12 months later. He spent his best years with Bristol Rovers, for whom he netted 13 goals in 44 games.

MURRAY, JAMES J.
Goalkeeper/inside-right: 8 apps
Born: Scotland, 1869 – Deceased
Career: Glasgow Rangers (1889), EVERTON (September 1891), Swindon Town (February 1893)
After failing to make headway in Scotland, Jock Murray made his League debut

for Everton at Bolton in October 1891, taking over from Gordon at inside-right. A year later, during an injury crisis at Goodison Park, he played in goal against Newton Heath (won 4–3), Accrington (1–1) and Bolton (lost 4–1).

MYHRE, THOMAS
Goalkeeper: 82 apps
Born: Sarpsborg, Norway, 16 October 1973
Career: Viking Stavanger/Norway (1992), EVERTON (£800,000, November 1997), Glasgow Rangers (loan, November–December 1999), Birmingham City (loan, March–May 2000), Tranmere Rovers (loan, December 2000), FC Copenhagen/Denmark (January 2001), Besiktas/Turkey (£375,000, November 2001), Sunderland (free, July 2002), Crystal Palace (loan, October 2003–January 2004)

Thomas Myhre – 6 ft 4 in. tall, 13 st. 12 lb in weight – was the first goalkeeper to be penalised for retaining the ball for longer than the stipulated six seconds, when he was playing for Norway in Euro 2000. Extremely agile with a safe pair of hands, he was already an international (one cap) before moving to Goodison Park, where he replaced Neville Southall, making his Premiership debut in a 0–0 draw with Leeds in December 1997. He kept his place in the side until giving way to Paul Gerrard and thereafter had to fight for first-team football, eventually switching to Denmark. By 2004 he had won 29 full caps, having also represented his country at youth and Under-21 levels.

NAYSMITH, GARY ANDREW
Left–back/Midfield: 103+12 apps, 6 goals
Born: Edinburgh, 16 November 1979
Career: Whitehill Welfare/Edinburgh (1995), Heart of Midlothian (professional, June 1996), EVERTON (£1.75m, October 2000)

Normally an attacking left-back and fine crosser of the ball, Gary Naysmith has also been deployed on the left side of midfield, performing admirably in both positions. He made 120 appearances for Hearts and helped them win the Scottish Cup in 1998 before moving to Goodison Park, making his Everton debut as a substitute at Newcastle in October 2000. One of the few Scotsmen to gain some credit during the disappointing period from 2001 to 2004, Naysmith has now represented his country at schoolboy, Under-21 (22 caps) and senior levels (20 caps).

NEVIN, PATRICK KEVIN FRANCIS MICHAEL
Wide midfield: 118+38 apps, 21 goals
Born: Glasgow, 6 September 1963
Career: Gartosch/Glasgow, Clyde (May 1981), Chelsea (£95,000, July 1983), EVERTON (tribunal set fee of £925,000, July 1988), Tranmere Rovers (loan, March–May 1992; signed for £300,000, August 1992; retired May 1998); chairman of the PFA; later chief executive of Motherwell

One of the most stylish, graceful and well-balanced footballers in his position during the 1980s, Pat Nevin was somewhat unorthodox on the field, being one of the game's great enigmas! He could lie dormant for long periods during a game and then burst into life, quickly becoming a match-winner when least expected. He certainly lacked consistency (much to the chagrin of his manager and supporters) and was dropped quite a few times from the first team, but in his day he gave defenders plenty to think about with his mazy dribbling skills, smart body swerve and electrifying pace over 30–40 yards. He made 91 appearances for Clyde (20 goals), with whom he gained a Scottish Second Division championship medal (1982) and 241 for Chelsea (46 goals), helping the Londoners win the Second Division title (1982) and the FMC (1984). He moved to Goodison Park after Chelsea and Everton failed to come to an agreement over a suitable fee (Blues' boss Colin Harvey valued Nevin at £500,000 – an independent tribunal said he was worth £925,000). He made his debut in a 4–0 home win over Newcastle on the opening day of the 1988–89 season and spent a shade under four years at Goodison Park before moving to Tranmere, shortly after Howard Kendall had returned to the club – after asking to go on the transfer list. He later opened his own website while also working as a match summariser on various radio and TV programmes, including Sky Sport and Channel 5. He also tried his hand at journalism. Capped by Scotland 28 times at senior level, he represented his country as a youth, played in five Under-21 and four 'B' internationals and took part in Euro 92, also helping the Scots qualify for the finals again in 1996, although not selected for the final 22. He amassed an exceptionally fine record: 750 appearances and over 130 goals, including 39 in 239 outings for Tranmere.

NEWELL, MICHAEL COLIN
Striker: 68+27 apps, 21 goals
Born: Liverpool, 27 January 1965
Career: Liverpool (juniors), Crewe Alexandra (professional, September 1983), Wigan Athletic (October 1983), Luton Town (£100,000, January 1986), Leicester City (£350,000, September 1987), EVERTON (£850,000, July 1989), Blackburn Rovers (£1.1m, November 1991), Birmingham City (£775,000, July 1996), West Ham United (loan, December 1996–January 1997), Bradford City (loan, March–May 1997), Aberdeen (£160,000, July 1997), Crewe Alexandra (March 1999), Doncaster Rovers (June 1999), Blackpool (February 2000; retired as a player, July 2001), Hartlepool United (manager, November 2002), Luton Town (manager, June 2003)

In his nomadic career, Mike Newell – always a willing worker, a physical presence with the capacity to pull defenders out of position – scored 166 goals in 655 games while assisting 12 different clubs. Signed by Everton to put pressure on Tony Cottee and to assist Graeme Sharp up front, he made his debut in a 2–0 defeat at Coventry in August 1989 and scored his first goal three days later in a 2–1 home win over Spurs. He was lured away from Goodison to link up with Alan Shearer at Blackburn. Not taking into account his loan exploits, one of his leanest spells came at St Andrew's (three goals in 20 games); he was an Associate Members' Cup winner with Wigan (1985) and a Premiership winner with Blackburn (1995) while also representing England in two 'B' and four Under-21 internationals.

NEWTON, HENRY ALBERT

Left-back: 85 apps, 6 goals
Born: Nottingham, 18 February 1944
Career: Nottingham Forest (junior, January 1960; professional, June 1961), EVERTON (£150,000 plus Tommy Jackson, October 1970), Derby County (£100,000, September 1973), Walsall (May 1977; retired with arthritis, May 1978); later ran a sub-post office in Derby after a hip operation

Henry Newton was a tremendous competitor, a no-nonsense performer, supremely confident on the ball, hard working and, above all, a player who never shirked a tackle. He put in many outstanding displays in the left-back position (and occasionally at left-half) and was, on several occasions, the star of the day. He made 315 appearances for Nottingham Forest before joining Everton, for whom he made his debut in a disastrous 4–0 defeat at Arsenal in October 1970.

Having represented England Under-23s and the Football League, he was on the verge of making the 1970 World Cup squad but missed out when Alf Ramsey named his final 22. He made 156 appearances for Derby and ended his career with over 575 games under his belt.

NEWTON, KEITH ROBERT

Full-back: 59 apps, 1 goal
Born: Manchester, 23 June 1941 – *Died*: June 1998
Career: Manchester youth football, Blackburn Rovers (amateur, April 1957; professional, October 1958), EVERTON (£80,000, December 1969), Burnley (June 1972), Morecambe (August 1978–May 1979)

Keith Newton was one of England's full-backs for the 1970 World Cup finals, beating his namesake Henry (q.v.) for a place. He started his career at Ewood Park as a gangling inside-forward and left a decade later as England's first-choice right-back, having been compared with Rovers' former full-back Bill Eckersley. An FA Youth Cup winner with Rovers in 1959, he scored 19 goals in 357 games before transferring to Everton, quickly helping the Blues win the League title, having made his debut against Derby in December 1969. Tall and athletic, he was a cultured defender, sharp in the tackle and noted for his excellent runs down the flank. He was also quick in recovery and was a fine header of the ball as well. Unfortunately, he left Merseyside, perhaps unexpectedly, after a disagreement with manager Harry Catterick over his role!

In 1973 he helped Burnley win promotion to the top flight and a year later was a beaten FA Cup semi-finalist with the Clarets. Having made his England debut against West Germany five months before the World Cup final, he eventually replaced ex-Everton star Ray Wilson in the national team and went on to win 27 caps, while also playing in four Under-23 games and representing the Football League. He and Henry Newton played together in nine League games for Everton.

NULTY, GEOFFREY OWEN

Midfield/centre-half: 28+5 apps, 2 goals

Born: Prescot, Liverpool, 13 February 1949

Career: Prescot schoolboy football, Stoke City (professional, July 1967), Burnley (free, July 1968), Newcastle United (£120,000, December 1974), EVERTON (£45,000, July 1978; retired May 1980, due to injury; appointed assistant manager at Goodison Park), Preston North End (assistant manager, December 1981–December 1983)

Never a headline-grabbing footballer, Geoff Nulty, nevertheless, was a dedicated professional, whose career spanned 13 years, during which time he amassed close on 300 senior appearances (259 in the Football League). With ex-Everton star Keith Newton, he helped Burnley win the Second Division title (1973) and reach the semi-finals of the FA Cup the following season. He had 127 outings with Newcastle before linking up again with his former boss Gordon Lee at Everton. The bond between player and manager was strong and after his retirement Nulty became Lee's assistant at both Goodison Park and Preston. He made his debut for the Blues against Chelsea in August 1978 and played his last game in the Merseyside derby in March 1980. Sadly, Nulty was stretchered off the field after severely damaging his left knee following a tackle by Liverpool's Jimmy Case. He never played again. As the holder of an Open University degree in social sciences, he was better prepared than most players to face life without football and has done well since leaving the game. It is said that Nulty owns half of Prescot on Merseyside.

NUTTALL, THOMAS ALBERT B.

Forward: 19 apps, 7 goals

Born: Bolton, February 1889 – Deceased

Career: Heywood United, Manchester United (May 1910), EVERTON (May 1913); guest for Stockport County during the First World War; St Mirren (August 1919), Northwich Victoria (January 1920), Southend United (July 1920), Leyland (1921), Northwich Victoria (May 1922–23)

While developing his game with Manchester United, Tom Nuttall scored ten goals in three successive reserve games. This sort of form prompted other clubs, including Everton, to take note, but it wasn't until 1913 that he moved to Goodison Park. Unfortunately, at 5 ft 8 in. tall and 10 st. 8 lb in weight, he lacked the required physique to take on the more sturdy defenders and was often overpowered by the men who marked him. He hit four goals in 16 League appearances during his time with United and scored twice on his debut for Everton in a 5–0 win over Derby in October 1913. His father, Jack Nuttall, was assistant trainer at Old Trafford before the First World War, and his younger brother, Harry, made over 300 appearances for Bolton and won three England caps (1928–29).

NYARKO, ALEX
Midfield: 31+7 apps, 1 goal
Born: Accra, Ghana, 15 October 1973
Career: Asante Kotoko/Ghana, Dawn Youngsters/Ghana, Sportul Studentese /Ghana, FC Basel/Switzerland (August 1995), Karlsruhe/Germany (August 1997), RC Lens/France (July 1998), EVERTON (£4.5m, August 2000), AS Monaco/France (loan, August 2001–May 2003); left EVERTON (May 2004)

A Ghanaian international, Alex Nyarko was likened, in many quarters, to Arsenal's Patrick Vieira. The pair may have been alike in style and physical build, but on the field there was no comparison whatsoever. In the pre-season build-up before his Premiership debut against Leeds in August 2000, Nyarko looked an elegant and classy midfielder and scored a fine goal with a wonderfully executed free-kick in a friendly against Manchester City. He followed that up with another exquisite finish against Spurs but then injuries disrupted his performances and after being unfairly red-carded at Ipswich and an unsavoury incident against Arsenal, he was loaned out to Monaco for two seasons. He was released by the club (May 2004), and not given a work permit.

O'CONNOR, JONATHAN
Defender: 3+2 apps
Born: Darlington, 29 October 1976
Career: EVERTON (apprentice, April 1992; professional, October 1993), Sheffield United (February 1998), Lincoln City (trial), Blackpool (October 2000–August 2002)

Tall, well-built and able to play at right-back or centre-half, Jon O'Connor was capped by England at both youth and Under-21 levels and made five Premiership appearances for Everton before moving to Bramall Lane. He made his debut for the Blues in a 2–0 defeat at Manchester United in February 1996.

O'DONNELL, JOHN
Full-back: 198 apps, 10 goals
Born: Gateshead, 25 March 1897 – Deceased
Career: Felling Colliery, Darlington (May 1922), EVERTON (January 1925), Blackpool (December 1930), Hartlepool United (May 1932), Wigan Athletic (1933–34), Dolphin FC (1934–35)

An ever-present in Everton's 1927–28 League championship-winning side, Jack O'Donnell was converted from centre-forward to full-back and spent two-and-a-half excellent seasons with Darlington before moving to Goodison to fill the left-back position vacated by Duggie Livingstone. He made his debut in a 2–1 home League defeat by Cardiff 48 hours after joining the club and went on to serve the Blues splendidly, having a few outings in the forward-line early in 1926–27. He made over 300 League appearances during his career.

O'HARA, ALBERT EDWARD
Outside-left: 31 apps, 2 goals
Born: Glasgow, 28 October 1935
Career: Falkirk, EVERTON (June 1958), Rotherham United (February 1960), Morton, (September 1961), Barnsley (July 1962–May 1965)
Eddie O'Hara played his best football with Barnsley, for whom he scored 36 goals in 127 League games. A useful winger who hugged the touchline, he did well with Falkirk and took over from Brian Harris at Goodison Park, making his debut for the Blues in a 2–0 League defeat at Leicester in August 1958. Subsequently replaced by Bobby Laverick.

O'KANE, JOHN
Defender/Midfield: 15+2 apps
Born: Nottingham, 15 November 1974
Career: Manchester United (apprentice, April 1991; professional, January 1993), Wimbledon (loan, June–September 1995), Bury (loan, October–November 1996 and January–March 1997), Bradford City (loan, October–November 1997), EVERTON (£250,000, January 1998), Burnley (loan, October–November 1998), Bolton Wanderers (November 1999), Blackpool (free, July 2001); Hyde United (June 2003)
After making 31 senior appearances in seven years, John O'Kane joined Everton, hoping to set himself up for a long and successful spell in the Premiership. After his debut for the Blues against West Ham in January 1998, he held his place in the side by playing with confidence and commitment. However, he wasn't selected at the start of 1998–99 and eventually left the club, doing reasonably well with Bolton and Blackpool. An FA Youth Cup winner with Manchester United (1992), he gained a Second Division championship medal with Bury (1997) and helped Blackpool carry off the LDV Vans Trophy (2002).

O'KEEFE, EAMONN GERARD
Forward/Midfield: 34+17 apps, 8 goals
Born: Manchester, 13 March 1953
Career: Stalybridge Celtic (1972), Plymouth Argyle (February 1974), Hyde United, then in Saudi Arabia, Mossley, EVERTON (July 1979), Wigan Athletic (January 1982), Port Vale (£10,000, July 1983), Blackpool (£10,000, March 1985), St Patrick's Athletic, Cork City, Chester City (March–May 1989), Bangor City (1990)
A sharp, enterprising forward or midfielder, Eamonn O'Keefe represented England at semi-professional level with Stalybridge Celtic before entering the Football League with Plymouth. He went on to win five caps for the Republic of Ireland (1981–85) and in March 1985 refused to play (on PFA advice) in a League game for Port Vale against Wrexham because he had been selected for international duty the following night. Soon afterwards he was sold to Blackpool. He still had an interesting career though, appearing in 210 League games and scoring 75 goals. His Everton debut was at left-half against Bolton

in December 1979 and he made his last appearance in a third-round FA Cup-tie against West Ham in January 1982.

OLDHAM, WILFRED
Centre-forward: 22 apps, 11 goals
Born: Liverpool, *circa* 1875 – Deceased
Career: EVERTON (professional, August 1898), Blackburn Rovers (May 1900), Padham, Oswaldwistle Rovers

Wilf Oldham possessed a fair amount of zip. He had a useful first season with Everton, scoring 11 goals in 19 League games, including the winner against Bolton on his debut in October 1898. He was replaced in the team by Wilf Toman at the end of the campaign and made only three more starts before leaving.

OLDROYD, DARREN
Right-back: 0+1 app.
Born: Ormskirk, 1 November 1966
Career: EVERTON (junior, April 1983; professional, November 1984), Wolverhampton Wanderers (August 1986), Southport (May 1987–May 1988); non-League football until 2000

Darren Oldroyd's only appearance for Everton was as a 'sub' against Nottingham Forest in May 1985 when he lasted only two minutes! He had ten outings with Wolves before injury forced him into non-League football, aged 21.

OLIVER, FRANK
Inside-left: 4 apps, 4 goals
Born: Southampton, *circa* 1882 – Deceased
Career: Southampton Beagles, Brentford, EVERTON (September 1905), Clapton Orient (August 1906–May 1912)

Deputising for Alex Young, Frank Oliver scored a hat-trick on his League debut for Everton against Notts County in October 1905. A lively forward, he found the net in his next game too (against Stoke) and came close to adding to his tally in his other two outings before returning to the reserves. He notched ten goals in 40 appearances for Orient.

O'NEILL, JAMES ANTHONY
Goalkeeper: 213 apps
Born: Dublin, Ireland, 13 October 1931
Career: Bulfin United/Dublin, EVERTON (trial, 1948–49; professional, May 1949), Stoke City (£5,000, July 1960), Darlington (March 1964), Port Vale (February 1965; free, May 1967), Cork Celtic (loan, December 1966–January 1967)

Jimmy O'Neill enjoyed a successful career. With a safe pair of hands, his commanding height made him a force whenever the ball was in the air and he was able to get down remarkably quickly to the low shot fired towards the corner of the net. After a successful trial at Goodison Park, he was taken on as a full-time professional and had to wait 12 months before making his League debut against Middlesbrough in August 1950. A regular in the side for virtually five years (December 1951–October 1956), he was replaced by Albert Dunlop. Rated one of the country's finest keepers, O'Neill won 17 caps for the Republic of Ireland before his transfer to Stoke, whom he helped win the Second Division title (1963). He made over 450 appearances for clubs and country.

ORR
Centre-forward: 1 app., 1 goal
Born: *circa* 1868 – Deceased
Career: EVERTON (September 1889–March 1890)
An unknown reserve, Orr scored on his League debut to earn Everton a point from a 2–2 draw at Derby in October in 1889.

OSMAN, LEON
Midfield: 3+4 apps, 1 goal
Born: Billinge, near Wigan, Lancashire, 15 May 1981
Career: EVERTON (apprentice, June 1997; professional, August 1998), Carlisle United (loan, October–December 2002), Derby County (loan, March–April 2004)
Leon Osman, an attacking midfielder, nimble and skilful, who was capped by England at both schoolboy- and youth-team levels, helped Everton win the FA Youth Cup in 1998. He made a surprise Premiership debut for Everton as a second-half substitute against Spurs in January 2003 and came off the bench against Aston Villa for his first home game three months later. A highly successful loan spell at Derby led to his first Premiership start at Wolves, when he scored after two minutes.

OSTER, JOHN MORGAN
Winger: 28+22 apps, 3 goals
Born: Boston, Lincolnshire, 8 December 1978
Career: Grimsby Town (apprentice, April 1995; professional, July 1996), EVERTON (£1.5m, July 1997), Sunderland (£1m, August 1999), Barnsley (loan, October 2001), Grimsby Town (loan, November–December 2002 and February–March 2003)
Honoured by Wales at four different levels, winning fourteen full, one 'B', nine Under-21 and youth caps, John Oster, a clever ball-player, had his best spell in Everton's first team during 1997–98, when he took part in 31 Premiership matches, scoring a late goal in a 4–2 home win over Barnsley. He made his debut for the Blues against Crystal Palace in August 1997 and helped Sunderland reach the First Division play-offs and FA Cup semi-final in 2004.

OWEN, LESLIE TERENCE
Forward/winger: 2 apps
Born: Liverpool, 11 September 1949
Career: EVERTON (apprentice, April 1965; professional, December 1966), Bradford City (June 1970), Chester City (June 1972), Cambridge United (August 1977), Rochdale (September 1977), Port Vale (July 1979), Northwich Victoria (May 1980), Oswestry Town

Never really given a chance at Goodison Park, Terry Owen played in two League matches for Everton in four years. He made his debut at Sheffield Wednesday in April 1968 and then appeared against Nottingham Forest soon afterwards when key players were rested ahead of the FA Cup final. He scored 41 goals in 176 League games for Chester and 21 in 83 for Rochdale, ending his senior career with 71 goals in 332 League games. His son is the current England striker Michael Owen.

OWEN, WILLIAM
Left-back/left-half/centre-half: 13 apps, 3 goals
Born: Brierley Hill, Dudley, March 1869 – *Died*: 1930
Career: Dudley Road Excelsior (1886), Loughborough (1889), Wolverhampton Wanderers (July 1893), Loughborough (August 1894), Wolverhampton Wanderers (July 1895), EVERTON (July 1898; retired May 1899)

Initially a full-back, Bill Owen made 19 appearances for Wolves in his first spell and 128 in his second when he switched to left-half, helping the Molineux club reach the 1896 FA Cup final (beaten by Sheffield Wednesday). A stern performer, he made his debut for Everton at centre-half against Blackburn in September 1898, partnering Richard Boyle in defence. After that, injuries affected his performances, forcing him to retire early.

PAGE, JOHN
Full-back: 10 apps
Born: Liverpool, 24 March 1886 – *Died*: 1951
Career: Rochdale (1909), EVERTON (July 1913), Cardiff City (May 1920), Merthyr Town (June 1926–May 1929)

Jack Page failed to make the breakthrough with Rochdale and was never a regular at Everton. He made 61 appearances for Cardiff and over 100 for Merthyr. A sturdy defender, he made his debut for the Blues at Tottenham in November 1913, conceding a penalty in a 4–1 defeat. He had two brothers, Louis and Tom (q.v.). Louis was a teenager with Everton (1915), who later played for Stoke, Northampton, Burnley, Manchester United and Port Vale and was capped twice by England in 1927. He later managed Newport and was also an England baseball international.

PAGE, THOMAS
Inside-forward: 7 apps, 2 goals
Born: Kirkdale, 15 November 1888 – *Died*: Gloucester, 26 October 1973
Career: Canada FC (Liverpool), Pembroke, Liverpool (trial), Rochdale (1912), EVERTON (September 1913), St Mirren (December 1913); guest for South

Liverpool during First World War; Port Vale (£400, June 1920), New Brighton (May 1929–May 1930)

Brother of Jack Page (q.v.), Tom Page – an England baseball international – was a clever inside-forward with flair and vision. He scored 65 goals in 298 outings for Port Vale after failing to do the business at Rochdale, St Mirren or Everton, for whom he scored on his debut against Middlesbrough in October 1913 (won 2–0).

PALMER, JOHN FREDERICK

Goalkeeper: 1 app.

Born: Liverpool, *circa* 1876 – Deceased

Career: EVERTON (August 1896), London junior football (April 1897–April 1898), Luton Town (August 1898–May 1899)

Reserve John Palmer made his only appearance for Everton in a 6–0 home League win over Burnley in November 1896 when he deputised for Charlie Menham. He also made one League appearance for Luton.

PALMER, WILLIAM

Outside-right or left: 23 apps, 2 goals

Born: Barnsley, 1888 – Deceased

Career: Barnsley (professional, July 1907), Mexborough Town (March 1908), Nottingham Forest (May 1909), Rotherham County (May 1910), Bristol Rovers (August 1912), EVERTON (July 1913), Bristol Rovers (August 1919), Gillingham (May 1922), Doncaster Rovers (June 1923–May 1924)

An efficient dual-purpose winger with good pace, Bill Palmer made his League debut for Nottingham Forest against Notts County in 1909. He joined Everton as cover for George Beare, George Harrison and Jimmy Houston and deputised for all three in his first season and for Harrison and Sam Chedgzoy in his second. His debut for the Blues was against Burnley in September 1913. During his career he scored 23 goals in over 125 games.

PARKER, ALEXANDER HERSHAW

Wing-half/right-back: 220 apps, 5 goals

Born: Irvine, Ayrshire, Scotland, 2 August 1935

Career: Kello Rovers/Kirkconnel (1950), Falkirk (professional, August 1952), EVERTON (£20,000, May 1958), Southport (£2,000, September 1965), Ballymena United (player–manager, January 1968–December 1969), Drumcondra (January 1970), Southport (trainer/coach, March 1970; then manager, May 1970–May 1971); later licensee in Runcorn

A Cup winner with Falkirk (1957) when he was voted Scotland's 'Player of the Year', Alex Parker developed into a constructive full-back, helping Everton win the League title in 1962–63, appearing in 33 games as Mick Meagan's partner. Scientific in his method and approach, he was a steady, efficient defender who was capped 15 times by Scotland (1955–58), while also appearing in six Under-23 internationals and representing the Scottish League eight times. He made his League debut for Everton at Aston Villa in October 1958, replacing Alan

Sanders in a 4–2 win. Parker is regarded as being one of the finest full-backs ever to play for the club.

PARKER, JOHN WILLIAM
Inside-forward: 176 apps, 89 goals
Born: Birkenhead, 5 July 1925 – *Died*: Lancashire, August 1988
Career: St Lawrence CYMS, EVERTON (amateur, December 1947; professional, December 1948), Bury (May 1956–May 1959)
Three times Everton's leading scorer, in 1951–52, 1953–54 and 1954–55, Johnny Parker was a tall, stylish inside-forward, able to use both feet with the ability to make and score goals, averaging one every two games for Everton. After being a regular in the second XI, he finally started his League career at the age of 26, when he made his debut on the left-wing (opposite Stanley Matthews) in a 2–0 home defeat by Blackpool in March 1951 in front of 61,000 spectators. Although relegation was suffered at the end of that season, he and the rest of the players battled on. He gained a regular place in the side in 1951–52 and played in the FA Cup semi-final a year later before helping the Blues regain their top-flight status in 1953–54, scoring 31 goals in 38 games including a four-timer in an 8–4 home win over Plymouth. Often criticised for being too casual, he was, nevertheless, widely regarded as being one of the more cultured players of his day.

PARKER, ROBERT NORRIS
Centre-forward: 92 apps, 71 goals
Born: Maryhill, Glasgow, 27 March 1891 – *Died*: 1950
Career: Jordan Hill FC (Glasgow), Possill Park, Glasgow Rangers (1909), EVERTON (November 1913), Nottingham Forest (May 1921–May 1923)
Top scorer with 36 goals when Everton won the First Division championship in 1914–15, Bobby Parker netted seven hat-tricks for the Blues (second highest behind Dixie Dean's 36). In a lengthy career he grabbed almost 200 competitive goals (183 in the League). Signed to replace Tommy Browell, he added the necessary punch to the attack and played exceedingly well alongside Joe Clennell and Bill Kirsopp and then Charlie Crossley and Stan Fazackerley. Described as being a 'dandy of a player' who liked to score in twos and threes, he was unlucky not to win an international cap. He netted 19 goals in 20 games for Rangers and made a scoring debut for Everton in a 1–1 home draw with Sheffield Wednesday a month after joining the club.

PARKER, THOMAS HUBERT
Outside-right: 7 apps
Born: Blackrod, 1901 – Deceased
Career: EVERTON (May 1926–May 1928)
A reserve at Everton, Tom Parker made his League debut against Bury at Gigg Lane in September 1926. Following the departure of Sam Chedgzoy, the Blues were struggling to find a replacement and during 1926–27 six players were utilised in the right-wing position, Ted Critchley finally claiming it ahead of Parker.

PARKINSON, HENRY
Left-half: 1 app.
Born: Liverpool, *circa* 1866 – Deceased
Career: EVERTON (season 1888–89)
A well-built, half-back reserve at Everton for the first season of League football, Parkinson's only game was against Accrington in December 1888, when he deputised for George Farmer.

PARKINSON, JOSEPH SIMON
Midfield: 105+2 apps, 4 goals
Born: Eccles, 11 June 1971
Career: Wigan Athletic (apprentice, June 1987; professional, March 1989), Bournemouth (£35,000, July 1993), EVERTON (£250,000, March 1994; retired injured, May 1999)
During his 12-year career, Joey Parkinson appeared in almost 300 games (239 in the Football League). A powerful, tough-tackling player with the ability to keep the ball, he was one of the first names on manager Joe Royle's team-sheet at Everton. He made his Premiership debut as a substitute against Aston Villa in August 1994 and a year later was an FA Cup and Charity Shield winner.

PARNELL, ROY
Full-back: 3 apps
Born: Birkenhead, 8 October 1943
Career: EVERTON (amateur, April 1958; professional, April 1960), Tranmere Rovers (August 1964), Bury (February 1967–May 1970)
Limited to three League games during his six years at Goodison Park, full-back Roy Parnell later made over 100 appearances for both Tranmere and Bury. His debut in League football was for Everton against Fulham in August 1961, deputising for Alex Parker.

PARRY, CHARLES F.
Full-back/wing-half/forward: 94 apps, 5 goals
Born: Llansilin, Denbighshire, 1870 – *Died*: Oswestry, 4 February 1922
Career: Llansilin, Chester St Oswald's, EVERTON (July 1889), Ardwick (November 1891), Liverpool Caledonian, EVERTON (December 1892), Newtown (November 1895), Aberystwyth Town (1899–1900), Oswestry United (1900–07; later groundsman and club caretaker, 1910–15); refereed in the Birmingham League (1907–10); also a publican, first in Newtown (starting in 1896) and then in Oswestry
Solid wing-half Charlie Parry was discovered playing junior football by Will Nunnerley, the FAW secretary. Everton wanted to sign him in 1888, but he was 'afraid' because he thought that he wasn't good enough for League football. However, a year later he did join the Blues and scored on his League debut in a 3–2 home win over Blackburn in September 1889. He developed into a classy footballer, able to play in a variety of positions from full-back to wing-half to centre and inside-forward. He was an ever-present in his first season with the

Blues and played in half of the matches the following year when he gained a League championship medal, before an injury interrupted his progress. After spells with Ardwick and Liverpool Caledonian (to regain full fitness), he returned to Goodison Park and immediately went into the side at left-back. He then suffered a painful knee injury but bounced back again. He won the Welsh Cup with Aberystwyth Town (1900) and later spent seven years in various capacities at Oswestry.

When playing up front, Parry earned the reputation for 'bashing goalkeepers', but he never let that worry him, not even at international level when gaining 13 caps for Wales (1891–98), occupying six different positions in the process. It was Parry who declared that 'first-class players are overworked and that the number of matches in which they have to take part is too great'. He also deplored the abolition of bonuses to players. He suffered from illness in his later years, and Everton generously played a friendly against Oswestry to raise funds for their former player. He died leaving a widow and six children.

PARRY, FRANK THOMAS
Outside-right: 13 apps
Born: Aigburth, Liverpool, 14 June 1898 – *Died*: Southport, 13 March 1973
Career: Seaforth FC, EVERTON (professional, November 1921), Grimsby Town (June 1926), Accrington Stanley (July 1927), Nelson (November 1929–June 1930)

Frank Parry understudied England right-winger Sam Chedgzoy at Goodison Park and then he had Charlie Devan and Jack Prior to contest the position with at Grimsby. He did much better with Accrington (ten goals in 81 appearances) and to a fair degree with Nelson. Described by the *Athletic News* as being a 'dainty winger with skill and polish', he made his senior debut for Everton against Manchester City on Boxing Day 1922 and his last outing, four years later, was against Aston Villa (April 1926). His father, Maurice Parry, played for Liverpool and Wales and his uncle, Tom Parry, also played for Wales and Oswestry.

PATERSON, JAMES PETER
Inside-forward: 5 apps, 1 goal
Born: Scotland, 1880 – Deceased
Career: Royal Albert, EVERTON (amateur, September 1901), Royal Albert (November 1901)

An amateur throughout his short career, Jim Paterson deputised for Jack Taylor. He made his League debut for Everton against Sheffield United in October 1901 and scored his only goal in English football against Blackburn later in the month.

PATRICK, JOHN
Goalkeeper: 1 app.
Born: Kilsyth, Scotland, 10 January 1870 – Deceased
Career: Grangemouth, Falkirk, St Mirren (1890), EVERTON (October 1896), St Mirren (November 1896–99)

After an injury to Harry Briggs, Jack Patrick was signed as cover for Bob Menham but made only one League appearance for Everton, keeping a clean sheet in a 6–0 home win over Burnley six weeks after his transfer. A Scottish international, capped in 1897 against England and Wales, he also represented the Scottish League. A St Mirren loyalist, he lived in a dwelling which was in the environs of the club's Love Street ground. He had an excellent physique and in the 1890s was described as being 'one of the best custodians that has ever represented Scotland'.

PAYNE, JAMES BOLCHERSON
Outside-right/inside-left: 6 apps, 2 goals
Born: Bootle, 10 March 1926
Career: Bootle Schools, Bootle ATC, Liverpool (amateur, 1942; professional, November 1944), EVERTON (£5,000, April 1956, retired, injured, February 1957); later owned a newsagent's/confectionery shop in Liverpool
Jimmy Payne scored 37 goals in 224 appearances for Liverpool, whom he represented in the 1950 FA Cup final (against Arsenal). Dubbed the 'Merseyside Matthews' at Anfield, he moved to Everton as insurance cover for Jimmy Harris and Wally Fielding, among others. Possessing excellent ball control and a deceptive body swerve, he gained an England 'B' cap as a 'Red' and made his debut for Everton against Blackpool at Goodison Park shortly after his transfer. However, niggling injuries (which had started at Liverpool) began to take the edge off his game and Payne was forced to retire early.

PEACOCK, JOHN
Wing-half/centre-forward: 161 apps, 12 goals
Born: Wigan, 15 March 1897 – *Died*: 1979
Career: Atherton, EVERTON (July 1919), Middlesbrough (September 1927), Sheffield Wednesday (August 1930), Clapton Orient (July 1931), Sleipner FC/Sweden (player–coach, March 1933; retired from playing, April 1934), Wrexham (trainer, July 1939–48)
'Joe' Peacock was an important member of Everton's rebuilding plans after the First World War. He had a couple of games at right-half, making his League debut against Sheffield Wednesday in January 1920 but was then switched to centre-forward and scored his first goal from that position against Sheffield United. Later moved to wing-half, he became one of the stars of the team, going on to appear in over 160 games for the Blues before transferring to Middlesbrough, with whom he won a Second Division championship medal (1928–29). In the summer following that season Peacock joined the England party on a continental tour and won three caps against France, Belgium and Spain. He made 55 appearances for Orient before coaching in Sweden.

PEARSON, JAMES FINDLAY
Midfielder/striker: 97+23 apps, 19 goals
Born: Falkirk, Scotland, 24 March 1953
Career: Gairdoch United, St Johnstone (amateur, June 1969; professional,

March 1970), EVERTON (£100,000, May 1974), Newcastle United (£75,000, August 1978; retired, injured, February 1980); returned with Barrow (April 1980), Gateshead (November 1981), North Shields (player–manager, June 1983), Gateshead (July 1984), Workington (October 1984), Whitley Bay (coach, November 1985–May 1988), Blyth Spartans (coach, November 1985–May 1988), North Shields (manager, June 1988); coach in Brunei; Gateshead (assistant manager, April 1989–May 1990); later worked in insurance, then for sportswear giants Nike, based in Washington (County Durham)

The slimly built, fair-haired Jim Pearson was useful as a midfielder or striker, being skilful with deft touches and always likely to find the net. Capped by his country at schoolboy- and youth-team levels, he made his debut as a 17-year-old north of the border and netted over 40 goals for St Johnstone while adding two Under-23 caps to his collection and being 'sub' for the Scottish League. He settled in quickly at Goodison Park, making his debut as a substitute in a second-round League Cup replay against Aston Villa, going on to score four goals in 31 appearances that season. He was switched to midfield in 1975–76 and the following year helped Everton reach the semi-final of the FA Cup, also playing in the second and third games of the League Cup final against Villa. Gordon Lee sold him to Newcastle, where he made an immediate impact before injury ruined his career. A respected professional in non-League circles, he guided Blyth Spartans to two Northern League titles.

PEJIC, MICHAEL

Full-back: 93 apps, 2 goals
Born: Chesterton, Staffs, 25 January 1950
Career: Chesterton and North Staffs Schools, Corona Drinks FC, Stoke City (apprentice, June 1966; professional, January 1968), EVERTON (£135,000, February 1977), Aston Villa (£225,000, September 1979; retired, injured, May 1980); became a farmer (unsuccessfully); Leek Town (manager, 1981–82), Northwich Victoria (manager, 1982–83), Port Vale (youth coach, July 1986; senior coach, December 1987–March 1992), FA coach and player development officer; Kuwait (coach), Chester City (manager, 1994–95), Stoke City (youth coach, 1995–99)

Son of a Yugoslav miner, aggressive full-back Mike Pejic was a thoughtful player who cleared his lines precisely, covered well, was totally committed and some say he was the fiercest tackler seen at Goodison Park for years. During a fine career he won four caps for England, appeared in eight Under-23 internationals and helped Stoke win the League Cup in 1972. He made over 400 appearances during his career (300 for the Potters). His debut for Everton was against his former club Stoke in February 1977 but he missed that season's League Cup final, having already played in the competition with the Potters. Partnering Dave Jones at full-back, he was outstanding during 1977–78 and was doing well again before suffering an injury against Leeds United in December 1978. He recovered but couldn't regain his first-team place (owing to the presence of John Bailey) and was subsequently transferred to Aston Villa. His brother, Mel Pejic, also played for Stoke and made over 400 League appearances for Hereford and 100 plus for Wrexham (1979–95).

PEMBRIDGE, MARK ANTHONY

Midfield: 91+10 apps, 4 goals
Born: Merthyr, 29 November 1970
Career: Luton Town (apprentice, April 1987; professional, July 1989), Derby County (£1.25m, June 1992), Sheffield Wednesday (£900,000, July 1995), Benfica/Portugal (free, July 1998), EVERTON (£800,000, August 1999), Fulham (£750,000, July 2003)

An industrious and versatile midfielder, usually deployed on the left-hand side of the park, Mark Pembridge was given a holding role in his last season with Everton and did well for both club and country, helping Wales reach the play-offs for Euro 2004. He made 70 appearances for Luton, 140 for Derby and 107 for Wednesday before his spell in Portugal. On returning to the Premiership, he made his debut for Everton as a substitute against Aston Villa in August 1999 and his first goal for the club was a belated Christmas present, banged home in a 5–0 win over Sunderland on Boxing Day of the same year. Honoured by Wales at schoolboy, Under-21 (1) and 'B' (2) team levels, Pembridge has now won over 50 senior caps.

PHELAN, TERENCE MICHAEL

Left-back: 25+3 apps
Born: Manchester, 16 March 1967
Career: Leeds United (apprentice, May 1983; professional, August 1984), Swansea City (free, July 1986), Wimbledon (£100,000, July 1987), Manchester City (£2.5m, August 1992), Chelsea (£900,000, November 1995), EVERTON (£850,000, January 1997–May 1999)

Eyebrows were raised when Everton boss Joe Royle signed Terry Phelan from Chelsea. But the Republic of Ireland international settled in at Goodison Park immediately and did well initially before suffering injury. Attack-minded, speedy and good on the overlap, and a replacement for the injured Andy Hinchcliffe, he made his debut for the Blues against Blackburn on New Year's Day 1997 and played in 15 Premiership games that season. However, he suffered from the injury curse that blighted the club during the late 1990s, and calf and knee problems curtailed his performances before he was released. Phelan gained 38 full caps and served his country at youth, Under-21, Under-23 and 'B' team levels. He made 450 appearances in senior football, including 198 for Wimbledon and 122 for Manchester City.

PICKERING, FREDERICK

Centre-forward: 115 apps, 70 goals
Born: Blackburn, 19 January 1941
Career: Blackburn amateur football, Blackburn Rovers (amateur, August 1956; professional, January 1958), EVERTON (£85,000, March 1964), Birmingham City (£50,000, August 1967), Blackpool (£5,000, June 1969),

Blackburn Rovers (£5,000, March 1971), Brighton and Hove Albion (trial, February–March 1972); retired May 1972; later worked as a fork-lift truck driver for a plastics firm near Blackburn

Burly centre-forward Fred Pickering had a fine career in League football, venturing all over the country. Initially a full-back before being converted into a striker, he was an FA Youth Cup winner with Blackburn in 1959 and during his first spell at Ewood Park scored 59 goals in 123 League games. He then produced the goods for Everton, bagging a hat-trick on his debut in a 6–1 win over Nottingham Forest in March 1964, following up two months later with another treble on his international debut for England in a 10–0 win over the USA in New York. He later added two more caps to his tally, playing against Northern Ireland and Belgium.

A well-built, powerful, pacy footballer, he quickly bedded himself into the first team at Goodison Park but unfortunately he missed out on England's glory year of 1966 and was an absentee from Everton's FA Cup final success that same year. He teamed up with future Everton star Bob Latchford and a young Trevor Francis at Birmingham. Besides his senior caps, Pickering also represented his country in three Under-23 internationals and played for the Football League XI. All told, he netted 168 goals in 354 League games, scored in seven successive FA Cup games for Everton (1965, 1966) and holds the record for most 'European' goals for the Blues (six). Pickering ballooned to over 16 st. after his playing days were over.

PINCHBECK, CLIFFORD BRIAN

Centre-forward: 3 apps
Born: Cleethorpes, 20 January 1925 – *Died*: 2 November 1996
Career: Scunthorpe United (junior 1942), EVERTON (professional, December 1947), Brighton and Hove Albion (August 1949), Port Vale (£3,500, November 1949), Northampton Town (November 1951), Bath City (May 1952), Salisbury

The tall figure of Cliff Pinchbeck covered for Harry Catterick and Jock Dodds at Everton, making his debut in the First Division against Derby in January 1948. After a season with Brighton (five goals in 14 games), he scored a hat-trick on his debut for Port Vale in a 4–0 home win over Millwall (November 1949), finishing as leading scorer that season. He went on to register 40 goals in 78 games for the Potteries club. He broke his ankle in his third game for Northampton.

PINKNEY, ERNEST

Outside-right: 8 apps, 1 goal
Born: Glasgow, 23 November 1887 – Deceased
Career: West Hartlepool, EVERTON (February 1910), Barrow (May 1912), Gillingham (July 1913), Liverpool (October 1915), Tranmere Rovers (1919–20), Halifax Town (July 1921), Accrington Stanley (June 1922; retired, injured, May 1923)

A positive winger, Ernie Pinkney was reserve to Jack Sharp at Goodison Park and made his League debut on the right flank against Bury in March 1910. His only goal for the Blues came in a 2–0 win at Preston in January 1911 when he occupied the inside-right berth. He struggled at Tranmere before netting three times in 30 League games for Halifax.

PINNELL, ARCHIBALD
Goalkeeper: 3 apps
Born: Liverpool, *circa* 1870 – Deceased
Career: EVERTON (August 1892), Preston North End (April 1894), Chorley (August 1894), Burnley (August 1898), New Brighton (March–April 1899), Argyle FC/Scotland (1899–1900)
One of five goalkeepers used by Everton during 1892–93, Archie Pinnell played in just three League games, making his debut in a 2–2 draw at Blackburn in September. He played once for Preston, helping them retain their First Division status after beating Notts County in a Test match. Towards the end of his career, Pinnell played on the right-wing.

PISTONE, ALESSANDRO
Full-back/centre-half: 67+8 apps
Born: Milan, Italy, 27 July 1975
Career: Vicenza/Italy (April 1992), Solbiatese/Italy (August 1993), Crevalcore/ Italy (July 1994), Vicenza/Italy (August 1995), Inter Milan/Italy (October 1995), Newcastle United (£4.3m, July 1997), EVERTON (£3m, July 2000)
An Italian Under-21 defender in 1996, Sandro Pistone made 63 appearances for Newcastle before transferring to Everton. A good reader of the game, with pace and crispness in his tackling, he was always seeking to get forward, especially from the left-back position, despite being prominently right-footed. He made his debut for the Blues against Leeds in August 2000 but then had a large chunk of that season and the next two wiped out through injury, suffering lengthy play-offs with knee-ligament damage and a hernia problem. He made 100 appearances in Italy before moving to St James's Park.

POINTON, NEIL GEOFFREY
Full-back: 125+13 apps, 5 goals
Born: Warsop, 28 November 1964
Career: Scunthorpe United (apprentice, April 1981; professional, August 1982), EVERTON (£75,000, November 1985), Manchester City (£600,000 July 1990), Oldham Athletic (£600,000, July 1992), Heart of Midlothian (£50,000, October 1995), Walsall (free, July 1998), Chesterfield (free, January 2000), Hednesford Town (June 2000)
After making 185 senior appearances for Scunthorpe, composed left-back Neil Pointon helped Everton win the League championship and Charity Shield in 1987. His debut for the Blues came in a 6–1 home win over Arsenal in November 1985, when he took over from Alan Harper, who had switched to the opposite flank. Kept out of the side by Paul Power and then Pat Van den Hauwe, he eventually became Gary Stevens's partner and formed an excellent back-line

with Kevin Ratcliffe and Dave Watson. Pointon made 90 appearances for Manchester City and played under Joe Royle in the Premiership for Oldham. He starred in 100 games for the Latics, following up with 77 outings for Hearts, 75 for Walsall (skippering the Saddlers to promotion from Division Two in 1999) and 12 for Chesterfield, amassing a career record of 684 senior appearances.

POLLOCK

Right-half: 1 app.
Born: circa 1866 – Deceased
Career: EVERTON (August 1888–April 1889)
Pollock's only League game during his short career was for Everton in a 6–2 defeat at Bolton in September 1888, when he deputised for Johnny Holt.

POTTS, HAROLD J.

Inside-forward: 63 apps, 16 goals
Born: Hetton-le-Hole, 22 October 1922
Career: Hetton, Burnley (November 1937); guest for Fulham and Sunderland during the Second World War; EVERTON (£20,000, October 1950; retired May 1956), Wolverhampton Wanderers (coach, July 1956), Shrewsbury Town (manager, June 1957–February 1958), Burnley (manager, February 1958–February 1970; general manager to February 1972), Blackpool (manager, December 1972–May 1976), Burnley (chief scout, July 1976; manager, February 1977–October 1979), Colne Dynamo (chief scout, 1980s)
Harry Potts was Everton's first £20,000 signing. An effective inside-forward, he scored 50 goals in 181 appearances for Burnley, gaining an FA Cup-winner's medal in 1947. The Turf Moor board turned down a £25,000 bid from Blackpool before selling him to the Blues. He made his Everton debut at Charlton in October 1950, partnering Tommy Eglington on the left-wing. His best season with the club was his first when he scored five goals in 29 games. He played once when promotion was gained from the Second Division in 1954.

He spent 12 years as manager at Turf Moor, guiding one of Burnley's greatest-ever sides into Europe as League champions and taking them to Wembley for the 1962 FA Cup final. Those were heady days for the Clarets, but Potts wasn't getting younger and in 1972 moved upstairs. He took over from Bob Stokoe at Blackpool and during his second spell at Turf Moor the Clarets won the Anglo-Scottish Cup. He was coach at Molineux under manager Stan Cullis.

POWELL, AUBREY

Inside-forward: 35 apps, 5 goals
Born: Lower Cwmtwrch, near Swansea, 19 April 1918
Career: Cwm Wanderers, Swansea Town (amateur, 1933–34), Leeds United (November 1935), EVERTON (£10,000, July 1948), Birmingham City (£7,000, August 1950); after refusing to sign for Wellington Town (August 1951), he retired to become a sweet shop 'rep', later running his own confectionery shop in Leeds

Aubrey Powell was Everton's first five-figure signing after the Second World War. He joined the Blues in readiness for the 1948–49 season, made his debut in a 3–3 home draw with Newcastle and helped the Blues escape relegation from the top flight. A dapper yet somewhat fragile-looking footballer, he was a wonderful dribbler and possessed a strong, right-foot shot. He twice fought back after doctors had written him off with serious injuries. During the Second World War he served in Belgium before returning to win eight full caps (two as an Everton player) and star in four Victory internationals for Wales. He scored 25 goals in 112 League games for Leeds.

POWER, PAUL CHRISTOPHER
Midfield: 69+2 apps, 7 goals
Born: Manchester, 30 October 1953
Career: Leeds Polytechnic, Manchester City (apprentice, September 1973; professional, July 1975), EVERTON (£65,000, June 1986–May 1988; coach to November 1990)

After making 437 appearances for Manchester City, left-sided midfielder Paul Power entered the twilight zone of his professional career with Everton, for whom he made his debut at Wembley, in the 1986 Charity Shield game against Liverpool. He had expected to see out his playing days at Maine Road after skippering one of City's finest post-Second World War sides but was surprisingly allowed to leave Maine Road with 12 months of his contract remaining. Signed by Blues' boss Howard Kendall, he had a wonderful first season at Goodison Park, making 49 appearances and scoring four goals, collecting a League championship medal in the process. After announcing his retirement, he stayed on as coach under manager Colin Harvey but lost his job when Kendall returned for a second time as boss. He led Manchester City in the 1981 FA Cup final defeat by Spurs and five years later lost another Wembley final when Chelsea won the FMC. He played for England against Spain in a 'B' international in 1981.

PRATT, CHARLES B.
Centre-half: 2 apps
Born: Birmingham, *circa* 1888 – Deceased
Career: Barrow (August 1907), EVERTON (August 1909), Exeter City (August 1910; retired May 1915; then trainer until 1922)

Rough and ready defender Charlie Pratt made two League appearances for Everton, lining up against Manchester United and Blackburn in April 1910, when he deputised for Jack Borthwick. He made 104 appearances for Exeter before becoming the Grecians' trainer. His brother, William Pratt, played for Birmingham in the 1890s.

PROUDFOOT, JOHN
Inside-right/centre-forward: 89 apps, 31 goals
Born: Scotland, *circa* 1872 – Deceased
Career: Partick Thistle (1894), Blackburn Rovers (February 1897), EVERTON (£100, August 1898), Watford (March 1902)

A craggy Scotsman, strong with a forceful approach, Jock Proudfoot did well north of the border with Partick before netting 14 goals in 37 games for Blackburn. After joining Everton, he went straight into the team alongside Edgar Chadwick, scoring on his debut in a 2–1 home win over his former club, Blackburn. He finished up as leading marksman in his first season (13 goals) and scored eight times the following year and ten in 1900–01 before losing his place to Alex Young, although he did get a few more outings when deputising for Jack Taylor and Jimmy Settle.

RADOSAVIJEVIC, PREDRAG
Forward: 25+28 apps, 4 goals
Born: Belgrade, Yugoslavia, 24 June 1963
Career: St Louis (USA), EVERTON (August 1992), Portsmouth (July 1994–May 1995); Kansas City Wizards/USA (1995–2004)
Affectionately known around Goodison Park as 'Preki', Predrag Radosavijevic, a Yugoslavian international, had two good seasons with the Blues, although he had to battle hard and long to win a place in the starting line-up, hence his total of substitute appearances. He made his League debut against Leeds in September 1992, having played against Rotherham in the League Cup three days earlier, and netted his first goal against Middlesbrough in April 1993 (his 20th game for Everton). His career flourished in America and he was voted 'Most Valuable Player' in the US Mid-League South in 1997 and again in 2003, at the age of 40!

RADZINSKI, TOMASZ
Striker: 85+16 apps, 26 goals
Born: Poznan, Poland, 14 December 1973
Career: Toronto Rockets/NASL (1989), St Catherine's FC/Belgium (1990), AS Roma/Italy (1992), Germinal Ekeren/Belgium (April 1994), RSC Anderlecht/Belgium (July 1998), EVERTON (£4.5m, August 2001), Fulham (£1.75m, July 2004)
After struggling with injuries during his first season at Goodison Park, when he played in only 29 matches, Canadian international (over 20 caps to date) Tomasz Radzinski bounced back in style and had a wonderful 2002–03, as partner to Kevin Campbell, and, at times, Wayne Rooney, netting 11 goals. A small, nippy and positive marksman, fleet of foot, he made his debut in the Premiership as a substitute against Liverpool in September 2001 and scored his first goal a fortnight later in a 5–0 home win over West Ham. A proven scorer before joining the Blues, Radzinski netted 42 times in 104 League games for Ekeren and 52 in 78 outings for Anderlecht.

RAFFERTY, DANIEL
Wing-half/outside-right: 7 apps
Born: 1885 – Deceased
Career: EVERTON (seasons 1907–10)
A reserve at Goodison Park, Dan Rafferty could play equally as well as a right-half or an orthodox outside-right, preferring the latter, from where he made his

League debut at Blackburn in March 1908, when he deputised for Jack Sharp. He played in both wing-half positions in 1909–10.

RAITT, DAVID
Right-back: 131 apps
Born: Buckhaven, Fife, Scotland, 1897 – Deceased
Career: Buckhaven Thistle, Army football (1914–18), Dundee (1919), EVERTON (May 1922), Blackburn Rovers (August 1928), Forfar Athletic (April 1929)
Only 5 ft 9 in. tall and weighing 11 st., David Raitt was a steady, reliable defender who was never out of place against tougher opponents. He learnt his football in the Army and represented the Scottish League as a Dundee player before transferring to Goodison Park, arriving at a dismal time for the Merseyside club, who had struggled against relegation all season. He made his League debut against Spurs in September 1922, partnering Jock McDonald and although his position was threatened when Duggie Livingstone was introduced and then Warney Cresswell, Riatt stuck it out, regained his first-team place and held on until Jasper Kerr arrived in 1926. He played six games in the Blues' championship-winning season of 1927–28.

RANKIN, ANDREW GEORGE
Goalkeeper: 105+1 apps
Born: Bootle, 11 May 1944
Career: EVERTON (amateur, June 1959; professional, October 1961), Watford (£20,000, November 1971), Huddersfield Town (December 1979–May 1981); now works as a warehouseman in Huddersfield
Andy Rankin was the first goalkeeping substitute used by Everton, coming on for Gordon West in an Inter-Cities Fairs Cup encounter against Nuremberg in October 1965. Understudying West for most of his stay at Goodison, he also suffered his fair share of injuries. He had his best spell in the first team between November 1963 and December 1964, making 42 appearances with his debut coming against Nottingham Forest at the start. Technically sound with fine reflexes and a safe pair of hands, Rankin had set his mind on quitting the game to join the police force but new Everton boss Harry Catterick persuaded him to continue in soccer and in the end the decision was right. His finest moment for the club was his save in the penalty shoot-out against Borussia Moenchengladbach that clinched victory in a European Cup-tie in 1970. After leaving the Blues, he played in 299 League games for Watford and 71 for Huddersfield. He gained one Under-23 cap for England.

RANKIN, BRUCE
Winger: 38 apps, 7 goals
Born: Glasgow, 21 July 1880 – *Died*: 1946
Career: Walton Council and St. Bernard's Schools (Liverpool), White Star Wanderers, Kirkdale FC, Tranmere Rovers (trial), EVERTON (December 1901), West Bromwich Albion (£500, February 1906), Manchester City

(£500, February 1907), Luton Town (1907–8), Egremont Social Club, Wirral FC, Wrexham (August 1908; retired May 1912)

Bruce Rankin was an easy-moving, graceful-looking wing-forward, clever on the ball and a player who could let fly with a useful, telling shot. He was never a regular performer in the Everton side, having his first game against Sheffield United in February 1902. He represented the North against the South in 1903 and in 1909 gained a Welsh Cup-winner's medal with Wrexham. He left WBA in a huff after being suspended and transfer-listed.

RANKIN, GEORGE

Left-back: 39 apps

Born: Liverpool, 29 January 1930 – *Died*: 1989

Career: EVERTON (amateur, April 1946; professional, August 1948), Southport (July 1956–May 1960)

Owing to the form of Gordon Dugdale and Jack Hedley and then George Saunders and Eric Moore, well-built full-back George Rankin had to wait until December 1950 before making his League debut for Everton against Derby at Goodison Park. He retained his place in the side for the remainder of that season before losing out to the former Rangers defender John Lindsay. He later did well with Southport, for whom he appeared in 144 League games in four seasons.

RATCLIFFE, KEVIN

Defender: 489+4 apps, 2 goals

Born: Mancot, Flintshire, Wales, 12 November 1960

Career: Shotton CP School, Deeside Primary School XI, Flint Under-13s and Under-15s, Wales Under-15s, EVERTON (apprentice, June 1977; professional, November 1978), Dundee, EVERTON (n/c, October 1992), Cardiff City (n/c, January 1993), Nottingham Forest (n/c, 1994), Derby County (n/c, January 1994), Chester City (September 1994; manager, August 1995); Shrewsbury Town (manager, November 1999; resigned May 2003)

Kevin Ratcliffe skippered Everton to two League titles and victory in both the FA Cup and European Cup-Winners' Cup finals. He also played in three losing FA Cup finals and five semi-finals, was ever-present in 1986–87 and is the only player to captain the Blues in four FA Cup finals. With 57 appearances to his name, he is second, behind Neville Southall (70), for most outings for Everton in the FA Cup and he's also made the third highest number of League Cup appearances for the club (46) behind Southall (65) and Graeme Sharp (48). He played in almost 500 matches for the Blues (359 in the League) and lined up in 32 Merseyside derbies (only Southall has more to his credit: 41). He played 11 times for the Blues at Wembley: four FA Cup finals, one League Cup final, four Charity Shield games, one Simod Cup final and one Zenith Data Systems Cup final, and two of his 59 full internationals for Wales (against England) were also at Wembley. Capped four times at youth and twice at Under-21 levels, he was a supreme servant to the Blues and was rewarded with a testimonial against Howard Kendall's Athletic Bilbao in April 1989.

RAWLINGS, JAMES SIDNEY DEAN
Outside-right: 2 apps
Born: Wombwell, Yorkshire, 5 May 1913 – *Died*: 1956
Career: Dick Kerr's XI. Preston North End (professional, March 1932), Huddersfield Town (March 1934), West Bromwich Albion (March 1935), Northampton Town (June 1936), Millwall (December 1937), EVERTON (November 1945), Plymouth Argyle (May 1946; retired December 1947)
Renowned for his cross-wing play, Sid Rawlings had a decent time away from Goodison Park, and during his 'League' career – severely disrupted by the Second World War – he appeared in 190 games and scored 69 goals. He joined Everton halfway through the transitional season of 1945–46 and played in both FA Cup games against his former club, Preston, in January 1946 as well as in 17 Regional League North games, netting two goals. His father, Bill Rawlings, won two England caps in the 1920s as a Southampton player.

REA, KENNETH WILFRED
Wing-half: 51 apps
Born: Liverpool, 17 February 1935
Career: EVERTON (amateur, April 1950; professional, June 1952), Runcorn (May 1959)
Nine years at Goodison Park, seven as a loyal professional, reserve wing-half Ken Rea had to wait until September 1956 before making his League debut, taking over the number six shirt from Cyril Lello for the game at Wolves. He made 18 appearances that season and 29 the following term, when he switched to the right-half berth.

REAY, HAROLD
Outside-right: 2 apps, 1 goal
Born: County Durham, 1870 – Deceased
Career: Newcastle United (1892), EVERTON (September 1893), Southampton (April 1895)
A reserve right-winger, Harry Reay's two games for Everton were against Bolton (League) on the last day of the 1893–94 season and Southport (FA Cup) in January 1895. He failed to make the first XI at Newcastle or Southampton.

REES, BARRIE GWYN
Wing-half/centre-forward: 4 apps, 2 goals
Born: Rhyl, Wales, 4 February 1944 – *Died*: summer 1965
Career: EVERTON (amateur, April 1959; professional, September 1961), Brighton and Hove Albion (January 1965)
Welshman Barrie Rees died in a car crash at the age of 21 while still a registered player with Brighton. He made four appearances for Everton, scoring on his debut at West Ham in October 1963, when he deputised at centre-forward for Alex Young.

REHN, JAN STEFAN
Midfield: 2+4 apps
Born: Stockholm, Sweden, 22 September 1966
Career: Djurgardens IF/Sweden, EVERTON (June 1989), IFK Gothenburg/Sweden (January 1990)
Swedish midfielder Stefan Rehn failed to impress during his stay at Goodison Park, making his League debut at Charlton in September 1989, when he wore the number six shirt in place of Norman Whiteside.

REID, DAVID
Half-back/inside-right/outside-left: 101 apps, 11 goals
Born: Glasgow, *circa* 1895 – Deceased
Career: Distillery, EVERTON (May 1920), Distillery (February 1927)
Signed to boost Everton's squad after an initial lacklustre post-First World War campaign, David Reid, who had done well in Ireland with Distillery, scored five goals in 21 League games for the Blues in 1920–21 when teaming up with Charlie Crossley, Joe Peacock and Stan Fazackerley. He had to work harder the following year before being tried on the left-wing, where he participated in 13 games, eventually reverting back to a defensive position.

REID, PETER
Midfield: 228+6 apps, 13 goals
Born: Huyton, Lancashire, 20 June 1956
Career: Bolton Wanderers (apprentice, June 1972; professional, May 1974), EVERTON (£60,000, December 1982), Queens Park Rangers (free, February 1989), Manchester City (free, December 1989), Southampton (n/c, September 1993), Notts County (n/c, February 1994), Bury (n/c, July–September 1994); Sunderland (manager, March 1995–October 2002); then a football summariser on Sky Sport; Coventry City (manager, April 2004)
Midfield workhorse Peter Reid won four medals with Everton (two League titles, one FA Cup victory and a European Cup-Winners' Cup triumph). Voted PFA 'Footballer of the Year' in 1985, he had a terrific engine and lasted every minute of every game he played in, never shirking a tackle and inspiring the players around him. He had already amassed 262 appearances for Bolton before making his debut for the Blues in a 3–1 home win over Nottingham Forest in December 1982, when he accompanied Kevin Sheedy and Steve McMahon in centre-field. After more than 200 outings for the Blues, he moved south to join QPR. When he retired, he had accumulated a record of 642 appearances and 41 goals. Capped 13 times by England and on six occasions by the Under-21s, Reid did well as a manager of Sunderland, guiding the Black Cats into the Premiership as First Division champions in 1999.

RENNIE, ALEXANDER
Goalkeeper: 4 apps
Born: Scotland, 1868 – Deceased
Career: EVERTON (August 1892–May 1893)
Alex Rennie was one of five players used between the posts by Everton during 1892–93, making his first appearance in a 5–3 home defeat by Sheffield Wednesday in November 1892.

RICHARDSON, KEVIN
Midfield: 125+20 apps, 20 goals
Born: Newcastle-upon-Tyne, 4 December 1962
Career: EVERTON (apprentice, June 1978; professional, December 1980), Watford (£225,000, September 1986), Arsenal (£200,000, August 1987), Real Sociedad/Spain (£750,000, July 1990), Aston Villa (£450,000, August 1991), Coventry City (£300,000, February 1995), Southampton (£150,000, September 1997), Barnsley (£300,000, July 1998), Blackpool (loan, January–February 1999; retired May 2000), Stockport County (assistant manager/coach, 2002–03)
Kevin Richardson performed consistently over the years, working tirelessly for every club he served. Capped once by England, he gained winner's medals with Everton in the FA Cup (1984), European Cup-Winners' Cup (1985) and League championship (1985), and followed up by collecting a second League championship prize with Arsenal (1989). He also played in Everton's Charity Shield-winning side of 1984 and a decade later skippered Aston Villa to victory in the League Cup final, becoming the first player ever in English football to win the three major trophies with different clubs. During his career Richardson amassed over 700 appearances at club level – 684 in England, the first as a 'sub' for Everton against Sunderland in November 1981, when he conceded a penalty. He scored 50 goals.

RIDEOUT, PAUL DAVID
Striker: 112+28 apps, 40 goals
Born: Bournemouth, 14 August 1964
Career: Priestlands School, Southampton and Hampshire Schools, Lawrence BC, Lymington, Southampton (schoolboy forms, 1979–80), Swindon Town (apprentice, June 1980; professional, August 1961), Aston Villa (£250,000, June 1983), Bari/Italy (£400,000, July 1985), Southampton (£430,000, July 1988), Swindon Town (loan, March–April 1991), Notts County (£250,000, September 1991), Glasgow Rangers (£500,000, January 1992), EVERTON (£500,000, August 1992), Red Star/France (August 1998), Tranmere Rovers (free, August 2000; retired May 2002); now lives in the USA
Paul Rideout achieved fame as a teenager when he scored a stunning goal playing for England schoolboys in the televised game against Scotland at Wembley. He was on Southampton's books at the time, but was allowed to join Swindon, returning to The Dell in 1988, having by then scored 75 goals in 250 matches while also gaining eight England youth and five Under-21 caps.

Rideout was a record 'sale' by Swindon to Aston Villa and his total fees had reached almost £2m by the time he signed for Everton. He made his debut against Sheffield Wednesday in August 1992 and at the end of the 1994–95 season had the pleasure of scoring the winning goal in the FA Cup final against Manchester United. In a fine career Rideout netted over 150 goals in almost 550 appearances. When Rideout made his League debut against Hull in 1980, he became Swindon's youngest-ever player, aged 16 years, 107 days.

RIGBY, ARTHUR
Inside/outside-left: 44 apps, 11 goals
Born: Chorlton, near Manchester, 7 June 1890 – *Died*: Crewe, 25 March 1960
Career: Manchester and Salford junior football, Stockport County (trial), Crewe
    Alexandra (August 1919), Bradford City (£1,200, February 1921), Blackburn
    Rovers (£2,500, April 1925), EVERTON (November 1929), Middlesbrough
    (May 1932), Clapton Orient (August 1933), Crewe Alexandra (August 1935;
    retired May 1937)
A cunning footballer, Arthur Rigby possessed all the tricks of the trade, being quick, tricky and an expert at crossing the ball on the run when occupying the left-wing position (his favourite). He was an FA Cup winner with Blackburn in 1928, gained a Second Division championship medal with Everton in 1931, won the Welsh Cup with Crewe in 1935 and was capped five times by England (1927–28). He made his debut for the Blues against Birmingham in November 1929 when he partnered Jimmy Stein on the left flank and scored twice in his next game, a 5–4 defeat by Leicester. In a lengthy career Rigby netted 107 goals in 468 League games – all this after playing in goal as a youngster! He was an electrician by trade.

RIGSBY, HERBERT
Inside-left: 14 apps, 5 goals
Born: Aintree, Liverpool, 22 July 1894 – *Died*: 1972
Career: Inglewood FC, Southport (briefly), EVERTON (January 1919),
    Swansea Town (1920), Southport (1921) Burscough Rangers, Marine,
    Hartley's FC
Bert Rigsby, a solid man with a strong shot, played his best football with Southport, for whom he scored ten goals in 49 League games in his second spell. He never quite fitted the bill at Goodison Park, despite scoring on his League debut at Bradford PA in September 1919, having netted five times (including a hat-trick against Rochdale) in four Lancashire Section games in the previous March and April.

RIMMER, NEIL
Midfield: 0+1 app.
Born: Liverpool, 13 November 1967
Career: EVERTON (apprentice, April 1984), Ipswich Town (professional,
    August 1985), Wigan Athletic (July 1988–May 1996)
Neil Rimmer's only appearance for Everton was as a 'sub' against Luton in May 1985. An England schoolboy and youth international, he was released before he

could sign as a full-time professional at Goodison Park. He scored ten goals in 190 League games for Wigan.

RIMMER, STUART ALAN
Forward: 3 apps
Born: Southport, 12 October 1964
Career: EVERTON (apprentice, April 1981; professional, October 1982), Chester City (January 1985), Watford (March 1988), Notts County (November 1988), Walsall (February 1989), Barnsley (March 1991), Chester City (August 1991), Rochdale (loan, August–September 1994), Preston North End (loan, December 1994); retired May 1998
A skilful, pacy footballer, former England youth international Stuart Rimmer was never really given a chance at Goodison Park. He made just three appearances for the Blues, making his League debut at Swansea in May 1982. He became Chester's all-time record goalscorer, finding the net 149 times in his two spells at that club and during his career bagged 198 goals in 580 games.

RING, THOMAS
Winger: 27 apps, 6 goals
Born: Glasgow, 8 August 1930 – *Died*: October 1997
Career: Glasgow schoolboy football, St Teresa's Boys' Guild (Glasgow), Springburn United, Glasgow Ashfield, Clyde (August 1949), EVERTON (£8,000, January 1960), Barnsley (£2,000, November 1961), Aberdeen (February 1963), Fraserburgh (July 1963), Stevenage Town (October 1963–May 1964)
A small, sprightly winger with good technique, Tommy Ring was an embodiment of the truth that size is not essential for footballing success. He compiled a fine goal-tally with Clyde, scoring 45 times for the club's two Scottish Second Division championship-winning sides of 1952 and 1957 and finding the net en route to their two Scottish Cup triumphs of 1955 and 1958. He made an excellent start in the Football League with Everton, setting up two goals on his debut in a 6–1 home win over Nottingham Forest in January 1960. His Goodison Park career was effectively ended when he broke his leg against Chelsea in October 1960. Capped 12 times by Scotland (1953–58), Ring also represented the Scottish League on eight occasions.

RIOCH, BRUCE DAVID
Midfield: 39 apps, 4 goals
Born: Aldershot, 6 September 1947
Career: Romsey Junior School (Cambridge), Cambridge and District Schools, Dynamo BC, Luton Town (apprentice, September 1962; professional, September 1964), Aston Villa (£100,000, with brother Neil, July 1969), Derby County (£200,000, February 1974), EVERTON (£180,000, December 1976), Derby County (£150,000, November 1977), Birmingham City (loan, December 1978), Sheffield United (loan, March 1979), Torquay United (player–coach, October 1980), Seattle Sounders (loan, March–June

1981), Torquay United (player–manager, July 1982–January 1984), Seattle Sounders (coach, July 1985–January 1986), Middlesbrough (assistant manager, January 1986; manager, March 1986–March 1990), Millwall (manager, April 1990–March 1992), Bolton Wanderers (manager, May 1992–May 1995), Arsenal (manager, June 1995–August 1996), Norwich City (manager, June 1998–April 2000), Wigan Athletic (manager, July 2000–May 2001)

Bruce Rioch was the first English-born player to captain Scotland and, indeed, was also the first £100,000 footballer in the Third Division when signed by Aston Villa. The son of a Scottish sergeant major, he was a dynamic, all-action, hard-shooting midfielder, who went on to win 24 full caps for Scotland while accumulating more than 600 appearances at club level. After helping Villa win the Third Division championship (1972) and Derby lift the First Division trophy (1975), he moved to Everton and made his debut at Coventry City in December 1976. Unfortunately, his stay at Goodison Park was all too brief and in less than a year he had been sold back to Derby. He took his first steps to becoming a successful manager at Torquay. He then guided Middlesbrough to promotion from the Third to the First Division in successive seasons but left Arsenal after 61 weeks (with Arsène Wenger ready to move in). He steered Bolton from the Second Division into the Premiership in three years.

RITCHIE, HENRY McGILL

Outside/inside-right: 30 apps, 5 goals
Born: Scone, Perthshire, Scotland, 27 October 1898 – Deceased
Career: Perth Violet, Hibernian (1915), EVERTON (£4,000, with Jimmy Dunn, April 1928), Dundee (February 1930), St Johnstone (October 1931; retired April 1934)

Twice a Scottish Cup finalist with Hibs (1923, 1924), Harry Ritchie was a shade too heavy for a winger but relished tussles with opponents when playing inside. He and Dunn were regarded as the best 'right-wing' pairing north of the border during the 1920s, and played together for their country against Ireland in 1928, Ritchie having gained his first cap against Wales five years earlier. He also represented the Scottish League on five occasions. Possessing an explosive shot (right-footed), he netted over 50 goals for the Easter Road club and set up one for Dixie Dean when making his Everton debut in a 3–2 win at Bolton in August 1928. He secured his first goal for the Blues two games later in a 4–0 home victory over Portsmouth. After losing his place in the forward-line to Ted Critchley, he returned to Scotland.

ROBERTS

Centre-half: 1 app.
Born: *circa* 1865 – Deceased
Career: EVERTON (season 1888–89)

Reserve centre-half Roberts's only League game for Everton was against Wolves in February 1889, when he deputised for Johnny Holt.

ROBERTS, JAMES
Outside-left: 1 app.
Born: Mold, 7 January 1891 – Deceased
Career: Mold Villa (August 1905), Mold Town (May 1907), Wrexham (August 1910), Crewe Alexandra (May 1913), EVERTON (April 1914), Tranmere Rovers (June 1920), Crewe Alexandra (August 1921), Wrexham (1922–23), Mold Town (1923–May 1926)
Jimmy Roberts top-scored for Mold Town as a youngster. Described as a 'spirited player' and reckoned to be an 'effective forward', he was often criticised for holding on to the ball too long. After gaining an amateur cap for Wales in his first season with Wrexham, he played in two senior internationals against Ireland and Scotland in 1913, scoring on his debut. After a decent season with Crewe it was thought that Roberts might succeed at a higher level when he joined Everton. Unfortunately, he never fitted in at Goodison Park and, with the First World War looming, he made only one appearance, replacing Bill Palmer in a 5–1 win at Aston Villa in February 1915.

ROBERTSON, HOPE RAMSEY
Defender/forward: 31 apps, 2 goals
Born: Glasgow, 17 January 1868 – Deceased
Career: Partick Thistle (September 1886), EVERTON (October 1890), Bootle (November 1892), Walsall Town Swifts (August 1894–January 1895)
A most versatile footballer, Hope Robertson played as defender and in three of the five forward-line positions. Having performed admirably for Partick, he moved to Goodison Park and made his League debut for Everton on the right-wing at Blackburn in November 1890. In his next game he lined up at centre-forward and scored the winning goal against Sunderland. The following season he played entirely as a half-back, before losing his place in the side to Jim Jamieson.

ROBERTSON, JOHN TAIT
Half-back: 36 apps, 1 goal
Born: Dumbarton, 25 February 1877 – *Died*: Milton, Hampshire, 24 January 1935
Career: Poinfield, Sinclair Swifts, Greenock Morton, EVERTON (October 1895), Southampton (May 1898), Glasgow Rangers (£300, August 1899), Chelsea (player–manager, April 1905–October 1906), Glossop North End (player–manager, October 1906–May 1909), Manchester United (reserve-team manager, June 1909–May 1926), coached on continent (1927–28)
Jacky (Jock) Robertson was still a teenager when he made his League debut against Bolton in April 1896. A powerful tackler, able to carry the ball upfield with authority, he was superb at heading and packed a powerful right-foot shot. After spending three years at Goodison Park, he linked up with ten other Scots at Southampton. One of the finest Scottish-born players of his time, he was a Southern League championship winner with Saints (1899), gained three Scottish League championship medals in succession with Rangers (1900, 1901

and 1902) and played in three Scottish Cup finals (1903, 1904 and 1905), collecting a winner's medal in the first. Capped 16 times by Scotland between 1898 and 1905, he also represented the Scottish League on six occasions and twice played for Glasgow against Sheffield. He scored 25 goals in 130 appearances for Rangers before moving into management with Chelsea.

ROBINSON, ALFRED J.

Inside-right: 1 app.
Born: Birkenhead, 30 January 1898 – Deceased
Career: EVERTON (August 1919), Tranmere Rovers (March 1920)
Reserve at Goodison Park, Alf Robinson's only League game for Everton was at inside-right (in place of Frank Jefferis) at Sheffield Wednesday in January 1920.

ROBINSON, NEIL

Right-back/Midfield: 17+4 apps, 1 goal
Born: Liverpool, 20 April 1957
Career: EVERTON (apprentice, June 1972; professional, May 1974), Swansea
    Town, (£70,000, October 1979), Grimsby Town (£20,000, September 1984),
    Darlington (July 1988–May 1989)
Neil Robinson made his League debut against Burnley in January 1976 but was unable to establish himself at Goodison Park. An efficient player, he was practically a regular in Swansea's 1981 Second Division promotion-winning side and also gained two Welsh Cup-winner's medals (1981, 1982).

ROBINSON, WILLIAM WALTER

Left-back/left-half: 7 apps
Born: Birkenhead, *circa* 1895 – Deceased
Career: EVERTON (August 1917), Chester (March 1920), Wrexham
    (February 1924)
Strong-tackling left-back Bill Robinson made 65 appearances for Everton during the last two First World War seasons. He was introduced to League football against Chelsea in August 1919 but failed to retain his position, replaced by Louis Weller. He came back as a left-half before moving to Chester.

ROBSON, THOMAS

Wing-half: 29 apps
Born: Morpeth, 1909 – Deceased
Career: Blyth Spartans (1926), EVERTON (April 1929), Sheffield Wednesday
    (October 1930), Yeovil and Petters United (April 1932), Northampton Town
    (August 1934), Kettering Town (1938–39)
A strapping defender, as hard as nails, Tommy Robson, an ex-miner, made his League debut for Everton in a 4–1 win at Portsmouth in September 1929, when he deputised for the injured Jerry Kelly. He retained the right-half berth until March 1930.

ROCHE, WILLIAM
Outside-right: 1 app.
Born: 1879 – Deceased
Career: EVERTON (July 1900–May 1902)
A reserve at Everton, Bill Roche's only senior outing for the Blues was in the First Division game at Aston Villa in September 1901.

ROONEY, WALTER FRANCIS
Wing-half: 18 apps
Born: Liverpool, 31 March 1902 – *Died*: 1963
Career: EVERTON (April 1924) Wrexham (August 1929–May 1930)
Walter Rooney deputised for George Brown, Hunter Hart, Joe Peacock and Albert Virr. A capable and trusty half-back, he never let the side down and made the first of his 18 appearances for Everton in a 3–1 win over Nottingham Forest in February 1925.

ROONEY, WAYNE
Forward: 48+29 apps, 17 goals
Born: Liverpool, 24 October 1985
Career: EVERTON (apprentice, April 2002; professional, February 2003), Manchester United (an estimated £25–27m, August 2004)
Only the third 16-year-old to play League football for Everton, Wayne Rooney made his Premiership debut against Spurs in August 2002. Two months later he became the youngest Premiership goalscorer when he cracked in a glorious winner against Arsenal at Goodison Park. Then in February 2003 he became the youngest player ever to win a full England cap, taking the field at the age of 17 years, 111 days in the friendly against Australia (beating James Prinsep's record by 141 days). Seven months later the irrepressible Rooney hit the headlines again by grabbing his first England goal in the European Championship decider against Macedonia to become his country's youngest-ever marksman. Short, stocky, confident in his own ability, he does tend to fly off the deep end at times and has already seen 'red' as well as collecting his fair share of yellow cards. Rooney, capped at youth level, has now represented his country in 15 full internationals (7 goals) and played very well in Euro 2004. He joined Manchester United in 2004 and scored a hat-trick on his debut.

ROOSE, LEIGH RICHMOND
Goalkeeper: 24 apps
Born: Holt, near Wrexham, 27 November 1877 – *Died*: France, 7 October 1916
Career: UCW Aberystwyth, Aberystwyth Town (1898), Druids (August 1900), London Welsh (soccer), Stoke (amateur, October 1901), EVERTON (November 1904), Stoke City (August 1905), Sunderland (January 1908), Huddersfield Town (April 1911), Aston Villa (August 1911), Woolwich Arsenal (December 1911), Llandudno Town (1912–14); joined the 9th Battalion Royal Fusiliers as a Lance Corporal (1914); was killed in action

The son of a Presbyterian minister, Dick Roose obtained his early education at the Holt Academy, where he was taught for a short time by H.G. Wells. He took a science degree at University College of Wales in Aberystwyth and learnt his goalkeeping skills with the town's football team, gaining a Welsh Cup-winner's medal almost immediately (1900). He was a sporting hero when playing for Druids before moving to King's College Hospital in London to train as a doctor, but despite his keen interest in bacteriology, he never qualified and remained a perpetual student. On joining Stoke, he thought nothing of travelling by train to the Victoria Ground, charging the cost to the club! He once took a horse and carriage to get to a game and on another occasion used someone's bicycle.

H. Catton ('Tityrus' of the *Athletic News*) described Roose as 'dexterous though daring, valiant though volatile'. Another writer was more expansive, stating: 'Few men exhibit their personality so vividly in their play as L.R. Roose. You cannot spend five minutes in his company without being impressed by his vivacity, his boldness, his knowledge of men and things – a clever man undoubtedly, but one entirely unrestrained in word or action. On the field his whole attention is centred on the game, he rarely stands listlessly by the goalpost even when the ball is at the other end of the enclosure, but is ever following the game keenly and closely.'

He was certainly a character, also a very wealthy man as well as being a marvellously gifted keeper, who was known on occasions to charge some 15–20 yards away from his goal to clear the ball if he thought his defenders were under pressure. He was unorthodox in style when dealing with shots hit straight at him, often double-punching the ball away or even heading it! After Stoke he went to Everton, where he replaced the Irish international Billy Scott and played his part as the Merseysiders reached the semi-final of the FA Cup and runners-up spot in the First Division in 1905. He certainly saved Sunderland from relegation during his time on Wearside and the club wanted to award him a testimonial match for his efforts, but the FA stepped in and scotched the idea because of Roose's amateur status. He had to settle instead for an illuminated address, presented to him by the mayor.

An inveterate practical joker, Roose once turned up for a match in Belfast with his hand heavily bandaged, moaning and groaning. With everyone in suspense, wondering whether he was fit or not, minutes before kick-off, to the disbelief of the press, he shouted out, 'I'm okay', quickly stripped off the dressing and went out and played a blinder!

An erratic genius, he never took the field wearing a clean pair of shorts, his boots used to last him for years and generally he had a scruffy appearance about him – but what a star!

He won 24 caps at 'senior' level for Wales, plus a handful as an amateur (it could and should have been far more in both instances). And quite often he would ask if he could stand down to allow eight times reserve Alf Edwards an opportunity to show his worth. But the FAW would have none of it! Roose, recruited by Everton when Billy Scott was injured, made his debut in a 1–0 home defeat by his future club Sunderland in November 1904. He played 24 times that season and made over 300 appearances during his career, and one suspects that he would have carried on longer had he lived!

ROSS, NICHOLAS JOHN
Centre-forward/left-back: 19 apps, 5 goals
Born: Edinburgh, 6 December 1862 – *Died*: Preston, 1931
Career: Heart of Midlothian (1880), Preston North End (July 1883), EVERTON (July 1888), Linfield (August 1889), Preston North End (September 1889–May 1894)

Nick Ross was desperately unlucky not to gain full international honours for his country – simply because Scotland in the 1880s completely ignored players based south of the border. He did, however, play in the first Inter-League game, for the Football League against the Football Alliance in April 1891. He had skippered Hearts before joining Preston, who converted him from a centre-forward into a brilliant left-back. He was in the Preston side beaten by West Brom in the 1888 FA Cup final and soon afterwards moved to Everton, making his debut against Accrington in September 1888 – being the Blues' first captain in the club's first game in the newly formed Football League. He missed only three games that season and then surprisingly moved to Ireland, only to return to Preston, with whom he stayed for another five years. He died of consumption. His brother, Jimmy Ross, played for Liverpool, Preston, Burnley and Manchester City.

ROSS, TREVOR WILLIAM
Midfield: 146+5 apps, 20 goals
Born: Ashton-under-Lyne, 16 January 1957
Career: Hartshead School, Lancashire Schoolboys, Arsenal (schoolboy forms, 1970; apprentice, May 1972; professional, June 1974), EVERTON (£170,000, November 1977), Portsmouth (loan, October–November 1982), Sheffield United (loan, December 1982), AEK Athens/Greece (July 1982), Sheffield United (January 1984), Bury (August 1984–May 1987)

An England schoolboy international, Trevor Ross gained one cap for Scotland at Under-21 level (through a parentage qualification) and made 67 appearances for the Gunners before his transfer to Goodison Park, where he eventually linked up in midfield with Martin Dobson and Andy King. He made his debut for the Blues against Derby in November 1977 and went on to serve the club well until his departure in 1983. During his career Ross appeared in over 350 competitive games but admitted that his move to AEK was the 'worst mistake of my life'.

ROUSE, FREDERICK WILLIAM
Centre-forward: 10 apps, 2 goals.
Born: Cranford, Middlesex, 28 November 1881 – *Died*: 1953
Career: Bracknell and District Schools, Southall, High Wycombe (1900), Wycombe Wanderers (season 1901–02), Shepherd's Bush FC (briefly), Grimsby Town (professional, March 1903), Stoke (£150, April 1904),

EVERTON (£750, November 1906), Chelsea (£850, October 1907), West Bromwich Albion (£250, May 1909), Croydon Common (September 1910), Brentford (May 1911), Slough Town (August 1912; retired 1915)

For a big man Fred Rouse was astonishingly nimble for a centre-forward, possessing good control, a useful shot and a witty sense of humour. He played for the Football League in 1905 and 1906 and during his League career scored 58 goals in 154 outings. He was a huge disappointment at Goodison Park, despite an impressive debut against Blackburn in November 1906, won 2–0.

ROWETT, GARY

Defender: 2+2 apps

Born: Bromsgrove, 6 March 1974

Career: Cambridge United (apprentice, April 1990; professional, September 1991), EVERTON (£200,000, March 1994), Blackpool (loan, January–March 1995), Derby County (£300,000, July 1995), Birmingham City (£1m, August 1998), Leicester City (£3m, July 2000), Charlton Athletic (£2.5m, May 2002; retired June 2003)

A strong, hard-tackling and skilful defender, Gary Rowett never got a chance at Goodison Park. He made his debut for Everton, as a substitute, in a 5–1 defeat at Sheffield Wednesday in April 1994 and later played in 120 games for Derby, 103 for Birmingham and 57 for Leicester before suffering back and knee injuries at Charlton.

ROYLE, JOSEPH

Striker: 273+3 apps, 119 goals

Born: Norris Green, Liverpool, 8 April 1949

Career: Liverpool and District Schools, EVERTON (apprentice, July 1964; professional, August 1966), Manchester City (December 1974), Bristol City (December 1977), Norwich City (£60,000, August 1980; retired, injured, April 1982), Oldham Athletic (manager, July 1982), EVERTON (manager, November 1994–March 1997), Manchester City (manager, February 1998–May 2001), Ipswich Town (manager, October 2002)

Joe Royle was the first 16-year-old to play League football for Everton, making his debut against Blackpool in January 1966, aged 16 years, 282 days. An ever-present and top scorer for the Blues in their League championship-winning season of 1969–70, with 23 goals in 42 games, he was actually leading marksman on five occasions during his time at Goodison Park. Strong and able to withstand the fiercest of challenges, he was also quick over short distances and was a fine header of the ball, being widely acknowledged in some quarters as the best post-war centre-forward to serve the club. Besides his championship medal, he also played in one Charity Shield victory, gained six full England caps – the first in 1971 against Malta, the last in 1977 against Luxembourg – collected ten at Under-21 level, played for his country's youth team and also represented the Football League. He was a loser in the 1968 FA Cup final but made up for that disappointment when, in 1976, he returned to Wembley to help Manchester City win the League Cup. Royle scored 152 goals in a total of

TOP: League Division One champions in 1969–70 under manager Harry Catterick

ABOVE LEFT: Alan Ball — England World Cup winner

ABOVE MIDDLE: Colin Harvey — player, manager and coach
at Goodison Park (© Terry Mealey Photography)

ABOVE RIGHT: Jimmy Husband, — goalscoring winger
who made his debut at the age of 17

TOP LEFT: Joe Royle, who scored over 100 goals for Everton, whom he later managed

TOP RIGHT: Gordon West — England international goalkeeper
and League championship winner

ABOVE LEFT: Ray Wilson — Alan Ball's 1966 World Cup-winning colleague

ABOVE MIDDLE: Howard Kendall — skilful midfielder who had
three spells as Everton manager

ABOVE RIGHT: Martin Dobson — signed from Burnley for £300,000 in 1974

TOP LEFT: Bob Latchford, who scored a goal almost every two games for the Blues

TOP RIGHT: Mick Lyons and Seamus McDonagh. Lyons appeared in over 450 games for the Blues in 12 years; McDonagh in just 48.

ABOVE LEFT: Duncan McKenzie — Everton's first 'overseas' signing

ABOVE RIGHT: Trevor Steven, an industrious midfielder who made 300 appearances for the Blues

TOP LEFT: John Gidman — right-back who also played for Liverpool and both Manchester clubs

TOP MIDDLE: Brian Kidd — one of the few players to get sent off in an FA Cup semi-final

TOP RIGHT: Billy Wright — well-built centre-half who also played for Birmingham City

ABOVE LEFT: Bruce Rioch — the last English-born player to captain Scotland (1978)

ABOVE RIGHT: Steve McMahon, who went from Everton to Aston Villa to Liverpool

TOP LEFT: Trevor Francis, the game's first million-pound footballer (1979)

TOP RIGHT: Andy Gray, who scored in both the FA Cup and European Cup-Winners' Cup finals for Everton

ABOVE LEFT: Adrian Heath — scorer of almost 100 goals in over 300 games for Everton

ABOVE MIDDLE: Derek Mountfield, who made over 150 appearances for the Blues mainly as a central defender

ABOVE RIGHT: Graeme Sharp — Scottish international striker, later manager of Oldham Athletic

TOP LEFT: Neville Southall chalked up a record 578 League appearances
for the Blues and 92 caps for Wales

TOP RIGHT: Kevin Ratcliffe — Everton's long-serving captain and Cup-final specialist

ABOVE LEFT: Peter Reid — a bargain £60,000 buy from Bolton Wanderers in 1982

ABOVE RIGHT: Norman Whiteside scored as a 17 year old
for Manchester United and Northern Ireland

TOP LEFT: Tony Cottee, who scored over 280 goals (99 for Everton) in a fine career

TOP MIDDLE: Gary Ablett — an FA Cup winner with both Everton and Liverpool

TOP RIGHT: Barry Horne — Wales international midfielder, capped 59 times

ABOVE LEFT: Peter Beardsley — England international forward who also
played for Liverpool and both Manchester clubs

ABOVE RIGHT: Dave Watson — long-serving defender who
made over 500 appearances for the Blues

TOP LEFT: Kevin Campbell — scorer of over 160 goals in English League and Cup football

TOP RIGHT: Duncan Ferguson rejoined Everton from Newcastle United for £3.75m in 2000

ABOVE LEFT: Thomas Graveson — Danish international midfielder
(over 50 caps) who played in Euro 2004

ABOVE MIDDLE: Gary Naysmith — Scotland international defender
bought for £1.75m from Hearts in 2000

ABOVE RIGHT: Unsworth made 350 appearances for Everton
before joining Portsmouth in 2004

473 League appearances before entering management with Oldham, whom he steered back into the First Division after an absence of more than 50 years. He then took the Latics to the League Cup final in 1990 (beaten by Nottingham Forest) and when he returned as boss at Goodison Park, he guided the Blues to FA Cup glory (1995). In 1999 he lifted Manchester City out of the Second Division and a year later led the Maine Road side back into the Premiership before losing his job to Kevin Keegan. He then guided Ipswich into the First Division play-offs in 2004.

RUSSELL, JOHN
Centre-half: 3 apps
Born: Liverpool, *circa* 1880 – Deceased
Career: EVERTON (May 1902), West Ham United (August–November 1902)
Reserve to centre-half Tommy Booth, Jack Russell made his League debut for the Blues at Bolton in November 1902. He did nothing at West Ham.

SAGAR, EDWARD
Goalkeeper: 497 apps
Born: Moorends, Yorkshire, 7 February 1910 – *Died*: Liverpool, 16 October 1986
Career: Thorne Colliery, Hull City (trial, 1928), EVERTON (March 1929; retired May 1953); became a Liverpool licensee
The oldest player ever to appear in a first-class game for Everton, Ted Sagar was 42 years, 281 days old when he took his final bow in a Second Division game at Plymouth in November 1952. Rather slim-looking and perhaps a shade underweight, Sagar was on the Goodison Park playing staff for 22 years, 302 days – a record for long service by any player with a single club. He actually remained with the Blues for 24 years and five weeks. An ex-miner, he took over from Bill Coggins in the Blues' goal and was a regular every season up to the Second World War, missing only one game when the League title was won in 1931–32, gaining a second championship medal in 1938–39 and an FA Cup-winner's prize in 1933. After 61 games during the Second World War, when free from Army duties in Denmark, Italy and Iraq, he regained his place in 1946 from George Burnett and was first choice for another five seasons. He amassed 463 League appearances and was capped four times by England (1935, 1936) – it should have been more, for Sagar was one of the finest goalkeepers of his era. An Everton legend, he made his debut for the Blues in a 4–0 home League win over Derby in January 1930 and became famous for his headlong dives towards the ball, regardless of how many players were blocking his path. He was a fine shot-stopper and had the uncanny ability to pluck high, looping balls out of the air with timely precision, completely without nerves. But for the lack of foresight on the part of Hull, Sagar may never have found his way to Goodison Park. As a youngster he was playing in the Doncaster Senior League for Thorne Colliery when an eagle-eyed Tigers' scout spotted his talent. He was given a trial at Anlaby Road but surprisingly was not taken on, allowing Everton to step in and sign him for nothing!

SALT, ERNEST T.
Goalkeeper: 4 apps
Born: Walsall, 10 February 1897 – Deceased
Career: Talbot Stead Tubeworks (Birmingham Combination), EVERTON (professional, November 1920), Accrington Stanley (July 1923), Wigan Borough (May 1925–May 1926)
Ernie Salt deputised for Tommy Fern in each of his four games for Everton, making his debut against Sunderland in January 1922. A relatively small man, he was nevertheless able to field high balls with authority, one press verdict saying he was 'Cool, confident and collected'. He made 72 League appearances for Accrington and 26 for Wigan.

SAMWAYS, VINCENT
Midfield: 22+6 apps, 4 goals
Born: Bethnal Green, east London, 27 October 1968
Career: East London and London Schools, Tottenham Hotspur (apprentice, April 1985; professional, November 1995), Wolverhampton Wanderers (loan, December 1995), Birmingham City (loan, February–March 1996), EVERTON (£2.2m, August 1994), Las Palmas/Spain (July 1996), Sevilla/Spain (August 2002), Walsall (August 2003)
Before moving to Goodison Park, Vinny Samways played in over 250 games for Spurs. A hard-working, enthusiastic midfielder, with stamina and skill, he gained England youth caps, played in five internationals at Under-21 level (the first in 1988) and was an FA Cup winner in 1991, playing extremely well after future Evertonian Paul Gascoigne had gone off injured. Making his debut for the Blues against Aston Villa in August 1994, he later played in one Charity Shield-winning team (scoring against Blackburn in 1995) before leaving Merseyside. Unfortunately, after some tussles with opponents and officials, seeing red a couple of times, he was dubbed as the 'hard man' of Spanish football before his return to England with First Division Walsall.

SANDERS, ALAN
Full-back: 63 apps
Born: Salford, 31 January 1934
Career: Salford and Manchester Boys, Manchester City (amateur, June 1949; professional, August 1955), EVERTON (July 1956), Swansea Town (November 1959), Brighton and Hove Albion (January 1963–May 1966)
Although he was registered as a player with Manchester City for six years, full-back Alan Sanders never appeared in the first team, his National Service counting mainly for that. He was 23 when he was given his League debut for Everton against Spurs in November 1957, taking over from Don Donovan, who switched to centre-half. A strong competitor, he made 29 senior appearances the following season before losing his place to Alex Parker. He made 92 League appearances for the 'Swans' and 80 for Brighton.

SANSOM, KENNETH GRAHAM
Left-back: 6+1 apps, 1 goal
Born: Camberwell, London, 26 September 1958
Career: Beaufoy School, South London and Surrey Schools, Leeds United (trial), Crystal Palace (1975), Arsenal (£1.2m, exchange-deal involving Clive Allen, August 1980), Newcastle United (£300,000, December 1988), Queens Park Rangers (June 1989), Coventry City (March 1991), EVERTON (February 1993), Brentford (March 1993), Chertsey Town (briefly), Watford (n/c, August–October 1994); now a TV pundit

A highly constructive left-back with power and pace, Kenny Sansom loved to race forward (given the chance) and deliver decisive crosses from deep. Not a big man, he was a very consistent and thoughtful player, never overrun or indeed 'roasted' by an opposing winger, being quick in recovery, alert, versatile and brilliant at times.

A Second Division championship winner with Crystal Palace (1979), he surprisingly won only one medal with Arsenal (League Cup, 1987). He skippered the Gunners and was their 'Player of the Year' in 1981. He appeared in 394 games for Arsenal, 197 for Palace and during a splendid career amassed in excess of 850 at club and international level, but only seven with Everton, for whom he made his debut at Sheffield Wednesday in February 1993.

Recognised by England at both schoolboy and youth levels, Sansom went on to become England's most capped full-back, starring in 80 internationals between 1979 and 1988, scoring one goal against Finland in a 5–0 win in October 1984. He also played in eight Under-21 matches, starred once for England 'B', represented the Football League and took part in the 1982 and 1986 World Cup finals.

SAUNDERS, GEORGE E.
Defender: 140 apps
Born: Birkenhead, 1 March 1918 – *Died*: 1982
Career: Merseyside junior football, EVERTON (amateur, March 1937; professional, February 1939; retired May 1952)

Recommended to Everton by Dixie Dean, George Saunders was a reliable, consistent, hard-working defender, respected on and off the terraces, whose safety-first tactics, by clearing the ball first time, was his trademark. He was a firm tackler, never dirty, and could get enormous distances with his headers. He played two seasons for Everton's 'A' team before signing professional and, owing to the Second World War, he had to wait until September 1946 before making his League debut against Arsenal in front of more than 40,000 fans at Goodison Park. Prior to that, he had appeared in one Regional League game against Liverpool in December 1939. A fine golfer, he was also the cousin of Ron Saunders (q.v.).

SAUNDERS, RONALD

Centre-forward: 3 apps
Born: Birkenhead, 6 November 1932
Career: Birkenhead and Liverpool Schools, EVERTON (amateur, April 1947; professional, February 1951), Tonbridge (July 1956), Gillingham (£800, May 1957), Portsmouth (£8,000, September 1958), Watford (£10,000, September 1964), Charlton Athletic (1965), Yeovil Town (general manager, May 1967–November 1968), Oxford United (manager, March–June 1969), Norwich City (manager, July 1969–November 1973), Manchester City (manager, November 1973–April 1974), Aston Villa (manager, June 1974–February 1982), Birmingham City (manager, February 1982–January 1986), West Bromwich Albion (manager, February 1986–September 1987)

Much was expected of centre-forward Ron Saunders when he gained England youth-team honours, but he never established himself at the top level and made only three League appearances for Everton, the first against Cardiff City in February 1955. After a spell with Tonbridge, he re-entered League football in 1957 with Gillingham and over the next ten years scored more than 220 goals (in over 400 games) with 207 coming in 388 League outings.

As a player, he was bold, tough and aggressive, but, as a manager, he was blunt, unyielding and a strict disciplinarian. Consequently, the teams that he managed often produced dull, unimaginative football. However, he collected a few prizes, and the best of the lot was winning the League championship with Aston Villa (1981). He then set them on their way to the European Cup final before rocking the boat and leaving for neighbours Birmingham City. Earlier, he had tasted League Cup success in 1975 and 1977 and was a beaten finalist in the same competition in 1973 and 1974, while winning the Second Division title in 1972 and taking the runner's-up spot in 1975. Later, he guided Birmingham into the top flight (1985).

SCHOFIELD, ALFRED JOHN

Forward: 13 apps, 2 goals
Born: Liverpool, 1874 – Deceased
Career: Liverpool junior football, EVERTON (August 1895), Newton Heath/Manchester United (August 1900; retired May 1907); played cricket in Blackburn, was a member of the East Lancashire team and a self-employed businessman

Alf Schofield made his League debut for Everton in March 1896 in a 3–2 home win over Preston. He could not hold down a first-team place at Goodison Park and was subsequently transferred to Newton Heath, where he replaced Billy Bryant on the left-wing. He did extremely well there, scoring 35 goals in 179 games, helping United gain promotion from the Second Division in 1906. A Manchester newspaper columnist wrote: 'Alf Schofield is a marvel at centering [sic] the ball and no small percentage of the team's goals have been due to his excellent work.' He retired from the game gracefully after another winger, Billy Meredith, had taken over centre stage. Schofield was awarded a benefit by United in March 1906 (against Barnsley).

SCOTT, ALEXANDER SILCOCK
Outside-right: 180 apps, 27 goals
Born: Falkirk, Scotland, 22 November 1936 – *Died*: September 2001
Career: Camelon Thistle, Bo'ness United, Glasgow Rangers (part-time, January 1954; professional, March 1955), EVERTON (£39,000, February 1963), Hibernian (£13,000, September 1967), Falkirk (June 1970–May 1972)
A League championship winner with Rangers on four occasions (1956, 1957, 1959 and 1961), Alex Scott also helped the Ibrox Park club lift the Scottish Cup (1960) and the League Cup (1961, 1962) while collecting a runner's-up medal in the latter competition in 1958. He was a League championship winner with Everton in 1962–63, contributing four goals in 17 games, and collected an FA Cup-winner's medal three years later. Tremendously fast and direct, he was certainly a menacing winger, who loved to cut inside his full-back and unleash a powerful shot on goal. He made his debut for the Blues against Leicester in February 1963, taking over from Billy Bingham, and his last appearance was on the left-wing against Manchester City in April 1967.
Capped 16 times by Scotland (1957–66), he also represented the Scottish League on seven occasions and played once for both the 'B' and Under-23 sides. He scored 108 goals in 331 appearances for Rangers.

SCOTT, PETER WILLIAM
Full-back: 48+2 apps, 2 goals
Born: Liverpool, 19 September 1952
Career: EVERTON (apprentice, September 1968; professional, July 1970), Southport (loan, January 1974), York City (£11,000, December 1975), Aldershot (£3,000, March 1979–May 1983)
Peter Scott made his League debut in August 1971 at Ipswich. After a solid first season when he appeared in 33 games, he had to fight for his place over the next three years. He became only the second York City player to receive international honours when winning the third of his ten caps for Northern Ireland, having gained the first two with Everton. He made 114 appearances for the Minstermen and over 120 for Aldershot while also becoming the latter's leading cap-winner.

SCOTT, WALTER
Goalkeeper: 18 apps
Born: Worksop, 1886 – *Died*: 16 September 1955
Career: Worksop Town, Grimsby Town (May 1907), EVERTON (£750, January 1910), Shelbourne (May 1911), Sunderland (July 1911), Belfast United (1915); guest for Brentford and Millwall during the First World War; Worksop Town (August 1919), Grimsby Town (February 1920), Gainsborough Trinity (June 1920–May 1922)
Outstanding for reliability and superb anticipation, Walter 'Buns' Scott saved three penalties playing for Grimsby against Burnley in February 1909. He linked up with Billy Scott, another goalkeeper, at Everton having made almost 100 appearances for the Mariners and played his first game for the Blues in the

Merseyside derby against Liverpool in February 1910. Always second choice at Goodison Park, he later represented the Irish League on five occasions.

SCOTT, WILLIAM
Goalkeeper: 289 apps
Born: Belfast, Northern Ireland, 1883 – Deceased
Career: Cliftonville (1901), Linfield (1903), EVERTON (July 1904), Leeds City (August 1912–April 1914); did not play after the First World War
Already capped six times by Northern Ireland before becoming an Everton player, Billy Scott spent eight years at Goodison Park, recommending his younger brother, Elisha, to Liverpool in the process. A wonderfully safe and reliable goalkeeper, he went on to play in another ten full internationals during his time with the Blues and finished up with 25 in his locker all together (collected between 1903 and 1913). An FA Cup winner in 1906 and a loser in 1907, Scott also collected three League Division One runner's-up medals (1905, 1909, 1912) and proved a mighty difficult man to replace, so well had he guarded the Blues' goal.

SEARGEANT, STEVEN CHARLES
Defender: 86+4 apps, 1 goal
Born: Liverpool, 2 January 1951
Career: EVERTON (apprentice, April 1967; professional, July 1968, contract cancelled, February 1978)
Steve Seargeant made his League debut for Everton against WBA in January 1972, wearing the number ten shirt when playing alongside Mick Lyons at the heart of the defence. A strong-looking footballer, he had to wait until the 1974–75 season before getting a decent run in the side, making 39 appearances in the left-back position. He held his place until halfway through the next campaign and thereafter had spasmodic outings before his release in February 1978, as the club was reasonably well off for defenders.

SETTLE, JAMES
Inside-forward/outside-left: 269 apps, 97 goals
Born: Millom, near Bolton, 1876 – Deceased
Career: Bolton junior football, Bolton Wanderers (August 1894), Halliwell FC (May 1895), Bury (January 1897), EVERTON (April 1899), Stockport County (May 1908; retired May 1909)
One of the game's most instinctive finishers during the early part of the twentieth century, Jimmy Settle was lightning-quick inside the penalty area and as one reporter wrote: 'often scores when the goalkeeper isn't looking'. He required little space in which to execute his trickery, was a wonderful passer of the ball and frequently carved open the tightest of defences with one 20 to 30-yard pass measured to a tee. A shade lethargic and indeed selfish on occasions, he spent nine years at Goodison Park, during which time he scored, on average, a goal every three games. He made his debut for Everton against Burnley in April 1899 (three days after joining the club from Bury) and, injuries apart, remained a regular in the side until 1906. He won six

England caps between 1899 and 1903, represented the Football League and starred in the 1906 and 1907 FA Cup finals, collecting a winner's medal in the first.

SHACKLETON, ALAN
Forward: 27 apps, 10 goals
Born: Padiham, Lancashire, 3 February 1934
Career: Bolton Wanderers (amateur, June 1949), Burnley (amateur, August 1951; professional, May 1954), Leeds United (£8,000, October 1958), EVERTON (September 1959), Nelson (May 1960), Oldham Athletic (£1,200, August 1961; retired through injury, June 1962)
A tidy marksman throughout his career, Alan Shackleton's League return was a good one – 51 goals in 97 games. Never a regular with any of his clubs, his best figures came at Turf Moor (18 strikes in 31 starts). He played alongside Don Revie in the Leeds' forward-line and scored seven times in ten outings for Oldham, including a hat-trick against Hartlepool in August 1961. He made his debut for Everton against Nottingham Forest in September 1959 and was first choice until February 1960, when changes were made to the front-line, Roy Vernon coming in at inside-left to partner Jimmy Harris.

SHARP, ALBERT
Defender: 10 apps
Born: Hereford, 8 January 1876 – *Died*: Liverpool, 2 November 1949
Career: Clyde Henry School, Hereford Comrades (April, 1893), Hereford Thistle (August 1894), Hereford Town (September 1895), Hereford Thistle (May 1886), Aston Villa (April 1897), EVERTON (August 1899), Southampton (May 1900), EVERTON (May 1901), Kirkdale (August 1904; reinstated as an amateur), Southport Central (January 1905; retired April 1907); appointed a director of EVERTON (with brother Jack, q.v.) in 1922
Older brother of the more famous Jack Sharp, Bert Sharp was never in the same class. A honest, hard-working defender nevertheless, he was versatile and a good athlete, who performed consistently well for each club he served, making 23 appearances for Villa and 22 for Saints before joining Everton. He made his League debut for the Blues against Derby in December 1899 with his brother lining up in front of him. He was also a useful cricketer, and in 1900 averaged 40 with the bat playing for Herefordshire.

SHARP, GRAEME MARSHALL
Centre-forward: 426+21 apps, 159 goals
Born: Eastercraigs, Glasgow, 16 October 1960
Career: Dumbarton (professional, October 1978), EVERTON (April 1980), Oldham Athletic (July 1991; player–manager, November 1994; retired as a player, May 1995, continued as manager until May 1997); now supporters' liaison officer at Goodison Park and pundit on local radio
Graeme Sharp won four medals with Everton – two League titles, one FA Cup victory and a European Cup-Winners' Cup triumph. He also played in three

losing FA Cup finals and was the club's top scorer in 1984–85, with 30 goals in 50 games, including 21 in the First Division. In fact, he was Blues' leading marksman four times (1981–82, 1982–83, 1984–85 and 1987–88).

One of only five players to have appeared in 50 or more FA Cup games for Everton (total: 54), he netted 20 goals in the competition – only the great Dixie Dean struck more (32). He also claimed 15 goals in 48 League Cup matches, placing him second in the list behind Bob Latchford (19), and he's the club's record post-Second World War goalscorer. Strong in the air and packing an explosive shot – just what a striker requires – Sharp made his League debut against Brighton in May 1980 and over the next 11 years gave the club and the supporters excellent value for money. Capped 12 times by Scotland and once at Under-21 level, he went to the 1986 World Cup finals in Mexico.

SHARP, JOHN SAMUEL
Outside/inside-right: 342 apps, 80 goals
Born: Hereford, 15 February 1878 – *Died*: Wavertree, Liverpool, 27 January 1938
Career: Clyde Henry School, Violet BC, Hereford Thistle (August 1895), Aston Villa (April, 1897), EVERTON (August 1899; retired May 1910); ran a sports shop in Liverpool, became wealthy and joined the board of directors at Goodison Park with his brother Bert in 1922; later club chairman
Jack Sharp represented England at both cricket and football. A short, thickset outside- or inside-right, a 'Pocket Hercules', he made only 24 senior appearances for Villa but scored 15 goals before transferring to Everton. With the Merseysiders he developed into an international quality player, gaining two full caps and representing the Football League. He was a regular in the Everton side for 11 years, amassing almost 350 appearances, the first against Sheffield United in September 1899. He also played in two FA Cup finals, collecting a winner's medal in 1906 and a loser's a year later. The famous referee Jack Howcroft, in the game for 30 years, rated Sharp as the best outside-right he ever saw play, better than Billy Bassett, Billy Meredith and even Stanley Matthews!

On the cricket field, Sharp played in three Test matches and hit a century against Australia at The Oval in 1909. He spent 26 years with Lancashire (1899–1925), scored over 22,700 runs (38 centuries), took 440 wickets and held 223 catches.

SHARPLES, GEORGE FRANK VINCENT
Wing-half: 10 apps
Born: Ellesmere Port, 20 September 1943
Career: EVERTON (apprentice, April 1959; professional, September 1960), Blackburn Rovers (March 1965), Southport (July 1971–May 1972)
George Sharples had Jimmy Gabriel and also Tony Kay to contest the wing-half positions with. Efficient and hard-working, he made his League debut for Everton against WBA in November 1960 (aged 17) and played his last game for

the club in a 6–0 defeat at Arsenal in December 1963. He made 113 appearances for Blackburn.

SHAW, STUART
Outside-right: 3 apps
Born: Liverpool, 9 October 1944
Career: Aintree Villa Colts, EVERTON (amateur, April 1960; professional, December 1961), Crystal Palace (December 1966), Southport (March 1967), Port Vale (July 1969), Morecambe (May 1970), Skelmersdale United, South Liverpool, Howard Sports, Fleetwood Heath
Stuart Shaw spent six and a half years as a reserve at Goodison Park, appearing in just three League games – at Blackburn in October 1964 and away to WBA and at home to Arsenal in September 1965 – deputising for Alex Scott each time.

SHEEDY, KEVIN MARK
Midfield: 356+12 apps, 97 goals
Born: Builth Wells, 21 October 1959
Career: Hereford Lads' Club, Hereford United (apprentice, April 1975; professional, October 1976), Liverpool (£80,000, July 1978), EVERTON (£100,000, August 1982), Newcastle United (free, March 1992), Blackpool (July 1993–May 1995), Blackburn Rovers (assistant coach, August 1995), Tranmere Rovers (assistant coach, July 1996), Hartlepool United (assistant coach, 2002–03)
Kevin Sheedy starred in 41 internationals for the Republic of Ireland as an Everton player, eventually totalling 45. He also gained one youth and five Under-21 caps in a near 20-year career that realised over 500 club appearances. He was on the losing side in three FA Cup finals (1985, 1986, 1989), scored in the 1985 European Cup-Winners' Cup final triumph over Rapid Vienna and collected two League championship winning medals in 1985 and 1987. Recognised as one of the finest midfield players of the 1980s, he had a frustrating time at Anfield, but after his move across Stanley Park (reluctantly sold by Reds' boss Bob Paisley) his career took off.

Combining inch-perfect passing with some deadly shooting, he made his senior debut for Everton in a 2–0 defeat at Watford in August 1982, and despite struggling at times with injuries, his name was always one of the first on the team-sheet when fully fit. He eventually lost his first-team place when Howard Kendall returned as manager in 1990.

SHERIDAN, JAMES
Inside-left: 20 apps, 4 goals
Born: Belfast, Northern Ireland, April 1884 – Deceased
Career: Cambuslang Hibernian, EVERTON (August 1902), Stoke (October 1904), New Brompton (December 1904)
Recruited in readiness for the 1902–03 season, skilful inside-forward Paddy Sheridan made his League debut for Everton at Wolves a month after arriving

at the club, replacing Jimmy Settle. He scored twice in 17 games that season, but got only spasmodic outings after that, being unable to oust Settle from the forward-line. Despite all this, Sheridan won five caps for Northern Ireland during his spell on Merseyside and later added a sixth to his tally with Stoke. He was the Blues' youngest international player before Wayne Rooney.

SHORT, CRAIG JONATHAN

Defender: 104+9 apps, 4 goals
Born: Bridlington, North Yorkshire, 25 June 1968
Career: Pickering Town, Scarborough (professional, October 1987), Notts County (£100,000, July 1989), Derby County (£2.5m, September 1992), EVERTON (£2.7m, July 1995), Blackburn Rovers (£1.7m, August 1999)

Although not the fastest of players, Craig Short is a brave and totally committed central defender who had already chalked up 379 senior appearances before joining Everton in the summer of 1995. He made his Blues' debut in the away Premiership game against Nottingham Forest two months after arriving at Goodison Park and went on to form a reliable and trustworthy partnership with Dave Watson. He played in 31 games that season, 26 the following term and 33 in 1998–99 before helping Blackburn win the League Cup in 2002. His brother, Chris Short, played for Scarborough, Notts County, Huddersfield and Sheffield United.

SIMMS, SAMUEL

Centre-forward: 2 apps, 1 goal
Born: Atherton, 1888 – Deceased
Career: EVERTON (June 1912), Swindon Town (June 1913), Leicester Fosse (June 1914), Swindon Town (July 1919), Gillingham (May 1921)

Essentially a reserve with each of his clubs, Sammy Simms scored on his League debut for Everton in a 2–1 League win at Blackburn on Boxing Day 1912. He netted five times in 17 starts for Leicester.

SIMONSEN, STEVEN PREBEN

Goalkeeper: 35+2 apps
Born: South Shields, 3 April 1979
Career: Tranmere Rovers (apprentice, May 1995; professional, October 1996), EVERTON (£3.3m, September 1998; released May 2004), Stoke City (July 2004)

Capped by England at youth and Under-21 levels, goalkeeper Steve Simonsen made 42 appearances for Tranmere before joining Everton as cover for Thomas Myhre. The following season Paul Gerrard arrived from Oldham and it wasn't until January 2000 that he finally made his Premiership debut, in the 2–0 defeat at Southampton. A fine shot-stopper, Simonsen then had to contest the goalkeeping position with Richard Wright – although injuries certainly affected his game at Goodison Park.

SIMPSON, ROBERT H.
Full-back: 23 apps
Born: Redcar, 1889 – Deceased
Career: Blackburn Rovers (May 1910), Bradford City (May 1911), EVERTON
    (September 1912), Wrexham (June 1919–May 1922)
Able to play on both flanks, Bob Simpson failed to make any impression at
Ewood Park or Bradford. He joined Everton as cover for Billy Stevenson and
John Maconnachie and made his League debut in place of the former in a 6–0
defeat at Newcastle in October 1912. He remained at Goodison Park throughout
the First World War, making a further 16 appearances in Regional matches.

SIMPSON, THOMAS
Outside-left: 1 app.
Born: Keyworth, 13 August 1879 – *Died*: Oldham, 19 December 1961
Career: Notts County (September 1899), Leicester Fosse (October 1902),
    EVERTON (May 1903–April 1904)
After making his League debut for Notts County and appearing in 28 first-class
matches for Leicester, left-winger Tommy Simpson moved to Everton, but, due
to the excellent form of England international Harold Hardman, had only one
outing, at Newcastle in January 1904.

SINGLETON, HARRY BERTRAM
Outside-left: 3 apps
Born: Prescot, Lancashire, January 1877 – *Died*: 5 July 1948
Career: Liverpool junior football, EVERTON (July 1900), Grimsby Town (May
    1902), New Brompton (May 1903), Queens Park Rangers (May 1904),
    Leeds City (May 1905–April 1907)
Well proportioned, Harry Singleton often made his presence felt with some
timely challenges on his opponents. He was reserve at Everton first to George
Turner and then to Lawrie Bell and was 23 when he made his League debut
against Sheffield United in February 1902. He netted seven goals in 45 League
games for Leeds.

SLOAN, DONALD
Goalkeeper: 6 apps
Born: Rankinston, Ayr, Scotland, 31 July 1883 – Deceased
Career: Ayrshire junior football, Belfast Distillery (1903–04), EVERTON (May
    1906), Liverpool (June 1908), Belfast Distillery (player–manager, July
    1909–May 1913)
An Irish League representative and Irish Cup winner before joining Everton,
Donald Sloan was never found wanting between the posts. No mean performer,
he was unlucky that his career coincided with Billy Scott at Everton and Sam
Hardy at Liverpool. He made his debut for the Blues against Blackburn in April
1907 and in 1910 collected a second Irish Cup-winner's medal.

SMALLEY, ROBERT EDWIN
Goalkeeper: 38 apps
Born: 1865 – *Died:* 1947
Career: Preston North End (1886), EVERTON (May 1887– August 1890); later worked as an accountant in Preston
After joining Everton from Preston, Bob Smalley took over from Charlie Joliffe and made his debut for the Blues against Notts County in October 1887. Nine months later – after 30 more appearances – he starred in the club's first-ever League game against Accrington. A well-built yet agile keeper, he kept his place in the side for two seasons before being replaced by Jack Angus.

SMALLMAN, DAVID PAUL
Forward: 23+3 apps, 6 goals
Born: Connahs Quay, Flintshire, 22 March 1953
Career: Deeside Schools, Shotton Westminster, Wrexham (apprentice, April 1969; professional, November 1971), EVERTON (£75,000, March 1975–May 1980), Wrexham (September 1980), Oswestry Town (January 1981), Bangor City (August 1981), Green Gully Ajax/Australia (for six years: 1982–88); Newtown (September–November 1988), Colwyn Bay (late 1988), Hawarden Rangers (1989–90), Deeside FC (manager, June 1990–May 1993); also coached Deeside non-League sides
David Smallman gained a Welsh Youth Cup-winner's medal at the end of his first season with Wrexham, going on to make his League debut in September 1972 – the first of 125 outings for the club (51 goals). Unfortunately, his time at Goodison Park was a nightmare! In five years he twice suffered a broken leg, the injuries ruining a seemingly glittering career as he was just beginning to establish himself in the Welsh national side (he won one youth, five Under-23 and seven full caps for his country altogether). Smallman made his senior debut for the Blues against Luton in April 1975 and, in fact, was on the treatment table for over 50 months during his time with Everton.

SMITH, DEREK LEONARD
Centre-half: 3+1 apps
Born: Liverpool, 5 July 1946
Career: EVERTON (apprentice, July 1961; professional, November 1963), Tranmere Rovers (March 1968–May 1970)
Derek Smith failed to establish himself in Everton's first XI, making only four League appearances, the first against Leeds in April 1966. He played at centre-half and centre-forward for Tranmere and scored 21 goals in 82 League games in just over two seasons.

SMITH, JOHN
Midfield: 2 apps
Born: Liverpool, 14 March 1953
Career: EVERTON (apprentice, April 1969; professional, September 1970), Carlisle United (June 1976), Southport (loan, February–April 1977)

England schoolboy international John Smith made two appearances for Everton in 1973–74, playing on the right-side of midfield against QPR (January 1974) and Southampton (April 1974).

SMITH, JOSEPH EDWARD

Forward: 10 apps
Born: West Stanley, County Durham, *circa* 1886 – Deceased
Career: West Stanley, Hull City (£10, September 1905), EVERTON (February 1912), Belfast Distillery (August 1913), Bury (December 1913), West Stanley (July 1919–May 1921)

Known universally as 'Stanley' – from his birthplace to distinguish him from another J. Smith (who was at Hull at the same time) – 'Joe' Smith was an adaptable player, thickset in build who could play on the right-wing, through the centre or in any of the inside-forward positions. Probably best on the right flank, he could cross a ball with great precision when running at full tilt and drew up a fine scoring record with the Tigers – 48 goals in 214 appearances. He had lost some of his dash by the time he arrived at Everton, for whom he made his debut in a 4–0 defeat at Manchester City in February 1912. He gained Irish Inter-League honours against the Football, Scottish and Southern Leagues in 1914.

SNODIN, IAN

Midfielder/full-back: 190+11 apps, 7 goals
Born: Rotherham, 15 August 1963
Career: Doncaster Rovers (apprentice, April 1979; professional, August 1980), Leeds United (May 1985), EVERTON (£840,000, January 1987), Sunderland (loan, October–November 1994), Oldham Athletic (January 1995), Scarborough (August 1997), Doncaster Rovers (player–manager, season 1998–99)

Younger brother of Glyn Snodin, who also played for Doncaster, Leeds, Oldham and Scarborough, Ian Snodin's playing career spanned 20 years, during which time he made over 570 appearances, including more than 200 for both Doncaster and Everton. He represented England as a youth and later won four Under-21 and two 'B' caps. He was a fine midfielder, always having a touch of class and was perhaps unfortunate to gain only one club medal – when Everton took the League championship in 1987. Already an experienced campaigner when he arrived at Goodison Park (having turned down a chance to join Liverpool), he made his debut for the Blues as a midfield substitute against Sheffield Wednesday in January 1987, having his first start a week later versus Nottingham Forest. With speed and composure as well as a fine attitude, he was successfully converted into a fine full-back and was called up for the England against Greece international in February 1989, but sadly had to withdraw due to injury. He never got another chance at senior level and spent most of the 1990–91 season and the whole of 1991–92 convalescing after severely damaging his hamstring.

SOUTHALL, NEVILLE
Goalkeeper: 750 apps
Born: Llandudno, Wales, 16 September 1958
Career: Llandudno Swifts, Conwy United, Bangor City, Winsford United, Bury
  (£6,000, June 1979), EVERTON (£150,000, July 1981), Port Vale (loan,
  January–February 1983), Southend United (loan, December 1997–February
  1998), Stoke City (free, February 1998), Doncaster Rovers (July 1998),
  Torquay United (free, December 1998), Bradford City (free, February 2000;
  retired April 2000); later coached the Wales Under-16 squad and was also
  joint-manager of the Welsh national team

Goalkeeper Neville Southall made a club record of 750 appearances for Everton
(266 consecutively between 1987 and 1993, including 212 in the League, of
which 207 were in the Premiership). He was an ever-present seven seasons and
in 1984–85 played in a record 62 senior matches for his club. His overall tally of
first-team outings was made up as follows: 578 League/Premiership, 70 FA Cup
and 65 League Cup (both records), 13 in European competitions and 24
'others'. He played in 41 Merseyside derbies (another record), helped win two
League championships (in 1985, when he was an ever-present, and 1987),
triumphed in two FA Cup finals (1984, 1995) and was victorious in the 1985
European Cup-Winners' Cup.

A runner-up in two other FA Cup finals, Southall, who was voted the
Football Writers' 'Player of the Year' in 1985, gained 92 caps for Wales (a record
for a goalkeeper and, indeed, for an Everton player) and, 15 months after leaving
Goodison Park, walked away with Torquay's 'Player of the Year' trophy.

On leaving school, Southall took a job with the local council, clearing gun
emplacements built during the Second World War. Almost immediately he
became one of the youngest players ever to appear in the Welsh League, aged
14, when placed in goal for Llandudno Swifts against Rhos Aelwyd in 1973.
After a spell at the Ritz Café in Llandudno, he worked on several building sites
as a hod carrier while trying to establish himself in the local side. He made good
progress, and after playing for Conwy and Bangor City he was signed by John
Williams, Winsford's shrewd manager. His solid and consistent displays in the
Northern Premier League prompted Bury to take him into the Football League
at the comparatively advanced age of 21. He never looked back after that – and
what a tremendous servant he was to Everton – signed for what was a bargain
fee by boss Howard Kendall, one of his first acquisitions after taking the hot seat
at Goodison Park. He played his first game for the Blues in place of Jim Arnold
at Ipswich in October 1981 and made his last appearance against Spurs in
November 1997. Standing over six feet tall and weighing on average 13 st. 8 lb,
he was a courageous goalkeeper whose reflexes for a big man were quite
exceptional. He was a fighter to the last, always urging on his colleagues, and he
once said: 'If you don't believe you can win, there is no point in getting out of
bed at the end of the day.'

SOUTHWORTH, JOHN

Centre-forward: 32 apps, 36 goals
Born: Blackburn, December 1866 – *Died*: 16 October 1956
Career: Inkerman Rangers (as a 12-year-old, 1878), Brookhouse Rangers, Brookhouse Perseverance (both nurseries for Blackburn Olympic), Higher Walton FC, Chester, Blackburn Olympic (August 1883; professional, August 1886), Vale of Lune (guest), Blackburn Rovers (September, 1887), EVERTON (£400, August 1893; retired April 1895)

In his first season with Everton (1893–94) Jack Southworth, a great and talented centre-forward with a heavy black moustache, finished up as top scorer. He also headed the First Division charts with 27 goals, including four against Sheffield Wednesday and six against West Bromwich Albion in successive matches – the latter creating a club record for the most in one game. Although illness and injury ruined his career on Merseyside, his record of 36 strikes in only 32 games makes him the Blues' champion marksman in terms of goals per game. In fact, during his career Southworth – fast, accurate with his shooting and, by no means least, showing complete unselfishness – bagged 158 goals in 165 League and Cup games (for Blackburn and Everton) and scored once in each of his three international outings for England (1899–92).

As a 16 year old he once scored six goals for Blackburn Olympic against Leigh and helped the team win the Lancashire Cup in 1885. He then won successive FA Cup-winner's medals with Blackburn Rovers (1890, 1891). So highly thought of was Southworth, that in 1892 Rovers arranged a testimonial for him, under floodlights against Darwen, using a white ball! A professional musician, Southworth played with the Halle Orchestra for many years and quit football for a short time while touring in Chester in the mid-1880s, before turning professional.

SPEED, GARY ANDREW

Midfield: 65 apps, 18 goals
Born: Hawarden, Flintshire, 8 September 1969
Career: Deeside Primary Schools XI, Hawarden GS, Leeds United (apprentice, April 1986; professional, June 1988), EVERTON (£3.5m, July 1996), Newcastle United (£5.5m, February 1998), Bolton Wanderers (July 2004)

Gary Speed ended his first full season in League football as a Leeds player (1989–90) as a regular member of the side, with a Second Division championship medal and a full international cap. On 19 May 1990 – having already won a youth cap – he played for Wales against Poland at Under-23 level – 24 hours later he gained his first full cap against Costa Rica when he came on as a substitute. Since then he's become a thoroughbred among professionals and has now won more than 80 senior caps while amassing almost 650 club appearances and netting close on 120 goals. Indeed, Speed was the first player to appear in 400 Premiership matches. A midfield player with pace, skill and vision, as well as being a fine header of the ball and having a useful right-foot shot, he also helped Leeds win the First Division title and Charity Shield in 1992 before transferring to Goodison Park. He scored on his debut for Everton in a 2–0 home Premiership victory over his future club Newcastle in August 1996 and during his time with the Blues produced some exhilarating performances when missing only one game in his first season on Merseyside. However, after again producing the goods during the first half of the following season, it was reported that Speed was unhappy at the club he had supported since his schooldays. Things came to a head when he refused to travel for an away game at West Ham and soon afterwards he was transferred to Newcastle. His departure from Goodison was fractious but he was prevented from giving his side of the story by agreeing to sign a non-disclosure contract for manager Bobby Robson.

SPENCER, HENRY GEORGE
Inside-right: 9 apps, 2 goals
Born: Southampton, 17 July 1895 – Deceased
Career: Southampton (trialist), EVERTON (May 1921), Wigan Borough (August 1922), Walsall (July 1924–April 1925)
Reserve Harry Spencer deputised in the main for Stan Fazackerley during his spell at Goodison Park. He made his League debut against Birmingham in September 1921 and played his last game against Chelsea in April 1922. He scored seven goals in 35 League games for Wigan but failed to make much headway with Walsall.

SPENCER, JOHN
Forward: 5+4 apps
Born: Glasgow, 11 September 1970
Career: Glasgow Rangers (apprentice, June 1986; professional, September 1987), Morton (loan, March–April 1989), Chelsea (£450,000, August 1992), Queens Park Rangers (£2.5m, November 1996), EVERTON (loan, March–April 1998; signed for £1.5m, May 1998), Motherwell (loan, October–December 1998, signed permanently January 1999)
A small, lively, bustling utility forward, John Spencer was already an established and experienced League and Scottish international when he joined Everton on loan in 1998, signed as a stop-gap by former Ibrox boss Walter Smith. He had represented his country at both schoolboy and youth-team levels before gaining three Under-21 and 14 senior caps as well as netting 70 goals north and south of the border. He made his debut for Everton against Blackburn in March 1998, and although he kicked off the following campaign, it soon became apparent that he wasn't going to fit into the manager's plans and left for Motherwell.

STANLEY, GARY ERNEST
Midfield: 61+2 apps, 1 goal
Born: Burton-on-Trent, 4 March 1954
Career: Derbyshire schools football, Chelsea (apprentice, April 1970; professional, March 1971), Fort Lauderdale Strikers/NASL (loan, May–July 1979), EVERTON (£300,000, August 1979), Swansea City (£150,000,

October 1981), Portsmouth (free, January 1984), Wichita Wings/USA (June 1986), Bristol City (August–October 1988)

An attacking midfielder player, recommended to Chelsea by ex-player Frank Upton, Gary Stanley helped the Londoners gain promotion from the Second Division in 1977 but never really established himself in the first team at Stamford Bridge. He moved on to ease the financial situation at Stamford Bridge, joining Everton after a brief spell in the NASL, making his debut for the Blues against Cardiff in a League Cup encounter in August 1979, following up soon afterwards with his League bow against Aston Villa. He manned midfield efficiently (with Steve McMahon and Asa Hartford), before switching to Swansea, who were battling hard in their first-ever season of top-flight football. Stanley quit competitive football in 1988 with more than 300 senior appearances under his belt (plus his games in America).

STEIN, JAMES

Outside-left: 217 apps, 65 goals

Born: Coatbridge, Lanarkshire, Scotland, 7 November 1907 – Deceased

Career: West Lothian, Blackburn Rovers (August 1924), Dunfermline Athletic (July 1925), EVERTON (£1,500, April 1926), Burnley (October 1936), New Brighton (June 1938–September 1939); did not play after the Second World War

Although he played briefly for Blackburn, Jimmy Stein first caught the eye when helping Dunfermline win the Scottish Second Division title and promotion in 1926. Everton pipped two other big-named clubs for his signature and he eventually replaced Alex Troup on the left-wing at Goodison Park, gaining a regular place in the first XI in 1929. He made his debut against Bolton in December of the previous year and scored his first goal for the club on the opening day of the 1929–30 League season, also against Bolton (won 3–2). An exciting player, full of dash and vigour, he was a model professional, a quiet man, possessing a long, raking stride and a powerful shot. An integral part of the Everton side that won the Second Division title in 1930–31 (ten goals scored in 28 games), Stein earned a League championship winning medal 12 months later (netting nine goals in 37 outings). Then, in 1933, he had a fine game when helping the Blues win the FA Cup in 1933, scoring in the 3–0 victory over Manchester City. A broken leg, suffered on Everton's 1935 summer tour to Switzerland, sidelined him until February 1936. He never really recovered full fitness and left Merseyside for Turf Moor ten months later. Completely out of context, the usually mild-mannered Stein was sent off playing for New Brighton and was subsequently fined three guineas (£3.15) but not suspended.

STEPHENSON, GEORGE

Right-half: 1 app.

Born: circa 1865 – Deceased

Career: EVERTON (July 1888–April 1889)

Stephenson's only appearance in League football was for Everton in a 4–0 defeat at Wolves in January 1889. (Some reference books have his surname as Stevenson.)

STEVEN, TREVOR McGREGOR
Midfield: 294+4 apps, 59 goals
Born: Berwick-on-Tweed, 29 September 1963
Career: Burnley (apprentice, June 1980; professional, September 1981), EVERTON (£300,000, July 1983), Glasgow Rangers (£1.5m, July 1989), Olympique Marseille/France (£4.5m, September 1991), Glasgow Rangers (September 1992; retired May 1999); later a football agent

Trevor Steven won 14 medals at club level – four with Everton (two League titles, one FA Cup victory and a European Cup-Winners' Cup triumph), nine with Rangers (five Scottish League titles and four League Cup successes) and a French League title with Marseille. He also played in three losing FA Cup finals (1985, 1986 and 1989) and top-scored for the Blues in 1986–87 (including 14 League goals in 41 games). Steven took 23 penalties for Everton (21 in the League) and missed only two. A decidedly right-sided midfielder with an attacking flare, he was monitored by Everton boss Howard Kendall for two years before his move to Goodison Park, making his debut for the Blues in a 1–0 home win over Stoke in August 1983. He bedded in quickly and was regarded as one of the finest individual talents ever to don the blue of Everton. He was a wonderful dribbler with excellent close control, and complemented Peter Reid superbly well in centre-field. Regarded as a creator of chances rather than a taker, he still scored some vital goals and it was he who crossed from the right for Andy Gray to head home Everton's decisive goal in the 1984 FA Cup final against Watford. Having already represented his country at youth and Under-21 levels, he won the first of his 36 full England caps against Northern Ireland in February 1985, played in the World Cup finals the following year and had close on 300 games for Everton before joining Rangers, after refusing to sign a new contract at Goodison. He made 184 appearances for Rangers (25 goals).

STEVENS, DENNIS
Inside-forward/wing-half: 145 apps, 23 goals
Born: Dudley, West Midlands, 30 November 1933
Career: Brierley Hill and Dudley Schoolboys, Manchester United (trialist), Bolton Wanderers (amateur, April 1949; professional, December 1950), EVERTON (£35,000, March 1962), Oldham Athletic (£4,000, December 1965), Tranmere Rovers (March 1967–April 1968); later ran a menswear shop in Bolton, where he still lives

An ever-present (with Alex Young) when Everton won the League title in 1962–63, Dennis Stevens had been an FA Cup finalist with Bolton Wanderers (against Manchester United) five years earlier. Initially an aggressive, smart and decisive inside-forward with an eye for goal, he made his debut for the Blues at Sheffield United in March 1962, taking over from Scottish international Bobby Collins. He later switched to right-half and even played at full-back. Capped twice by England at Under-23 level, he also represented the Football League and netted 113 goals in 457 League games. Stevens is also the cousin of the great Duncan Edwards.

STEVENS, GEORGE LEOPOLD

Centre-forward: 2 apps
Born: Wallasey, 18 March 1910 – *Died*: 1987
Career: Wallasey Trams FC, New Brighton (amateur, December 1930; professional, January 1931), EVERTON (£500, June 1932), Southend United (£100, November 1933), Stockport County (£150, June 1936), Crewe Alexandra (July 1938–September 1939); guest with Oldham Athletic (1943–44); did not play after 1945

Leo Stevens was a tram conductor before turning to professional football with New Brighton. Slim, fair-haired with good pace and a strong right-foot shot, he scored 33 goals in 54 appearances for the 'Rakers' before joining Everton as cover for Dixie Dean. He made only two starts for the Blues, the first against Manchester City in February 1933, the second against Leeds United two months later. Thereafter he continued to hit the target and when the Second World War arrived (which ended his career) he had claimed 112 goals in 180 appearances, helping Stockport win the Third Division (N) title in 1937. Stevens was one of 13 children; two of his five brothers, John and Bill, played for New Brighton.

STEVENS, MICHAEL GARY

Right-back: 293+1 apps, 14 goals
Born: Barrow-in-Furness, 27 March 1963
Career: EVERTON (apprentice, April 1979; professional, March 1981), Glasgow Rangers (£1.25m, July 1988), Tranmere Rovers (£350,000, September 1994; retired June 1998); now a physiotherapist

Gary Stevens helped Everton win two League titles (1985, 1987), the FA Cup (1984) the European Cup-Winners' Cup (1985) and two Charity Shields (1984, 1985). Then with Rangers he collected six Scottish League championship-winning medals in succession: (1989–94), one Scottish Cup (1992) and three League Cup-winner's medals (1989, 1991, 1994).

A positive, hard-working, assured and reliable right-back, he had a terrific engine and, despite venturing upfield on several overlaps, he was always there at the back when danger threatened. He did exceptionally well in Everton's Central League side and made his First Division debut against West Ham in October 1981 when he replaced Billy Wright. He returned to the second XI, where he bided his time until eventually securing the number two spot from Brian Borrows a year later. He was called into the England World Cup squad in 1986, having gained the first of his 46 full caps against Italy on a US tour in June 1985. He also played in one 'B' international and on his retirement in 1998 had amassed 736 club and international appearances.

STEVENS, THOMAS

Outside-left: 5 apps
Born: Scotland, *circa* 1888 – Deceased
Career: Clyde, EVERTON (March 1912), Clyde (May 1912); did not play after the First World War

With Harold Uren sidelined, Everton brought in Tom Stevens, who made his debut in a 3–0 home win over Woolwich Arsenal in March 1912. He returned to Clyde rather rapidly!

STEVENSON, ALEXANDER ERNEST
Inside-left: 271 apps, 90 goals
Born: Dublin, Ireland, 9 August 1912 – *Died*: 1985
Career: Dolphin FC/Dublin, Glasgow Rangers (professional, August 1930), EVERTON (£37,000, January 1934), Bootle (May 1949–May 1950)
Alex Stevenson scored seven goals in 12 games for Rangers before moving to Goodison Park. A wily, brainy player, clever ball-juggler (one of the best of his generation) and as nimble as a mountain goat, he could create an opening out of nothing and often scored a goal in the same way. He was a great 'supplier', first to Dixie Dean and then to Tommy Lawton, and a splendid partner to Jackie Coulter before the Second World War. Stevenson, who helped Rangers win the Scottish crown in 1933–34 (11 games), was a League championship winner with Everton in 1938–39, scoring ten goals in 36 outings. On the international front, he won 17 full caps for Northern Ireland and seven with Eire, his last in 1948–49 and played in one Victory international against Scotland (1946). He made his debut for Everton against Arsenal in February 1934.

STEVENSON, WILLIAM
Full-back: 125 apps
Born: Accrington, 1886 – Deceased
Career: Accrington Stanley (May 1903), EVERTON (July 1907–May 1913)
A confident, strong and resolute full-back, Billy Stevenson made his debut for Everton against Newcastle United in December 1907 when he replaced the injured Walter Balmer. He continued to deputise in both full-back positions until gaining a regular place in the side during the second half of the 1910–11 season, when he partnered first Robert Balmer and then Jock Maconnachie. He missed only six games when the Blues finished runners-up in the First Division the following season and was the mainstay of the side until replaced by new signing Bob Thompson during the early stages of the 1913–14 campaign.

STEWART, ALEXANDER
Half-back/inside-left: 19 apps, 1 goal
Born: Greenock, Scotland, 1869 – Deceased
Career: Grenalmond FC, Rosebury FC, Greenock Morton (1887), Burnley (August 1889), EVERTON (December 1892), Nottingham Forest (July 1893), Notts County (March 1897), Bedminster (July 1898), Northampton Town (July 1899), Burnley (August 1901), Leicester Fosse (player/trainer, August 1902–May 1905)
Alec Stewart was a player with a neat and polished style, a valuable member of every side he played with, although his stay at Goodison Park was a relatively short one. He made well over 250 appearances (211 in the Football League)

during his 16 years in the game. Able to occupy both wing-half positions and inside-left, he was a Lancashire Cup-winner with Burnley (1890). He made his debut for Everton against his future club, Notts County, in December 1892 and scored his only goal in a 2–1 defeat against another of his future clubs, Nottingham Forest, the following month.

STEWART, WILLIAM SEYMOUR
Left-half: 137 apps, 6 goals
Born: Arbroath, Scotland, *circa* 1867 – Deceased
Career: Strathmore (1884), Arbroath (1886), Black Watch team (1887–88), Belfast Distillery (1889), Preston North End (August 1890), EVERTON (August 1893), Bristol City (May 1898–April 1900)
As a member of the Black Watch team, mustachioed Billy Stewart gained an Army Cup-winner's medal and while stationed with the Royal Scots Greys in Ireland he helped Belfast Distillery to lift the Irish Cup. Preston then bought him out of the Army and he played for them for three years before moving to Goodison Park in 1893. He had the ability to deliver an exceptionally long throw-in, whereby he used to run up to the touchline and then jump in the air to get thrust before delivering the ball – but this technique was subsequently outlawed. He also possessed a powerful kick and would often send the ball up to 80 yards downfield with one mighty clearance. He made his League debut for Everton against Sheffield United in September 1893 and retained his place in the side until moving to Bristol City, whom he skippered in his first season. Stewart was a Lancashire Cup winner on five occasions – twice with Preston and three times with Everton – and he also played in the Blues' 1897 FA Cup final.

STORRIER, DAVID
Centre-half/full-back: 65 apps
Born: Arbroath, 25 October 1872 – Deceased
Career: Arbroath (1890), EVERTON (February 1894), Celtic (May 1898), Dundee (1901), Millwall Athletic (September 1902–April 1904)
A commanding presence on the pitch, Dave Storrier was a tall, solid 13 st. 6 lb defender who feared no one. He had 'pith of foot' wrote one reporter – a tribute to his masterful and forceful kicking. Certainly a wonderful player, able to occupy both full-back positions as well as centre-half, he made his Everton debut in the pivotal slot against Stoke in March 1894. However, injuries affected his game for long periods, although he was a regular in the side in 1896–97 (playing in the FA Cup final). He gained three caps for Scotland (against England, Ireland and Wales in 1899), made two appearances for the Scottish League and played for Glasgow against Sheffield in the annual Inter City match. Twice a Scottish Cup winner with Celtic (1899, 1900), he appeared in 40 games for the Glasgow club.

STOWELL, MICHAEL

Goalkeeper: 1 app.
Born: Preston, 19 April 1965
Career: Leyland Motors, Preston North End (professional, February 1985), EVERTON (free, December 1985), Chester City (loan, September 1987), York City (loan, December 1987), Manchester City (loan, February 1988), Port Vale (loan, October 1988), Wolverhampton Wanderers (loan, March 1989), Preston North End (loan, February 1990), Wolverhampton Wanderers (£250,000, June 1990), Bristol City (free, June 2001; retired June 2003)

Signed as cover for Neville Southall, Mike Stowell made one senior appearance for Everton, taking Southall's place for the home Simod Cup-tie against Millwall in December 1988. He remained loyal to the club, having several loan spells to keep him focused on the game and to participate in competitive action. After leaving Goodison Park, he broke Bert Williams's record for the most appearances by a Wolves goalkeeper (448). Standing 6 ft 2 in. tall, he possessed fine reflexes, good positional sense and was a fine shot-stopper. In November 1990 Stowell hired a tractor to beat severe snow drifts in the Midlands in order to report for international duty in Algeria with the England 'B' team.

STRETTLE, SAMUEL

Full-back: 4 apps
Born: Warrington, *circa* 1885 – Deceased
Career: EVERTON (May 1906), Chesterfield (April 1909), Exeter City (August 1913–May 1920), Northwich Victoria (August 1920; retired May 1922)

Reserve Sam Strettle deputised for Walter Balmer in successive League games against Bolton and Sheffield United in March 1907 and played only twice over the next two seasons before moving to Chesterfield. He made 114 appearances for Exeter either side of the First World War.

STUART, GRAHAM CHARLES

Midfielder/forward: 137+24 apps, 31 goals
Born: Tooting, London, 24 October 1970
Career: Chelsea (apprentice, April 1987; professional, June 1989), EVERTON (£850,000, August 1993), Sheffield United (£850,000, November 1997), Charlton Athletic (£1.1m, March 1999)

An attacking midfielder, who can also play as an out-out-forward, Graham Stuart is hard-working with a goalscoring touch, who made over 100 appearances for Chelsea before moving to Goodison Park. He made his debut for the Blues against his future club Sheffield United in August 1993, taking his place in the engine room alongside Mark Ward and Peter Beagrie (on the left). His value to the club was inestimable and in four and a half years played in over 160 senior games, gaining an FA Cup-winner's medal in 1995, having earlier represented England at both youth and Under-21 levels, gaining five caps in the latter category. His two goals on the last day of the 1993–94 season (in a 3–2 win over Wimbledon) kept Everton in the Premiership. In 2000 he helped Charlton reach the Premiership as Division One champions and has since taken his career appearance-tally close to the 500 mark.

STUBBS, ALAN
Defender: 99+7 apps, 3 goals
Born: Liverpool, 6 October 1971
Career: Bolton Wanderers (apprentice, April 1988; professional, July 1990), Celtic (£3.5m, July 1996), EVERTON (free, July 2001)
Alan Stubbs has had his fair share of health problems over the years but what a marvellous defender he has proved to be. A rugged, hard-tackling centre-back, he made 237 appearances for Bolton and 153 for Celtic, with whom he won two Scottish League titles and two League Cups before his move to Everton. A boyhood 'Blue', he has since captained the team regularly. He bedded into his position at the heart of the Blues immediately and produced some outstanding performances while also scoring some superb goals from set-pieces and with his own dead-ball shooting. A fine header of the ball, he achieved his personal ambition by skippering the Blues in the Premiership in 2002–03. An England 'B' international (one cap), he made his debut at Charlton in August 2001 and reached the milestone of 500 appearances in 2004.

STYLES, ARTHUR
Full-back: 26+1 apps
Born: Liverpool, 3 September 1949
Career: Liverpool Boys, EVERTON (apprentice, August 1965; professional, August 1967), Birmingham City (February 1974, in the deal involving Bob Latchford and Howard Kendall), Peterborough United (July 1978), Portsmouth (July 1979–May 1980)
Archie Styles looked a good prospect at Goodison Park, but his career stagnated and he was restricted to only 27 first-team appearances in nine years. After moving to St Andrew's as a makeweight in the Latchford–Kendall deal he found it hard to hold down a first-team place and made only 82 appearances in four and a half years before lowering his standards and signing for Peterborough. Capped by England at schoolboy and youth-team levels, he made his debut for Everton against Wolves in December 1972, when he took over from Henry Newton.

SUGG, FRANK HOWE
Full-back/centre-half/centre-forward: 10 apps
Born: Ilkeston, 11 January 1862 – *Died*: 1933
Career: Bolton Wanderers (briefly, 1882–83), The Wednesday (1883–84), Derby County (November 1884), Burnley (March 1885), EVERTON (September 1888), Burnley (March–April 1889)
Frank Sugg could and would play anywhere to get a game of football. He was 26 when he joined Everton, having played for four major clubs prior to the introduction of the Football League. He made his debut for the Blues at centre-

forward against Aston Villa in October 1888 and lined up in four different positions during his stay on Merseyside.

SUTHERLAND, JOHN FRANCIS
Full-back: 8 apps
Born: Cork, Ireland, 19 February 1932
Career: Evergreen FC/Ireland, EVERTON (professional, May 1950), Chesterfield (June 1957), Crewe Alexandra (November 1958–May 1960)
A reserve at Goodison Park, John Sutherland had to wait until September 1956 before making his League debut at right-back against Wolves at Molineux. He played in 147 League games for both Chesterfield and Crewe.

SUTTON, WILLIAM W.
Goalkeeper: 1 app.
Born: 1871 – Deceased
Career: EVERTON (July 1894–May 1895)
Reserve Bill Sutton's only League game for Everton was in the 2–2 draw at Derby in January 1895, when he deputised for Dick Williams.

TAL, IDAN
Winger: 14+19 apps, 2 goals
Born: Beer Sheva, Israel, 12 February 1975
Career: Maccabi Petach Tikva/Israel (May 1996), Hapoel Tel Aviv/Israel (July 1998), Merida/Israel (August 1999), EVERTON (£700,000, October 2000), Rayo Vallecano/Spain (September 2002)
An old-fashioned winger, tricky and hard-working, Idan Tal began well enough at Goodison Park but then lost his way, and although he stayed at the club, he subsequently moved to Spain. Capped 28 times by Israel before his move to Goodison Park, Tal had also netted 17 goals in 121 League games while playing domestic football in his homeland. He made his Premiership debut in a 1–0 win at Newcastle in October 2000.

TANSEY, JAMES
Full-back: 142 apps
Born: Liverpool, 29 January 1929
Career: St Gerard's RC School (Liverpool), EVERTON (amateur, June 1945; professional, May 1948), Crewe Alexandra (June 1960–April 1961)
A compact full-back, sure-footed with good pace, Jimmy Tansey spent 15 years at Goodison Park – the first eight playing in the intermediate and reserve teams. He made his League debut against Notts County in March 1953 (deputising for Jimmy Lindsay) and it wasn't until the 1955–56 campaign that he finally established himself in the side, aged 26. He had three excellent seasons as partner to right-back Don Donovan before losing his place to John Bramwell. Tansey was evacuated to Wales during the Second World War. His younger brother, Gerard, was an Everton reserve (1951–55) and later played for Tranmere.

TAYLOR, EDWARD HALLOWS

Goalkeeper: 42 apps
Born: Liverpool, 17 March 1887 – *Died:* Manchester, 5 July 1956
Career: Marlborough Old Boys (Liverpool), Liverpool Balmoral, Oldham Athletic (professional, February 1912), Huddersfield Town (June 1922), EVERTON (February 1927), Ashton National (March 1928), Wrexham (November 1928; retired through injury May 1929); later worked in the cotton trade in Manchester

Despite standing only 5 ft 7 in. tall, Ted Taylor was one of the game's most scientific goalkeepers. Twice a League championship winner with Huddersfield (1924, 1926), he added a third to his collection with Everton (1928) and was capped six times by England (1922–26) as well as being an amateur international trialist (1912). A quick thinker without any noticeable weaknesses, he was successful to a large extent because he studied his opponents. He made his debut for the Blues against Liverpool at Anfield in February 1927 in front of 53,000 fans.

TAYLOR, JOHN DANIEL

Half-back/outside, inside or inside-right: 456 apps, 80 goals
Born: Dumbarton, 27 January 1872 – *Died:* West Kirby, Liverpool, 1949
Career: Dumbarton Athletic (1891), St Mirren (August 1894), EVERTON (July 1896; retired in May 1910); returned to South Liverpool (1912); did not play after the First World War

Scottish international Jack Taylor played in three FA Cup finals for Everton (1897, 1906, 1907), gaining a winner's medal in his second. He also played in six semi-finals for the Blues and with a total of 56 appearances to his credit (48 in succession) he is one of only five players to have appeared in over 50 or more FA Cup games for the club. He began his career as a centre-forward, played regularly on the right-wing before settling down to become a tower of strength at the heart of the Everton defence. A strong all-rounder who had an estimable personal character, he coaxed the best out of those around him and was without doubt an inspirational footballer. He scored from the right-wing berth on his League debut for Everton in a 2–1 home win over Sheffield Wednesday in September 1896. He was a regular in the side right up until March 1910 – when playing in the FA Cup semi-final for Everton against Barnsley at Manchester, he was struck in the throat by the ball. He suffered severe damage to the larynx, an injury from which he never fully recovered, and he quit top-flight football that summer. He won five full caps for his country (1892–95) and also appeared in six Inter-League games. With Dumbarton, he twice won the Scottish League title (joint in 1891 and 1892). He was killed in a road accident.

Taylor is the only Everton player to have made 100 consecutive appearances from his debut – 5 September 1896 to 24 March 1899.

TELFER, GEORGE ANDREW
Forward: 91+24 apps, 22 goals
Born: Liverpool, 6 July 1955
Career: EVERTON (amateur, July 1970; professional, August 1972), San Diego/NASL (July 1979), Scunthorpe United (December 1981), Altrincham (1982), Preston North End (n/c, August–September 1983), Runcorn, Barrow; then football in the community officer for the Merseyside Youth Association from October 1984

George Telfer was a speedy forward, direct and aggressive, who, besides creating chances for his colleagues, scored some stunning goals himself, especially for Everton. He made his League debut for the Blues in December 1973 against Arsenal and that season his form was excellent, receiving rave reports and hints that he could well be a future England international. Indeed, everything seemed to be going smoothly for him until Duncan McKenzie arrived on the scene to take over his position. He gritted his teeth and stayed on at Goodison, pledging to regain his place. He failed to do so, and after turning down a move to Chester, who were willing to pay £30,000 for him in November 1980 to replace Ian Rush (sold to Liverpool), he chose to visit the NASL before returning to League football with Scunthorpe.

TEMPLE, DEREK WILLIAM
Forward: 276+1 apps, 84 goals
Born: Liverpool, 13 November 1938
Career: Lancashire Boys, EVERTON (amateur, April 1955; professional, August 1956), Preston North End (£35,000, September 1967–May 1970)

Derek Temple was the star of Everton's 1966 FA Cup final victory over Sheffield Wednesday when he raced away to score the winning goal to clinch one of the great post-Second World War fight-backs at Wembley. Not all that big, he was nevertheless a powerful and pacy player who possessed a strong right-foot shot. An England schoolboy international (1953–54), he was outstanding in Everton's Colts' team and in one season netted 70 goals, including a handful of double hat-tricks and two five-timers, duly winning an international youth cap. He made his senior debut against Newcastle in March 1957 and established himself in the first team in 1963. Two years later he won his only cap against West Germany in Nuremberg. He scored 14 goals in 76 League outings for Preston.

THOMAS, ANTHONY
Full-back/Midfield: 8+2 apps
Born: Liverpool, 12 July 1971
Career: Tranmere Rovers (apprentice, July 1977; professional, February 1989), EVERTON (£400,000, August 1997), Motherwell (£150,000, December 1998)

Tony Thomas made well over 300 appearances for Tranmere and played at Wembley when Rovers won the Leyland DAF Trophy in 1990. An attacking full-back, strong in the tackle when required and able to deliver damaging crosses into the danger zone, he struggled with a stream of injuries at Goodison Park, including a tedious thigh problem. As a result, he managed only nine first-team outings under boss Joe Royle before his departure to Motherwell, sold by Walter Smith. He made his Premiership debut against Crystal Palace in August 1997.

THOMAS, DAVID

Outside-left: 84 apps, 6 goals
Born: Kirkby-in-Ashfield, 5 October 1950
Career: Burnley (amateur, April 1966; professional, October 1967), Queens Park Rangers (£165,000, October 1972), EVERTON (£200,000 August 1977), Wolverhampton Wanderers (October 1979), Vancouver Whitecaps/NASL (June 1980), Middlesbrough (March 1982), Portsmouth (July 1982–May 1985)

Darting, weaving left-winger Dave Thomas won 8 full (all with QPR) and 11 Under-23 caps for England, as well as representing his country at youth-team level. In a fine career, spanning 15 years, he scored over 60 goals in more than 500 games, 179 with Burnley, where he won the FA Youth Cup (1967) and became the youngest-ever Burnley player (in the top flight) when at the age of 17 he made made his debut against Everton, also in 1967. His transfer from Turf Moor to QPR was a record for both the clubs and he helped the Londoners finish runners-up to his former club in the Second Division in 1973–74. He moved to Everton full of promise and made his debut for the Blues against Nottingham Forest in August 1977, scoring his first goal three weeks later in a 5–1 win at Leicester. He played very well during his two years on Merseyside before his departure to Wolves – part of a wholesale clearout at Goodison Park. He never really adapted to life or the surroundings at Molineux and after less than eight months went over to play in the NASL, returning to wind down his career at both ends of the country.

THOMAS, EDWARD

Inside-forward: 93 apps, 41 goals
Born: Newton-le-Willows, 23 October 1933 – *Died*: Allestree, Derby, 12 November 2003
Career: EVERTON (amateur, April 1949; professional, October 1951), Blackburn Rovers (February 1960), Swansea Town (July 1962), Derby County (August 1964), Leyton Orient (September 1967–March 1968); later worked for an insurance company while also giving dedicated support to his local Catholic church

Always a relaxed player, Eddie Thomas was an accurate marksman who bagged 133 goals in League and Cup football during his professional career. He spent almost 11 years at Goodison Park and made his senior debut against Manchester United in March 1957 in front of 34,000 spectators. It was surprising when he was allowed to leave Goodison Park, signed by ex-Everton defender Johnny Carey, then manager of Blackburn. He scored in each of his first six League games for Swansea and drew up a fine partnership with Alan Durban at The Vetch Field.

THOMAS, MICHAEL REGINALD
Midfield: 11 apps
Born: Mochdre, Powys, Wales, 7 July 1954
Career: Mochdre and Newtown Schools, Welshpool District Boys, Pentre Youth Club, Wrexham (amateur, 1969; apprentice, July 1970; professional, April 1972), Manchester United (£300,000 November 1978), EVERTON (£450,000 player/exchange deal involving John Gidman, August 1981), Brighton and Hove Albion (£400,000 November 1981), Stoke City (£200,000 August 1982), Chelsea (£75,000 January 1984), West Bromwich Albion (£100,000 September 1985), Derby County (loan, March–May 1986), Wichita Wings/USA Indoor League (£35,000 August 1986), Shrewsbury Town (August 1988), Leeds United (£10,000, June 1989), Stoke City (loan, March 1990; signed on a free, August 1990), Wrexham (July 1991–May 1993), Conwy United (briefly, early in 1993–94), Inter Cardiff (1995–96), Portmadoc (manager/coach); later manager of a soccer coaching school near Wrexham (late 1990s); soccer summariser for Century Radio (Manchester)

Mickey Thomas was a hard-working, industrious midfield dynamo, who in 24 years played on more than 80 different grounds, in 15 countries, scored 101 goals in 729 appearances and gained two Under-21, one Under-23 and 51 full caps for Wales. A Welsh Cup winner with Wrexham in 1972, 1975 and 1978, he also helped that club win the Third Division title in 1978 and afterwards played for Manchester United in the 1979 FA Cup final and gained a First Division runner's-up medal in 1980. He was in the Chelsea team that clinched promotion to the First Division in 1983–84 and two years later, in 1985–86, helped Derby rise from Division Three. After his debut for Everton against Birmingham in August 1981, Thomas failed to settle down at Goodison Park and left after barely three months at the club, following a dispute with manager Howard Kendall when he refused to play in a reserve game. Prior to joining Inter Cardiff in 1995, Thomas served an 18-month jail sentence for handling counterfeit money.

THOMAS, WILLIAM W.
Goalkeeper: 1 app.
Born: *circa* 1870 – Deceased
Career: EVERTON (July 1892–April 1894)
Bill Thomas made only one League appearance for Everton – in a 3–0 defeat at WBA in October 1892, when both David Jardine and Archie Pinnell were unavailable.

THOMPSON, ROBERT
Left-back: 1 app.
Born: Liverpool, *circa* 1870 – Deceased
Career: EVERTON (August 1892–April 1893)
A reserve with Everton, Thompson's only League outing was in a 5–0 defeat at Preston in December 1892 when he deputised for Arthur Chadwick.

THOMPSON, ROBERT
Right-back: 89 apps
Born: Bells Close, Newcastle, 1890 – *Died*: Liverpool, 1958
Career: Scotswood FC (August 1909), Leicester Fosse (May 1911), EVERTON
   (with George Harrison, April 1913), Millwall (July 1921), Tranmere Rovers
   (May 1922–May 1923)
The powerful Bob Thompson helped Everton win the League title in 1914–15,
when he formed a fine full-back partnership with John Maconnachie. He made
a further 87 first-team appearances for the Blues during the First World War
and after the hostilities went on to play in nine League games for Millwall and
35 for Tranmere.

THOMSEN, CLAUS
Midfielder/central defender: 18+7 apps, 1 goal
Born: Aarhus, Denmark, 31 May 1970
Career: Aarhus/Denmark (1989), Ipswich Town (£250,000, June 1994),
   EVERTON (£900,000, January 1997), AB Bagsvaerd/Denmark (March
   1998), BK Copenhagen/Denmark
A Danish international, capped 14 times before joining Everton and twice while
at Goodison Park, Claus Thomsen, 6 ft 3 in. tall and 13 st. 6 lb in weight, was
equally at home in defence or midfield. He had appeared in almost 100 games
for Ipswich when Joe Royle signed him to boost his squad. He made his debut
for the Blues against Arsenal in January 1997 but three months later had the
misfortune to concede an own-goal in the 1–1 draw with Liverpool. He did not
figure in Howard Kendall's plans when he returned as boss.

THOMSON, GEORGE MATTHEWSON
Full-back: 77 apps, 1 goal
Born: Edinburgh, 19 October 1936
Career: Heart of Midlothian (1956), EVERTON (November 1960), Brentford
   (November 1963–May 1968)
A League championship winner with both Hearts and Everton, George
Thomson was a well-built defender who competed vigorously throughout a long
career which saw him amass in excess of 300 senior appearances north and south
of the border, including 162 in League football as a Brentford player. A Scottish
League representative, he was 24 when he moved from Tynecastle to Goodison
Park and made his debut for the Blues against Arsenal in November 1960,
taking over at left-back after Tommy Jones had struggled with injury. He
switched his allegiance to Griffin Park after Mick Meagan had settled in as Alex
Parker's full-back partner.

THOMSON, JOHN ROSS
Left-half: 296 apps, 5 goals
Born: Thornton, Renfrewshire, Scotland, 6 July 1906 – *Died*: Carnoustie,
   Scotland, 1979
Career: Thornton Rangers Juveniles, Thornton Rangers, Dundee (May 1925),

EVERTON (March 1930; retired December 1939); later returned to guest for Aldershot, Fulham and Carnoustie during the Second World War; then Manchester City (manager, July 1947–November 1950); later a licensee in Carnoustie until November 1974

Jock Thomson gained three League championship medals with Everton – two for First Division triumphs in 1931–32 and 1938–39 (the latter as captain) and his first when the Second Division title was won in 1930–31. He also helped the Blues win the FA Cup in 1933. A six-footer, strong and aggressive, he made his Blues' debut against West Ham in March 1930 (lost 2–1) and was capped by Scotland against Wales in October 1932; he also represented the Scottish League. He left his managerial post at Maine Road soon after Manchester City had been relegated to the Second Division. He was keen on films and boxing.

THOMSON, SAMUEL
Forward: 3 apps, 1 goal
Born: Lugar, Ayrshire, Scotland, 14 February 1862 – *Died*: Preston, 23 December 1943
Career: Lugar Boswell, Glasgow Rangers (1884), Preston North End (July 1885), Wolverhampton Wanderers (May 1890), EVERTON (August 1891), Accrington (October 1891; retired, injured, April 1892); later worked in Preston

A double-winner with Preston in 1888–89 and recipient of a second League championship medal the following season, Sam Thomson was a dashing, all-purpose forward, able to adapt to whatever circumstances prevailed. He had done reasonably well in non-competitive football with Rangers, gaining two full caps for Scotland (against Wales and Ireland in 1884). He then scored ten goals in 34 League games for Preston and nine in 21 games for Wolves before making his debut for Everton against WBA in September 1891 (lost 4–0). He failed to settle on Merseyside and spent the rest of that season with Accrington before retiring.

TIE, LI
Midfield: 36+4 apps
Born: Liaoning, China, 18 September 1977
Career: Liaoning Bodao/China, EVERTON (loan, August 2002; signed July 2003)

Li Tie, capped over 80 times by his country, was, at 6 ft, unusually tall for a Chinese player. Nevertheless he gave a good account of himself in the Premiership, producing some impressive performances as a feisty and industrious midfielder. He had a keen eye for an opening and created several goals for his front men. Unfortunately, he was sidelined for three months after fracturing his leg with the China squad in February 2004.

TILER, CARL
Defender: 23 apps, 1 goal
Born: Sheffield, 11 February 1970
Career: Barnsley (YTS, June 1986; professional, February 1988), Nottingham

Forest (£1.4m, May 1991), Swindon Town (loan, November 1994), Aston Villa (£750,000, October 1995), Sheffield United (£650,000, March 1997), EVERTON (£500,000, November 1997), Charlton Athletic (£700,000, September 1998), Birmingham City (loan, February 2000), Portsmouth (£250,000, March 2001; released May 2003)

Before joining Everton, Carl Tiler, a strong, tall, dominant defender, had already gained 13 England Under-21 caps and made over 200 appearances, despite spending three years in the shadows at Nottingham Forest. He arrived at Goodison Park during an injury crisis and made his debut against Spurs 48 hours after signing. He retained his place at the heart of the defence for the remainder of the season but was then transferred to Charlton soon after Walter Smith took over as manager. He helped both the Valiants and Portsmouth reach the Premiership in 2000 and 2003 respectively.

TODD, COLIN

Utility: 35 apps, 1 goal

Born: Chester-le-Street, County Durham, 12 December 1948

Career: Chester-le-Street Boys, Sunderland (apprentice, April 1965; professional, December 1966), Derby County (£180,000, February 1971), EVERTON (£333,000, September 1978), Birmingham City (£300,000, September 1979), Nottingham Forest (£70,000, August 1982), Oxford United (February 1984), Vancouver Whitecaps/NASL (May–October 1984), Luton Town (retired June 1985), Whitley Bay (manager, July 1985), Middlesbrough (reserve-team coach, May 1986; chief scout/assistant manager, September 1986; manager, March 1990–June 1991), Bradford City (assistant manager, January 1992), Bolton Wanderers (assistant manager, June 1992; joint manager with Roy McFarland, January 1995; upgraded to manager, November 1996–May 1999), Swindon Town (manager, May–November 2000), Derby County (manager, August 2001–January 2002), Bradford City (manager, June 2004)

An FA Youth Cup winner with Sunderland, Colin Todd developed into a superb footballer, self-assured, confident, a superb reader of the game and, above all, a true professional. He amassed more than 700 appearances at club and international level during a 20-year career, and that tally included 293 League outings for Derby and 173 for Sunderland. His appearance-record with Everton was moderate, although his performances were excellent. Versatile to the extent that he could play as an orthodox right-back, as a resilient wing-half, as a rock-solid centre-half or as a midfielder. Capped 27 times by England, he also represented his country in youth and Under-23 matches and played for the Football League XI. He won two League championship medals with Derby (1972, 1975), helped Birmingham gain promotion from the Second Division (1980) and was voted 'Footballer of the Year' in 1975. He played in 35 games for Everton, making his debut against Wolves in September 1978 when he replaced Terry Darracott at right-back. He is the oldest player ever to appear in a League game for Oxford United, aged 35 in 1984. As a manager, Todd took Bolton up to and down from the Premiership.

TOMAN, WILFRED
Forward: 29 apps, 10 goals
Born: Bishop Auckland, 1873 – Deceased
Career: Victoria Athletic, Aberdeen, Dundee, Victoria United, Burnley (November 1896), EVERTON (April 1899), Southampton (June 1900), EVERTON (July 1901), Stockport County (January 1904), Newcastle United (amateur, August 1906), Scottish junior football (1909–14); did not play after the First World War

A clever centre-forward with an eye for goal, Wilf Toman netted 37 goals in 88 games for Burnley before spending a season at Goodison Park. He continued to find the net on a regular basis, scoring in his second game for the Blues, having made his debut in a 0–0 draw with his former club, Burnley, in April 1899. He formed useful partnerships with both Jimmy Settle and Jack Proudfoot the following season before moving to Southampton, with Everton retaining his registration. After helping Saints win the Southern League title, he returned to Goodison Park and scored on his 'second' debut (against Manchester City) before suffering a serious leg injury which sidelined him for two and a half years. He struggled to regain full fitness and after brief sojourns with Stockport and Newcastle, he returned to live in Scotland.

TOMLINSON, JOHN
Outside-right: 2 apps
Born: Bebington, 26 June 1934
Career: EVERTON (amateur, May 1947; professional, June 1952), Chesterfield (June 1957–May 1959)

A reserve at Goodison Park, Jack Tomlinson, who was capped by England at youth-team level, played in just two First Division matches for Everton, deputising for Tony McNamara each time. He made his debut in a 0–0 draw at Newcastle in November 1956 and played in a 5–1 defeat by Aston Villa two months later. He scored five goals in 47 League games for Chesterfield.

TREBILCOCK, MICHAEL
Forward: 15 apps, 5 goals
Born: Gunnislake, 29 November 1944
Career: Tavistock, Plymouth Argyle (professional, December 1962), EVERTON (£23,000, December 1965), Portsmouth (January 1968), Torquay United (July 1972–May 1973), Weymouth (season 1973–74); emigrated to Australia; Western Suburbs/Sydney (manager, 1975–79); later worked as a delivery driver for a filter-cleaning company in Newcastle, New South Wales, earning £240 per week, while also running an over-35s team, playing his last game in 1994

Mike Trebilcock received a belated 21st birthday present – an FA Cup-winner's medal – after scoring twice for Everton in their 3–2 victory over Sheffield Wednesday in 1966, when manager Harry Catterick preferred him to Fred Pickering. Malcolm Allison signed him for Plymouth and he netted 29 goals in 81 games for the Pilgrims before joining Everton on New Year's Eve 1965, making his debut against Spurs 24 hours after his transfer. Unfortunately, he found it difficult to secure a first-team place at Goodison Park and after appearing in only 15 games in two years he switched 300 miles south to sign for Portsmouth.

TRENTHAM, DOUGLAS HAROLD
Outside-left: 17 apps, 7 goals
Born: Chirbury, *circa* 1915
Career: Chirbury, Mickle Trafford FC, EVERTON (professional, December 1936), Ellesmere Port Town (March 1939–44); did not play after the Second World War

Doug Trentham was 21 when he made his League debut for Everton against Blackpool in September 1937. He took over the left-wing berth from Jackie Coulter and did well until losing his place to new signing Wally Boyes (recruited from WBA). His elder brother, Bert Trentham, was a professional with WBA (1929–37), helping the Baggies gain promotion and win the FA Cup in 1931.

TROUP, ALEC
Outside-left: 260 apps, 35 goals
Born: Forfar, Scotland, 4 May 1895 – *Died*: Forfar, Scotland, 1951
Career: Forfar Athletic, Dundee (April 1915), EVERTON (January 1923), Dundee (February 1930; retired May 1933); later ran a clothes shop in Forfar

An ever-present in Everton's 1927–28 League championship-winning side (ten goals scored), the diminutive and determined Alec Troup – 5 ft 5 in. tall and known affectionately as 'Wee Troupie' – often dazzled the opposition with his clever ball play. Owing to a weak collarbone, he usually played with his shoulder heavily strapped as it continually slipped out of joint. Yet he still bravely took his fair share of buffeting from the hefty defenders, and often came up with a smile, or, failing that, a telling cross which often led to a goal – Dixie Dean benefiting enormously from his precise centres. A Scottish international, gaining five full caps (1920–26), he also twice represented the Scottish League.

TURNER, DAVID
Right-back: 1 app.
Born: Derby, 26 December 1948
Career: EVERTON (apprentice, April 1965; professional, October 1966), Southport (May 1970–May 1973)

During his time with Everton, David Turner made only one League appearance, deputising for Tommy Wright against Chelsea in April 1968 when manager Harry Catterick rested key players ahead of the FA Cup final with WBA. He played in over 70 games for Southport.

TURNER, GEORGE
Outside-left: 2 apps
Born: Mansfield, 5 May 1910 – Deceased
Career: Sneiton FC, Notts County (April 1929), Luton Town (June 1931),

EVERTON (October 1932), Bradford City (March 1933), Luton Town (August 1935), Northampton Town (March 1936–May 1937)

Another reserve-team player with Everton, George Turner covered for Jimmy Stein and made just two League appearances, the first against WBA on New Year's Eve 1932. During his career Turner scored 11 goals in almost 70 games.

TURNER, JOSEPH HENRY

Forward: 36 apps, 9 goals

Born: Burslem, Stoke-on-Trent, 2 March 1872 – *Died*: Southampton, 20 November 1950

Career: Newcastle Swifts (April 1893), Dresden United (August 1894), Southampton St Mary's (April 1895), Stoke (May 1898), EVERTON (April 1900), Southampton (May 1901), New Brompton (June 1904), Northampton Town (August 1906), Eastleigh Athletic (1907), South Farnborough Athletic (1909); later employed by a Stoke brewery

Joe Turner joined Southampton for 30 shillings (£1.50) a week after two seasons in Staffs non-League football. He had electrifying speed and was described as a 'dashing winger' who scored a high number of goals for a player in his position, including 74 in 153 games in his two spells with Saints and 15 in 60 outings for Stoke. He helped Southampton reach the 1902 FA Cup final and win successive Southern League titles (1903, 1904). He partnered Jimmy Settle on the left-flank at Everton, making his debut at Preston in September 1900. Early in 1901, he returned to The Dell for a first-round FA Cup-tie and scored in Everton's 3–1 win over his former club.

TURNER, ROBERT FREWN

Outside-left: 34 apps, 1 goal

Born: Leicester, 15 July 1885 – *Died*: Darlington, 15 February 1959

Career: Leicester Imperial (1903), Leicester Fosse (March 1905), EVERTON (April 1909), Preston North End (July 1911), Darlington (June 1912), Coventry City (June 1914); did not play after the First World War; emulated his father, Frew, by playing County cricket for Leicestershire (1909–11)

Bob 'Leggy' Turner scored on his Everton debut against Liverpool in April 1909.

A speedy, hard-shooting left-winger, his transfer to Goodison Park was controversial in that Turner was reported to the FA for claiming an illicit £100 signing-on fee. He was found guilty and fined £50 and he didn't receive his signing-on fee either!

Turner was married soon after joining Everton, and the wedding was attended by several (if not all) of his former Leicester team-mates – shortly before Fosse crashed 12–0 to Nottingham Forest in a League game! In a varied career, Turner, the joker in the pack, scored eight goals in 59 games for Leicester (his best return) and he helped Darlington win the Northern Eastern League before moving to Coventry. Turner's younger brother, Richard Turner, played for Leicester as well as Portsmouth and Leyton.

TYRER, ALAN

Midfield: 10 apps, 2 goals
Born: Liverpool, 8 December 1942
Career: EVERTON (amateur, April 1958; professional, December 1959), Mansfield Town (July 1963), Arsenal (August 1965), Bury (August 1967), Workington (July 1968–May 1976)

Alan Tyrer was aged 17 years, 137 days old when he scored for Everton against Leeds in April 1960 – having made his First Division debut three months earlier against Fulham. A reserve at Goodison Park, he went on to make 41 League appearances for Mansfield before having a brief spell at Highbury, signed by the former England captain Billy Wright. He did very little at Gigg Lane but made up for lost time by accumulating an excellent record with Workington (255 appearances, 23 goals).

UNSWORTH, DAVID GERALD

Defender: 314+36 apps, 40 goals
Born: Chorley, Lancashire, 16 October 1973
Career: EVERTON (apprentice, April 1990; professional, June 1992), West Ham United (£1m, August 1997), Aston Villa (£3m, July 1998), EVERTON (£3m, August 1998), Portsmouth (free transfer, July 2004)

After scoring on his League debut for Everton as a substitute against Spurs in April 1992 while still only 19, David Unsworth is now the club's joint most successful penalty-taker of all time (with Trevor Steven) with 23 conversions to his name (and three misses). Possessing a terrific shot, besides his spot-kicks, he has also scored other goals with powerful shots from outside the area. He appeared in more Premiership games than any other Everton player (304), ahead of Dave Watson (223) and Neville Southall (207) – after his move to Villa Park lasted barely a fortnight! After moving to West Ham in 1997, he failed to settle in London and agreed a move to the Birmingham-based club only to realise that his old employers (Everton) had coveted his signature. After pleading with the Villa hierarchy, Unsworth was allowed to move back to Goodison Park for the same price (£3m) without ever kicking a ball for the Midlanders. He immediately carried on displaying the competitiveness he had done before leaving the club in 1997 and although injuries affected his performances from time to time, he has been a wonderful servant to the Blues. Capped as a teenager at youth-team level, he then proceeded to gain six Under-21 caps and has played once for the full England team, starting against Japan in the Umbro Trophy at Wembley in 1995, the same year he helped Everton win the FA Cup and the Charity Shield. He stayed in the Premiership with Portsmouth in 2004.

UREN, HAROLD JOHN

Outside-left: 24 apps, 3 goals
Born: Barton Regis, Bristol, 23 August 1885 – *Died*: 7 April 1955
Career: Northern Nomads, Hoylake FC, Liverpool (amateur, July 1907; professional, September 1909), EVERTON (February 1912 in exchange for

Billy Lacey and Tom Gracie), Wrexham (May–October 1913); did not play after the First World War

Very tricky and difficult to dispossess, for a winger Harold Uren was stocky and well built, weighing over 12 st. Everton valued him highly, and went to great lengths to secure his signature in 1912. He had already scored twice in 43 games for Liverpool but he never quite hit it off at Goodison Park and left the club after 15 months and 24 appearances, his debut coming against Bolton 48 hours after his transfer from Anfield. He never got a game with Wrexham.

VAN DEN HAUWE, PATRICK WILLIAM ROGER

Full-back/defender: 200+1 apps, 3 goals

Born: Dendermonde, Belgium, 16 December 1960

Career: Birmingham City (apprentice, April 1977; professional, August 1978), EVERTON (£100,000, September 1984), Tottenham Hotspur (£595,000, August 1989), Millwall (September 1993), Notts County (February–May 1995); now lives in South Africa

Pat Van den Hauwe played in four FA Cup finals in the space of six years – three with Everton (1985, 1986, 1989) and one with Spurs (1991), gaining a winner's medal in the last. A ferocious tackler, his only goal in 143 appearances for Birmingham came in a 2–1 home win over Arsenal in March 1983. Former Everton favourite Howard Kendall brought him to Goodison Park in 1984 and he made his debut against the Gunners at Highbury 24 hours after signing. He played at Wembley in the FA Cup final against Manchester United at the end of his first season when he also gained a League championship medal. A year later Van den Hauwe received a League runner's-up medal before adding a second First Division championship prize to his collection in 1987. By this time he had also won the first of 13 full caps for Wales, having been on the verge of being called up into the Belgium national side by manager Guy Thees after he had seen him in action at Old Trafford in 1985. After pencilling him in as an over-age player for the Under-21 match against Spain, Thees found out that Van den Hauwe had unwittingly signed away his birthright by opting out of National Service. This, of course, led to press speculation as to which of the British nations would pursue him and eventually he teamed up with Everton colleagues Kevin Ratcliffe and Neville Southall in the Welsh side, making his debut in a World Cup qualifier against Spain at Wrexham. Two years after joining Spurs, at long last, he finally got his hands on an FA Cup-winner's medal when the London club defeated Nottingham Forest. He went on to appear in 125 games for Spurs over a period of four years. His father, René, kept goal for Belgium.

VARADI, IMRE

Striker: 28+6 apps, 7 goals

Born: Paddington, London, 8 July 1959

Career: Paddington and Central London Schools, Letchworth Garden City, Letchworth Town, FC 75/Hitchin, Sheffield United (apprentice, July 1975; professional, April 1978), EVERTON (£80,000 March 1979),

Newcastle United (£125,000, August 1981), Sheffield Wednesday (£150,000 plus David Mills, August 1983), West Bromwich Albion (£285,000, June 1985), Manchester City (October 1986, exchange deal involving Robert Hopkins), Sheffield Wednesday (September 1988, exchange for Carl Bradshaw), Leeds United (£50,000, February 1990), Luton Town (loan, March–April 1992), Oxford United (loan, January–February 1993), Rotherham United (March 1993), Boston United (May 1995), Mansfield Town (n/c, August 1995), Scunthorpe United (n/c, August 1995), Matlock Town (player–manager, November 1995–May 1996), Guiseley (player–coach, late 1996), Denaby United (player–coach, January 1997–May 1998); Stalybridge Celtic (assistant manager–coach, season 1998–99); later became a football agent, and worked for the PFA

'Ray' Varadi was a natural goalscorer, finding the net consistently for virtually every club he served. A favourite at most of his ports of call, he was fast, alert and keen-eyed and was a promotion-winner with Wednesday in 1984 before helping Leeds take the Second Division title in 1990. Two years later he played in three games when the League championship found its way to Elland Road. Unfortunately he never quite established himself at Goodison Park, despite some useful performances. Indeed, he was handed only six outings at senior level in his first season. He made his debut for the Blues (as a 'sub') against Feyenoord in the second leg of a first-round UEFA Cup-tie in October 1979 and followed up with his League debut against Coventry City (also as a substitute) a few days later. He had a good run in the side as Peter Eastoe's strike-partner from December 1980 until May 1981, at which point, after a proposed transfer to Benfica had fallen through, he joined Newcastle, signed by Arthur Cox. During his career, Varadi netted 151 goals in 419 League games. His brother, Fernando Varadi, played for Fulham.

VAUGHAN, ALFRED
Centre-half: 1 app.
Born: Liverpool, 1885 – Deceased
Career: EVERTON (July 1897–May 1899)
A reserve centre-half for two seasons at Goodison Park, Alf Vaughan's only League game and, indeed, the only one of his career was against Preston in January 1899.

VEALL, RAYMOND JOSEPH
Outside-left: 11 apps, 1 goal
Born: Skegness, 16 March 1942
Career: Skegness, Doncaster Rovers (professional, March 1961), EVERTON (September 1961), Preston North End (May 1965), Huddersfield Town (December 1965–May 1966)
Ray Veall's League career was relatively short – lasting just five years, during which time he appeared in 53 games and scored eight goals. He joined Everton after some impressive displays for Doncaster but after playing reasonably well in

his first two games at the start of the 1962–63 season (against Burnley and Manchester City, both won) he was replaced by Johnny Morrissey on the left-wing. Thereafter, despite some excellent displays in the second XI, he found it difficult to regain his place, making nine appearances before leaving for Preston in 1965.

VERNON, THOMAS ROYSTON

Inside-left: 203 apps, 111 goals
Born: Ffynnongroew, Holywell, Wales, 14 April 1937 – *Died*: 4 December 1993
Career: Rhyl Grammar School XI, Flintshire Boys, Mostyn YMCA Juniors, Welsh YMCA, EVERTON (trialist), Blackburn Rovers (amateur, May 1954; professional, March 1955), EVERTON (£27,000 plus Eddie Thomas, February 1960), Stoke City (£50,000, March 1965), Halifax Town (loan, January–February 1970), Cape Town FC/South Africa (briefly, late 1970); Great Harwood (1970–72); later ran an antiques business but sadly in later life suffered with arthritis in the hip and the spine

Roy Vernon, a forceful inside-forward, noted for his powerful and accurate shooting, was Everton's top scorer four seasons running in major competitions, 1960–64, notching 24 in 41 League games in 1962–63 when the Football League championship came to Goodison Park. He was also a very useful penalty-taker, being successful with 19 out of 20 spot-kicks he took for the Blues (all matches). Capped 32 times by Wales (1957–68), Vernon, who was a superbly gifted player with added pace, perception and dribbling skills, enjoyed a memorable partnership in the Everton attack with Alex Young. He was the dressing-room joker and probably the only player who could smoke a cigarette in the shower! He made his debut for the Blues against Wolves in February 1960.

VIRR, ALBERT EDWARD

Left-half: 127 apps, 3 goals
Born: Liverpool, 1902 – *Died*: 1959
Career: Lyndholm, EVERTON (professional, April 1922; retired, injured, May 1929)

A local find, Ted Virr got very few chances to show his worth during the early stages of his career at Goodison Park. However, he bided his time in the reserves and eventually established himself in the first XI, making 39 appearances in the League championship-winning side of 1927–28 when he played exceptionally well alongside Hunter Hart and Jerry Kelly. He was forced to retire early with a serious knee injury. He made his Everton debut against Spurs in January 1925.

WAINWRIGHT, EDWARD FRANCIS

Forward: 228 apps, 76 goals
Born: Southport, 22 June 1924
Career: High Park FC (Southport), Southport (trialist), EVERTON (amateur, August 1939; professional, March 1944), Fleetwood Town (guest, 1940–43), Rochdale (June 1956; retired July 1959); became a licensee

Loaned to Fleetwood as a teenager (to aid his development and gain experience of competitive football), Eddie Wainwright improved rapidly. He played a lot of representative football in the Army and when he returned to Goodison Park he went straight into Everton's first team, making his debut in a wartime game against Manchester United in September 1943. Lining up alongside Tommy Lawton and Joe Mercer, he went on to appear in 66 'war' games for the Blues, scoring 36 goals. He then established himself in League football during 1946–47, although he didn't have the greatest of starts, being on the losing side 2–0 against Brentford in his first-ever game in the competition. An intelligent, skilful ball-player of the 'quicksilver type', he had a strong, direct shot and scored almost 50 goals in the first four post-war seasons up to May 1950, when he went on tour to the USA and Canada with the FA party, while also playing for the Football League against the Irish League. Unfortunately the latter years of his Everton career were dogged by injuries, Wainwright never making a full recovery following a fractured-leg mishap, which he suffered in a tackle with Chick Musson of Derby in December 1950. He did eventually regain full fitness and went on to score 27 goals in 100 League games for Rochdale before retiring.

WAKENSHAW, ROBERT ANDREW

Forward: 2+3 apps, 1 goal
Born: Ashington, Northumberland, 22 December 1965
Career: Ponteland BC, EVERTON (apprentice, April 1982; professional, December 1983), Carlisle United (£20,000, September 1985), Doncaster Rovers (loan, March–April 1986), Rochdale (September 1986), Crewe Alexandra (June 1987–May 1988)

Capped seven times by England at Under-19 level, Ron Wakenshaw scored on his League debut against Manchester United in May 1984 and was still an 18-year-old when he played in his first European Cup-Winners' Cup games as a substitute against UC Dublin five months later. Basically regarded as a reserve forward during his three years at Goodison Park, he failed to lock himself into a regular routine with any of the clubs he served and withdrew from League football in 1988 with 85 appearances under his belt (16 goals).

WALKER, JOHN

Right-back/wing-half/centre-half: 3 apps, 1 goal
Born: Alexandria, Dumbartonshire, Scotland, *circa* 1869 – Deceased
Career: Vale of Leven (1886), Grimsby Town (June 1888), Gainsborough Trinity (briefly, 1892), EVERTON (July 1893), Manchester City (October 1894), Leicester Fosse (May 1895; retired April 1900)

Jack Walker, a versatile defender, joined Grimsby during the Mariners' Football Alliance days and was with them when they entered the Football League. He spent just the one season at Everton, making his debut in place of Johnny Holt in a 4–2 win over Aston Villa in September 1893. He suffered a broken shin playing for Leicester against his former club Grimsby in April 1899 and never recovered full fitness. He was subsequently awarded a benefit match (against Everton) in October of that same year, but sadly only £75 was raised.

WALL, ALEXANDER
Inside-forward: 17 apps, 3 goals
Born: Liverpool, 31 October 1899 – *Died*: 1978
Career: Booth Secondary School Old Boys, EVERTON (professional, May 1919), Swindon Town (May 1925–April 1927)

A skilful player, Alex Wall had done well in non-League circles and was all set to join Everton when the First World War commenced. When he finally signed professional forms at Goodison Park, he was almost 20 and had to wait until February 1920 before making his League debut against Oldham, when he partnered Sam Chedgzoy on the right-wing. He remained loyal to the club for six years before spending two seasons with Swindon.

WALSH, DEREK
Right-back/Midfield: 1 app.
Born: Hamilton, 24 October 1967
Career: EVERTON (apprentice, April 1983; professional, October 1984), Hamilton Academical (March 1988), Carlisle United (August 1988), Hamilton Academical (May 1993)

Reserve utility player Derek Walsh tasted competitive football with Everton just once, making his First Division debut on the left side of midfield at Luton on the last day of the 1984–85 season, taking over from Kevin Sheedy ahead of the FA Cup final. A talented player, he scored six goals in 121 League games during his five years at Carlisle and played with David Moyes at Hamilton (1993–94).

WALSH, MICHAEL ANTHONY
Forward: 26 apps, 3 goals
Born: Chorley, 13 August 1954
Career: Chorley, Blackpool (November 1971), EVERTON (August 1978), Queens Park Rangers (March 1979, exchange for Peter Eastoe), Porto/Portugal (£175,000, August 1980–May 1985)

In February 1975, Mickey Walsh scored one of the greatest goals ever seen at Bloomfield Road (or indeed on BBC TV). With three minutes remaining of a League game, he raced clear from the halfway line to bury a shot into the Sunderland net to earn his side a 3–2 win and duly earned him the 'Goal of the Season' award. He complemented Wyn Davies up front for the Seasiders, for whom he notched 76 goals in 194 appearances before moving to Everton, making his debut for the Blues in a 1–0 win at Chelsea in August 1978 when partnering Bob Latchford up front. A Republic of Ireland international (22 caps), after leaving QPR he had a decent spell with Porto, playing in the European Cup-Winners' Cup final against Juventus in 1984.

WALSH, MICHAEL THOMAS
Defender: 22 apps
Born: Manchester, 20 June 1956
Career: Bolton Wanderers (apprentice, June 1972; professional, July 1974),

EVERTON (£900,000 plus Seamus McDonagh, August 1981), Norwich City on loan, October–November 1982), Burnley (loan, December 1982), Fort Lauderdale Strikers/NASL (May 1983), Manchester City (October 1983), Blackpool (£6,000, February 1984), Bury (free, July 1989–May 1990); later Southport (manager)

Capped five times by the Republic of Ireland at full international level, Mick Walsh had a fine career, amassing in excess of 500 appearances in top-class football, including 201 for Bolton and 181 for Blackpool. A well-built, physically strong defender, he partnered Sam Allardyce at the heart of the Bolton defence and then played alongside Mick Lyons during his time at Goodison Park. He made his debut for Everton against Birmingham in August 1981 but then lost his way and his place halfway through the season when Billy Wright was switched from left-back and Mark Higgins came in to accompany Kevin Ratcliffe and/or Gary Stevens and Brian Borrows.

WARD, MARK WILLIAM

Midfield: 93+1 apps, 7 goals
Born: Huyton, 10 October 1962
Career: EVERTON (apprentice, April 1978; professional, September 1980), Northwich Victoria (free, May 1981), Oldham Athletic (£10,000, July 1983), West Ham United (£250,000, August 1985), Manchester City (£1m, December 1989), EVERTON (£1.1m, August 1991), Birmingham City (loan, March 1994; signed for £500,000, August 1994; player–coach, August 1995), Huddersfield Town (free, March 1996), Wigan Athletic (n/c, September 1996; retired May 1997); later Northwich Victoria (manager)

Midfield dynamo Mark Ward made more than 500 appearances (463 in the Football League) and scored over 60 goals during a career spanning almost 20 years. Released by Everton as a teenager, he won semi-professional honours for England as a 'Vics' player before joining the Latics in 1983. He did well at Boundary Park, West Ham (over 200 games) and at Maine Road before rejoining Everton, signed by manager Howard Kendall. He made his debut for the Blues against Nottingham Forest soon after arriving at Goodison Park, partnering Kevin Sheedy and John Ebbrell in centre-field. He was a virtual ever-present during that season but lost his way in 1992–93 before re-establishing himself the following year, only to be transferred to Birmingham after a loan spell at St Andrew's.

WARD, MITCHUM DAVID

Full-back/Midfield: 22+7 apps
Born: Sheffield, 19 June 1971
Career: Sheffield United (apprentice, June 1987; professional, July 1989), Crewe Alexandra (loan, November–December 1990), EVERTON (£850,000, November 1997), Barnsley (£20,000, July 2000), Lincoln City (March 2003)

There's no doubt that Mitch Ward played his best football and, indeed, had his best days at Sheffield United. A versatile right-sided ball-winner, he was one of the first names on the Blades' team-sheet before suffering a punctured lung and fractured rib playing against Notts County towards the end of March 1995. He recovered full fitness and went on to make 172 appearances for the Bramall Lane club prior to his transfer to Everton. After making his debut for the Blues in a Premiership match against Chelsea in November 1997, a tedious ankle injury restricted him to under 30 outings overall.

WAREING, WILLIAM
Half-back: 69 apps, 6 goals
Born: Southport, *circa* 1888 – Deceased
Career: Chorley, Preston North End (August 1910), EVERTON (October 1912), Swindon Town (March 1920–May 1925)
A well-built, strong-tackling, reliable half-back, able to perform on the right or in the centre of the middle line, Bill Wareing gave Everton splendid service for ten years and besides his senior outings for the club he also played in 127 regionalised matches during the First World War. He made his League debut for Preston against Manchester City in September 1910 and played his first game for the Blues against Newcastle in October 1912. He was a regular in the side during his first season at Goodison Park but was then reserve to Tom Fleetwood and Jimmy Galt until the League was suspended in 1915. He made over 160 appearances for Swindon.

WARMBEY
Centre-half: 1 app.
Born: 1865 – Deceased
Career: EVERTON (season 1888–89)
Reserve to Jimmy Holt during Everton's first season in League football, the unknown Warmbey played only once in the first team – against Aston Villa in September 1888.

WARZYCHA, ROBERT
Winger: 60+26 apps, 8 goals
Born: Wielun, Poland, 20 June 1963
Career: Gornik Zabrze/Poland, EVERTON (March 1991–May 1994), Columbus Crew/USA (player, then player–coach)
Robert Warzycha made his League debut for Everton against Nottingham Forest in March 1991. Already an experienced and well-established Polish international, injuries and country commitments apart, he enjoyed a 20-month spell in the first team and scored some important goals, including a brace in only his second outing for the club, away to Aston Villa (won 2–0). He left Goodison Park after losing his form and being dropped to the bench.

WATSON, DAVID
Defender: 523+6 apps, 38 goals
Born: Liverpool, 20 November 1961
Career: Liverpool (apprentice, April 1977; professional, May 1979), Norwich

City (£100,000, November 1980), EVERTON (£900,000, August 1986, player–caretaker-manager March–May 1977; retired as player, March 2001), Tranmere Rovers (manager, April 2001–September 2002)

Of Dave Watson's senior appearancs for Everton, 223 were in the Premiership. He also took part in 30 Merseyside derbies. Sold for peanuts by Liverpool without ever playing a senior game for the Reds, he had over 260 outings for Norwich, whom he helped win the League Cup and Second Division championship in successive seasons (1985, 1986) before switching to Goodison Park. He moulded himself into the Blues' defence alongside Kevin Ratcliffe, after making his debut against Nottingham Forest in the opening game of the 1986–87 League season. The backbone of the side, he was brilliant when the League title was won in 1987 and was captain when the FA Cup came to Merseyside in 1987. He also played in two Charity Shield-winning sides (1987, 1995), was capped 12 times by England and on seven occasions at Under-21 level. He retired (aged 39) with 808 club and international appearances in his locker.

WATSON, JOHN

Full-back: 44 apps
Born: Dundee, Scotland, 1876 – Deceased
Career: Dundee Wanderers (1897), New Brompton (September 1898), Dundee (May 1899), EVERTON (March 1900), Tottenham Hotspur (£1,000, May 1902–May 1908)

After experience at home in Dundee and with New Brompton (now Gillingham) he had two and a half years as Everton's regular left-back, making his debut for the Blues against Derby in April 1900. However, after forming a fine partnership with Walter Balmer, injury cost him his place in the side midway through the 1901–02 season and although he recovered full fitness and regained his position, he was persuaded to make the move to Spurs at the end of the campaign. A solid, hard-kicking defender, he made 200 appearances for Spurs, helping them win the London League (1902), the Western League (1903) and gain entry into the Football League (1908).

WATSON, JOHN GORDON

Outside-right/inside-left: 2 apps
Born: Wolsingham, County Durham, April 1912 – Deceased
Career: Combois FC, Blyth Spartans (1930), EVERTON (January 1933), Coventry City (September 1934), Crystal Palace (May 1936), Ashington (May 1937); did not play after the Second World War

An Everton League debutant against Middlesbrough in April 1933, Jack Watson was a reserve forward during his 20-month stay at Goodison Park. He made only 16 appearances for Coventry and 12 for Palace before moving to Ashington in 1937.

WATSON, ROBERT
Outside/inside-forward: 22 apps, 6 goals
Born: Liverpool, *circa* 1866 – Deceased
Career: EVERTON (August 1887), Gorton Villa (October 1889)
Scorer of ten goals in 14 games in his first season with Everton, Bob Watson had made his debut at inside-left in a first-round FA Cup-tie against Bolton in October 1887 before playing his initial League game on the right-wing against Aston Villa in September 1888. A sprightly forward, with good control, he was then switched to inside-right and had a sound first season of League action before losing his place to Welsh international Charlie Parry.

WATSON, STEPHEN CRAIG
Utility: 100+9 apps, 16 goals
Born: North Shields, 1 April 1974
Career: North Shields schoolboy football, Newcastle United (apprentice, June 1990; professional, April 1991), Aston Villa (£4m, October 1998), EVERTON (£2.5m, July 2000)
A consistent and versatile footballer, calm under pressure, and a player who never gives less than 100 per cent every time he takes the field, strong running right-back or midfielder (even attacker) Steve Watson made 255 senior appearances for Newcastle and 54 for Aston Villa before his transfer to Goodison Park. He made his debut for Everton against Leeds in August 2000 and when fully fit has been a regular in the side ever since. He was honoured by England at youth, Under-21 (12 caps) and 'B' team levels during his time at St James's Park.

WATSON, THOMAS GORDON
Left-half/left-back: 66 apps, 1 goal
Born: Wolsingham, County Durham, 1 March 1914 – *Died*: 2001
Career: Washington BC, Blyth Spartans, EVERTON (January 1933; retired through injury March 1949; remained with club until 1997, serving as trainer, in promotions department, as barman, steward and stadium guide)
Gordon Watson succeeded veteran Jock Thomson in the Everton line-up during the club's League championship-winning season of 1938–39, appearing in 16 games. Unfortunately the Second World War arrived and so he had no real chance of making much headway at Goodison Park, although he made an extra 200 plus first-team appearances during the hostilities. He remained at the club until 1949, acting mainly as a reserve after the war when he also turned out at left-back and right-half. He made his League debut for Everton at Brentford in January 1937, and played his last game in October 1948 against Burnley. Watson served Everton FC for 44 years.

WAUGH, DAVID
Forward: 7 apps, 2 goals
Born: *circa* 1866 – Deceased
Career: Burnley (July 1887), EVERTON (July 1888, released May 1889)

One of Everton's reserve forwards during the first season of League football, David Waugh made his debut in their opening fixture against Accrington on 8 September 1888. He was injured early in the campaign and was sidelined for quite some time before returning late on to occupy the left-wing position. He was not retained for the following season: Alf Milward was switched to take Waugh's place on the flank.

WEAVER, WILLIAM WALTER
Left-half, forward: 22 apps, 3 goals
Born: Birkenhead, 9 November 1898 – *Died*: Accrington, 8 June 1965
Career: Royal Ivanhoe, South Liverpool (1915), Burnley (professional, August 1919), EVERTON (December 1924), Wolverhampton Wanderers (October 1926), Accrington Stanley (December 1927; retired through injury, May 1928); chose to live and work in the Lancashire town

Basically a left-winger, Walter Weaver could also occupy the inside-left position as well as the left-half berth. Strong and determined, he did exceptionally well during his five years at Turf Moor, scoring 18 goals in 116 matches, helping Burnley finish runners-up in the First Division (1920) and win the League title the following season (making 27 appearances). He took over briefly from Alec Troup on Everton's left-flank but failed to hold down a regular place in the side and was subsequently transferred to Wolves, where he linked up with his brother Reg, who also played for Newport, Chelsea, Bradford City and Chesterfield.

WEBBER, KEITH JAMES
Centre-forward: 6 apps, 1 goal
Born: Cardiff, 5 January 1943 – *Died*: September 1983
Career: Barry Town, EVERTON (professional, February 1960), Brighton and Hove Albion (£17,000, April 1963), Wrexham (£4,500, September 1964), Doncaster Rovers (£6,000, July 1966–April 1969), Chester (September 1969), Stockport County (July 1971–May 1972)

Keith Webber, a well-built centre-forward with tightly cropped hair, was reserve to Frank Wignall and Alex Young, scored on his Everton debut against Walsall in a second-round League Cup-tie in October 1960 and made his first League appearance at home to Chelsea the following February. After leaving Goodison Park, he netted over 90 goals in almost 300 outings, having his best spell with Wrexham (36 strikes in 86 games). As a lad, Webber – whose biggest thrill was playing for Everton against Liverpool in the Liverpool Senior Cup final before a crowd of 54,000 – took part in a Welsh schools rugby trial.

WEIR, DAVID GILLESPIE
Defender: 176+8 apps, 7 goals
Born: Falkirk, Scotland, 10 May 1970
Career: Celtic Boys' Club, Falkirk (professional, August 1992), Heart of Midlothian (July 1996), EVERTON (£250,000, February 1999)

A solid and reliable and certainly underrated defender, David Weir is also an excellent reader of the game who appeared in 149 competitive games for Falkirk and 117 for Hearts before moving to Goodison Park. He made his debut in the Premiership as a substitute in a 5–0 home win over Middlesbrough in February 1999, and, after settling into the way of life on Merseyside, he missed only six games in the next three seasons, then formed a fine partnership with Alan Stubbs before injury ruined his 2003–04 season. Capped 40 times by Scotland, Weir was a First Division and B&Q Cup winner with Falkirk in 1994 and a Scottish Cup-winner with Hearts in 1998.

WEIR, JAMES

Wing-half: 21 apps
Born: Edinburgh, 1864 – Deceased
Career: Hibernian, Third Lanark, EVERTON (September 1887), Sunderland
    Albion (October 1889)
Jim Weir made his debut for Everton against Bolton in a first-round FA Cup replay in October 1887. He appeared in his first League game nine months later against Aston Villa and remained a regular in the side during that initial League campaign. A well-proportioned defender, able to play in both wing-half positions, he was associated with the Blues for two years.

WELDON, ANTHONY

Inside-left: 74 apps, 13 goals
Born: Croy, Scotland, 12 November 1900 – Deceased
Career: Kilsyth Rangers, Airdrieonians (£5, December 1924), EVERTON
    (£2,000, March 1927), Hull City (£1,000, June 1930), West Ham United
    (£1,000, June 1931), Lovells Athletic (May 1932), Rochdale (August 1933),
    Dundalk (player–coach, July 1934), Bangor/Northern Ireland
    (player–manager, November 1934–May 1936)
Tony Weldon was a clever inside-forward, a shade on the small side but nevertheless a sprightly competitor who fitted in nicely alongside the burly figure of Dixie Dean and was a fine partner for Alec Troup on the left-hand side of the park. He succeeded two excellent Scottish internationals at Airdrie (Willie Russell and Hughie Gallacher) before making a scoring debut for the Blues against Leeds in March 1927. He enjoyed his best season at Goodison Park when the League championship was won in 1927–28, playing in 38 games and scoring seven goals. He lost his place to Tommy Johnson during the 1929–30 campaign and subsequently moved to Hull City. His son-in-law, Jim Storrie, played for Leeds in the 1960s.

WELLER, LOUIS CHARLES

Full-back/wing-half: 70 apps, 2 goals
Born: Stoke-on-Trent, 7 May 1887 – *Died*: 1952
Career: Chesterfield (April 1907), EVERTON (March 1910), Chesterfield
    (September 1910), EVERTON (March 1911–May 1922)
Louis Weller made only one appearance for Everton during his first spell at Goodison Park. Taking over from Harry Makepeace at left-half, he celebrated with a goal at Blackburn. On his return to the club he went straight into the side

270

against the reigning League champions Aston Villa and played five times at the tail-end of that season. However, he made only one appearance in 1911–12 and none at all the following year and had to wait until the final quarter of 1913–14 before having another run in the team. He struggled to retain his place during the last campaign before the First World War, yet after serving his country during the hostilities, he returned to Merseyside and had 29 first-team outings in 1919–20 before drifting back into the second XI.

WEST, GORDON

Goalkeeper. 402 apps
Born: Darfield, Barnsley, 24 April 1943
Career: Don and Dearne Schools/Barnsley, Blackpool (amateur, May 1958; professional, April 1960), EVERTON (£27,000, March 1962; retired, May 1973); made a brief comeback with Tranmere Rovers (1975, later on the groundstaff at Prenton Park); subsequently employed as security officer at RAF Woodvale, Formby, Lancashire (1980s/90s)

Signed from Blackpool for a then British record fee (for a goalkeeper), Gordon West missed only four games when Everton won the League championship in 1962–63 and was an ever-present when gaining a second championship medal in 1969–70. An FA Cup-winner with the Blues in 1966 against Sheffield Wednesday, he was a disappointed loser two years later against WBA.

A debutant for the Seasiders at the age of 17, he had only 33 first-class appearances under his belt when he moved to Goodison Park, where he replaced Albert Dunlop, playing his first game for the Blues in a 4–0 home win over Wolves (March 1962). Well-built with good hands, he was confident on his line but was perhaps not the most composed of goalkeepers, although in his day he could be brilliant, spectacularly hurling himself across his area to keep out shots and headers with effective abandon. He won England youth recognition and was later capped three times by his country at senior level (1969). However, he refused to join Sir Alf Ramsey's squad for the 1970 World Cup finals in Mexico, choosing to stay at home with his family. He was once refused a job on the Barnsley groundstaff.

WHITE, THOMAS ANGUS

Centre-forward/inside-right/centre-half. 204 apps, 66 goals
Born: Pendleton, Manchester, 29 July 1908 – *Died*: Liverpool, 13 August 1967
Career: Southport Council School, Trinity Old Boys, Southport (amateur, August 1923; professional, September 1925), EVERTON (February 1927), Northampton Town (October 1937), New Brighton (February 1938; retired May 1938); later worked in Liverpool's dockyard and died as a result of his injuries received in an accident while employed there

The versatile Tommy White won fame as a defender during his schooldays before switching to being an orthodox centre-forward with Southport. He then moved back to right-half at Goodison Park and prior to leaving the Blues had also played in his first position at centre-half. Not a tall man, he was nevertheless an aggressive performer. He had many admirers and made his League debut for the Blues against West Ham United in October 1927, scoring twice in a 7–0 win. However, he had to wait until November 1928 before his second outing, at right-half against Sheffield United at Bramall Lane. He netted ten goals in ten games when Everton won the Second Division title in 1931 and claimed 18 goals in 23 outings the following season when the League championship came to Goodison Park. In 1933 he won his only England cap at centre-half against Italy in Rome, playing behind his club colleague Albert Geldard in a 1–1 draw. That same year he toured the continent with the FA. An excellent swimmer, he was also keen on tennis and enjoyed a round of golf.

WHITE, WALTER
Wing-half/inside-forward: 52 apps, 13 goals
Born: Hurlford, Ayrshire, 15 May 1882 – *Died*: London, 8 July 1950
Career: Hurlford Thistle (1897), Bolton Wanderers (April 1902), EVERTON (December 1908, with Bob Clifford), Fulham (October 1910; retired May 1924); remained in the Fulham area
Before moving to Goodison Park, Scottish international Walter 'Wattie' White scored 94 goals in 217 League and Cup games for Bolton, gaining a FA Cup runner's-up medal in 1904 and collecting two full caps against England. He made his debut for the Blues against Sheffield United 48 hours after moving from Burnden Park and, injury apart, kept his place in the side until the end of the 1909–10 season, when Bill Lacey was preferred in the inside-right berth. A small but smart and skilful ball-player, he then moved to Fulham, where he stayed for 13 years, amassing 203 appearances for the Cottagers, having his last outing in February 1923, aged 40.

WHITEHEAD, JOHN
Goalkeeper: 2 apps
Born: Liverpool, *circa* 1871 – Deceased
Career: Bootle, EVERTON (November 1892), Liverpool (March 1895–April 1896)
A reserve with both Merseyside clubs, Jack Whitehead deputised for Dick Williams in successive League games for Everton against Darwen and Newton Heath in January 1894. After moving across Stanley Park, he made his debut for the Reds in a test match against Bury, which they lost and were then relegated to the Second Division.

WHITESIDE, NORMAN
Forward/Midfield: 35+2 apps, 13 goals
Born: Belfast, Northern Ireland, 7 May 1965
Career: West Belfast Schools, Manchester United (apprentice, June 1981; professional, July 1982), EVERTON (£750,000, August 1989; retired with knee injury, May 1991); later Northwich Victoria (assistant manager, 1991–92); now a chiropodist
Norman Whiteside – from Belfast's Crumlin Road – made his League debut for Manchester United as a 16-year-old against Brighton in April 1982. Then, as a

late 17th birthday present, he scored on his first full outing for the club at home to Stoke in mid-May.

He proved to be one of the great discoveries of the 1980s and his rise to the top was nothing less than meteoric – just like Roy of the Rovers! He was spotted by United scout Bob Bishop in 1980 after netting over 150 goals in local junior football (including 102 in one season). He quickly stepped up a grade to professionalism and overtook George Best as the youngest-ever Irishman to don the famous red jersey.

Named in Billy Bingham's Northern Ireland squad for the 1982 World Cup finals in Spain, Whiteside received his international baptism against Yugoslavia in Zaragoza to become the youngest player at 17 years, 41 days ever to figure in the World Cup finals, taking over from Pele. He turned out to be one of the stars of the tournament. He followed up in 1983 by scoring the only goal of a tight League Cup final when United beat Liverpool (making him the youngest-ever scorer in a major Wembley final). He then poached the winner against Arsenal in the FA Cup semi-final and then notched one of four goals that United put past Brighton to win the Cup final replay.

At the age of 19 he rattled in a hat-trick when West Ham were thumped in the quarter-final of the 1985 FA Cup competition and in the final his sensational goal earned the ten men of United victory over his future club, Everton.

In 1986 Whiteside once more appeared in the World Cup finals and he went on to take his tally of international caps to 36 with United. After scoring 68 goals in 278 games for United, he demanded a move, following a rift with new boss Alex Ferguson. He was subsequently transferred to Goodison Park, with whom he added two more caps to his collection. Whiteside played his first game for the Blues against Coventry in August 1989 and netted his first goal against Southampton three games later.

Unfortunately, he was injured at Chelsea in April 1990 and although he returned to action the following season, he was never the same player. After breaking down again at Wimbledon in the November, he was advised to take early retirement at the age of 26.

Whiteside certainly had a temper, a mean streak, which earned him the tag of 'Nasty Norman' by the press – several brushes with officialdom after skirmishes on the pitch saw him receive several red and yellow cards, resulting in a batch of suspensions.

He later became Sammy McIlroy's number two at Northwich Victoria, eventually quitting football to become a chiropodist, concentrating, not unnaturally, on footballers' problems while also working on the hospitality side at Old Trafford.

WHITLEY, JOHN

Goalkeeper: 14 apps
Born: Seacombe, Cornwall, April 1880 – *Died*: London, 1955
Career: Liskeard YMCA (1897), Darwen (1898–99), Aston Villa (May 1900), EVERTON (August 1902), Stoke (September 1904), Leeds City (April

1906), Lincoln City (September 1906), Chelsea (September 1907; retired May 1914; club trainer to May 1939)

Jack Whitley was a sound and competent goalkeeper who deputised for Billy George at Villa Park. He then served as understudy to George Kitchen during his two years at Goodison Park, making his league debut for Everton in a 0–0 draw at Grimsby on Christmas Day 1902. He later helped Chelsea win promotion to the First Division (1912), making 138 appearances for the Londoners. As a trainer, he was a father figure to generations of young players at the club and when he raced on to the pitch, his shining bald head and flapping coat-tails were very much part of the Chelsea scene during the inter-war years. He spent 32 years at the 'Bridge'.

WHITTLE, ALAN
Forward/Midfield: 87+3 apps, 27 goals
Born: Liverpool, 10 March 1950
Career: EVERTON (apprentice, April 1966; professional, July 1967), Crystal Palace (£100,000, December 1972), Sheffield United (free, July 1976), Leyton Orient (September 1976), FC Persepolis/Iran (May 1977), Leyton Orient (April 1979); Bournemouth (n/c, January–April 1981); then football in Australia

In a 15-year career (in England) the versatile, gritty Alan Whittle made 279 appearances and scored 59 goals, having his best spell with Palace (24 goals in 122 outings). Blond-haired, strong-running with a terrific engine, he graduated through the ranks at Goodison Park before making his League debut in a 6–2 win at WBA two months before the 1968 FA Cup final.

His first two goals for the club came in a 4–0 home League Cup win over Tranmere Rovers in September 1968. Then, after helping the Blues win the First Division championship in 1970 (making 15 appearances and scoring six goals in six games during the run-in), he followed up by having his best season at Goodison Park, playing in 30 games, including outings in the European Cup. He was sold to Palace on the same day Everton's manager Harry Catterick signed Joe Harper from Aberdeen. In fact, it was somewhat ironic that Catterick had described Whittle as 'the greatest Everton discovery of all time', hailing him initially as the 'new Denis Law'.

WIGNALL, FRANK
Centre/inside-forward: 38 apps, 22 goals
Born: Blackrod, near Chorley, Lancashire, 21 August 1939
Career: Horwich RMI, EVERTON (amateur, May 1958; professional, May 1960), Nottingham Forest (June 1963), Wolverhampton Wanderers (March 1968), Derby County (February 1969), Mansfield Town (November 1971), King's Lynn (July 1973), Burton Albion (August 1974), Qatar (national coach, October 1974–78), Shepshed Charterhouse (manager, July 1981–March 1983)

Frank Wignall's career spanned 15 years and in that time he scored over 125 goals in more than 350 appearances (107 in 322 League games). Well-built and physically strong, he was still an amateur when he netted on his League debut for Everton against Burnley in September 1959, and 13 months later he had the pleasure of scoring the Blues' first League Cup hat-trick – against Tranmere Rovers. Capped twice by England against Wales and Holland in 1964, Wignall also represented the Football League and played for an FA XI against Mexico, and four years after leaving Goodison Park, helped Nottingham Forest finish runners-up in the First Division and reach the semi-finals of the FA Cup (1967). He was a key player for Derby when they lifted the Second Division title in 1969 under Brian Clough's management. He managed Shepshed Charterhouse during a purple patch in the club's history.

WILDMAN, WILLIAM

Full-back: 2 apps
Born: Liverpool, 1883 – Deceased
Career: EVERTON (March 1904), West Ham United (June 1906)
Reserve Bill Wildman spent a little over two years at Goodison Park, during which time he deputised for Walter Balmer in the League game against Middlesbrough in January 1905 and for Jack Crelley against Sheffield Wednesday at the end of the year.

WILKINSON, JONATHAN MONTAGUE

Centre-forward/outside-right: 12 apps, 2 goals
Born: Esh Winning, County Durham, 18 July 1908 – *Died*: Newcastle-upon-Tyne, 19 September 1979
Career: Esh Winning, Durham City, Crook Town (February 1927), Newcastle United (£50, May 1927), EVERTON (£675, June 1929), Blackpool (March 1931), Charlton Athletic (£500, February 1933–May 1940)
Auburn-haired 'Monte' Wilkinson, an ex-pit boy, was hot property as a youngster in County Durham. Nimble of foot with an eye for goal, he was quickly snapped up by Newcastle United, signed as understudy to the great Hughie Gallacher. He scored 11 goals in 27 games for the Geordies and the club's supporters believed he deserved a better deal but was sold to Everton after two years at St James's Park. He made his debut for the Blues against Manchester City in September 1929 but had to wait until November of the following year before notching his first goal, in a 4–0 win over Wolves. With Dixie Dean leading the attack, Wilkinson was used as an outside-right during his second season at Goodison Park. He went on to score 50 goals in 235 games for Charlton, playing an important role in the Valiants' rise from the Third Division to runners-up spot in the First Division in 1937. Wilkinson served in Burma during the Second World War and later resided in Lincoln, before returning to the north-east, where he became a cinema manager in Washington.

WILKINSON, PAUL

Centre-forward: 31+14 apps, 15 goals
Born: Grimoldy, near Louth, Lincolnshire, 30 October 1964
Career: Lincolnshire schools football, Grimsby Town (apprentice, April 1981;

professional, November 1982), EVERTON (£250,000, March 1985), Nottingham Forest (£200,000, March 1987), Watford (£300,000, August 1988), Middlesbrough (£550,000, August 1991), Oldham Athletic (loan, October–November 1995), Watford (loan, December 1995), Luton Town (loan, March–April 1996), Barnsley (July 1996), Millwall (£150,000, September 1997), Northampton Town (free, July 1998–June 2000); coached in Qatar (2001–02); now a garage owner in Nottingham

When he retired from first-class football at the end of 1999–2000, Paul Wilkinson looked back on a fine career that saw him score 197 goals in 653 senior games, including 66 in 202 outings for Middlesbrough and 56 in 155 for Watford. Fast and dangerous, especially strong in the air, he had sufficient strength to withstand the strongest of challenges. An England Under-21 international (capped four times), he scored for Grimsby in the 90th minute at Goodison Park in a League Cup-tie in November 1984. And after leaving Blundell Park, he netted a Charity Shield winner for Everton in 1986, having made his debut for the Blues as a substitute against Southampton in March 1985. Two months later he scored the winner in the Merseyside derby. He had one good season at Goodison Park – when the League title was won in 1986–87 – playing in 28 games, coming off the bench 11 times. He later helped Middlesbrough twice reach the Premiership (1992, 1995).

WILLIAMS, BENJAMIN DAVID

Full-back: 139 apps

Born: Penrhiwceiber, Glamorgan, 29 October 1900 – *Died*: Bridgend, 5 January 1968

Career: Penrhiwceiber FC (1919), Cardiff City (trial, 1923), Swansea Town (£25, February 1925), EVERTON (£7,500, December 1929), Newport County (August 1935; player–coach, May 1937; retired May 1938); returned to the colliery where he had begun his working life; afflicted by senile dementia in the 1960s

A speedy defender, strong in the tackle, Ben Williams made his mark with Swansea before joining Everton, whom he helped regain their First Division status and then win the League championship in 1931–32, appearing in 33 matches as partner to Warney Cresswell. He unfortunately missed the 1933 FA Cup final through injury. A Welsh international, capped ten times between 1928 and 1935, the last six as an Evertonian, Williams was not willing to accept the terms offered to him by Cardiff and joined Swansea instead, earning £4 per week with an additional 10 shillings (50p) for first-team appearances. He was transferred to Goodison Park when the Vetch Field club got into financial difficulties. He made the first of his senior appearances for Everton against Derby in January 1930, deputising for Warney Cresswell, who later moved to the left-back berth. As a youngster during the First World War, before establishing himself as a footballer, Williams won boxing fame in his home port of Penrhiwceiber.

WILLIAMS, GEORGE GRAHAM

Outside-left: 33 apps, 6 goals

Born: Southsea, near Wrexham, Wales, 31 December 1935

Career: Wrexham and District Schools, Wrexham (amateur), Oswestry Town, Bradford City (professional, August 1955), EVERTON (£5,000, March 1956), Swansea Town (February 1959), Wrexham (July 1964), Tranmere Rovers (August 1966), Port Vale (July 1968), Wellington Town (May 1969), Runcorn (1970–71); later a carpenter (in Wrexham) and was one of Denbighshire's most accomplished golfers

Welsh schoolboy international left-winger Graham 'Flicka' Williams went on to gain five full caps for his country and also played once for the Under-21 side. Introduced to League football by Bradford City manager Peter Jackson, he was Everton's first big-money signing for seven years when signed as cover for Irishman Tommy Eglington. One of the smallest players in the game, he was a brave and tricky customer and quickly settled into his new surroundings, making his debut in the First Division against Sunderland in March 1956 in front of almost 50,000 fans at Goodison Park. Unfortunately the club failed to do him justice and only intermittent outings followed before his transfer to Swansea in 1959. A Welsh Cup winner in 1961, he broke his leg in February of the following year, and this injury kept him out of action for two seasons. He re-established himself at Wrexham before winding down his senior career at Prenton Park and Vale Park.

WILLIAMS, OWEN

Left-half: 2 apps

Born: Holyhead, Wales, 12 October 1896 – Deceased

Career: South Liverpool, EVERTON (August 1919), Wigan Borough (July 1920), Holyhead (August 1921), Wigan Borough (March 1924–May 1926)

A reserve at Goodison Park, Owen Williams deputised for Alan Grenyer in home League games against Arsenal in October 1919 and Manchester United in March 1920. He made over 60 appearances in his two spells with Wigan Borough.

WILLIAMS, RICHARD

Goalkeeper: 70 apps

Born: Chesterfield, *circa* 1869 – Deceased

Career: Bromborough Port, EVERTON (May 1891), Luton Town (June 1895), Glossop North End (August 1898–May 1900)

Initially, 6 ft 2 in. goalkeeper Dick Williams joined Everton as cover for David Jardine, for whom he deputised in ten games during his first season at Goodison Park, making his First Division debut against Derby County in late October. He was still regarded as second choice the following term before establishing himself in the side in 1893–94, when he missed only four matches. Courageous and a safe handler of the ball with long reach, he moved on after Jack Hillman arrived from Burnley. He made 30 League appearances for Luton and 52 for Glossop.

WILLIAMS, WILLIAM

Outside-right or left: 24 apps, 5 goals
Born: Liverpool, *circa* 1874 – Deceased
Career: EVERTON (professional, January 1894), Blackburn Rovers (May 1898), Bristol Rovers (August 1900), Newton Heath/Manchester United (August 1901–May 1902)

Bill Williams, 5 ft 8 in. tall and 11 st. in weight, scored on his League debut for Everton against Stoke in January 1895. He spent four seasons at Goodison Park without ever establishing himself as a regular in the first XI. He then made his first appearance for Blackburn against Everton and later scored twice in Bristol Rovers' record 15–1 FA Cup win over Weymouth in 1900. He made only four appearances for Manchester United.

WILLIAMS, WILLIAM DAVID

Inside-left: 41 apps, 14 goals
Born: Manchester, 16 November 1898 – *Died*: 1926
Career: Darwen (1919), EVERTON (May 1922), Blackpool (March 1925–May 1928)

A dashing inside-forward with a positive approach, Billy Williams spent the first three post-First World War seasons with Darwen before making his League debut for Everton in a 2–0 defeat at Newcastle on the opening day of the 1922–23 campaign. A week later he scored his first goal when the Blues won the return fixture 3–2 at Goodison Park. He retained his position in the front-line until knocked down by injury in February 1923. He returned to first-team duty later but was never the same player and eventually moved to Blackpool, for whom he scored 123 goals in 27 appearances.

WILLIAMSON, DANIEL ALAN

Midfield: 17 apps
Born: West Ham, London, 5 December 1973
Career: West Ham United (apprentice, April 1990; professional, July 1992), Doncaster Rovers (loan, October–December 1993), EVERTON (August 1997; contract cancelled, May 1999)

Danny Williamson was described as a polished youngster from London's East End when signed by Everton in 1997. He had already scored five goals in 58 outings for the Hammers as well as three times in 16 outings on loan with Doncaster. He made his debut for the Blues against his former club (West Ham) in August 1997 but then became 'missing in action' during his first season at Goodison! He had been a regular in the side until December but then suffered hamstring and foot injuries that kept him out for the rest of the campaign. He failed to regain full fitness and his contract was subsequently cancelled by the club.

WILSON, ALAN

Midfield: 2 apps
Born: Liverpool, 17 November 1952
Career: EVERTON (apprentice, April 1969; professional, July 1970), Southport

(July 1975), Torquay United (June 1978), Northwich Victoria (August 1979) Six years a reserve at Goodison Park, Alan Wilson made only two first-team appearances, lining up in midfield against Coventry in October 1971 and Derby in April 1973. He scored 13 goals in 134 League games for Southport.

WILSON, DAVID

Inside-forward/outside-left: 5 apps
Born: Lochgelly, Scotland, 1883 – Deceased
Career: Lochgelly Rangers (1898), Buckhaven United (1899), Cowdenbeath (1901), East Fife (1902), Gainsborough Trinity (May 1904), Heart of Midlothian (1905), EVERTON (£800, May 1906, with brother George, q.v.), Portsmouth (June 1907)

David Wilson unfortunately never adapted to life in the Football League. A useful enough utility forward, he made only a handful of appearances for Everton, his first at Newcastle in September 1906 and his last against Derby in April 1907.

WILSON, GEORGE W.

Outside-left: 34 apps, 4 goals
Born: Lochgelly, near Dunfermline, Scotland, 1884 – *Died*: Canada, 2 June 1960
Career: Buckhaven United (1900), Cowdenbeath (1902), Heart of Midlothian (May 1903), EVERTON (£800, May 1906 with brother David, q.v.), Belfast Distillery (loan, August–October 1907), Newcastle United (£1,600, November 1907), Raith Rovers (£250, July 1919), East Fife (1920), Albion Rovers (1922), Raith Rovers (manager, June 1926–February 1927), St Andrew's FC/Vancouver (Canada)

A month after gaining a Scottish Cup-winner's medal with Hearts, George Wilson – one of the biggest names north of the border, noted by one commentator as being a 'purest football gem' – signed for Everton, along with his brother David. Already a full international with four caps under his belt, he later added two more to his collection (one with the Blues, one with Newcastle) and had the distinction of playing for both the Scottish League and Irish League sides. After his Football League debut for Everton in a 9–1 home win over Manchester City in September 1906, he partnered his brother for the first time (in England) when the Blues lost 1–0 to his future club Newcastle a fortnight later. Wilson, affectionately known as 'Wee Geordie', was short in stature but highly skilled and assertive. He produced some excellent displays in both the inside-left and left-wing positions but was then sensationally left out of Everton's FA Cup final side that season (1907). Soon afterwards he joined Newcastle for a record fee of £1,600 and became a much-loved personality at Gallowgate, United's attractive style suiting his talent down to a tee. He made 218 first-team appearances during his 12 years on Tyneside, helping the Magpies win the League title in 1909 and reach three FA Cup finals. He collected a winner's medal in 1910 to become one of only a handful of footballers who have won both the Scottish and English Cups. He served in the Royal Navy during the First World War.

WILSON, IAN WILLIAM
Midfield: 36+14 apps, 2 goals
Born: Aberdeen, Scotland, 27 March 1958
Career: Aberdeen (junior, 1974), Dundee, Elgin City, Leicester City (£30,000, April 1979), EVERTON (£300,000, September 1987), FC Kocaelispor/Turkey (August 1989), later Peterhead/Scotland (manager)
Blending constructive and combative play in the middle of the park, influential playmaker Ian Wilson spent eight years at Filbert Street before transferring to Goodison Park. Predominantly left-footed, he scored 19 goals in 318 appearances for the Foxes, setting up chances galore for strikers Gary Lineker and Alan Smith, among others. He gained a 'B' cap, followed by two at senior level for Scotland in 1987 and overall produced some excellent displays for the east Midland side. After his switch to Everton, he scored on his debut at home to Rotherham in a League Cup-tie in September 1987 and soon afterwards played in his first League game for the Blues against the FA Cup holders, Coventry. An FA Cup finalist against Liverpool in May 1989, he left Goodison Park three months later.

WILSON, RAMON, MBE
Full-back: 151+3 apps
Born: Shirebrook, Derbyshire, 17 December 1934
Career: Langwith Boys' Club, Langwith Juniors/Mansfield, Huddersfield Town (amateur, May 1951; professional, August 1952), EVERTON (£40,000 plus Mick Meagan, July 1964), Oldham Athletic (July 1969), Bradford City (player–coach, July 1970; caretaker-manager, September–November 1971); later undertaker as well as running a 15-acre farm with his wife in Yorkshire
Ray Wilson was England's left-back when the World Cup was won in 1966 and lost his place in the national team through injury, replaced by Keith Newton, later to join Everton. Cool under pressure, assured in his play, he had a wonderful left foot and was quick to recover while also possessing accurate distribution. He learned his football under Bill Shankly at Huddersfield before Harry Catterick signed him for Everton in a player-exchange deal involving Mick Meagan, who was valued at £15,000. He made his debut for the Blues against Stoke in August 1964, gained an FA Cup-winner's medal against Sheffield Wednesday in 1966 but was a loser in the same competition two years later. Regarded as one of the finest left-backs of his generation, he played in 63 full internationals for his country, represented the Football League and appeared in 283 games for Huddersfield, being the Terriers' most-capped player. He was named Ramon after the film star Ramon Navarro.

WILSON, WALTER
Left-back: 1 app.
Born: *circa* 1865 – Deceased
Career: EVERTON (season 1888–89)
A reserve left-back, Wilson played only once for Everton, taking Nick Ross's

position on the last day of the inaugural League season against Blackburn in March 1889, when the Blues won 3–1.

WINTERHALDER, ARTHUR
Outside-left: 4 apps
Born: Oxford, 1885 – Deceased
Career: West Ham United (September 1904), EVERTON (August 1907), Preston North End (May 1908)
Able to occupy either flank but preferring the left, Arthur Winterhalder spent just one season at Goodison Park. He deputised for Harold Hardman in each of his four League outings, the first coming in September 1907 against his future club, Preston, for whom he later appeared in 56 League games (six goals).

WOLSTENHOLME, SAMUEL
Right-half: 170 apps, 8 goals
Born: Little Lever, Lancashire, 1878 – Deceased
Career: Farnworth Alliance, Horwich, EVERTON (professional, October 1897), Blackburn Rovers (May 1904), Croydon Common (August 1908), Norwich City (May 1909–May 1913); coached in Germany from 1914 and later interned
Described as being 'a brainy and thoughtful right-half, as nimble as a squirrel' – Sam Wolstenholme, a fine passer of the ball, always trying to be inch-perfect, was usually able to counter the wiles of the most trickiest of adversaries. Making his League debut for Everton against Stoke in January 1898, he finally established himself in the side during the second half of the following season and went on to make 170 senior appearances for the Blues before transferring to Blackburn. He played in 117 games in four years at Ewood Park and then added a further 180 to his tally with the Southern League side Norwich. He was capped three times by England (1904, 1905).

WOOD, GEORGE
Goalkeeper: 126 apps
Born: Douglas, Lanarkshire, 26 September 1952
Career: Balmoral Hydrolics, East Stirlingshire (professional, April 1970), Blackpool (£10,000, January 1972), EVERTON (£145,000, August 1977), Arsenal (£150,000, August 1980), Crystal Palace (free, May 1983), Cardiff City (January 1988), Blackpool (loan, March–May 1990), West Bromwich Albion (guest, May 1990), Hereford United (August 1990), Merthyr Tydfil (1992), Mid-Cardiff FC, Inter-Cardiff (player–manager, mid-1990s)
An apprentice stonemason before taking up soccer, George Wood, at his peak (mid-1970s), stood 6 ft 3 in. tall and weighed 14 st. – and there weren't too many heftier goalkeepers in the game at that time. Sound in judgement, courageous and able to achieve a remarkable distance when clearing his lines, he replaced John Burridge at Bloomfield Road and made 117 League appearances in his first spell there before moving to Goodison Park, where he took over from Dai Davies and David Lawson. Manager Gordon Lee had been searching for a keeper for quite a

while and Wood fitted the bill, making his debut for the Blues against Nottingham Forest in August 1977. Two years later he was rewarded for some excellent displays with three Scottish caps (against England, Northern Ireland and Argentina). Halfway through the 1979–80 season he lost his place to Martin Hodge, leaving for Highbury at the end of the campaign. After a spell with Palace, he gained a Welsh Cup-winner's medal with Cardiff before returning for a loan spell at Blackpool. He was 40 years of age when he hung up his jersey in 1992 with over 500 senior appearances behind him. Wood is also a keen ornithologist.

WOODHOUSE, ROLAND THOMAS
Inside-forward: 2 apps
Born: Leyland, 15 January 1897 – *Died*: 1969
Career: Lancaster Town, Preston North End (April 1919), EVERTON (September 1926), Wrexham (May 1927), Halifax Town (June 1930), Chorley (1931)
Seven and a half years a player at Preston North End, and a good one at that, inside-forward Roly Woodhouse scored 61 goals in 238 games for Preston before moving to Goodison Park at the age of 29. Black-haired, well-built with a strong shot in both feet, he made his debut for Everton against Blackburn in October 1926. However, he couldn't dislodge 'Art' Dominy or Bobby Irvine from the inside-forward berths, and after one more game (on the right-wing against Burnley) he moved to Wrexham, for whom he struck 27 goals in 130 games.

WOODS, LEONARD GEORGE
Outside-left: 4 apps
Born: *circa* 1882 – Deceased
Career: EVERTON (seasons 1906–08)
A reserve at Goodison Park, Woods played in only four League games for Everton, standing in for Harold Hardman against Blackburn (for his debut in November 1907) and later against Sunderland, Arsenal and Notts County (all in December 1907).

WOODS, MAURICE
Defender: 8 apps, 1 goal
Born: Skelmersdale, Lancashire, 1 November 1931
Career: Burscough (October 1946), EVERTON (amateur, April 1947; professional, November 1949), Blackburn Rovers (£6,000, November 1956), Hakoah/Australia (June 1963), Drumcondra (coach, briefly, 1965), Luton Town (July 1965), Stockport County (July 1966; later trainer, then manager, April 1970–December 1971), Hellas/Australia (coach), Southport (coach, 1974–75)
Unable to establish himself at Goodison Park, 'Matt' Woods, who was barely 6 ft tall and weighed less than 13 st., became a colossus at the heart of the Blackburn defence, making 307 appearances. Groomed by Everton since the age of 15, he made his League debut against Fulham in May 1953, when he deputised for Tommy Clinton. However, over the next three years he made only

seven more senior appearances before switching his allegiance to Blackburn, whose manager Johnny Carey pulled off one of the transfer coups of the decade. With Ronnie Clayton to his right and Mick McGrath to his left, Woods formed one of the best half-back lines in Rovers' history. He played in the 1960 FA Cup final defeat by Wolves and also represented the Football League during his time at Ewood Park. After moving 'down under' in 1963, Woods went on to captain the Australian national team. He coached Drumcondra during the Irish club's European Cup preparations in 1965.

WRIGHT, BERNARD PETER

Centre/inside-forward: 10+1 apps, 2 goals
Born: Birmingham, 17 September 1952
Career: Birmingham City (amateur, 1968), Walsall (professional, September 1971), EVERTON (February 1972), Walsall (January 1973), Bradford City (February 1977), Port Vale (£9,000, June 1978), Kidderminster Harriers (May 1980), Trowbridge Town, Cheltenham Town, Worcester City, Gloucester City

After being rejected by Birmingham, burly striker Bernie Wright had made only 15 League appearances (two goals) for Walsall before his transfer to Goodison Park – after impressing in a fourth-round FA Cup-tie at Goodison Park in January 1972. He made his debut for Everton in the Merseyside derby against Liverpool in March 1972 but less than a year later he returned to Fellows Park due to disciplinary reasons! Everyone's dream of a powerhouse front man, Wright, with his thick sideburns, was one of the biggest and best Walsall strikers over the years. He went on to take his record with the Saddlers to 48 goals in 196 outings and in 1978–79 was Port Vale's top marksman, going on to net 24 times in 81 outings for the Potteries' club.

WRIGHT, MARK ANDREW

Defender: 1 app.
Born: Manchester, 29 January 1970
Career: EVERTON (apprentice, April 1986; professional, June 1988), Blackpool (loan, August–September 1990), Huddersfield Town (March 1991), Accrington Stanley (April 1992), Wigan Athletic (November 1993–May 1995)

After only one League game for Everton, when he deputised for Dave Watson in a 1–0 home win over QPR in April 1990, giving away a last-minute penalty (saved by Neville Southall), reserve defender Mark Wright moved to Huddersfield, for whom he made 32 appearances. He later had 30 games for Wigan.

WRIGHT, RICHARD IAN

Goalkeeper: 41 apps
Born: Ipswich, 5 November 1977
Career: Ipswich Town (apprentice, April 1994; professional, January 1995), Arsenal (£6m, July 2001), EVERTON (£3.5m, July 2002)

After helping Arsenal complete the double in 2002, England international goalkeeper Richard Wright left Highbury for Goodison Park, where he immediately took over the number one position from Steve Simonsen, making his debut for the Blues against Totthenham Hotspur at Goodison Park in August 2002.

He made 291 appearances for Ipswich during his seven years at Portman Road, earning 15 Under-21 caps to go with those he won at schoolboy- and youth-team levels. He later added two senior caps to his collection, playing against Malta in 2000 and Holland in 2001. It was anticipated that Wright would succeed David Seaman between the posts at Arsenal, but manager Arsène Wenger had other ideas and allowed him to move to Goodison Park. A shot-stopper par exellence, Wright was well on his way to reaching the milestone of 400 appearances in 2004.

WRIGHT, ROBERT

Centre-forward: 1 app.
Born: *circa* 1880 – Deceased
Career: EVERTON (August 1904), Burnley (September 1907–May 1908)

A reserve at Everton, Bob Wright's only League outing for the club was against Bolton in March 1906, when he deputised for Alex Young in a 3–2 defeat. Switched to right-half by Burnley, he had only two outings for the Clarets – against Hull and Derby in September 1907.

WRIGHT, THOMAS JAMES

Right-back: 374 apps, 4 goals
Born: Liverpool, 21 October 1944
Career: Liverpool Schools, EVERTON (amateur, August 1961; professional, March 1963; retired through injury, May 1974); later worked on Merseyside docks

Tommy Wright was a compact right-back, defensively strong, a sure kicker with a good sense of awareness. He enthused on the overlap, was quick to recover and was generally solid in his all-round play. An FA Cup winner with Everton in 1966 and a beaten finalist two years later, he was an ever-present when helping the Blues win the League championship in 1969–70, being part of a superb defence that also included fellow England internationals Gordon West (in goal), Keith Newton and Brian Labone. Wright appeared in more than 370 matches for Everton, his first against Blackpool in October 1964 (in place of Scottish international Alex Parker) and his last against Wolves in April 1973, when he suffered a knee injury which eventually led to his premature retirement at the age of 29. At international level, he won 11 full caps for England (1968–70) and gained a further seven at Under-23 level, having earlier represented his country as a schoolboy. He played in the 1970 World Cup finals in Mexico. Tommy Wright and William Wright (q.v.) are uncle and nephew, respectively.

WRIGHT, WILLIAM
Defender: 196+2 apps, 10 goals
Born: Liverpool, 28 April 1958
Career: EVERTON (apprentice, June 1974; professional, January 1977), Birmingham City (free, June 1983), Chester City (loan, February–March 1985), Carlisle United (August 1986), Morecambe (July 1988–May 1989)

Billy Wright was a stocky, compact, hard-tackling centre-half (or left-back), whose career spanned 15 years (1974–89), during which time he amassed well over 400 senior appearances and around 500 in all games. After almost 200 senior outings for Everton, for whom he made his League debut as a substitute against Leicester in February 1978, he became captain and chief penalty-taker with Birmingham. A big favourite with the fans at Goodison Park and St Andrew's, he developed weight problems during his last year with the Midland club and at that point, 'Wrighty' knew his career was slowly drawing to a close. Indeed, he left Goodison Park after being controversially dropped for a game at Ipswich for being overweight. Capped twice by England 'B' and on six occasions at Under-21 level, he helped Birmingham win promotion from the Second Division in 1985.

WRIGHT, WILLIAM P.
Centre-forward: 2 apps
Born: Seaforth, *circa* 1890 – Deceased
Career: St Mirren (1912), EVERTON (October 1914), Tranmere Rovers (March 1915), Exeter City (August 1920), Huddersfield Town (December 1920), Mid-Rhondda United (1921–22)

Signed as cover for Joe Clennell and Bob Parker, Bill Wright made two League starts for Everton during his stay at Goodison Park. He made his debut in a goalless draw with Sheffield United in late January 1915 and lined up in the 4–3 home defeat by Oldham just prior to his departure.

WYLIE, THOMAS G.
Forward: 21 apps, 5 goals
Born: Maybole, Ayrshire, Scotland, 5 August 1870 – *Died*: Bristol, *circa* 1955
Career: Maybole FC, Glasgow Rangers (April 1888), EVERTON (December 1890), Liverpool (1892), Bury (1893–94), Bristol City (August 1897–May 1898); became a Football League linesman and later a referee; later ran a thriving newsagent's business in Bristol

Tom Wylie was a very competent footballer. Able to play on the right-wing or inside, he was always able to spot a scoring opportunity and netted five goals in 11 games for Rangers before moving to Goodison Park. He made his debut for Everton against Wolves shortly after signing and in his second game blasted in four goals in a 6–2 win at Derby as the Blues headed towards the League title. When he left Everton, Wylie became Liverpool's first professional player but he never made the first XI at Anfield. He later helped Bury win the Second Division title (1895) and, in fact, he played his best football with the Shakers, for whom he scored 15 goals in 73 League games. Capped once by Scotland against Ireland in 1890, he also played in seven Inter-City matches for Glasgow.

XAVIER, ABEL
Defender: 45+4 apps
Born: Mozambique, 30 November 1972
Career: PSV Eindhoven/Holland, EVERTON (£1.5m, September 1999), Liverpool (£800,000, January 2002), Galatasaray/Turkey (loan, January–May 2003, signed August 2003)

When making his Premiership debut for Everton against Sheffield Wednesday in September 1999, Portuguese international defender Abel Xavier became only the second player whose surname begins with the letter 'X' to appear in a League game in England – the first was Davide Xausa for Stoke a year earlier. Already an experienced campaigner, having played for Portugal at Under-16, Under-18, Under-21 and senior levels (20 caps gained in the latter category), he had a good, solid first season at Goodison Park before losing his form and his place, eventually transferring to Liverpool, seemingly a snip-of-a-signing by Gérard Houllier! It was not – and after 21 games for the Reds he was loaned out to Galatasaray for five months, hoping to regain his form.

YOBO, JOSEPH
Defender: 53+4 apps, 2 goals
Born: Kano, Nigeria, 6 September 1980
Career: Mechelen/Belgium (1997), Standard Liège/Belgium (August 1998), Olympique Marseille/France (July 2001), EVERTON (£4.5m, August 2002)

Signed by Everton initially on a one-year contract, Joseph Yobo showed from the outset that he was an international class player and an excellent purchase by Everton boss Walter Smith. After a freak accident on the training ground, he finally made his Premiership debut against Fulham in September 2002 and thereafter was in superb form, his muscular presence, composure and strong heading ability adding something special to the Everton defence. He played in the African Nations Cup in 2003 and 2004 before returning to continue his fine defensive work with Everton.

YOUDS, EDWARD PAUL
Defender/Midfield: 6+4 apps
Born: Liverpool, 3 May 1970
Career: EVERTON (apprentice, June 1986; professional, June 1988), Cardiff City (loan, December 1989), Wrexham (loan, February–May 1990), Ipswich Town (£250,000, November 1991), Bradford City (£175,000, January 1995), Charlton Athletic (£550,000, March 1998), Huddersfield Town (free, July 2002), Gray's Athletic (June 2003)

Always showing a no-nonsense attitude, especially when playing at the heart of the defence, Eddie Youds never quite made it at Goodison Park, having just ten League outings, the first as a substitute against Norwich in December 1990. After moving to Portman Road, he made 59 appearances for Ipswich and followed up with 99 for Bradford and 62 for Charlton before assisting Huddersfield. He helped the Addicks climb back into the Premiership as First Division champions in 2000.

YOUNG, ALEX

Inside/centre-forward: 272+3 apps, 89 goals
Born: Loanhead, Midlothian, Scotland, 3 February 1937
Career: Newtongrange Star, Heart of Midlothian (professional, August 1955), EVERTON (£42,000, November 1960), Glentoran (£10,000, player–manager, August 1968), Stockport County (£14,000; player–assistant manager, November 1968; retired as a player, August 1969); later worked as a hooks and tassles man for a curtain manufacturing company with branches in Carlisle, Edinburgh and the Shetland Islands

Unlike a lot of orthodox centre-forwards, Alex Young – an Everton hero to this day and nicknamed 'the Golden Vision' – was a class act, a real artist with a delicate touch, clever movement and style who used his tremendous ball skills to make up for a lack of weight. He was twice a League championship winner with Hearts (1958, 1960) and once with Everton in 1962–63, scoring 22 goals as an ever-present. He also helped the Blues win the FA Cup in 1966. The club's first-ever £40,000 signing, Young made his debut against Spurs in December 1960 and scored his first two goals in a 3–1 win over Blackburn in March 1961. He gained six Scottish international caps (1959–61) – one as an Evertonian – played twice for the Scottish League side and six times for the Under-23s. Douglas Lamming wrote of Young in his booklet *Who's Who of Scottish Internationals*: 'a golden haired aristocrat among footballers with his subtleties and grace. Almost deified by Everton supporters who rightly felt he ideally suited their club's traditional style.'

YOUNG, ALEX SIMPSON

Inside-forward: 314 apps, 125 goals
Born: Slamannan, Scotland, 23 June 1880 – *Died*: Portobello, Edinburgh, 17 September 1959
Career: Paisley St Mirren (August 1899), Falkirk (July 1900), EVERTON (July 1901), Tottenham Hotspur (June 1911), Manchester City (November 1911), South Liverpool (August 1912), Burslem Port Vale (briefly, 1913)

Alex 'Sandy' Young top-scored for Everton in five successive seasons (1903–08) and topped the charts again in 1910–11. He was an FA Cup winner in 1906 when he scored the only goal in the final to beat Newcastle United, and gained two caps for Scotland, against England in 1905 and Wales two years later. An imposing, muscular centre-forward, with a heart of gold, he made his League debut for the Blues against Aston Villa in September 1901 – having learned the business north of the border with St Mirren and Falkirk. He scored four times in a 9–1 win over his future club Manchester City in September 1906 and weighed in with 29 goals that season, firing in another 21 the following year. He was still in pretty good form when, in 1911, he was transferred to White Hart Lane. He netted three times in five starts for Spurs but then surprisingly asked for and got a free, being unable to settle in London. He unfortunately failed with his efforts at Manchester City, South Liverpool and, indeed, Port Vale, and in 1914 emigrated to Australia. A year later Young was charged with the wilful murder of his brother and in June 1916 was found guilty of manslaughter, evidence having been produced from football officials in England that during his playing career he had been subject to fits of temporary insanity. He was sentenced to three years' imprisonment but was not released immediately on the completion of his sentence but kept in custody on the grounds of 'mental weakness'. It was quite some time before he returned to Scotland.

YOUNG, ROBERT THOMSON
Defender: 41 apps, 8 goals
Born: Swinhill, Stonehouse, Lanarkshire, Scotland, 7 September 1886 – *Died:* Scotland, 1955
Career: Paisley St Mirren (September 1901), West Ham United (July 1907), Middlesbrough (October 1908), EVERTON (May 1910), Wolverhampton Wanderers (August 1911; retired May 1914 due to injury and ill health)
Craggy Scot Bob Young was a solid, uncompromising defender, playing in his home country, in London, the Midlands, the north of England and on Merseyside. Well built, physically strong and muscular, he signed for Everton at the age of 23, having already appeared in more than 100 competitive games (including 44 for West Ham and 37 for Middlesbrough). He made his debut for the Blues against Spurs at Goodison Park in September 1910 and netted his first goal a month later in a 2–1 win over Bury. He appeared in 73 games for Wolves before suffering a bad knee injury from which he never recovered.

WARTIME GUESTS

The following are some of the many guest players who assisted Everton during the First and Second World Wars:

1915—18
R. McNeal (West Bromwich Albion, later England)
J. Shelton (Manchester United, Liverpool)

1939—46
E.W. Anderson (Wolves, Torquay, West Ham)
L.L. Ashcroft (Tranmere)
T.A. Astbury (Chester)
R. Beattie (Preston)
T. Bond (local)*
J.K. Boothway (Manchester City, Crewe)
J. Carey (Manchester United, Irish international, later manager of Everton, Blackburn, Plymouth)
F. Curran (Southport, Bristol City, Bristol Rovers, Accrington Stanley, Torquay)
R.W. Dell (Manchester City, Mansfield, Blackburn)
R. Dunkley (Stoke)
G.S. Glidden (Sunderland, Port Vale, Reading, Clapton Orient)
W.W. Hall (Liverpool)
W. Hallard (Bury)
N. Higham (local)
H. Jones (Preston, WBA)
S. Jones (local)
R.L. Keen (local)
R. Kinnell (local)
J.S. Lees (local)
J.W. Logan (Charlton, Darlington, Barnsley)
N. Low (Liverpool, Newport, Norwich)
G. Makin (local)
J.M. McIntosh (Blackpool)
J. Morris (Manchester United, Leicester)
G. Murphy (Bradford City, Hull)

G. Mutch (Manchester United, Preston, Burnley)
W. Owen (Manchester City, Tranmere, Newport)
T. Peters (Bury, Leeds)
J.S.D. Rawlings (Preston, Huddersfield, WBA)
F. Roberts (Bury)
E. Rogers (Wrexham, Arsenal)
A. Rosenthal (Tranmere Rovers)
A. Smith (local)
F. Soo (Stoke)
E.A. Steele (local)
P. Turner (Chester)
T.K. Urmston (local)
T. Waring (Aston Villa, Barnsley, Wolves, Tranmere)
E. Williams (local)
* Bond was Everton's last Second World War guest.

EVERTON MANAGERS

1888–89	William E. Barclay*
1889–1901	Dick Molyneux*
1901–18	William C. Cuff*
1918–19	W.J. Sawyer*
1919–35	Thomas H. McIntosh*
1936–48	Theo Kelly†
1948–56	Cliff Britton
1956–58	Ian Buchan‡
1958–61	Johnny Carey
1961–73	Harry Catterick
1973–77	Billy Bingham
1977–81	Gordon Lee
1981–87	Howard Kendall
1987–90	Colin Harvey
1990–93	Howard Kendall
1994	Mike Walker
1994–97	Joe Royle
1997–98	Howard Kendall
1998–2002	Walter Smith
2002 to date	David Moyes

* Held position of secretary–manager

† Appointed club's first-ever official team manager in May 1939, having previously served as secretary/manager since 1935

‡ Team coach, rather than team manager

MANAGERS' NOTES

- Cliff Britton, Harry Catterick, Billy Bingham, Howard Kendall, Colin Harvey and Joe Royle all played for Everton before becoming the club's manager (see under respective player biographies).
- Ian Buchan, a Scottish amateur international, was a former Loughborough College lecturer in physical education and was a surprise appointment. He was tragically killed in a car crash in Glasgow in 1965, aged 45.
- Johnny Carey was a defender with Manchester United (344 appearances: 1936–53), who also played for Home Farm. He then managed Blackburn (1953–58) and after leaving Goodison was in charge of Leyton Orient (1961–63), Nottingham Forest (1963–68) and Blackburn again, as joint manager with Eddie Quigley (1969–71). Voted 'Footballer of the Year' in 1949, he won the FA Cup and League championship with Manchester United in 1948 and 1952 respectively, gained 29 caps for the Republic of Ireland and seven for Northern Ireland, and also played for the Rest of the World against Great Britain. As manager, he was twice a Second Division runner-up: 1958 with Blackburn and 1962 with Orient.
- Harry Catterick (12 years in charge) has been Everton's longest-serving manager.
- Kelly was in charge when the League championship was won in 1939, thus allowing Everton to retain the trophy for a record seven years. He reverted back to being club secretary in 1948 when Britton became manager.
- Gordon Lee was a full-back with Aston Villa (1955–66) and player–coach of Shrewsbury before managing Port Vale (1968–74). After a season in charge of Blackburn, he bossed Newcastle (1975–77) and on leaving Everton took over the reins at Preston (1981–83), later coaching in Iceland, the Middle East and at Leicester, where he twice acted as caretaker-manager. He was a League Cup winner in 1961 and loser in 1963 with Villa and as manager was also a runner-up in the same competition in 1976 (with Newcastle) and 1977 (with Everton). He guided Port Vale to promotion from Division Four in 1970 and Blackburn to the Third Division championship in 1975.
- David Moyes made over 400 League appearances as player serving with Celtic (from 1980), Cambridge United (1983), Bristol City (1985), Shrewsbury (1987), Dunfermline (1990), Hamilton (1993) and Preston (1993–98). He became manager at Deepdale (after a spell as assistant to Gary

293

Peters) and moved to Goodison Park after guiding North End to the Second Division title in 2000 and First Division play-offs a year later.

- Walter Smith is now assistant manager to Sir Alex Ferguson at Old Trafford. He played two League games for Rangers (1956–58) and also starred for Dumbarton and Dundee United. He retired to become assistant manager at Tannadice in 1982 (under Jim McLean). He eventually succeeded McLean in the hot seat and in 1986 was appointed assistant manager to Graeme Souness at Ibrox Park. Upgraded to manager in 1991, he saw seven League titles won by the 'Gers, plus three Scottish Cups and three League Cups, including the treble in 1993. He resigned halfway through the 1997–98 season but remained a club director. He moved to Goodison Park in 1998 and remained in charge for almost four years, during which time financial constraints severely marred his progress.

- Mike Walker won four Under-23 caps as a goalkeeper for Wales. A player with Reading, Shrewsbury, York, Watford, Charlton and Colchester in that order (1963–82), he was then coach, assistant manager and manager at Layer Road before taking over as manager of Norwich's second team in 1988, being upgraded to senior manager at Carrow Road in 1992. He was a Third Division championship winner with Watford in 1969 and gained promotion to the Third Division with Colchester five years later. His son, Ian, ex-Spurs and now Leicester, is also a goalkeeper.

BIBLIOGRAPHY

I have referred to several books to clarify certain relevant statistics including facts and figures, individual players' details and, indeed, stories and match reports from past seasons regarding Everton FC. There are some conflicting facts, stats and other information in these sources and I have made judgement as to what is likely to be correct.

The list:

AFS Who's Who: 1902–03, 1903–04, 1907–08, 1909–10 (Essex: AFS Statisicians)

Barwick, B. and G. Sinstadt (1988), *The Great Derbies: Everton against Liverpool* (London: BBC Books)

Bell, D. and G. Buckland (2001), *Everton: The Ultimate Book of Stats & Facts* (Liverpool: The Bluecoat Press)

Everton: Champions (brochure) 1970

FA Official Yearbooks: 1951–2000 (London: The Football Association)

Gibbs, N. (1988), *England: The Football Facts* (Exeter: Facer Books)

Gibson, A. and W. Pickford (1905), *Association Football and the Men Who Made It*, 4 vols (London: Caxton Publishing Company)

Goldsworthy, M. (1969), *The Encyclopaedia of Association Football* (London: Robert Hale & Co.)

Hugman, B.J. (1998), *The PFA Premier and Football League Players' Records: 1946–1998* (Hertfordshire: Queen Anne Press)

Hugman, B.J. (1995–2001 [published annually], *Footballers' (PFA) Factfile, 1995–96, 1996–97, 1997–98, 1999–2000, 2000–01, 2001–02* (Hertfordshire: Queen Anne Press)

Johnson, F. (1935), *Football Who's Who* (London: Associated Sporting Press)

Joyce, M. (2002), *Football League Players' records, 1888–1939* (Nottingham: SoccerData Publication/Tony Brown)

Keith, J. and P. Thomas (eds) (1973), *A–Z of Mersey Soccer* (Manchester: Beaverbrook Newspapers Ltd of Liverpool)

Lamming, D. and M. Farror (1972), *English Internationals Who's Who, 1872–1972* (London: Robert Hale & Co.)

Platt, M. (2003), *The Essential History of Everton* (London: Headline Book Publishing)

Pringler, A. and N. Fissler (1996), *Where Are They Now?* (London: Two Heads Publishing)

Rogers, K. (1989), *Everton Greats* (Edinburgh: John Donald Publishers Ltd)

Rollin, J. (1985), *Soccer at War, 1939–45* (London: Willow Books/Collins)

Rollin, J. (ed.), *Rothmans Yearbook, 1970–2002*, vols 1–32 ([1970–91 London: Queen Anne Press; [1992–2002] London: Headline Publishing)

Ross, I. and G. Smailes (1993), *Everton: A Complete Record* (Derby: Breedon Books)

Williams, T. (ed.), *Football League Directory: 1985–89* (London: Daily Mail)

OTHER PUBLICATIONS

AFS Bulletins

Everton 'home' programmes: 1920–2004

Everton magazines/handbooks

Liverpool Daily Post

Liverpool Echo

I've also referred to many national newspapers, club histories and *Who's Who* publications, autobiographies and biographies of players and managers and a number of soccer reference books for confirmation of certain factual points.